Recipes and Recollections
from the American South

A Gracious Plenty

JOHN T. EDGE

**FOR THE CENTER FOR THE STUDY OF SOUTHERN CULTURE
AT THE UNIVERSITY OF MISSISSIPPI**

An Ellen Rolfes Book

G. P. Putnam's Sons
New York

To those unsung propagators of Southern culture—Southern cooks

G. P. Putnam's Sons
Publishers Since 1838
a member of
Penguin Putnam Inc.
375 Hudson Street
New York, NY 10014

Library of Congress Cataloging-in-Publication Data

Edge, John T., date.
    A gracious plenty : recipes and recollections from the American South / John T. Edge for the Center for the Study of Southern Culture at the University of Mississippi.
        "An Ellen Rolfes Book."
        p.   cm.
    ISBN 0-399-14534-6
    1. Cookery, American—Southern style. 2. Food habits—Southern States. 3. Southern States—Social life and customs.   I. University of Mississippi. Center for the Study of Southern Culture.   II. Title.
    TX715.2.S68E32   1999   99-24119 CIP
    394.1'0975—dc21

Printed in the United States of America

10 9 8 7 6 5 4 3 2 1

This book is printed on acid-free paper. ∞

BOOK DESIGN BY RENATO STANISIC

ACKNOWLEDGMENTS

....

The authors thank John Egerton, Bill Ferris, Jessica Harris, Mary Hartwell Howorth, Richard Howorth, Scott McCraw, Steve McDavid, Sarah Dixon Pegues, Cynthia Shearer, John Martin Taylor, Charles Reagan Wilson, and the sponsors, speakers, volunteers, and attendees at the 1998 Southern Foodways Symposium for their invaluable contributions. Thanks also to those selfless Southerners who gave of their time to share the meal memories printed herein. For her recipe compilation and transcription skills, thanks go to Carol Boker. Without the gracious consent of the many organizations whose recipes fill these pages, this book would not have been possible. A thousand times, thanks. And finally, praise and appreciation for the tireless work of agent Liv Blumer, editor John Duff, and project shepherd and font of wisdom Ann Abadie, associate director of the Center for the Study of Southern Culture. Without the combined efforts of these friends and colleagues, you would not be holding this book in your hands today.

AUTHORS' NOTE

....

We think that the best cookbooks are storybooks, their purpose as much to document the communal draw of the meal table as to show the curious cook how to bake a gravity-defying biscuit or stir up a tasty kettle of Brunswick stew. When all the dishes have been cleared from the table, these recipes remain, a tangible link to a time, a place, a people.

In *A Gracious Plenty,* we share with you, the reader, our recipes. But what is more, we share with you our memories of meals past, of dinner on the grounds after a morning in church, of bombast and barbecue as savored at a political picnic, of snacking on fruitcake and coffee on a cold winter afternoon. If the recipes are the flesh and bones of our book, then the heart and soul is most assuredly these meal memories—recollections from people you know, like bluesman B. B. King, and people you should know, like catfish farmer Ed Scott. In retelling their tales we share with you what it means to live beneath that mythical Mason-Dixon divide, what it means to be a Southerner.

Eudora Welty once observed that the deeper one goes into the heart of a region, the more one transcends its boundaries. And so it is with the South as we see it, a region, indeed a culture, not as much bound by borders as defined by attitude and opinion, history and heritage.

The recipes found herein are from a broad variety of sources. For the most part they are drawn from community cookbooks, those compilations of recipes authored not by one but by many, not by chefs but by cooks. To us, these spiral-bound books are the voice of an unsung people. With the publication of *A Gracious Plenty* we welcome you to a seat at our Southern table. And we proudly sing the praises of the cooks who went before us.

John T. Edge, Ellen Rolfes, and the Center for the Study of Southern Culture

P.S. We have made every effort to locate the groups and individuals who originally published these recipes. But addresses change, organizations cease operations and then re-form. If we have failed to give proper credit to your group, please write to us in care of the publisher.

THE "AMERICA EATS" PROJECT MATERIAL

....

Between July 1935 and June 1942, the federal government employed hundreds of white-collar workers in fieldwork efforts that have yet to be equaled in this country. First conceived as a means of work relief for unemployed writers and newspapermen, the Federal Writers Project—along with sister projects devoted to the arts, theater, and music—was an integral part of President Franklin D. Roosevelt's New Deal programs.

Though most recognized for the authorship of state guidebooks like *Mississippi: A Guide to the Magnolia State,* the Federal Writers Project also undertook a variety of lesser-known but equally ambitious projects. Among those was a book-length survey of American foodways, initially slated for publication in 1942. To be titled *America Eats* and edited by Louisiana writer Lyle Saxon, the book was intended as "an account of group eating as an important American social institution; [and] its part in development of American cookery as an authentic art."

The scope of the book was to be national, yet the emphasis was to be regional, even local. Unprecedented in their concentration on "food events," the project's developers discouraged the compiling of recipes out of context, instead encouraging writers to compile remembrances and participant observations of "family reunions, political barbecues, fish fries, box-supper socials, coon hunt suppers, cemetery cleaning picnics, chittlin feasts at hog-killin' time," among others. Scattered throughout *A Gracious Plenty* are excerpts from these dispatches, written by a variety of Southerners, ranging from Kate Hubbard to Eudora Welty. Understood within the context of time, they provide a compelling portrait of the food habits of the past.

CONT

INTRODUCTION

....

The South: Where, Who, and What's for Dinner

Charles Reagan Wilson

This Thanksgiving is a busy one for my father-in-law. He is hosting more than forty relatives for a family reunion built around food and the holiday. He is Lebanese Mississippian by ancestry, his mother's family having come from Beirut. She is ninety-four, the matriarch of the family, a sweet, dominating presence at this occasion. My father-in-law fries Cajun turkeys—whole turkeys or turkey breasts cooked in sizzling peanut oil for less than an hour, coming out juicy on the inside because of a rich marinade and the hot oil sealing in the flavor. He and his nephew, who has come to Mississippi from Washington State for this event, also make kibbee, that wonderful Lebanese meat dish. We have stuffed grape leaves and cabbage rolls, reflecting the family's heritage, but also oyster dressing and sweet potato casserole, which reflect their heritage as Southerners.

The meal and the family embody much for me about the South: the diversity that belies the simple stereotypes of the region and yet the underlying power of its way of life to make its citizens into identifiable Southerners. What Southerners have for dinner, or other meals, reflects the geography of the region and its culture.

Defining the South must take into account, though, the varieties of Southern experiences. "The South" appears at times, for example, as essentially a historical term—the eleven states of the Confederacy. But Kentucky and Missouri were slave states in 1861 and shared many customs and attitudes with people farther south. Defining the South through the Confederate experience is tidy, but the South's ways often have transcended that definition. The U.S. Census Bureau classifies the South as the Confederate states plus Maryland, Kentucky, Oklahoma, Delaware, and Washington, D.C. For the federal government to place the nation's capital inside the South seems a bureaucrat's irony, and a Southern triumph, but it also indicates that locating "the South" may take more than a map.

Virginia is Southern at its historical sites, but in places near Washington it is also a part of the Northeastern megalopolis. How does the world of south Florida fit into a South identified with moonlight and magnolias? Where is the dividing line between East Texas and West Texas, between "Southern" and "Western" spheres? Willie Morris once told me that one Texan he met knew exactly where that line was—Conroe, Texas—because west of that small central Texas town bar fights were indoors and east of Conroe bar fights were outdoors.

The South's borders are problematic precisely because the diversity of the region grew out of geography. The imagery that outsiders create of the South often suggests a monolithic place. Television's *The Dukes of Hazzard,* for example, takes place in one supposed Southern county with mountains, hills, swamps, alligators, and every other stereotypical symbol associated with the region in general but with no real place.

The South can be seen more productively, perhaps, as a collection of regions. The Appalachians, the Alleghenies, the Blue Ridge, and the Ozarks are the Mountain South. The Upland South has been a place of hill-country farmers, the tobacco business, and textile mills. The Lowland South is the Deep South, a place of cotton growing, the blues, warm Gulf Coast breezes, Florida beaches, and Latin rhythms. The urban South has been the center of the New South, from Atlanta newspaper editor Henry Grady in the 1880s to Andrew Young today. One could chart more specific landscapes in Cajun Louisiana, the Kentucky bluegrass, the Mississippi Delta, and the Piney Woods.

Each place is defined by its food as well as its terrain. Barbecue provides a classic example. All Southern regions can affirm the importance of this gift of the hog. North Carolinians cook it so long that it falls apart, and they insist on serving it shredded on hamburger buns. South-central Kentucky restaurants often serve slices of pork shoulder as barbecue, with bones in, dipped in sauce, and accompanied by white bread. Texans barbecue sausage links. Sometimes barbecue is not even pork. Those same Texans barbecue beef brisket in tribute to the cows that have been a part of their way of life for so long, and some Kentuckians feast on mutton barbecue.

The South is its regions and their food traditions, but it is more than that. The South is above all its people, and here one finds the best expression of the region's diversity. Two groups have dominated the South for close to four centuries—the descendants of British ancestors and those of African origins. Both groups are as blueblooded as any America has produced, given their time on this land. English settlers first appeared in the South in 1607, and the first Africans were brought in 1619. White and black Southerners made their own distinctive contributions to the everyday cuisine that would become known in the 1960s as "soul food."

Native Americans had been here even earlier, providing the foundational diet that would grow into Southern food. They shared with Europeans and Africans their knowledge of wild and domesticated food plants common in the Southern environment. Native American maize, or corn, became the most popular food for humans and animals in the South and the fundamental staple in the regional diet.

While other American regions ate wheat bread, the South embraced cornbread. The names of cornmeal recipes make a fine litany: remember the pones, muffins, griddle cakes; recall the corn dodgers, hoecakes, hush puppies. The Indians invented the precursor to the grits I have for Saturday morning breakfast.

Food defines the South through the historical contributions of early peoples who created a Hog Belt and a Corn Belt. But this is not the whole story, either. If the South is its people, then later arrivals also must be counted. The South missed the massive waves of immigration in the nineteenth century, which would transform the United States into a multicultural nation. But one cannot dismiss the presence of ethnic groups and their overlapping ethnic and regional identities. One finds historic Jewish communities in Charleston and Savannah and prominent Jewish families throughout the region. Germans came to North Carolina in the colonial era, went down the Great Wagon Road from Pennsylvania into the Shenandoah Valley and into the Southern backcountry a little later, and in another wave, settled in central Texas in the mid-nineteenth century. The Cajuns are in south Louisiana, and their claims on the Southern identity are hard to ignore, especially for anyone who loves to eat, drink, and dance to the music.

Food shows the way these ethnic identities become intertwined with regional identities. Eli Evans, in chronicling the story of Jewish Southerners, told of the young Alabama man who remembered his mother serving "kosher grits," a good emblem in memory of his self-consciousness. When I was in school in central Texas, I remember going to the Oktoberfest in New Braunfels, which had been settled by Germans in the nineteenth century. I bought a German sausage that had been wrapped in a tortilla and put on a stick—a Southwestern eclecticism that I probably would not have found in Munich.

Southerners have sometimes taken the South with them and planted Southern colonies or individual identities outside of the region. Like the Irish, they have frequently been in exile. Thousands of defeated Confederates escaped "Yankee rule" after the Civil War and departed for South America. Their descendants still eat grits in Brazil. Playwright Julian Green's Virginia-born mother raised him as a Southerner even though he grew up in France after she had married and moved there. The South has exported talent, for generations of people left the often-dismal regional economy and the too-often brutal social system to seek opportunities elsewhere. Expatriate writers and intellectuals have taught or have seized publishing opportunities in the North, but Southerners like C. Vann Woodward and Robert Penn Warren living in the North have given classic expressions of the Southern identity.

Enclaves of working-class people from the South live in Northern cities. The movement of the South's disadvantaged out of the region in the twentieth century represented a massive human migration, but they took much of the South's culture with them. When music critic Robert Palmer visited Muddy Waters in south Chicago in the 1970s, the blues legend showed him his garden in the back, where he was growing turnip greens and sweet potatoes. The South remained down home even in Chicago. The South even took root in California; the Okies and Arkies who left the South in the Depression planted Southern culture in the West in the 1930s. Bakersfield later became known as Nashville West because country music singers such as Merle Haggard and Buck Owens emerged there.

If Southern diversity is rooted in geography and migration, Southern unity has rested in a rich mythology. The legends of the Old South, the Lost Cause of the doomed Confederacy, the tragedy of Reconstruction, the superiority of white supremacy, and now the triumphs of the Sunbelt—all have insisted that Southerners have somehow been a special people, irrespective of the evidence that this world has often been a vale of tears for them.

The South of history reflects the words in the Book of Job that man is born to sorrow as the sparks fly upward. Generations of white Southerners lived with the moral taint of slavery and legal segregation in an American nation dedicated to democratic ideals. They knew the humiliation of Confederate defeat. Black Southerners saw the dashing of their hopes for true freedom after Emancipation. And all people in the region lived with the debilitating effects of widespread poverty, disease, and illiteracy. What some Southerners ate for dinner was sometimes nutritionally not enough, and dietary deficiencies were a tragic accompaniment of rural poverty. The simplicities of myth may have especially appealed to people struggling with such adversities.

Out of these mythic and historical forces came the identity of the Southerner, and celebrating the region's foodways became a way to express Southern pride. Woe to the non-Southerner who would disparage grits or collards. Not everyone who lives in the South today, though, has a self-identity as a Southerner. American homogenization has blurred regional boundaries, through national networks of communication, transportation, and consumer marketing. Our biscuits often now come out of the can, just as in Maine or Minnesota. Yet recent studies suggest that the self-conscious Southern identity is still alive. Despite the end of the one-party South, Jim Crow laws, the predominance of country living, the cotton economy, and other regional landmarks, Southerners continue to nurture their sense of Southernness through festivals, sporting events, popular culture, and even political attitudes.

Today, that Southern identity includes the well-educated, well-traveled, city-living, media-viewing middle-class Southerner. He or she may be thought of as a regional version of the yuppie. This lifestyle includes adapting traditional versions of Southern homes (whether columned or dogtrotted), growing azaleas and magnolias, and reading regional magazines on their decks to learn about the South and its traditions. The Southern identity also has room now for black Southerners who know that understanding their distinctive heritage requires exploring the South's history and claiming it as their own. The region acknowledges the foundational role that black Southerners played in defining a South, and the contemporary South embraces its biracial culture seen in the blues and country music, and in the writing of a William Faulkner and a Richard Wright or a Margaret Walker Alexander and a Dorothy Allison. Nowhere is this biracial legacy more apparent than in cooking and eating.

Southerners still show their regional identity through the books they write, the music they sing, the jokes they laugh at, and yes, the food they eat—all suggesting that they retain a distinctive style and a recognizable way of viewing life. In the old days, food was sometimes a way to divide the South's people. Laws forbade blacks and whites eating together. Farm women, in another instance, often prepared the main meal of the day but waited until the men had eaten to sit down themselves. But food also has represented healing. When someone dies, mourners bring food to the grieving family. The spiritual meaning of food in the South is perhaps best seen on Sundays. Dinner on the grounds brings together a church community in a symbol of wholeness. Sunday dinner at home has been a shared ritual of different Southerners for generations, reinforcing family ties over chicken and gravy. Breaking cornbread together and drinking sweet tea have been Southern sacraments, outward symbols of a deeper communion. Food in the South, and the shared importance of it to family and community among many kinds of Southerners, represents a peculiar resource for fellowship among the people of the South.

A native of Tennessee, educated in Texas, Charles Reagan Wilson is the director of the Center for the Study of Southern Culture at the University of Mississippi.

APPETIZERS

WHY COMMUNITY COOKBOOKS MATTER

I'm one of those people who read cookbooks the way other people read travel writing: I may not ever make the recipe, but it's fun to read about it, and to speculate on what kind of people would. . . . Any cookbook, read in its entirety, creates its own imagined view of the world.

MARGARET ATWOOD, LITERARY GASTRONOMY

Why Community Cookbooks Matter

....

Community cookbooks—those clunky, spiral-bound, gravy-spattered volumes—are as Southern as sweet tea. They may get comparatively little critical respect, but they are much relied upon in Southern kitchens. Whether full of white-glove standards like cheese straws, tomato aspic, and deviled eggs, or a collection of casseroles bound together by that ubiquitous duct tape of culinary creation called cream of mushroom soup, community cookbooks are a voyeur's treat, a window into the everyday life and foods of a group of churchgoers, a clutch of quilters, or a league of ladies inclined toward service.

The first community cookbooks (also called compiled cookbooks, fundraising cookbooks, or regional cookbooks) were published during the Civil War as a means of raising funds for the treatment of wounded soldiers and the support of families who lost sons and fathers—and farms—to the ravages of battle. In the years following the war, as a new generation of cooks struggled to make do and make dinner, the compilation and sale of such cookbooks spread. Soon, seemingly every charitable organization, from the United Daughters of the Confederacy to Tuskegee Institute, was selling cookbooks. By the close of the nineteenth century, more than two thousand community cookbooks were in print.

At first glance, the books are almost formulaic in their intent, organization, and content. Yet a closer look at the foods selected for inclusion, the names ascribed to the dishes, and the tales told of meals past reveals as much about the community of the compilers as any local history could.

Thumbing through *Food for Body and Soul,* published by the Ladies Ministries of the Highway 5

Church of God, Nauvoo, Alabama, one finds much the same recipes as in a secular book of recipes published by a garden club in faraway Charlotte, North Carolina. Squash casserole, corn pudding, and three different types of coleslaw; pickled peaches, bread-and-butter pickles, and salmon croquettes; fried chicken, cornbread dressing, and tuna noodle casserole—they're all there. And the recipes, slight variations aside, are much the same.

Look a little closer, though, at the cookbook from the ladies of Nauvoo and you are likely to spot a dish or two that may tell you something of people and place. Take the meaty Coal Miner's Pie, submitted by Rose Pullins, or Strike Survival, a recipe for black-eyed pea croquettes submitted by Barry Woods. Both bespeak the region's past, when coal from local mines fueled the steelmaking furnaces in nearby Birmingham, once touted as the "Pittsburgh of the South." Today Birmingham's economy is flush with white-collar workers, but these recipes live on, a culinary tribute to a not-too-distant past.

The best of these cookbooks suggest an honesty of craft, a frank love of simple foods cooked simply, of one-pot meals unadorned by pretense. The titles read as honestly as the recipes within—*My Mother Cooked My Way Through Harvard with These Creole Recipes,* from Oscar Rogers of Natchez, Mississippi; *Soybeans and Peanuts,* from the Hampton Institute of Hampton, Virginia; and that perennial favorite, *Charleston Receipts,* from the Junior League of Charleston, South Carolina—no fuss, no foie gras, no beluga, or osetra.

For the most part, the recipes featured in *A Gracious Plenty* are drawn from community cookbooks. We do this purposefully, un-abashedly, and with great humility, for we believe that the collected recipes reflect a greater Southern community, one that is neither black nor white, rich nor poor, but united in the love of good food and fellowship.

BENNE SEED WAFERS

Sesame seeds, called benne by the Wolof people of Africa, came with the slaves to South Carolina, and are the classic ingredient in these wafers.

YIELD: 50 WAFERS

1 cup firmly packed brown sugar
½ stick (⅛ pound) unsalted butter or margarine
1 egg, lightly beaten
½ cup flour
¼ teaspoon salt
⅛ teaspoon baking powder
1 cup toasted sesame seeds
1 teaspoon fresh lemon juice
½ teaspoon vanilla

Preheat the oven to 325°. Grease a cookie sheet. Combine the brown sugar and butter in a medium bowl and beat until creamy. Stir in the egg, flour, salt, and baking powder. Stir in the sesame seeds, lemon juice, and vanilla. Drop by teaspoonfuls onto the cookie sheet, 2 inches apart. Bake for 15 minutes, or until the wafers are brown around edges. Let cool 1 minute on the cookie sheet, then place on a cooling rack.

Black Family Reunion Cookbook
National Council of Negro Women
Washington, D.C.

Cheese Straws

These pastry strips are sometimes twisted before baking to give a more festive appearance.

YIELD: 6 DOZEN

8 ounces extra-sharp cheddar cheese, grated
1 stick (¼ pound) unsalted butter, softened
½ teaspoon salt
⅛ to ¼ teaspoon cayenne pepper
1½ cups flour
Paprika
Salt

Preheat the oven to 350°. Mix the cheese, butter, salt, cayenne, and flour into a dough that is soft and pliable. Squeeze through a cookie press with a number-1 disk; make long strips and place on an ungreased shiny cookie sheet. Bake for 20 minutes. Cut into 2-inch pieces while still warm, but let cool on the pan. Sprinkle lightly with paprika and salt. Store in an airtight container.

Upper Crust
Junior League of Johnson City
Johnson City, Tennessee

Stuffed Celery

Pimiento cheese shows up more commonly slathered between two slices of bread, but we Southerners enjoy it in a multitude of fashions.

YIELD: 20 TO 25 APPETIZERS

4 stalks celery, washed and scraped
Pimiento Cheese (see recipe below) or cream
  cheese, at room temperature
Paprika, pimientos, olives, chopped nuts (op-
  tional)
Mayonnaise (optional)

Fill the hollows of the celery with soft pimiento cheese. Season with paprika, pimientos, olives, or chopped nuts, if desired, and mayonnaise to soften if desired. Smooth off even with a knife. Chill for several hours. Before serving, cut into slices about 1 inch thick. Stick each with a toothpick.

The Memphis Cookbook
Junior League of Memphis
Memphis, Tennessee

Pimiento Cheese

Pimiento cheese is a sandwich spread that gained popularity with the advent of the country store and the availability of hoop cheese. This recipe, from Mary Hartwell Howorth, owes its uniqueness to a little yard grazing.

24 ounces shredded extra-sharp cheddar cheese
1 (7-ounce) jar sliced pimientos

REYNOLDS PRICE

THE PLEASURES OF PIMIENTO

I've failed in a long effort to trace the origins of pimiento cheese, but it was the peanut butter of my childhood—homemade by Mother. I suspect it is a Southern invention (I've seldom met a non-Southerner who knew what it was, though they take to it on contact). In any case, prepared versions can be bought to this day in Southern supermarkets—most of them made apparently from congealed insecticides. Last year, once I'd acquired a Cuisinart, I rebelled and tried to reconstruct Mother's recipe. I've made a change or two, in the interest of midlife zest, but I think any child of the thirties and forties (from, say, Baltimore down) will recall its glory and bless my name.

Grate a pound or more of extra-sharp cheddar cheese. Chop coarsely one jar of pimientos (four ounces, more if you like) with one or two cloves of garlic. Mix into the grated cheese with plenty of freshly ground pepper and a minimum of salt; then gradually add enough homemade mayonnaise (maybe three tablespoons) to form a stiff chunky paste. Sometimes I add a little lemon juice or a very little wine vinegar or Tabasco—nothing to disguise the bare cheese and peppers and good mayonnaise. I've been caught eating a pound in two days (though it keeps well), especially if life is hard. On rough brown bread, it's a sovereign nerve salve.

Reynolds Price, a native of Macon, North Carolina, is the author of more than twenty-five works of literature, including, most recently, Roxanna Slade, *a novel. This selection originally appeared in* The Great American Writers' Cookbook, *edited by Dean Faulkner Wells and published by Yoknapatawpha Press.*

Dried sage
Freshly ground black pepper
¼ to ½ cup yard onions, chopped
3 tablespoons homemade mayonnaise

Put the grated cheese in a bowl. Drain the pimientos thoroughly in a colander and add to the cheese. Add enough sage to blanket the pimientos. Add sugar, and then go outside and weed the yard onions—those scrawny scallions that pop up in even the most manicured of lawns—pulling up a couple of handfuls. If they are not in season, use the green tops of green onions. Grind a healthy amount of pepper into the mix, and add the onions. Bind it with the mayonnaise and serve on wheat or rye bread.

Howorth Family Collection
Oxford, Mississippi

BENEDICTINE SPREAD

First made popular by Louisville caterer Jennie Benedict, this heady spread is little seen outside Kentucky.

YIELD: ABOUT 5 CUPS

1 cucumber, peeled and seeded
1 small sweet onion
4 (8-ounce) packages cream cheese, at room
    temperature
4 ounces (½ cup) sour cream
½ cup mayonnaise
Salt to taste
1 or 2 drops green food coloring
Dill, to taste (optional)

Purée the cucumber and onion in the blender; combine with the cream cheese in a 2-quart mixing bowl. Add the sour cream and mayonnaise. Add salt to taste. Add enough food coloring to make the mixture light green in color. Mix in the dill, if using. Serve as a dip or with party rye for sandwiches.

What's Cooking in Kentucky
Irene Hayes
Hueysville, Kentucky

EGGPLANT CAVIAR

Eggplants here take center stage. This versatile fruit, found in the peak season during August and September, becomes an elegant appetizer.

YIELD: ABOUT 2 CUPS

2 large eggplants
Salt
Freshly ground pepper
½ to 1 cup salad oil
½ onion, grated

Preheat the oven to 350°. Pierce the eggplants with a skewer to prevent bursting during baking. Place the eggplants on a cookie sheet and bake for about 45 minutes, or until soft. Let cool and

peel. Chop the pulp coarsely; season to taste with salt and pepper. Blend salad oil with the eggplant until the eggplant cannot absorb any more. Mix in the onion. Serve in a bowl with black bread or wheat crackers.

La Piñata
Junior League of McAllen
McAllen, Texas

TEXAS CAVIAR

Forget beluga. Southerners crave this concoction of more mundane ingredients.

YIELD: 4 TO 5 CUPS

1 quart (32 fluid ounces) black-eyed peas,
   cooked, rinsed, and drained
1 small onion, minced
1 tablespoon minced fresh green chile pepper
1 large clove garlic, crushed
½ cup red wine vinegar
⅓ cup oil
½ teaspoon salt
½ teaspoon sugar
¼ teaspoon freshly ground black pepper
Pimientos, for garnish

Mix all ingredients except pimientos in a bowl. Cover and refrigerate for at least 2 days. Before serving, garnish with pimientos. (The Texas Caviar will keep up to 2 weeks.)

More Calf Fries to Caviar
Janel Franklin and Sue Vaughn
Tahoka, Texas

GUACAMOLE

A classic example of Hispanic assimilation into the Southern food culture.

YIELD: ABOUT 1 CUP

2 avocados, peeled and chopped
3 tablespoons picante sauce or salsa
2 tablespoons mayonnaise
1 tablespoon fresh lemon juice
½ teaspoon Worcestershire sauce
Dash of garlic

Mix all the ingredients in a blender. Keep tightly covered until serving time to prevent discoloration. Spoon into a serving bowl. Serve with blue corn chips.

Calf Fries to Caviar
Janel Franklin and Sue Vaughn
Tahoka, Texas

BLACK BEAN SALSA

This salsa can be served with tortilla chips, as a salad, or as a relish to accompany pork or beef. It will keep several weeks, but if you are planning to keep it more than three days, add the tomatoes the day of serving.

YIELD: 8 CUPS

3 (16-ounce) cans black beans, drained and
   rinsed
1 (8-ounce) can white shoepeg corn, drained
1 (8-ounce) can yellow corn, drained

1 red bell pepper, diced

1 green or yellow bell pepper, diced

2 large tomatoes, seeded and chopped

3 (10-ounce) cans Rotel tomatoes with green
   chiles, drained

1 cup seeded, chopped jalapeños

½ red onion, finely chopped

½ large bunch cilantro, chopped

¼ cup red wine vinegar

Juice of 1 lemon

2 large cloves garlic, finely chopped

¼ teaspoon salt, or to taste

⅛ teaspoon cayenne pepper, or to taste

⅛ teaspoon chili powder, or to taste

⅛ teaspoon cumin, or to taste

Combine all the ingredients and refrigerate in nonmetallic container.

The Artful Table
Dallas Museum of Art League
Dallas, Texas

ARTICHOKE DIP

The quintessential upscale Southern appetizer, served from New Orleans, Louisiana, to Norfolk, Virginia.

YIELD: 3 CUPS

3 to 4 cups cooked artichoke hearts
    or 2 (15-ounce) cans artichoke hearts,
    drained and chopped
1 cup grated Parmesan cheese
1 cup mayonnaise
Minced onions to taste

Preheat the oven to 350°. Combine the artichokes, cheese, and mayonnaise, mixing well. Stir in the onion to taste. Spoon into an 8-inch square baking dish. Bake until bubbly and lightly browned. Serve hot with assorted crackers.

Among the Lilies
First Baptist Church of Atlanta
Atlanta, Georgia

VIDALIA ONION DIP

Time was that Southerners with a taste for these super-sweet onions stored them in pantyhose, with a knot tied between each bulb to keep them separated. Now, with new storage techniques, we enjoy this Georgia crop year-round, and there's nary a pair of pantyhose in sight.

YIELD: 10 TO 12 SERVINGS

2 cups finely chopped Vidalia onions
2 cups grated Swiss or Gruyère cheese
1½ to 2 cups mayonnaise

Preheat the oven to 325°. Mix all the ingredients in a bowl; spread evenly in shallow baking dish.

Bake for 20 minutes. Serve with crackers or toast squares.

Windows
Brenau College Alumnae Association
Gainesville, Georgia

SUNDAY DEVILED EGGS

In the South, when we say "deviled" we don't mean hot. A dash of mustard enlivens this Sunday dinner standard.

YIELD: 12 SERVINGS

12 hard-cooked eggs
Mayonnaise
Salt
Pepper
Celery salt
Worcestershire sauce
Paprika
Caviar, for garnish (optional)

Peel the eggs, then cut them in half lengthwise. Carefully remove the yolks to a separate container. Crush the yolks and add mayonnaise to moisten. Add salt, pepper, celery salt, Worcestershire, and paprika to taste; mix well. Spoon the filling into the whites, cover well, and refrigerate. Remove from the refrigerator 30 minutes before serving. (Never serve on silver platter, or tarnish will occur.) Garnish with caviar, if desired.

Worth Savoring
Union County Historical Society
New Albany, Mississippi

Dill-Stuffed Deviled Eggs

In the South, "Come on in" is an invitation to eat and an expression of hospitality.

Yield: 16 servings

8 hard-cooked eggs, peeled
½ cup finely chopped purple onion
⅓ cup chopped fresh dill or 2 tablespoons dried
¼ cup mayonnaise
¼ cup sour cream
¼ cup Dijon mustard
Salt and freshly ground black pepper to taste

Slice the eggs in half lengthwise and remove the yolks. Mash the yolks with a fork until smooth. Blend in the onion, dill, mayonnaise, sour cream, mustard, salt, and pepper. Spoon the mixture into egg white halves, cover well, and chill.

Come On In!
Junior League of Jackson
Jackson, Mississippi

Hot Crab Meat Puffs

A taste of elegance courtesy of the sea, a coastal Southerner's other backyard garden.

Yield: 3 to 4 dozen

2 egg whites, stiffly beaten
1 cup mayonnaise
1 cup crab meat, flaked
1 teaspoon fresh lemon juice

½ teaspoon Worcestershire sauce
¼ teaspoon Tabasco
Toast rounds
Paprika

Preheat the broiler. Combine the egg whites, mayonnaise, and crab meat in a bowl. Add the lemon juice, Worcestershire, and Tabasco. Spoon onto toast rounds. Sprinkle with paprika, and broil until bubbly.

A Cook's Tour of the Azalea Coast
Auxiliary to the New Hanover-Pender County
  Medical Society
Wilmington, North Carolina

Pickled Oysters with Tangy Seafood Sauce

Pickling was once a way to preserve perishables. In this dish, it's all about flavor.

Yield: 8 servings

2 pints oysters, with their liquid
¼ cup white vinegar
Salt to taste
Pinch of allspice
6 whole cloves
Pinch of mace
Cayenne pepper to taste
Crackers, for serving
Tangy Seafood Sauce, for serving
  (recipe follows)

Remove the oysters from their liquid, reserving the liquid, and wash the oysters. Put the oyster liquid in a saucepan and add the washed oysters. Add the vinegar and then the salt, allspice, cloves, mace, and cayenne. Bring to a boil, turn down the heat, and simmer until the oysters curl. Remove the oysters and put in a medium bowl. Return the liquid to a boil and immediately remove from the heat. Allow to cool slightly and then pour over the oysters. Cover and refrigerate overnight. Drain the oysters and serve with crackers and Tangy Seafood Sauce.

TANGY SEAFOOD SAUCE

1 cup prepared chili sauce
1 teaspoon fresh lemon juice
½ teaspoon Worcestershire sauce
Prepared horseradish sauce to taste

Combine all the ingredients in a bowl. Let stand in refrigerator overnight to blend flavors.

Dining by Fireflies
Junior League of Charlotte
Charlotte, North Carolina

OYSTERS ROCKEFELLER

Originally created in 1899 at Antoine's Restaurant in New Orleans, Louisiana, this rich treatment of oysters is now enjoyed throughout the region.

YIELD: 6 SERVINGS

½ (10-ounce) package frozen chopped spinach
6 green onions
2 stalks green celery

⅓ bunch parsley
⅓ head lettuce
1 stick (¼ pound) unsalted butter, at room
  temperature
¾ cup bread crumbs
1 tablespoon Worcestershire sauce
1 tablespoon anchovy paste
Dash of hot sauce
1½ tablespoons anise-flavored liqueur
¼ teaspoon table salt
Rock salt
3 dozen oysters
¼ cup grated Parmesan cheese

Place the spinach, onions, celery, parsley, and lettuce in a blender; mince finely. Mix together the butter and ¼ cup of the bread crumbs in a large bowl. Add the minced greens and stir to mix. Add the Worcestershire sauce, anchovy paste, hot sauce, liqueur, and table salt. Mix thoroughly.

Make a bed of rock salt in each of 6 pie plates. Place in the oven for 20 minutes at 450°. Keep the oven on. Drain the oysters from their shells. Place the oysters back on the half shell, arranging 6 oysters in each pan of salt. Spread 2 tablespoons of sauce over each oyster. Combine the Parmesan cheese and remaining ½ cup bread crumbs; top each oyster with 1 teaspoon of the mixture. Bake at 450° for about 25 minutes, or until lightly browned.

Recipes and Reminiscences of New Orleans
Parents Club of Ursuline Academy
New Orleans, Louisiana

CONFEDERATES ON HORSEBACK

Says Bethany Ewald Bultman, "This recipe was found in an 1873 Natchez cookbook, and hand-written in the margin was 'It got us through the WAR.' It didn't say which war."

YIELD: 12 SERVINGS

24 small rounds of bread
Unsalted butter
24 drained oysters
24 thin slices of bacon spread with anchovy
   paste

Preheat the oven to 400°. Toast the bread rounds and butter them lightly. Wrap each oyster in bacon and secure with a toothpick. Bake for about 5 minutes or until the bacon is crisp. Drain well and remove the toothpicks. Serve on the toast rounds.

Cook with a Natchez Native
Bethany Ewald Bultman
Natchez, Mississippi

PICKLED SHRIMP

YIELD: 10 TO 12 SERVINGS

2½ quarts water
3 tablespoons salt
15 to 20 whole allspice
6 to 8 peppercorns
⅛ teaspoon black pepper
Juice and zest of ½ lemon
15 to 20 cloves
6 cloves garlic, sliced
3 small onions, sliced
2 large stalks celery, crushed or broken
2 large bay leaves
2 pinches dried thyme or 1 sprig
   fresh thyme
Several sprigs of parsley
A few bits of dried red pepper
1 tablespoon Worcestershire sauce
2 to 2½ pounds raw large shrimp
4 medium onions, thinly sliced
A handful of bay leaves
Sauce (recipe follows)
Crackers, for serving

Season 2½ quarts water with 3 tablespoons of salt; then add all the ingredients except the shrimp, the 4 medium sliced onions, the bay leaves, and the sauce. Bring to a boil and allow to simmer 20 minutes. Add the shrimp and bring to a boil again; lower the heat and simmer 12 to 15 minutes. Let the shrimp cool, then shell and devein them. In a large pan, arrange the shrimp in layers with the sliced onions and bay leaves. Pour the sauce over the layers. Cover the pan and refrigerate at least 24 hours. To serve, arrange the mixture on a large platter. Serve with cocktail picks and crackers.

SAUCE

1¼ cups salad oil
¾ cup warmed white vinegar
1½ teaspoons salt
2½ teaspoons celery seed
2½ teaspoons capers, with their juice
Dash of hot sauce

¼ cup Worcestershire sauce

1 tablespoon prepared yellow mustard

Combine all the ingredients in a bowl; mix thoroughly.

River Road Recipes
Junior League of Baton Rouge
Baton Rouge, Louisiana

SHRIMP PASTE

We have a way with leftovers, a remnant of the days when nothing went to waste, especially the prized shrimp.

YIELD: 4 CUPS

2 (8-ounce) packages (2 cups) cream cheese,
   at room temperature
Juice of 1 lemon
1 large onion, grated
1 teaspoon salt
Cayenne pepper to taste
1 cup ketchup
1 cup cooked diced shrimp
Tiny biscuits or potato chips,
   for serving

Place the cheese in a blender with all the ingredients except the shrimp; mix well. Gently stir the shrimp into the cheese mixture. Serve with tiny biscuits or potato chips.

Good Cookin' from the Heart of Virginia
Junior League of Lynchburg
Lynchburg, Virginia

HAM SPREAD

YIELD: 6 TO 8 SERVINGS

2 cups ground ham
½ cup mayonnaise
2 hard-cooked eggs, chopped fine
½ cup sweet pickle relish
2 tablespoons chopped onion
Dash of ground cloves
Party rye bread, for serving

Combine all the ingredients in a bowl. Mix well and chill. Serve with party rye bread.

Little Bit Different!
St. John's Episcopal Church
Moultrie, Georgia

HOT SAUSAGE BALLS

Most Southerners savor sausage balls that taste simply of cheese and meat. This recipe adds an interesting twist.

YIELD: 30 TO 40 APPETIZERS

1 pound hot country sausage
2 cups sauerkraut
3 ounces cream cheese, at room temperature
1 egg, lightly beaten
½ cup milk
1 tablespoon chopped parsley (optional)
¾ cup fine, dry bread crumbs

Crumble the sausage. Cook and drain well. Drain the sauerkraut and snip into pieces. Combine the sausage, sauerkraut, and cream cheese. Refrigerate until cool. Preheat the oven to 450°. Mix the egg and milk together. Mix the parsley, if using, with the bread crumbs. Roll the sausage mixture into balls. Dip each ball in the egg-and-milk mixture and roll in the bread crumbs. Bake for 10 minutes. Serve hot.

Tea-Time at the Masters
Junior League of Augusta
Augusta, Georgia

PORK BALLS PRYTANIA

Turner Catledge, a Mississippian, became managing editor and director of The New York Times. *He offered this recipe to* The Great American Writers' Cookbook *"not so much as a product of the genius of a 'great writer' but by one who has enjoyed these tidbits between many drinks, where they fit best."*

YIELD: ABOUT 3 TO 4 DOZEN

1 pound cheddar cheese, grated
1 pound hot country sausage
3 cups Bisquick

Preheat the oven to 350°. Mix all the ingredients; roll into bite-sized balls and place on a cookie sheet. Bake for 12 minutes. (Uncooked balls can be stored in the freezer and heated when needed.)

The Great American Writers' Cookbook
Dean Faulkner Wells
Oxford, Mississippi

CUCUMBER SANDWICHES

A delight for teatime in the South, especially on a warm spring or summer afternoon.

YIELD: 20 TO 24 SERVINGS

2 large cucumbers, peeled and finely grated
1 tablespoon salt
1 rounded tablespoon mayonnaise
1 rounded tablespoon sour cream
1 rounded tablespoon room-temperature cream cheese
⅛ teaspoon green onion flakes
⅛ teaspoon dillweed
Dash of black pepper
1 small onion, finely chopped
1 loaf sliced white bread, crusts removed

Combine the cucumbers and salt in a bowl and chill for a few hours. Wring the moisture from the cucumbers with your hands. Chop the cucumbers. Mix the mayonnaise, sour cream, and cream cheese with the cucumber in a medium bowl. Add the green onion flakes, dillweed, black pepper, and onion. Cut each slice of bread into quarters. Spread the cucumber mixture on each quarter to make an open-faced sandwich.

A Second Serving
Junior League of Charleston
Charleston, West Virginia

TOMATO SANDWICHES

If the tomatoes aren't vine-ripe, don't even bother.

YIELD: 20 SANDWICHES

40 slices white bread, frozen
Unsalted butter, at room temperature
Mayonnaise
Small vine-ripe tomatoes, peeled and sliced
   (enough tomatoes to yield 20 slices)
Salt and black pepper to taste
Chopped fresh basil

Cut 2- to 3-inch rounds from the frozen bread slices and spread with butter, then mayonnaise. Using half the bread rounds, place a tomato slice on each. Sprinkle the tomato slice with salt and pepper and a little basil. Top each sandwich with one of the remaining bread rounds.

Note: Butter keeps the bread from becoming soggy.

Party Potpourri
Junior League of Memphis
Memphis, Tennessee

Radish Sandwiches

Yield: 2 dozen

*8 radishes, trimmed, plus 4 to 6 radishes,
    trimmed and thinly sliced, for garnish*
6 ounces cream cheese
2 tablespoons unsalted butter
1 tablespoon parsley leaves
1 teaspoon snipped chives, fresh or freeze-dried
Fresh lemon juice
Salt and freshly ground black pepper
6 to 9 slices dark bread
Coarse salt

For the filling, grate the 8 radishes in a food processor or on a hand grater. Place in a colander and squeeze out all the excess liquid. Cream the cream cheese and butter in the food processor until well blended and fluffy; add the grated radishes, parsley, chives, and lemon juice and salt and pepper to taste, flavoring this filling assertively. Cut the bread into small rounds, spread with the filling, and garnish with the thinly sliced radishes. Put a pinch of coarse salt on top of each. Chill and serve.

One of a Kind
Junior League of Mobile
Mobile, Alabama

Boiled Peanuts

There was a time when community "peanut boilings" were as common as barbecues and fish frys in the Deep South.

Yield: 6 to 8 servings

*4 pounds green peanuts, in their shells (see
    Note)*
6 quarts water
6 to 10 tablespoons salt

Wash the green peanuts and place in a large pot with water and salt. Cover and bring to a boil. Boil slowly for 1½ to 2 hours. The water should be briny. More water and salt can be added if necessary while cooking. Test for doneness after 1½ hours. The peanuts should be soft but not mushy inside. Rinse in plain (unsalted) water. Drain well.

Note: Green (fresh) peanuts are available mostly in the early autumn. After cooling the boiled peanuts, you can freeze them in plastic bags. When ready to serve, simply reheat to a boil and drain.

Savannah Style
Junior League of Savannah
Savannah, Georgia

Virginia Roasted Peanuts

In Virginia, peanuts serve as fodder for Smithfield hogs, from which come those famous Smith-

field hams, but they taste grand to us humans, too.

YIELD: 2 CUPS

2 cups shelled raw peanuts, with skins on
2 tablespoons unsalted butter, melted
Salt to taste

Preheat the oven to 350°. Place the peanuts on a cookie sheet in a single layer. Bake 15 to 20 minutes, or until golden brown, stirring occasionally. Remove from the oven and pour the butter over the hot peanuts, stirring to coat. Drain on a brown paper bag and salt to taste while warm.

Very Virginia
Junior League of Hampton Roads
Newport News, Virginia

SPICED PECANS

Pecan trees, though native to the western regions of the South, are grown in a wide band that stretches from Texas to North Carolina.

YIELD: ABOUT 3 ½ CUPS

1 cup sugar
¼ cup water
1 tablespoon unsalted butter
1 teaspoon cinnamon
3 cups pecan halves

Mix the sugar, water, butter, and cinnamon in a saucepan. Place over medium heat and bring to a boil. When the mixture starts to boil, cook ex-

actly 2 minutes, stirring constantly. Pour in the pecans; stir quickly until the pecans are coated and all the syrup is absorbed. Pour out on sheet of waxed paper. Separate. Let cool and serve.

Note: Ground black pepper can be added to taste.

The Stuffed Griffin
Utility Club
Griffin, Georgia

SOUSE

During hog-killing time, nothing is wasted. The skin, ears, and noses are used to make souse, which is sliced and served with salad greens.

Take the skin from hogs and place in a large pot. Add ears and noses if desired. Cover with water and cook over an open fire until the skins are very tender. Grind; then add vinegar, salt, cayenne, and sage to taste. Pour into large shallow pans. The souse will congeal and can be cut in blocks.

The Smithfield Cookbook
Junior Woman's Club of Smithfield
Smithfield, Virginia

HOG'S HEAD CHEESE

Another example of eating every part of the hog but the squeal.

YIELD: 8 TO 10 SERVINGS

Souse

The worst part of making souse is getting the pig feet and the head ready to cook. The hard tips of the feet are removed and the tough snout cut off. The feet and head are carefully scraped and cleaned, until there is not one single bristle left to appear later in the souse. This done, the head and feet are boiled in a large pot until the meat is so tender that it falls away from the bone. Then take out every bit of bone and gristle, leaving a mass of perfectly tender meat. To this mass add salt and pepper and sage to suit the family taste and work in thoroughly. Pack the meat down in bowls and lay a weight on each bowl. When it is cold the souse will be jelled solidly, and should be sliced and served cold. A delicious dish. But, do not deceive yourself to the point of believing that you may safely eat all you want.

Collected by Kate C. Hubbard, in Possum & Pomegranate *for the Federal Writers Project "America Eats"*

Head, ears, and feet of a hog
1 tablespoon salt
1 tablespoon black pepper
1 tablespoon cayenne
3 cups finely chopped green onions
2 cups finely chopped parsley

Remove the eyes and brains from the head and split the head in half. Wash and scrape the head thoroughly, removing the excess fat. Singe the pig feet; wash and scrape. Singe, wash, and clean the ears thoroughly with hot water. Place all the pieces of the hog in a large pot; cover with hot water. Boil until the meat drops from the bones. Reserve 2 cups of the broth. Put the meat through a meat grinder. Add the salt, pepper, cayenne, broth, green onions, and parsley to 5 pounds of meat. Place in pans; press with weights and refrigerate overnight. Slice; store in jars covered with vinegar.

Cajun Cooking
Lafayette, Louisiana

CRACKLIN'S

Memere and Mam Papaul had to hide these from the children so there would be enough left to use in homemade bread for the family's supper.

YIELD: 5 POUNDS

1 pint water
5 pounds pork fat, diced

Place the water and pork in a deep black iron pot. Place over medium heat. Cook for about 1 hour, or until the water has evaporated and the fat has fried tender, brown, and crisp. Drain. Store in a covered jar. Eat as a snack or with grits, or use in cracklin' biscuits or cornbread.

Mam Papaul's Country Creole Basket
Nancy Tregre Wilson
Baton Rouge, Louisiana

BEVERAGES

·······················

DRINKS AND DRINKING IN THE SOUTH

*Southerners will drink wet and vote dry,
so long as any citizen can stagger to the polls.*

WILL ROGERS

Drinks and Drinking in the South

....

The South is a land of beguiling and bewitching contradictions. Poverty and plenty, hostility and hospitality, sobriety and sottedness alike have defined our people and our ways. Rather than temper our contradictions, we have instead resolved to revel in them. How else can you explain a region where many spend their Saturday nights in the honky-tonk and their Sunday mornings in church?

Despite claims to the contrary, drinks and drinking are not newly arrived Northern imports. Rather, alcoholic beverages and the Southern enjoyment thereof have a storied history south of the Mason-Dixon divide.

Soon after Pennsylvania whiskey makers fled south to frontier Kentucky in the 1790s, bent on escaping a newly levied excise tax on their home-distilled rye whiskeys, a new beverage came to the fore, as innovators like Dr. James Crow and the Reverend Elijah Craig began distilling a beverage very similar to what we now think of as bourbon, taking advantage of Kentucky's natural resources: limestone spring–fed water, forests of oak trees, and row after crop row of corn.

Today, a whiskey made from at least 51 percent corn that has been distilled to a maximum of 160 proof and then aged for at least two years at no more than 125 proof in charred, new oak barrels earns the right to be called bourbon. If the aging, at least, is done in Kentucky, you've got Kentucky bourbon.

It is not merely to the manufacture of America's premier whiskey that Southerners lay claim. No, by some accounts, the cocktail itself was invented in the South. According to New Orleanians, Antoine

Peychaud, a French-born apothecary, deserves credit for first concocting the cocktail. Sometime in the late 1790s, Peychaud began brewing a tonic, oftentimes called bitters, purported to settle the stomach and relieve other ills.

The story goes that Peychaud took to combining his bitters with a bit of Sazerac brandy and served the resulting potable in *coquetiers,* delicate china egg cups. Soon, the custom caught on with saloons in New Orleans, and *coquetier* was elided in that Brooklynese New Orleans dialect to cocktail. Some even argue that the standard drink measure of a jigger owes its origins to Peychaud's little egg cups.

It was not until the middle years of the nineteenth century that the prohibition movement took hold down South. But to be sure, it was here that it would find fervor. Twentieth-century populist Mississippi politician Theodore Bilbo made a lunge for the temperance vote when he declared that liquor "steals strength from the body, robs the mind of reason, kills love in the heart, drives peace from the soul, withers beauty in its blossom, and lights the funeral pyre of the deepest pit of hell. Its wrath is all-consuming; hate is its minister, and desolation marks the way that the demon has taken in his march of destruction." Never mind that he was known to take a tipple.

Five years before national Prohibition took effect, Alabama, Georgia, Kentucky, Louisiana, Mississippi, North Carolina, Tennessee, and West Virginia were dry. Even today, when a Southerner inquires as to whether a particular locale is wet or dry, chances are the query has little to do with the relative humidity and a lot to do with whether local laws allow one to whet one's whistle with a spot of liquor.

Southerners are, as a rule, comfortable with the contradictions, despite the strange bedfellows sometimes engendered. In many regions of the South, hard liquor is still not sold—at least in the open. In an uproarious evisceration of Southern culture, essayist Florence King may have explained it best when she told of an acquaintance who observed, "The Baptists and the bootleggers have always been hand in glove 'round here. Neither of 'em wanted anybody to drink legal hooch. It was bad for both their business, you might say."

SUN TEA

The house wine of the South.

YIELD: 1 QUART

3 tea bags
1 quart cold water

Put the tea bags into a clear glass quart jar filled with water. Set in the sun for several hours.

Huntsville Entertains
Historic Huntsville Foundation
Huntsville, Alabama

SWEET MINT ICED TEA

Most Southerners prefer sweet tea; however, the sugar and mint can be eliminated.

YIELD: 1 GALLON

1¾ cups sugar
2 cups boiling water
9 tea bags
Juice of 5 lemons
2 or 3 mint sprigs

Dissolve the sugar in the boiling water. Remove from the heat. Add the tea bags. Steep for 5 minutes. Remove the tea bags and add the lemon juice and mint sprigs. Add enough water to make 1 gallon. Chill and serve over ice in tall glasses.

The Southern Gourmet
Virginia Clower Robbins
St. Louis, Missouri

Lemonade

For a while during the presidential campaign in the summer of 1976, Amy Carter, daughter of Jimmy and Rosalynn, ran a lemonade stand in Plains, the way children in small towns have done for generations. Hers, however, had to close because too many customers clamored for this cooling beverage.

YIELD: 3 QUARTS

6 lemons
1½ cups sugar
2½ quarts water
Ice cubes

Roll the lemons with the hands, breaking cells to release juice. Slice 2 lemons thinly. With the handle of a wooden spoon, pound ½ cup of the sugar into the sliced lemons. Slice the remaining lemons thinly onto the first lemons, adding the remaining sugar. Let stand for 30 minutes; add water and stir. Add ice cubes.

Miss Lillian and Friends
Beth Tartan and Rudy Hayes
Plains, Georgia

Tennessee Lemonade

With a dash of Tennessee whiskey, lemonade takes on a new kick.

YIELD: 6 SERVINGS

1½ cups sugar
½ cup boiling water
1 cup fresh lemon juice
5 cups cold water
Dash of Jack Daniel's to taste (optional)
6 lemon slices
Ice cubes
Fresh mint leaves, for garnish

Combine the sugar and boiling water in a 2-quart pitcher and stir until the sugar is dissolved. Add the lemon juice; cover and store in the refrigerator at least 6 hours (but not more than 24) until ready to use. Add the cold water, and the Jack Daniel's if desired, when ready to serve. Fill the rest of the pitcher with the lemon slices and ice cubes. Pour over ice in 12-ounce glasses. Garnish with mint.

Drop Dumplin's and Pan-Fried Memories
Angie Thompson Holtzhouser
Lilbourn, Missouri

Muscadine Acid

Muscadines, the South's noble native grapes, are known for their musky sweetness.

YIELD: 50 OR 60 SERVINGS

12 pounds muscadines, thoroughly crushed
1 quart boiling water
Sugar
5 ounces tartaric acid
Crushed ice, for serving
Cold water, for serving
Sugar, for serving (optional)

Combine the muscadines and the 1 quart boiling water and let stand 12 hours or overnight; then strain. Measure the juice, and add an equal amount of sugar. Add the tartaric acid; bottle and seal.

   To serve as a beverage, add 2 tablespoons bottled mixture to a glass of crushed ice; fill with cold water. Add sugar, if desired.

Worth Savoring
Union County Historical Society
New Albany, Mississippi

CREOLE DRIPPED COFFEE

In making dripped coffee, it is essential to have a drip coffee pot and a dark roasted coffee, ground rather fine. With boiling water, scald the pot and the dripper. For every cup of coffee, allow 2 heaping tablespoons of grounds. Every 2 or 3 minutes, pour 2 tablespoons boiling water over the grounds until the desired quantity is made.

De Bonnes Choses à Manger
St. Matthew's Guild
Houma, Louisiana

CAFÉ BRÛLOT

An after-dinner drink long popular in New Orleans, brûlot *means "burnt brandy" in French. The well-outfitted dining room comes equipped with a flameproof brûlot bowl.*

YIELD: 4 SERVINGS

1 (4-inch) cinnamon stick
12 whole cloves
Peel of 2 oranges, cut in thin slices
Peel of 2 lemons, cut in thin slices
6 teaspoons sugar
8 ounces warmed brandy
2 ounces warmed curaçao
1 quart strong black coffee

In a brûlot bowl or chafing dish, mash the cinnamon, cloves, orange and lemon peels, and sugar with a ladle. Add the brandy and curaçao; stir together. Carefully ignite the brandy and mix until the sugar is dissolved. Gradually add the black coffee and continue mixing until the flame dies out. Serve in demitasse or brûlot cups.

Bayou Cuisine
St. Stephen's Episcopal Church
Indianola, Mississippi

Pear Wine

Though probably not altogether legal under Mississippi's rigid prohibition laws, pear wine is a common homemade beverage of real quality. Sand or "pineapple" pears are so plentiful that they frequently rot on the ground or are sold as low as ten cents per bushel on the trees.

Juice may be obtained raw by grinding and pressing the fruit. The commoner and better way is to dice fruit, including some of the peel, and stew slowly in limited water till tender, squeeze out juice through bags, strain very carefully, add 2½ to 3 pounds sugar per gallon, put into narrow-mouth glass, stone or wooden containers, leave open for several days till fermentation is well started; cork (leaving a vent for gasses—preferably rubber tube with end immersed in water); store in cool dark place; cork tightly when vinous fermentation ceases (2 to 3 weeks). Improves with further aging.

Good ripe fruit, cleanliness, freedom from dregs or floating particles, proper moderate temperature, and exclusion of air, so that alcohol does not escape or acetic (vinegar) fermentation set in, are important factors toward best results.

Clarence Kerns
Gulfport, Mississippi, 1941
Collected by Kate C. Hubbard in Possum & Pomegranate
for the Federal Writers Project "America Eats"

PLANTER'S PUNCH

The perfect drink to slake the thirst on one of those days when an egg fries easily on the sidewalk.

YIELD: 4 SERVINGS

Crushed ice
4 jiggers fresh orange juice
8 jiggers canned pineapple juice
4 jiggers water with 4 tablespoons sugar
4 jiggers light rum
4 jiggers dark rum
Cherry or orange slices, for garnish

Mix the crushed ice, orange juice, pineapple juice, sugared water, and light rum together in 4 tall glasses. Pour the dark rum on top. Garnish each serving with a fruit slice.

Party Potpourri
Junior League of Memphis
Memphis, Tennessee

SYLLABUB

Frothy and white, this sweet, downy cloud of a drink packs a real punch. Syllabub is best three or four days old; it will keep in the refrigerator.

YIELD: ABOUT 12 SERVINGS

Lemon peel
1 cup sweet wine
1 cup Madeira
1 quart heavy cream

6 tablespoons fresh lemon juice
Sugar to taste
Nutmeg

Soak the lemon peel in the sweet wine and
Madeira until the flavor is extracted; discard the
peel. Whip the cream until it begins to hold its
shape. Gradually whisk in the wines, lemon
juice, sugar, and nutmeg. Chill. Heap into glasses
to serve.

Inverness Cookbook
All Saints Episcopal Guild
Inverness, Mississippi

ORANGE BLOSSOM SYRUP

YIELD: ABOUT 3 CUPS

3 cups water
2 cups sugar
1 pint orange blossoms, rinsed and drained

Bring the water and sugar to a boil in a
saucepan. Add the orange blossoms; cover and
set aside for 20 minutes. Pour the syrup through
a colander; discard the blossoms. Place the syrup
in a bottle and refrigerate. Serve 1 ounce over ice
or mix with 1 quart vodka and serve over ice.

Mam Papaul's Country Creole Basket
Nancy Tregre Wilson
Baton Rouge, Louisiana

ARTILLERY PUNCH

*From the British tradition comes this punch that
packs a wallop.*

YIELD: 6 GALLONS,
OR ABOUT 80 TO 90 SERVINGS

1½ gallons sweet wine
½ gallon rum
1 quart gin
1 quart brandy
½ pint Benedictine
1½ quarts rye whiskey
1½ gallons strong tea
2½ pounds dark brown sugar
Juice of 18 oranges
Juice of 18 lemons
1 large bottle maraschino cherries
1 case Champagne

Combine all the ingredients except the Champagne about 36 to 48 hours before serving time.
Add the chilled Champagne when ready to serve.

The James K. Polk Cookbook
Polk Memorial Auxiliary
Columbia, Tennessee

MILK PUNCH

A New Orleans favorite during winter holidays. It's a soothing drink after a night of partying.

YIELD: 8 SERVINGS

2 quarts vanilla ice cream
1½ cups brandy
¼ cup sugar
2 teaspoons vanilla
2 cups cold milk
Nutmeg, for serving

Let the ice cream soften. Blend with the remaining ingredients except the nutmeg. Place to keep cool in the freezer until 1 hour before serving. Grate some nutmeg on top after pouring the milk punch into the glass.

Dodwell's Cookbook
Mary Dodwell
New Orleans, Louisiana

HOLIDAY EGGNOG

Eggnogs and other frothy, milky drinks are a legacy of our British forefathers.

YIELD: 20 SERVINGS

6 eggs, separated
1 cup sugar
1½ cups cognac, Cointreau, or Grand Marnier
½ cup light rum
1½ quarts milk
3 cups heavy cream, whipped
Nutmeg, for serving

Our Southern Receipt

Persimmon Beer

Native Americans have long favored persimmons for beermaking, and during times of privation, persimmon seeds were roasted and then ground as a coffee substitute.

Remove the seeds from enough ripe persimmons to make a bushel of fruit without the seeds. Line a wooden keg with clean corn shucks. Mash up the persimmons with half a bushel of corn meal and half a bushel of sweet potato peelings. Put in the keg and cover with water. Cover and allow to stand till the taste is right and then bore a hole in the top of the keg and draw off the beer. If you put a piece of cornbread in a cup and fill up the cup with persimmon beer, you'll have something highly satisfactory. Indulge cautiously until you learn your capacity.

Collected by Kate C. Hubbard in Possum & Pomegranate *for the Federal Writers Project "America Eats"*

Beat the egg yolks until thick and lemon-colored. Add the sugar gradually, beating constantly. Still beating, add the cognac and rum gradually. Chill 1 hour, stirring occasionally.

Beat the egg whites until stiff. Add the milk to the cognac mixture slowly and fold in the whipped cream and egg whites. Store in covered jars in the refrigerator a day or so before serving. Ladle when serving to distribute "fluff." Sprinkle each serving with grated nutmeg. Keeps, covered, 3 days in the refrigerator.

Almost Heaven
Junior League of Huntington
Huntington, West Virginia

PLAY MAMA'S CHRISTMAS EGGNOG

Natchezians adore open houses, particularly during the Christmas season. Eggnog is traditionally served at that time, and it's delicious at Play Mama's house. Play Mama is Katherine Grafton Miller, the originator of the Natchez Pilgrimage.

YIELD: 20 SERVINGS

18 eggs, separated
2 cups sugar
Fifth bourbon whiskey
2 quarts heavy cream, unbeaten
Nutmeg

Beat the egg yolks. Add the sugar, whiskey, and whipping cream, beating constantly. Beat the egg whites. Gently fold into the yolk mixture. Serve in a silver punch bowl and sprinkle with nutmeg.

Variation: To make this recipe less rich, use no egg yolks—only 9 egg whites—and substitute half-and-half for the whipping cream.

Cook with a Natchez Native
Bethany Ewald Bultman
Natchez, Mississippi

CHAMPAGNE PUNCH

Some Southerners would never do this to Champagne; others lap it up.

YIELD: 3¼ QUARTS

1 lemon, thinly sliced
1½ cups sugar
2 cups fresh lemon juice or fresh concentrate
2 fifths dry Sauternes, chilled
1 fifth Champagne, chilled
½ cup Cointreau
½ cup brandy

Make an ice ring for the punch bowl by filling a 2-quart ring mold with lemon slices and water. Freeze
　Stir the sugar into the lemon juice until dissolved and chill. To serve, pour lemon-and-sugar mixture, Sauternes, Champagne, Cointreau, and brandy into the punch bowl and stir to mix. Add the ice ring.

Dinner on the Diner
The Junior League of Chattanooga
Chattanooga, Tennessee

St. Cecilia Punch

This powerful punch was the traditional drink served at annual balls of the St. Cecilia Society, founded in Charleston in 1762.

YIELD: 80 TO 90 SERVINGS

6 lemons
1 quart brandy
1 pineapple
1½ pounds sugar
1 quart green tea
1 pint dark rum
1 quart peach brandy

4 quarts Champagne
2 quarts carbonated water

Slice the lemons thin and cover with brandy. Allow to steep for 24 hours.

Several hours before serving, slice the pineapple into the bowl with the lemon slices. Add the sugar, tea, rum, and peach brandy; stir well. Add the Champagne and carbonated water right before serving.

Charleston Receipts
Junior League of Charleston
Charleston, South Carolina

GENERAL SIMON BOLIVAR BUCKNER

THE PERFECT MINT JULEP

A mint julep is not the product of a formula—it is a ceremony and must be performed by a gentleman possessing a true sense of the artistic, a deep reverence for the ingredients, and a proper appreciation for the occasion. It is a *rite* that must not be entrusted to a novice, a statistician, or a Yankee. It is a heritage of the Old South, an emblem of hospitality, and a vehicle in which noble minds can travel together upon the flowerstrewn paths of a happy and congenial thought.

So far as the mere mechanics of the operation are concerned, the procedure, stripped of its ceremonial embellishments, can be described as follows: Go to a spring where cool, crystal-clear water burbles from under a bank of dew-washed ferns. In a consecrated vessel, dip up a little water at the source.

Follow the stream through its banks of green moss and wildflowers until it broadens and trickles through beds of mint growing in aromatic profusion and waving softly in the summer breeze. Gather the sweetest and tenderest shoots and gently carry them home. Go to the sideboard and select a decanter of Kentucky bourbon. . . . An ancestral sugar bowl, a row of silver goblets, some spoons, and some ice and you are ready to start.

Into a canvas bag, pound twice as much as ice as you think you will need. Make it fine as snow, and keep it dry and do not allow it to degenerate into slush.

Into each goblet put a slightly heaping teaspoonful of granulated sugar, barely cover this with spring water, and slightly bruise one mint leaf into this, leaving the spoon in the goblet. Then pour elixir from the decanter until the goblets are about one-fourth full. Fill the goblets with snow ice, sprinkling in a small amount of sugar as you fill. Wipe the outside of the goblets dry and embellish copiously with mint.

Then comes the important and delicate operation of frosting. By proper manipulation of the spoon, the ingredients are circulated and blended until nature, wishing to take a further hand and add another of its beautiful phenomena, encrusts the whole in a glistening coat of white frost. Thus harmoniously blended by the deft touches of a skilled hand, you have a beverage eminently appropriate for honorable men and beautiful women.

In a letter to a fellow general, General Simon Bolivar Buckner shared this receipt. Richard Barksdale Harwell, author of The Mint Julep, *postulates that someone else may have composed the receipt, but we will never know. General Buckner was killed in World War II.*

MAGNOLIAS

A variation on the mimosa theme.

YIELD: 8 SERVINGS

3¼ cups fresh orange juice, chilled
1 fifth Champagne, chilled
⅓ cup Grand Marnier
Orange slices or mint sprigs, for garnish

Combine the juice and Champagne in a large bowl or pitcher. Pour into 8 glasses; drizzle 2 teaspoons Grand Marnier over each. Garnish as desired. Serve immediately.

Celebrations on the Bayou
Junior League of Monroe
Monroe, Louisiana

WINTER WASSAIL

Germanic influences can be seen—and tasted—throughout the Hill Country of Texas.

YIELD: 15 TO 18 SERVINGS

4 cups apple cider
2 cups cranberry juice
½ cup fresh orange juice
2 cups vodka
1 cup brandy
1 teaspoon whole allspice
1½ teaspoons whole cloves
2 cinnamon sticks
Cranberries (optional)

Our Southern Receipt

Mint Julep

Says Eudora Welty, "In Columbus, Mississippi, hospitality at many plantation homes always includes mint juleps. The drink symbolizes the charm of the Old South, when life was less strenuous than it is today—when brave men and beautiful women loved and laughed and danced the hours away."

YIELD: 1 SERVING

½ lump sugar
1 tablespoon water
1 mint leaf
Crushed ice
Bourbon whiskey
Mint sprig

In a silver goblet, dissolve the sugar in the water. Bruise the mint leaf between your fingers and drop it into the dissolved sugar. Stir well and remove the mint leaf. Fill a goblet with crushed ice. Add bourbon whiskey to the top. Garnish with a mint sprig. Let goblet stand until frosted. Serve immediately.

Mr. and Mrs. T. C. Billups, "Whitehall"
Columbus, Mississippi
Collected by Eudora Welty for the Federal Writers Project
"America Eats"

Combine all the ingredients except the cranberries in a large saucepan. Heat until warm. Strain. Serve in a punch bowl and garnish with cranberries, if desired.

Necessities and Temptations
Junior League of Austin
Austin, Texas

Sangria Fresca

Paul Adams grew up in central Kentucky. Through his late wife, Evy, he learned the secrets of Cuban cuisine, melding his Southern experiences with her Havana memories.

Yield: 4 to 6 servings

1 bottle of red wine, chilled
1 cup club soda, chilled
Juice of 1 lemon
1 lemon, thinly sliced

Pour the chilled wine into a pitcher and add the chilled club soda, lemon juice, and thin slices of lemon. Serve over ice in a wineglass.

La Cocina Cubana Sencilla
Paul L. Adams
Louisville, Kentucky

Ramos Gin Fizz

First made by New Orleans bar owner Henry Ramos, this cocktail is a Carnival season favorite.

Yield: 1 serving

White of 1 egg
1 teaspoon fresh lime juice
1 teaspoon fresh lemon juice
2 teaspoons confectioners' sugar
1 tablespoon carbonated water
1 tablespoon heavy cream
A few drops orange flower water
1 jigger of gin
Finely crushed ice

Place all the ingredients in blender and blend well.

Recipe Jubilee!
Junior League of Mobile
Mobile, Alabama

Sazerac

Still popular in New Orleans where the Fairmont Hotel's Sazerac Bar serves up the quintessential version of this anise-flavored cocktail.

Yield: 1 serving

1 lump sugar
1 teaspoon water
1 dash of bitters
1 jigger of bourbon

1 dash anise-flavored liqueur
Cracked ice
1 slice lemon peel

Muddle the sugar and water in one glass. Add the bitters and bourbon. Stir. Twirl the liqueur in the second glass, fill with cracked ice, and add the lemon peel. Pour the bourbon mixture over ice.

Recipes and Reminiscences of New Orleans II
Parents Club of Ursuline Academy
New Orleans, Louisiana

JULEPS

The mint julep is among the most widely discussed and most debated recipes in the whole realm of mixed drinks. It is almost impossible to find two experts who agree on the way it should be made, and to recommend a certain method is inevitably to bring down on your head the wrath of some other julep school. May we say, however, that these two recipes have proved exceedingly popular?

ORIGINAL KENTUCKY MINT JULEP

Put 12 sprigs fresh mint in bowl. Cover with confectioners' sugar and just enough water to dissolve the sugar; crush with wooden pestle. Place half the crushed mint and liquid in the bottom of a crackled glass tumbler, or in a sterling silver or pewter tankard. Fill the glass half full of finely crushed ice. Add the rest of the crushed mint and fill the remainder of the glass with crushed ice. Pour in fine bourbon until the glass is brimming. Place in the icebox for at least an hour (preferably two or three, if you can wait that long). Decorate with sprigs of mint covered with confectioners' sugar when ready to serve.

GEORGIA MINT JULEP

4 sprigs fresh mint, plus additional for garnish
½ tablespoon confectioners' sugar
1½ jiggers of bourbon whiskey

Place the mint, sugar, and whiskey in a glass; fill with crushed ice and stir gently until the glass is frosted. Decorate with sprigs of mint.

Irwin S. Cobb's Own Recipe Book
Irwin S. Cobb
Louisville, Kentucky

NGER
DER COOLER
A DRIER PIPE
EMIUM
NS
ACK!
SK
LBS.
ROUGH CUT
48 LBS.
CAROLINA
BES
SELF-RISING
LOUR
CAROL
D CO.,
TON, N.
12 LBS.
SHENANDOAH
MILLING COMPANY, INC
None Better
Robert E. Lee
Finest Patent Flou
QUALITY BLEACHED UNEXCELLED
NORFOLK, VA.

BREADS

....

LIFE BENEATH THE HOT BREAD LINE

It's an old tale that the South is known as the land of the hot biscuit and the cold check. Yet a part of the placidity of the South comes from the sense of well-being that follows the heart-and-body-warming consumption of breads fresh from the oven. We serve cold baker's bread to our enemies, trusting that they will never impose on our hospitality again.

MARJORIE KINNAN RAWLINGS, *CROSS CREEK COOKERY*

Life Beneath the Hot Bread Line

....

Though it was the biscuit that stirred the writer Rawlings, she might as well have taken up her pen in praise of cornbread, ash cake, johnnycake, spiderbread, corn pone, or hoecake. No matter the grain, whether it be wheat flour for buttermilk biscuits or cornmeal for hoecakes, the Southern tongue calls out for *hot* breads. Fresh from the oven, split open, and slathered with butter, a treat both trivial and transcendent, hot breads bespeak neither race nor class.

Instead, the penchant for hot breads is a delineator of providence and province, a talisman of one's belonging to the Southland. The Mason-Dixon line, observed onetime Tennessee governor Bob Taylor, "is the dividing line between cold bread and hot biscuit."

The breads of the South serve yeoman's duty—as foil for sausage-laced sawmill gravy, as sponge to sop potlikker from the bottom of a bowl, or as ballast in what a friend once termed a Hillbilly Smoothie (a tumbler full of buttermilk and cornbread best eaten with a long-handled iced tea spoon). Sure, you can dress them up, add a bit of cheese or a couple of eggs to the batter, but what you are left with is much the same: quick bread served simply, and—if you do it right—served hot.

Much ink has been spilled and many trees felled over the question of why Southerners have such an affinity for hot breads. To anyone who has ever endured a protracted Sunday dinner blessing while seated at his grandmother's table, flanked on one side by a linen-shrouded basket of biscuits and on the other by a platter of skillet cornbread steaming forth billows of butter-scented promise, the reason is as obvious as it is elemental: because they taste best that way.

Those who persist in their questioning of why Southern bread isn't up to snuff unless it's hot are left with a number of scenarios to ponder. Perhaps the most plausible is that it is a legacy of the days when corn was virtually the sole grain of the South and cornbread the true staff of Southern life.

Prior to around 1880, wheat flour was a comparatively precious commodity consigned to the status of a sometime indulgence, while cornmeal was the stuff of daily sustenance. The problem was that cornbread didn't keep well. Yesterday's cornbread might make a fine dressing, but few would want a stale hunk of it on their dinner plate. So rather than splurge on wheat flour and store-bought leavening, Southern breadmakers opted to bake cornbread daily and serve it piping hot as proof of its freshness. With the Southern penchant for hot bread thus established, the practice soon carried over to the baking of yeast-fueled, baking powder–leavened biscuits and rolls. So goes the story.

No matter the story, the fact remains that when a Southerner reaches for a biscuit or a square of cornbread, he usually reaches for two, ever mindful of that oft-repeated invitation to eat: "Take two and butter 'em while they're hot."

HOT-WATER CORNBREAD

South of the Mason-Dixon line, some people call this first cousin to the hush puppy "dog bread."

YIELD: 8 TO 10 PONES

1 cup white cornmeal
1 teaspoon salt

About 1 cup boiling water
Bacon drippings

Combine the cornmeal and salt in a bowl. Stir in enough boiling water to allow the mixture to reach the proper consistency. With wet hands, shape the corn mixture by tablespoonful into flat pones or into flat little rolls. Fry the corn pones on both sides in the bacon drippings until crisp and brown, turning several times.

Hospitality
Harvey Woman's Club
Palestine, Texas

CORNBREAD FROM GEORGETOWN, ARKANSAS

Georgetown is a community of about seventy-five people located on the White River. This recipe originated with a cook employed on a nearby plantation.

YIELD: 8 SERVINGS

2 eggs
1 cup buttermilk
1 cup white cornmeal
1 teaspoon salt
2 tablespoons flour
¼ teaspoon baking soda
1 teaspoon baking powder
1 tablespoon bacon drippings or oil

Preheat the oven to 425°. Beat the eggs in a bowl. Add the buttermilk, then the cornmeal, and mix. Add the salt, flour, baking soda, and baking

powder. Mix thoroughly. Place the drippings or oil into a 9-inch iron skillet. Heat the skillet in the oven.

Pour the batter into the hot skillet. Put it in the oven and bake the cornbread for 10 to 15 minutes. Place it under the broiler for a few minutes to brown the top slightly. Turn the cornbread out upside down on a plate. Cut it like a pie, and serve immediately.

Concerts from the Kitchen
Arkansas Symphony Orchestra Society Guild
Little Rock, Arkansas

Corn Light Bread

Add a bit of flour to cornbread, bake it in a loaf pan instead of a skillet, and presto, you have corn light bread.

Yield: 1 loaf

2 cups cornmeal
1 cup flour
1 cup sugar
1 teaspoon salt
1 teaspoon baking soda
2 cups buttermilk
1 tablespoon vegetable shortening, melted

Preheat the oven to 350°. Grease a 9x5-inch loaf pan. Mix the cornmeal, flour, sugar, and salt together in a large bowl. In a small bowl, add the baking soda to buttermilk. Gradually add the buttermilk to the dry ingredients. Stir in the vegetable shortening. Pour into the prepared pan. Cover with foil. Bake for 20 minutes. Remove the foil and continue baking for 40 minutes. Remove from the oven and let sit for 10 minutes before serving.

Great Performances
Symphony League of Tupelo
Tupelo, Mississippi

Jalapeño Cornbread

Chiles from our Hispanic neighbors to the west enliven this Southern starch.

Yield: 1 loaf

3 cups cornbread mix
2¼ cups milk
½ cup oil
3 eggs, lightly beaten
1 large onion, chopped
2 tablespoons sugar
1 cup cream-style corn
½ cup chopped jalapeño
1½ cups grated cheese
4 ounces bacon, fried and crumbled
¼ cup chopped pimientos
1 clove garlic, chopped

Preheat the oven to 400°. Grease a 9x9-inch pan or a 9x5-inch loaf pan. Mix all the ingredients together in a large bowl. Place in the prepared pan. Bake for 35 minutes.

La Piñata
Junior League of McAllen
McAllen, Texas

ELIZABETH SPENCER

HOT BREADS AND BISCUITS

I recall hot breads as being an absolute requirement of my childhood. Pans of corn-bread, cornbread muffins, and—at special times—corn sticks, baked in little cast-iron molds shaped like ears of corn. Those little sticks always were so nice and crisp.

With the lesser ingredients, dog bread was made. It was unlike cornbread in that no buttermilk or soda was added, and certainly no eggs. It was the coarsest gruel imaginable, cooked up in hot iron skillets, then cut up for the dogs, and served with gravy on top.

We used to go to the grist meal to get our cornmeal, which we bought in enor-mous tins of five gallons or more. I remember it as very fine, very white. It had to be white, never yellow. When I first started publishing, I would go to New York and they would—quite self-consciously—order cornbread for me. It was always yellow. I never could quite figure out what they were trying to do.

The other hot breads we loved were biscuits. My father used to say that the bis-cuit dough was as old as his and my mother's marriage, because when they first mar-ried they lived with her parents and took dough from her parents' home to the house they bought. A little bit of dough from each batch of biscuits survived and was used in the next batch. And so on. Soon there was a whole generation of doughs de-scended from that first batch. My, those biscuits were good, steaming hot, fresh from the oven, with a bit of butter.

Elizabeth Spencer, a native of Carrolton, Mississippi, is the author of numerous novels, including The Night Travelers, *and* Landscapes of the Heart, *a memoir.*

Beaten Biscuits

Says Eudora Welty, "As far back as the 1840s, old plantations along the Tombigbee River centered their social life in Aberdeen, Mississippi, and recipes used in those days, such as this one, are still being made today."

YIELD: ABOUT 3 DOZEN

4 cups flour, measured before sifting
¾ cup lard
1 teaspoon salt
4 teaspoons sugar
Enough ice water and milk to make a stiff
   dough (about ½ cup)

Combine all ingredients. Break (knead) 150 times until the dough pops. Roll out and cut with a biscuit cutter; prick with a fork. Bake on a baking sheet at 400°. When biscuits are light brown, turn off the heat and leave them in the oven with the door open until they sink well, to make them done in the middle.

Mrs. C. L. Lubb
Aberdeen, Mississippi
Collected by Eudora Welty for the Federal Writers
Project "America Eats"

BUTTERMILK BISCUITS

The backbone of any Southern meal, the bread most often broken at breakfast time, biscuits are our answer to the French baguette.

YIELD: ABOUT 16 BISCUITS

2 cups sifted flour
¼ teaspoon baking soda
¼ teaspoon salt
2 teaspoons baking powder
4 tablespoons and 1 teaspoon lard or shortening
½ cup buttermilk

Preheat the oven to 450°. Sift together the sifted flour, baking soda, salt, and baking powder. Work in the lard with your fingers until the mixture resembles cornmeal. Stir in the buttermilk. Turn the dough out on a floured board and knead only until dough can be rolled. Roll out ½ inch thick and cut with a floured cutter. Prick the top of each biscuit with a fork. Bake for 8 minutes.

The Memphis Cookbook
Junior League of Memphis
Memphis, Tennessee

BEST ANGEL BISCUITS

Queenie Dixon, of the Eastside Homemaker Club, has contributed numerous recipes to the Lafayette County Extension cookbooks since the 1950s. Some say her biscuits are so light, they let you taste heaven.

YIELD: ABOUT 2 DOZEN

1 package active dry yeast

¼ cup warm water

5 cups self-rising flour

1 teaspoon baking soda

1 cup vegetable shortening

2 cups buttermilk

Preheat the oven to 425°. Dissolve the yeast in the warm water. Sift together the flour and baking soda in a large bowl; cut in the shortening. Stir the dissolved yeast into the buttermilk. Combine the buttermilk mixture with the flour mixture; mix all ingredients and knead well. Roll out and cut biscuits. Bake until done.

Note: You can divide dough into two or three portions, as it will keep in refrigerator several days.

Holiday Foods
Lafayette Extension Homemakers Cookbook
Oxford, Mississippi

FOOD PROCESSOR BISCUITS

An adaptation suited to the modern bride.

YIELD: 14 BISCUITS

2 cups flour

2 teaspoons baking powder

1 teaspoon salt

¼ teaspoon baking soda

3 to 4 tablespoons chilled lard or vegetable shortening

1 cup buttermilk

Preheat the oven to 475°. Place the metal blade in the bowl of a food processor and add the flour, baking powder, salt, and baking soda. Whirl a few seconds to mix. Add the lard. Process until the mixture resembles coarse crumbs, about 10 seconds. Add the buttermilk and process until just combined.

Turn the dough out onto a floured surface. Turn over a few times until surface of dough is no longer sticky. Do not knead; use as little flour as possible. Roll or pat into ½-inch thickness. Cut the biscuits with a floured cutter. Bake for 10 minutes or until brown.

Puttin' on the Peachtree
Junior League of DeKalb
Decatur, Georgia

SWEET POTATO BISCUITS

YIELD: 18 TO 20 BISCUITS

3 cups flour, plus additional for flouring the rolling surface

¾ cup sugar

1 tablespoon salt

3 teaspoons baking powder

1½ teaspoons allspice

1 teaspoon cinnamon

¾ cup shortening

2 cups mashed sweet potatoes

⅓ cup milk

Preheat the oven to 450°. In a large bowl, mix together the flour, sugar, salt, baking powder, allspice, and cinnamon. Cut in the shortening until the mixture resembles coarse meal. Stir in the

TERRY KAY

HOW TO COOK BISCUITS

I have a sense of respect for those little spiral-bound cookbooks. There is one that my wife and I use a great deal, called *Cook and Love It,* published by the Mother's Club at the Lovett School in Atlanta back in 1976. I think it used to have a blue cover, which has been lost from so much use.

It's full of real simple, very fine little recipes. When you open it up, you can tell which recipes we cook because my wife has underlined things, and of course there's grease splattered on the pages. The page with the squash casserole on it has ketchup smeared on it. You know, I always thought my mother taught my wife how to cook these things, but it looks like she's learned from *Cook and Love It.*

My mother was renowned for her cooking. She was just a remarkable cook. She taught my sisters, and they, in turn, have passed it down again. And so have I. We recall things our mother did, how she cooked, what she cooked. And then you tinker, you play with the memory of how your mother did it. Now it's my turn. My grandson, Jordan, is eight and just loves to get in the kitchen. The other day he made muffin biscuits. I was there with him, but he did it all himself, mixing the mayonnaise, and flour, and milk. Then he poured the mixture into muffin tins and soon enough—piping hot biscuits.

But baking biscuits is not always that easy. My favorite scene in my book *To Dance with the White Dog* is the biscuit-cooking scene, where the old man decides to try to make biscuits like his wife used to:

> *It would not be hard to bake biscuits, he thought. He had sat at the kitchen table hundreds of times and watched her at the cabinet, her hands flashing over the dough and it did not seem a hard thing to do. He knew the ingredients she used.*
>
> *He stood at the cabinet and took the wood mixing bowl and scooped three cups of flour from the flour bin, and then he measured out two teaspoons of baking powder and a teaspoon of baking soda and a teaspoon of salt and he mixed it together with his hands. Then he took up a palmful of shortening from the can and dropped it into the middle of the flour mixture, but it did not seem enough and he added another palmful and he began to knead the*

shortening and flour mixture together, but it was greasy and stuck to his hands.

The dog watched him from the doorway leading into the middle room. "Don't think I know what I'm doing, do you?" he said to the dog. "'Think I forgot about the buttermilk, don't you?" He had forgotten, and talking to the dog reminded him. He pulled across the room on his walker and took the buttermilk from the refrigerator and returned to the cabinet and began to pour the milk over the wad of dough. "Ought to be enough," he judged aloud. "Can't be that hard to make biscuits." He kneaded the buttermilk into the shortening-and-flour mixture, and the dough came like glue—sticking to his fingers. "Need some more flour," he said profoundly to the dog. The dog tilted her head curiously.

He worked for another thirty minutes with the dough, adding flour and buttermilk and shortening until it caked on his fingers, and then he decided the dough was firm enough and he rolled it out on waxed paper and cut it with the cutter. He had fifty-two biscuits. "Great God," he said in amazement. "I just wanted two or three."

The biscuits were not eatable. They were flat and hard and were colored a murky yellow. He put one in front of the dog and the dog sniffed and looked up at him sadly and trotted away. "Don't know what's good, do you?" he said. He wiped butter across the top of two of the biscuits and poured molasses over them and cut one with his knife and tasted it. He spit the biscuit from his mouth and sat at the table and laughed silently.

She would be laughing, too, he thought. Or scowling. Thinking him an old fool for trying to do something that she had done with ease. Got to get one of the girls to show me how to cook biscuits, he decided. Can't be that hard.

Terry Kay grew up in Royston, Georgia, and now makes his home down the road in Athens. His most recent novel is The Kidnapping of Aaron Greene.

sweet potatoes. Add the milk and stir until the dry ingredients are moistened.

Turn the dough out onto a floured surface; roll to ½-inch thickness. Cut the dough with a 2-inch biscuit cutter. Place on a greased cookie sheet and bake for 12 to 15 minutes.

Uptown Down South
Junior League of Greenville
Greenville, South Carolina

MOTHER WALKER'S POTATO ROLLS

This recipe was published in 1982, when Mother Walker was eighty-three. These rolls gain a bit of heft from the addition of potatoes.

YIELD: ABOUT 1 DOZEN

¼ cup milk
¼ cup shortening
Scant ¼ cup sugar
½ cup riced potatoes, hot
1 teaspoon salt
1 yeast cake
¼ cup lukewarm water
1 egg
1 egg yolk
2½ cups flour
Unsalted butter, for serving

Put the milk, shortening, and sugar in a saucepan and heat just to the scalding point. Remove from the heat and add the hot riced potatoes and salt. Let cool to lukewarm. Dissolve the yeast in the lukewarm water. Add the yeast mixture to the milk mixture. Beat the egg and the egg yolk until well mixed and add to the milk mixture. Stir in ½ cup of the flour. Cover and let rise in a warm place until light. Beat in the remaining 2 cups flour and let rise again until about doubled in bulk.

Turn out onto a floured board and roll to a ¼-inch thickness. Cut with a biscuit cutter and fold into a pocketbook shape, pressing the edges down. Let rise again.

Bake at 425° for 12 to 15 minutes, depending on the size of the rolls. Brush with butter while hot.

Southern Legacies
Nancy Patty Walker
Starkville, Mississippi

GRANDMOTHER WALTON'S ROLLS

YIELD: 12 SERVINGS

1 package active dry yeast
1 cup warm water
1 teaspoon salt
3 tablespoons sugar
3 tablespoons oil
3 cups flour
½ stick unsalted butter, melted

Dissolve the yeast in warm water. In a bowl, combine the salt, sugar, and oil. Add the yeast and water; stir well. Add the flour and stir. Let rise for 1 hour in the bowl.

Make into rolls. Dip each roll in melted butter. Fill two 9-inch cake pans with rolls. Let rise in the pan. Bake at 425° for 12 minutes.

Cookin' in the Little Easy
Oxford-Lafayette Humane Society
Oxford, Mississippi

SALT-RISING BREAD

Salt is added for the extra leavening lift in this loaf bread.

YIELD: 4 LOAVES

1 large potato, peeled and sliced thin
¼ cup cornmeal
6¼ cups flour, plus additional, if needed
1 teaspoon baking soda
1 teaspoon baking powder
½ cup plus 1 tablespoon plus 1 teaspoon sugar
2 cups boiling water
1 tablespoon plus ½ teaspoon salt
¾ cup vegetable shortening
4 cups hot milk

Place the potato slices in a large jar. Sprinkle with the cornmeal, ¼ cup of the flour, ½ teaspoon of the baking soda, ½ teaspoon of the baking powder, and 1 tablespoon of the sugar. Add the 2 cups boiling water. Let stand overnight in a warm place—about 108°. (It will have a distinctive odor by morning.)

The next morning, discard the potato and pour the liquid into a deep 2-quart pan. Now combine 3 cups of the remaining flour, the ½

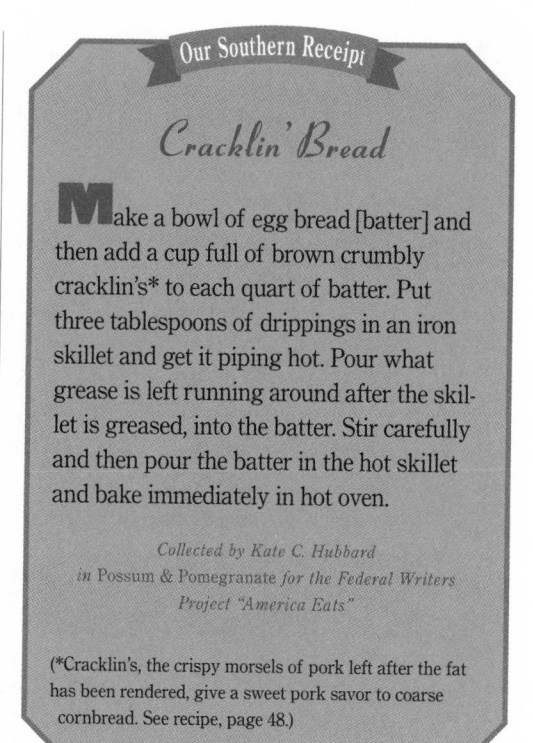

Our Southern Receipt

Cracklin' Bread

Make a bowl of egg bread [batter] and then add a cup full of brown crumbly cracklin's* to each quart of batter. Put three tablespoons of drippings in an iron skillet and get it piping hot. Pour what grease is left running around after the skillet is greased, into the batter. Stir carefully and then pour the batter in the hot skillet and bake immediately in hot oven.

Collected by Kate C. Hubbard
in Possum & Pomegranate *for the Federal Writers Project "America Eats"*

(*Cracklin's, the crispy morsels of pork left after the fat has been rendered, give a sweet pork savor to coarse cornbread. See recipe, page 48.)

teaspoon remaining baking soda, the ½ teaspoon remaining baking powder, the 1 teaspoon sugar, and ½ teaspoon of the salt. Stir into the potato water and allow to rise to the top of the pan (108° is perfect).

Sift the remaining 3 cups flour into a large bowl; add the remaining ½ cup of sugar and the remaining tablespoon of salt. Blend in the shortening. Pour the risen batter into the flour mixture and add the hot milk. Mix to a soft dough, using additional flour, if needed, to handle easily. Knead the dough 20 minutes. Shape into 4 loaves and place in 4 greased loaf pans. Let rise until double in size.

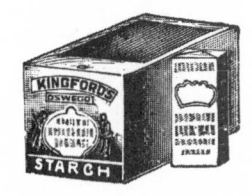

Preheat the oven to 400° and bake for 10 minutes. Reduce the heat and bake at 350° for 1 hour, or until brown and done. Wrap in bread cloth or towel while warm.

Global Feasting, Tennessee Style
Phila Hach
Knoxville, Tennessee

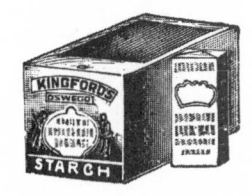

GRANDMOTHER OUTLAW'S CRACKLIN' BREAD

YIELD: ABOUT **10** TO **12** PATTIES

1 medium sweet potato
2 cups cornmeal
1 cup cracklin's

Preheat the oven to 400°. Peel the potato and cut it into small pieces. Boil until tender. Remove the potato, reserving the cooking water. Combine the cornmeal and cracklin's in a mixing bowl. Pour enough potato water over the cornmeal mixture to form a batter. Add the potatoes and fold twice. Form large patties. Bake on a cookie sheet for 35 minutes, or until done.

Festival Cookbook
Humphreys Academy Patrons
Belzoni, Mississippi

SALLY LUNN

A baker in seventeenth-century Bath, England, Sally Lunn was renowned for her breads, of which this delicacy is a distant cousin. So goes the story.

Y I E L D :   1 5   S E R V I N G S

1 package active dry yeast
¼ cup lukewarm water
1 teaspoon sugar
6 tablespoons unsalted butter, plus additional, melted, for basting the loaf
6 tablespoons lard or vegetable shortening
1 cup milk
4 cups flour
⅓ cup sugar
2 teaspoons salt
4 eggs

Dissolve the yeast in the warm water; add the sugar and set aside.

Heat the 6 tablespoons butter, the lard, and the milk together in a saucepan; stir until the butter and lard are melted. Let stand until luke-warm (105° to 110°).

Sift together the flour, sugar, and salt.

Beat the eggs thoroughly and combine with the milk mixture and the yeast mixture. Beat well. Add the flour mixture and beat well.

Set the bowl in a pan of hot water to rise. Leave a wooden spoon in the batter and cover all with a kitchen towel. Every 20 minutes, beat the dough down; then put it back in the pan of hot water, cover with towel, and let rise again. It will rise after every beating. Do this at least 3 hours. (The wonderful texture is achieved by this beating.)

After the last beating, put the dough in a well-greased Bundt or other tube pan, cover with a towel, and let rise again (about 1½ hours). Bake at 325° for 45 to 60 minutes. Baste with melted butter during the last 10 minutes of baking.

The Sally Lunn freezes beautifully wrapped in foil. Remove from the freezer 1 hour before serving; heat in a 350° oven for 20 to 30 minutes in the foil.

Southern Sideboards
Junior League of Jackson
Jackson, Mississippi

Spoon-bread

2 cups of corn meal
2½ cups of boiling water
2 tablespoons of butter
1½ cups of buttermilk
1 teaspoon soda
½ teaspoon of salt
2 eggs

Scald the meal with the boiling water and let it cool. Add the butter, soda, buttermilk, salt, and eggs well beaten. This batter will be very thin. Pour into well-buttered baking dish and bake 40 minutes at 350 degrees. Eat at once, before bread falls, serving it out of its baking dish with a spoon. Take a cold rainy day in the late fall, and garnish it with a supper of spoon-bread, smoked sausage, hominy, and blackberry jam, and you have an evening in which you can readily understand why it is that the people in Spain do as they do when it rains. They just let it rain.

Collected by Kate C. Hubbard in Possum & Pomegranate *for the Federal Writers Project "America Eats"*

SPOON BREAD

A constant in our kitchens from Colonial times to the present, spoon bread owes its name either to the Native American word for porridge, suppawn, *or to the utensil with which it is best served.*

YIELD: 8 SERVINGS

4 cups milk
1 cup cornmeal
2 tablespoons unsalted butter, plus additional
    for serving
1¾ teaspoons salt
4 eggs, separated

Preheat the oven to 375°. Scald the milk; stir into the cornmeal in the top of a double boiler. Cook about 5 minutes, or until the mixture has the consistency of thin mush. Add the butter and salt. Beat the egg yolks; fold into the batter. Beat the egg whites lightly and fold into the batter. Pour into a greased 1½-quart baking dish. Bake for about 45 minutes. Serve in the baking dish with plenty of butter.

Bless Us Cooks
Grace–St. Luke's Episcopal Church
Memphis, Tennessee

SCALDED HOECAKES

YIELD: 8 SERVINGS

1 cup cornmeal (plain or self-rising)
¼ cup chopped onion
¼ cup chopped green pepper
½ teaspoon salt
2¼ cups boiling water

In a small bowl, mix the cornmeal, onion, pepper, and salt. Pour boiling water over the meal mixture and let stand for 10 minutes. Drop by the tablespoonful on a hot, lavishly greased griddle.

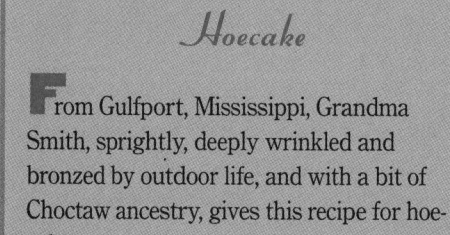
Hoecake

From Gulfport, Mississippi, Grandma Smith, sprightly, deeply wrinkled and bronzed by outdoor life, and with a bit of Choctaw ancestry, gives this recipe for hoecake.

"Take you about a quart of meal, a teaspoon salt (it mightn't be salt enough for you an' again it might), make it up (not too soft) with water (some folks use hot water to make it stick together but I don't have no such trouble iffen I bake it good an' brown—an' to my mind hot water gives it a gummy taste), put in a hot pot or pan that's well greased (Indians used to use hot stones), pat it down with you spoon flat, let it lie over that fire till you know there is a good crust on the under side, turn it over an' brown the other side, then eat."

Collected by Kate C. Hubbard in Possum & Pomegranate *for the Federal Writers Project "America Eats"*

Turn only once, when nicely browned. Drain and serve piping hot.

The James K. Polk Cookbook
Polk Memorial Auxiliary
Columbia, Tennessee

FLUFFY MATZO BALLS

Dumplings go kosher!

Yield: 10 matzo balls

4 eggs, separated
½ cup cold water
⅓ cup peanut oil or chicken fat
1 teaspoon salt
Dash of pepper
1¼ cups matzo meal

Beat the egg whites with a rotary beater until slightly fluffy. Beat or mix the egg yolks with the cold water until foamy. Combine the egg whites and the egg yolk mixture and beat with the rotary mixer until combined and foamy. Add the oil, salt, and pepper to the egg mixture and beat well. Add the matzo meal and stir with a fork until thoroughly combined. Let stand overnight, or at least 2 hours, in the refrigerator.

Lightly grease your hands with a little oil and form balls. Do not try to form perfect balls; just shuffle the matzo ball from one hand to another like a hot potato, or it will fall apart. Drop into 1½ quarts or more simmering salted water. If the water is boiling too rapidly, the matzo balls will fall apart. Cover the pot and cook for 20 minutes. (Do not lift the top off the pot, or you will have matzo rocks!)

From Generation to Generation
Sisterhood of Temple Emanu-El
Dallas, Texas

BILL FERRIS

PULLED FROM THE ASHES

Southern foods are inextricably bound to memories of our childhood experiences—the memories of pungent, mouthwatering smells rising from dishes cooked in the oven and over open flames, dishes that we, as children, were forbidden to touch or taste lest we interfere with the work of our elders.

At times we children were given special privileges, allowed to share foods that opened doors to a magical world. Such is my memory of the hoecake and of Amanda Gordon, the person who introduced me to it. Nicknamed "Feb" because she had been born in the month of February, a custom familiar among her ancestors of African heritage, Feb accorded me special privileges perhaps because I was the eldest of the children, or perhaps because of my fascination with foods and cooking. I remember ever so vividly her long nimble fingers shelling peas and butter beans at a small table where I still dine and where her spirit still resides. I remember how she cocked her head and squinted her eyes toward me, serving notice that I must follow her instructions and learn at her knee.

At an early age I recall looking into the kitchen where Feb worked, seeing her open the oven door and pull out a metal sheet covered with hot biscuits. Delicious and beautiful as the biscuits were, my eye was drawn to the larger piece of bread that had been baked beside these biscuits. That, Feb explained to me, was a hoecake, a bread that she had learned to cook when she was a child. Her mother cooked over an open hearth in her home, and when the coals were hot, she placed a large piece of dough on the blade of her hoe and slid it under a bed of hot coals and ashes. A few minutes later she took the hoe handle, slid the blade back under the ashes, and pulled the cooked bread from the fire. Once the ashes and small coals were dusted off, the freshly baked hoecake was ready to eat. The hoecake drew Feb back to childhood memories of her mother working in the kitchen, an association that I was blessed to be privy to as a child under her tutelage.

Through its smell, its taste, its eating, the hoecake bound my white child's world with the rich culture of black families who nurtured me on our farm in Warren County, Mississippi, isolated on a gravel road fifteen miles from Vicksburg.

Bill Ferris is founding director of the Center for the Study of Southern Culture at the University of Mississippi and chairman of the National Endowment for the Humanities.

HUSH PUPPIES

Here's the story we grew up hearing down South: On a fish fry by the levee or maybe it was on a riverbank, fishermen cooking up the afternoon catch took to frying bits of batter in the hot oil intended for the fish. They tossed the little morsels to the yelping dogs with the admonishment, "Hush, puppy!"

YIELD: 2 DOZEN

1 cup flour
1 cup cornmeal
1 tablespoon sugar
1 teaspoon baking soda
1 teaspoon baking powder
1 teaspoon salt
1 egg
1 onion, chopped
1 cup buttermilk
3 to 4 cups oil

In a large bowl, combine the flour, cornmeal, sugar, baking soda, baking powder, and salt. Add the egg, onion, and buttermilk; mix well. Heat the oil to hot but not smoking. Drop the batter by tablespoonfuls into the hot oil and fry until golden brown, about 2 minutes on each side.

Sensational Seasons
Junior League of Fort Smith
Fort Smith, Arkansas

Our Southern Receipt

Ash Cake

Make a hoecake out'n meal, salt, a little grease, and some boilin' water. Shape wid yo' hands. Pull out some live coals out of de fire place. Wrap cakes in a collard leaf, place on de coals coverin' wid some more not so hot. Let dem bake about 15 minutes. Dey's sho fitten'.

Collected by Kate C. Hubbard in Possum & Pomegranate *for the Federal Writers Project "America Eats"*

SPICY HUSH PUPPIES

YIELD: 3 DOZEN

1 cup cornmeal
½ cup corn flour
½ cup all-purpose flour
1 tablespoon baking powder
½ teaspoon dried thyme
¼ teaspoon dried oregano
½ teaspoon salt
1 teaspoon cayenne pepper
½ cup finely chopped green onions
2 teaspoons minced garlic
1 jalapeño pepper, chopped
2 eggs, lightly beaten
2 tablespoons vegetable oil
1 cup milk
Vegetable oil for deep frying

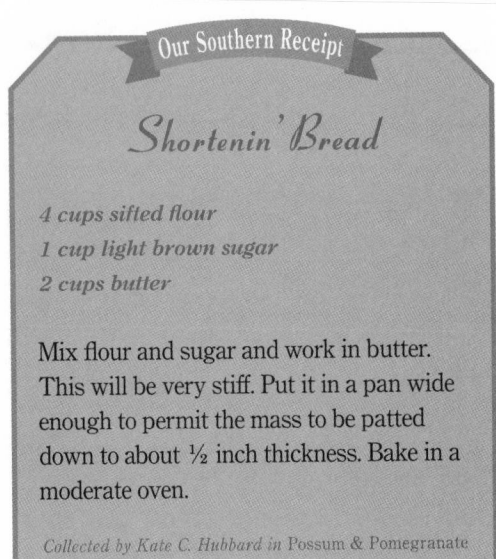
Shortenin' Bread

4 cups sifted flour
1 cup light brown sugar
2 cups butter

Mix flour and sugar and work in butter.
This will be very stiff. Put it in a pan wide
enough to permit the mass to be patted
down to about ½ inch thickness. Bake in a
moderate oven.

Collected by Kate C. Hubbard in Possum & Pomegranate
for the Federal Writers Project "America Eats".

Mix the cornmeal, corn flour, all-purpose flour,
baking powder, thyme, oregano, salt, and
cayenne in a bowl. Add the green onions, garlic,
and jalapeño. Add the eggs and mix well. Bring
the 2 tablespoons oil and the milk to a boil in a
large, heavy saucepan. Add the flour mixture.
Cook until thickened, stirring constantly. Chill
for 1 hour.

Heat the vegetable oil to 350° in a large skillet or deep fryer. Drop the batter by tablespoonfuls into the hot oil. Deep-fry until dark brown.
Drain on paper towels.

Apron Strings
Junior League of Little Rock
Little Rock, Arkansas

AUNT EFFIE'S CUSTARD JOHNNY CAKE

With the publication of Cross Creek *and* The
Yearling, *Florida writer Marjorie Kinnan Rawlings set our national stomach to rumbling. With*
Cross Creek Cookery, *she taught us how they ate
down on the swamp.*

YIELD: 4 TO 6 SERVINGS

1 cup cornmeal
½ cup flour
2 tablespoons sugar
1 teaspoon baking soda
1 teaspoon salt
1 cup buttermilk
2 eggs, well beaten
1 cup milk

Preheat the oven to 350°. Grease a rectangular
baking pan. Mix and sift together the cornmeal,
flour, sugar, baking soda, and salt in a large
bowl. Beat in the buttermilk, then stir in the
eggs. Add the milk, blending quickly. Pour into
the prepared pan. Bake for about 35 minutes.
Serve immediately, cutting into squares at the
table. The custard will rise to the top in baking.

Cross Creek Cookery
Marjorie Kinnan Rawlings
Cross Creek, Florida

FRENCH MARKET BEIGNETS

Long a treat sold by street vendors in New Orleans, these fluffy, yeasty, sugary indulgences are our answer to the doughnut.

YIELD: 10 TO 12 SERVINGS

1 cup milk, scalded
2 tablespoons margarine or vegetable
  shortening
1 tablespoon firmly packed dark brown
  sugar
1 tablespoon granulated sugar
1 package granulated yeast
3 cups enriched plain flour
1 teaspoon nutmeg
1 teaspoon salt
1 large egg
Oil for deep frying
Confectioners' sugar

Heat the milk in a saucepan to the scalding stage. Do not let it scorch. Stir often. Place the margarine in a large mixing bowl and add the brown sugar and granulated sugar. Pour in the scalded milk and stir until the margarine is melted. Let cool to lukewarm. Add the yeast and stir until the yeast is dissolved. Sift together the flour, nutmeg, and salt. Gradually add about half the flour mixture to the milk mixture to form a batter. Add the egg and beat thoroughly. Stir in the remaining flour mixture. Cover and set aside to allow to double in bulk (about 1 hour).

Knead gently. Roll out on a floured board to a ¼-inch thickness. Cut into diamond shapes. Cover. Let rise in a warm place for 30 minutes to 1 hour.

Deep-fry in hot oil (385°), turning only once. Drain and dust with confectioners' sugar. Serve warm.

Recipes and Reminiscences of New Orleans
Parents Club of Ursuline Academy
New Orleans, Louisiana

CINNAMON ROLLS

YIELD: ABOUT 1 DOZEN

½ cup vegetable shortening
2 cups milk, plus additional for frosting
½ cup sugar
½ teaspoon salt
2 eggs, beaten
1 package active dry yeast
½ cup warm water
5 to 6 cups plain flour
Cinnamon
Sugar
Dark brown sugar
Pats of unsalted butter
Confectioners' sugar

Combine the shortening and 2 cups milk in a saucepan. Heat to almost scalding and then let cool. Add the sugar, salt, and eggs. Dissolve the yeast in the warm water and add to the mixture. Add flour until the dough handles easily. Place the dough in a greased bowl; cover. Let rise until doubled in size.

Punch the dough down and roll it out like a large pie crust. Combine equal amounts of cinnamon and sugar in a small bowl. Sprinkle the dough with the cinnamon-sugar mixture. Roll it up like a jelly roll. Slice it into 1-inch-thick circles. Coat the bottom of cake pans with brown sugar. Top the brown sugar with the butter pats. Run the pans in the oven to melt the butter. Place the cinnamon rolls on top of the brown sugar. Let rise in a warm place.

Preheat the oven to 350° and bake until brown. Combine confectioners' sugar with enough milk to make a spreadable frosting. Frost the rolls while still warm.

Delta Dining, Too
Delta Academy Mothers Club
Marks, Mississippi

RICE WAFFLES

The test of a waffle in the old days used to be that "you could pick it up with a pin." Why anyone should want to do just that has never been explained, but somebody was always sure to mention it when the waffles were complimented. Even when they had to be brought across the yard from the kitchen "annex," they always arrived in this crisp condition.

YIELD: 1 DOZEN WAFFLES

2 eggs, separated
1 cup cooked rice

2 tablespoons unsalted butter, melted

2 cups flour

2 heaping teaspoons baking powder

1 teaspoon salt

A little milk, if needed

In a large bowl, beat the yolks; add the rice, butter, flour, baking powder, and salt. Add a small amount of milk if the batter is too thick. Beat the egg whites until stiff peaks form; fold into the batter. Cook batter on a waffle iron.

The Savannah Cookbook
Harriet Ross Colquitt
Savannah, Georgia

BANANA NUT BREAD

Bananas arrived late in the South but soon insinuated their way into many a dish. This version of banana nut bread benefits from an indigenous crop, the pecan.

YIELD: 8 TO 10 SERVINGS

½ cup unsalted margarine

1½ cups sugar

2 eggs, beaten

1 teaspoon vanilla

2 cups cake flour, measured after
    sifting

½ teaspoon salt

½ teaspoon baking soda

¼ cup milk

3 small or 2 large bananas, mashed
    to a pulp

1 cup chopped pecans

In a large bowl, cream the margarine and sugar. Add the eggs and vanilla. Beat until fluffy.

Sift together the sifted flour, salt, and baking soda. Add the dry ingredients to the sugar mixture alternately with the milk, bananas, and nuts, beating well after each addition.

Preheat the oven to 350°. Line a 6½x10½-inch loaf pan with waxed paper. Pour the batter into the pan and bake for 50 minutes, or until brown and a toothpick inserted in the center comes out clean. This bread keeps well in plastic wrap and also freezes well.

River Road Recipes II
Junior League of Baton Rouge
Baton Rouge, Louisiana

ZUCCHINI BREAD

This bread benefits from grated zucchini, a summer squash of Italian origin and first cousin to our crooknecks and pattypans.

YIELD: 2 LOAVES (32 SERVINGS)

1 whole egg plus 2 egg whites, lightly whipped

1½ cups sugar

⅓ cup oil

⅔ cup nonfat plain yogurt

1 tablespoon vanilla

2 cups flour

1 tablespoon cinnamon

2 teaspoons baking soda

¾ teaspoon salt

½ teaspoon baking powder

2 cups grated zucchini

⅓ cup chopped walnuts

Preheat the oven to 350°. Grease 2 loaf pans.

Blend the eggs, sugar, oil, yogurt, and vanilla in a large bowl. In a separate bowl mix the flour, cinnamon, baking soda, salt, and baking powder and add to the egg mixture. Add the zucchini and walnuts. Fill the prepared pans about two-thirds full with batter. Bake for 45 minutes.

Variation: Substitute for 1 cup of the zucchini ½ cup grated carrot, 1 large apple finely chopped, and 1 tablespoon fresh orange zest.

River Road Recipes III
Junior League of Baton Rouge
Baton Rouge, Louisiana

BLUEBERRY MUFFINS

YIELD: 1 DOZEN

½ stick unsalted butter
1 cup sugar
1 egg
1 teaspoon vanilla
1⅓ cups flour
2 teaspoons baking powder
¾ teaspoon cinnamon
½ teaspoon salt
1 cup milk
1 cup blueberries, picked over

Preheat the oven to 350°. Grease and flour a 12-cup muffin pan.

Cream the butter and sugar in a large bowl; add the egg and vanilla. Combine the flour, baking powder, cinnamon, and salt in a bowl. Add to the creamed mixture alternately with the milk, mixing well after each addition. Add the blueberries. Fill the muffin cups three-fourths full. Bake for 30 minutes.

Treasures of the Smokies
Junior League of Johnson City
Johnson City, Tennessee

SWEET POTATO MUFFINS

YIELD: 12 MUFFINS

1 sweet potato (about 12 ounces)
1 tablespoon unsalted butter
Pinch of salt
½ cup milk
2 eggs, well beaten
2 cups flour
1 teaspoon baking powder

Boil the sweet potato until done. Preheat the oven to 350°. Mash the sweet potato very well. Pass through a colander to free from all lumps. Add the butter and salt and whip well. Add the milk and eggs. Combine the flour and baking powder. Add enough of the flour mixture to the creamed mixture to make a soft batter. Bake in lined muffin pans for about 30 minutes.

The Historical Cookbook of the American Negro
National Council of Negro Women
Washington, D.C.

FRENCH TOAST

Down Louisiana way, where French is still spoken here and there, folks know this by the name of pain perdu, *or lost bread, for it is bread that would be lost to the trash if it were not for this recipe.*

YIELD: 4 SERVINGS

¼ cup milk
2 tablespoons sugar
½ teaspoon vanilla
1 egg, lightly beaten
4 slices bread (sandwich or French)
2 tablespoons unsalted butter
Confectioners' sugar
Maple syrup, for serving

Stir the milk, sugar, and vanilla into the egg. Dip the bread in the egg mixture. Make sure both sides are well coated. Melt the butter on a griddle. Brown the French toast lightly on both sides. Sprinkle with confectioners' sugar. Serve with maple syrup.

Variation: Sprinkle with a sugar-cinnamon mixture.

Delta Dining, Too
Delta Academy Mothers Club
Marks, Mississippi

SALADS & SALAD DRESSINGS

....

SOUTHERN HOSPITALITY AS HIGH ART

A salesman who travels southern Georgia and Alabama was told of a boardinghouse in a small town in his territory that had great food. One day he saw some cars parked outside of a house that looked right and went in. There were about ten people sitting at a big dining table heaped with food. He took an empty chair. He was a chatty type, and so were they. They passed the platters, and he ate his fill. When he stood up and asked the lady at the head of the table how much he owed her, she said, "Oh, you don't owe anything. This is a private home. We hope you enjoyed your dinner."

GAIL GREENBLATT

Southern Hospitality as High Art

....

The South is a land of myth and fable, of raggedy Confederate soldiers and brave conductors on the Underground Railroad, of every town's Tara and no man's shotgun shack, of moonlight, magnolias, and moonshine. Foremost among those myths of the South both old and new is that of Southern hospitality. This is not to say that hospitality as doled out down South is merely a figment of a fertile imagination. Rather, the hospitality is real, the manners seemingly innate.

We *do* say "thank you" and "please" with greater frequency. We *are* more inclined to use "sir" and "ma'am" when addressing our elders, even if the difference in age is measured in months rather than decades. And it is still considered common courtesy to meet the gaze of anyone you pass on the street with a nod of the head, a smile, or a word of greeting. As one interloper observed, "People down South are incredibly polite. Even their war was civil."

The kindness shown to strangers, friends, and family owes its origins to a time when hospitality was a pragmatic response, made by frontier families starved for diversion and welcomed by travelers in desperate need of accommodation. More recently, as folks both black and white began to travel by car, a picnic basket or shoe box full of fried chicken and deviled eggs by their side, they took what was often a circuitous route, dictated by which cousin had a spare bedroom or which friend had a foldout couch. It has only been in the last fifty or so years that white Southerners have been able to freely travel the South, secure that decent places to eat and sleep were in the offing, while for black Southerners such accommodations have been universally available to only the most recent generation of travelers.

Through the years, it has been at the table that Southern civility and hospitality truly took center stage. No matter whether you grew up eating dinner on pine-plank boards or supper on Great-Aunt Lizzie's prized mahogany-inlaid twelve-seater, you were taught early—and if you were initially inattentive, reminded often—to keep your elbows off the table, your peas off your knife, and your young opinions to yourself. When guests were present, these dictates were gospel: The prime pieces of fried chicken were to be offered first to what we all called "company," every request to pass a platter was preceded by the word "please," and you had best not be caught snagging a second piece of pecan pie before a guest had been served hers first.

All was done—all manners taught, the second pot of tomatoes put on to stew, the extra squash casserole put in the oven to warm—for the benefit of others, and with the knowledge that when you found yourself in their home, you could expect to be treated much the same. Though there are few Southerners who would hold up Blanche DuBois, Tennessee Williams's troubled heroine from *A Streetcar Named Desire,* as a paragon of Southern manners and hospitality, there are few among us who have not, from time to time, depended "on the kindness of strangers."

ASPIC VEGETABLE SALAD

Of tomato aspic, John Martin Taylor, author of Hoppin John's Lowcountry Cooking, *says, "Tomato aspic is the one salad eaten with frequency at the beginning of the traditional Lowcountry meal. Savory aspics have long been held in esteem by the French and in the Lowcountry, where they are as varied as souse."*

YIELD: 6 TO 8 SERVINGS

4 cups V-8 juice or tomato juice
2 (3-ounce) packages lemon gelatin
½ teaspoon seasoned salt
2 tablespoons fresh lemon juice
2 tablespoons firmly packed dark brown
*   sugar*
2 to 3 cups raw vegetables (any combination:
*   cucumbers, spring onions, celery, carrots,*
*   cauliflower, mushrooms, canned artichokes,*
*   and pimiento-stuffed olives)*
Lettuce, for serving (optional)
Mayonnaise, for topping (optional)

Bring the V-8 juice to a boil in a large saucepan. Add the gelatin, seasoned salt, lemon juice, and brown sugar. Allow to dissolve completely. Let cool. Arrange the vegetables in a 2-quart baking dish; pour the liquid gelatin mixture over the vegetables and chill until firm. Serve on lettuce with mayonnaise topping, if desired.

A Cook's Tour of the Azalea Coast
Auxiliary to the New Hanover–Pender County
    Medical Society
Wilmington, North Carolina

COLESLAW

From the Dutch koolsla, *meaning cabbage salad, comes this favorite Southern salad.*

YIELD: 8 SERVINGS

¾ *cup mayonnaise*
¼ *cup sour cream*
Juice of 1 large lemon (about ¼ cup)
¼ *cup sugar*
½ *teaspoon salt*
1 *medium cabbage, shredded*
2 *carrots, cut in julienne strips*
1 *green bell pepper, cut in julienne strips*
5 *green onions, minced, including green portion*
½ *cup dry-roasted peanuts*

In a small bowl, mix the mayonnaise, sour cream, lemon juice, sugar, and salt. In a large bowl, combine the cabbage, carrots, bell pepper, green onions, and peanuts. Pour the mayonnaise dressing over the salad and toss well to coat. Cover and refrigerate for several hours. Drain off most of the dressing before serving. Serve chilled.

Augusta Cooks for Company
Augusta Council of the Georgia Association for
    Children and Adults with Learning Disabilities
Augusta, Georgia

OCILLA COLESLAW

Ocilla is a small Georgia town best known for its annual Sweet Potato Festival. The coleslaw from these parts ranks right up there, too. Prepare this slaw a day ahead for best flavor.

YIELD: 20 SERVINGS

1 *cup corn oil*
1 *cup sugar*
1 *cup apple cider vinegar*
2 *teaspoons celery seed*
2 *teaspoons dry mustard*
Salt and pepper to taste
1 *large cabbage, coarsely shredded*
1 *large onion, sliced in rings*
2 *green bell peppers, coarsely chopped*

Combine the oil, sugar, and vinegar in an enamel or stainless steel saucepan. Bring to a boil, lower the heat, and simmer for 5 minutes. Add the celery seed, mustard, salt, and pepper. Let cool slightly. Combine the cabbage, onion, and bell pepper with the marinade in a glass or china bowl. Let stand in the refrigerator for 24 hours.

How to Cook a Pig
and Other Back-to-the-Farm Recipes
Betty Talmadge
Lovejoy, Georgia

MUSTARD

CRUNCHY CABBAGE APPLE SLAW

Y I E L D : 8 S E R V I N G S

½ cup sour cream
1 tablespoon vegetable oil
2 tablespoons apple cider vinegar
1 tablespoon plus 2 teaspoons sugar
1 teaspoon celery seed
¾ teaspoon salt
¼ teaspoon dry mustard
4 cups shredded cabbage
1 medium red apple, chopped
¼ cup finely chopped green bell pepper
2 tablespoons finely chopped onion

In a small bowl, combine the sour cream, oil, vinegar, sugar, celery seed, salt, and dry mustard and mix well. In a large bowl, combine the cabbage, apple, green pepper, and onion. Pour the sour cream mixture over the vegetables and toss to mix. Cover and refrigerate until ready to serve. Toss again just before serving.

The Black Family Dinner Quilt Cookbook
National Council of Negro Women
Washington, D.C.

RED CABBAGE SLAW WITH LEMON-CELERY SEED DRESSING

Cabbage is good for more than mayonnaise-bound coleslaw, as evidenced by this ruddy version.

Y I E L D : 6 S E R V I N G S

4 cups finely shredded red cabbage
1 large mild onion, sliced
2 tablespoons firmly packed dark brown sugar
½ teaspoon salt
¼ cup fresh lemon juice
2 tablespoons honey
1 teaspoon Dijon mustard
1 teaspoon celery seed
¼ cup oil

In a large bowl, toss the cabbage with the onion, brown sugar, and salt. In a small saucepan, combine the lemon juice, honey, mustard, and celery seed and bring to a boil. Lower the heat, add the oil, and simmer for 2 minutes. Pour the hot dressing over the cabbage mixture and stir to combine. Cover and chill for 24 hours before serving.

Concerts from the Kitchen
Arkansas Symphony Orchestra Society Guild
Little Rock, Arkansas

FLORIDA ORANGE AND AVOCADO SALAD

Avocados, the bottom note of this cool summertime salad, are called alligator pears by many Floridians.

Y I E L D : 6 S E R V I N G S

½ teaspoon grated orange zest
¼ cup fresh orange juice
½ cup vegetable oil
2 tablespoons sugar
2 tablespoons red wine vinegar
1 tablespoon fresh lemon juice

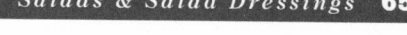
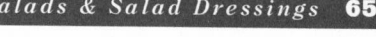

½ teaspoon salt

1 medium head iceberg lettuce

1 small cucumber, peeled and sliced thin

1 Florida avocado, peeled and sliced

2 medium oranges, separated into segments,
   or 1 (11-ounce) can mandarin oranges,
   chilled and drained

2 tablespoons sliced green onion

¼ cup broken walnut pieces

½ cup grated cheddar cheese

Croutons

Combine the orange zest, orange juice, oil, sugar, vinegar, lemon juice, and salt in a jar; shake well. Refrigerate just long enough to chill slightly.

Tear the lettuce into bite-sized pieces; place in a large bowl. Add the remaining ingredients. Toss with the dressing; serve.

Tampa Treasures
Junior League of Tampa
Tampa, Florida

SUMMER FRUIT SALAD

YIELD: 6 TO 8 SERVINGS

4 bananas, cut into large pieces

2 oranges, sliced

½ pineapple, cut into spears

½ cantaloupe, sliced

1 cup blueberries, picked over

½ cup strawberries, sliced

¼ small watermelon, cut in wedges

⅓ cup sour cream

⅓ cup mayonnaise

2 bananas, peeled and mashed

1 tablespoon honey

2 tablespoons almonds, toasted and finely
   chopped

Arrange the cut and sliced fruit on a plate. Combine the remaining ingredients in a sauceboat and serve with the fruit.

Fare by the Sea
Junior League of Sarasota
Sarasota, Florida

FRUIT SALAD WITH HONEY-POPPY SEED DRESSING

YIELD: 8 SERVINGS

4 oranges

2 grapefruit

2 avocados

½ cup cider vinegar

¼ cup vegetable oil

¼ cup olive oil

6 tablespoons honey

1 tablespoon poppy seeds

Salt and pepper

1 head Boston or red leaf lettuce

Peel and section the oranges and grapefruit. Peel the avocados and slice them thinly. Mix the fruits together in a bowl. Set the avocado pits in with the fruit and refrigerate for up to 4 hours.

Make the dressing by combining the remaining ingredients, except the lettuce, in a jar. Shake well. Let the dressing sit at room temperature for the flavors to blend. To serve, remove the avocado pits from the bowl of fruits; toss the fruit with the dressing. Mound the salad lightly on plates lined with lettuce.

Concerts from the Kitchen
Arkansas Symphony Orchestra Society Guild
Little Rock, Arkansas

ORANGE AND ONION SALAD

YIELD: 8 SERVINGS

4 medium oranges
½ cup diced Vidalia onion
2 teaspoons sugar
2 teaspoons dry mustard
1 teaspoon salt
1 teaspoon garlic salt
1 teaspoon paprika
1 teaspoon oregano

¼ cup lemon juice
2 tablespoons salad oil
3 tablespoons water
Lettuce leaves, for serving
Coarsely ground black pepper

Peel the oranges and cut each into six slices. Put the orange slices and diced onion in a plastic bag or glass dish. Combine the remaining ingredients, except the lettuce leaves and pepper, in a blender. Whirl for several seconds to mix. Pour over the orange slices and onion. Marinate for at least 1 hour in the refrigerator. To serve, arrange three orange slices and some onion on some lettuce leaves. Pour some marinade over each serving. Sprinkle with black pepper. Serve cold.

Concerts from the Kitchen
Arkansas Symphony Orchestra Society Guild
Little Rock, Arkansas

GREEN BEAN SALAD

Marinated salads, such as these, are favorites on steamy summer days, when a blanket of humidity seems to smother the whole of the Southland.

YIELD: 4 SERVINGS

1 tablespoon vinegar
1 tablespoon salt, or to taste
1 tablespoon salad oil
2 (1-pound) cans whole green beans, drained
1 purple onion, sliced
½ cup sour cream
1 tablespoon fresh lemon juice
½ cup mayonnaise
1½ teaspoons dry mustard
1 tablespoon horseradish

Mix the vinegar, salt, and oil in a large bowl and marinate the green beans and the onion in the mixture for 1 hour; drain. Combine the sour cream, lemon juice, mayonnaise, mustard, and horseradish in a small bowl. Toss with the green beans and onion.

Wild About Texas
Cypress-Woodlands Junior Forum
Spring, Texas

TOMATO SALAD

For heaven's sake, use vine-ripe tomatoes, rather than those pink cardboard aberrations they sell in most grocery stores.

YIELD: 4 TO 6 SERVINGS

5 medium-size ripe tomatoes, sliced ¼ inch
  thick
¼ cup olive oil
¼ cup vegetable oil
1 tablespoon red wine vinegar
1 tablespoon fresh lemon juice
1 clove garlic, crushed
1 tablespoon dried basil
1 teaspoon salt
Freshly ground black pepper
1 bunch green onions, chopped
1 tablespoon chopped parsley

Arrange the tomato slices overlapping on a platter. Mix the olive oil, vegetable oil, vinegar, lemon juice, garlic, basil, salt, and pepper in a small bowl. Spoon over the tomatoes. Combine the green onions and parsley. Sprinkle over salad. The salad can be made ahead and refrigerated.

Southern Accent
Junior League of Pine Bluff
Pine Bluff, Arkansas

Festive Corn and Black-Eyed Pea Salad

The slave trade brought the versatile black-eyed pea to the United States

YIELD: 4 SERVINGS

1 (14½-ounce) can corn kernels, drained
1 (15-ounce) can black-eyed peas, rinsed and
    drained
½ cup thinly sliced celery
1 medium red bell pepper, cored, seeded, and
    chopped
4 green onions, sliced thin
¼ cup vegetable oil or salad oil
3 tablespoons red wine vinegar
2 teaspoons honey
1 teaspoon fresh lemon juice
½ teaspoon salt
½ teaspoon ground black pepper
½ teaspoon red chili powder

In a large bowl, combine the corn, black-eyed peas, celery, bell pepper, and green onions. Set aside.

Combine the oil, vinegar, honey, lemon juice, salt, black pepper, and chili powder in a tightly covered container and shake until the dressing is well blended.

Pour the dressing over the vegetables and toss well. Cover and refrigerate at least 1 hour, stirring occasionally. Toss before serving.

Mother Africa's Table
National Council of Negro Women
Washington, D.C.

Ramps, Bacon, and Bear Lettuce

Ramps, wild onions resembling scallions, grow throughout the Southern Appalachians and are considered by many an excellent spring tonic or pick-me-up. While this relative of the leek has a mild taste, its lingering aftershocks define herbal halitosis.

YIELD: 2 SERVINGS

4 slices bacon
12 to 16 ramps
Bear, branch, or wild lettuce, torn in pieces

Fry the bacon until crisp and remove from the pan, reserving the drippings. Crumble the bacon. Cut the tops from the ramps, wash them, peel away the outer skin, and dice. Combine the ramps and lettuce in a bowl. Pour the bacon and hot drippings over the ramps and lettuce as dressing.

Campsite to Kitchens
Outdoor Writers Association of America
Memphis, Tennessee

EDNA LEWIS

POKE SALLET AND OTHER GREENS

Growing up, we always gathered wild things to eat. My brothers would pick watercress by the burlap bagful and hang it in the meat house to keep. Watercress would grow up under the snow, and after the snow melted and before the watercress bloomed, we would pick it too. We loved lamb's quarters, a meaty green that runs along the ground, and rape, too, with its very mild taste. Sometimes we would pick dandelions and mix them with other greens.

We doted on poke sallet. Poke was the first green of the season. You know it's not really poisonous, especially if you get it before the bloom unfurls. We would pick it along the fence line by the roadside where it grew. The birds would eat the seed and then go roost on the fence post where they would litter. Soon enough, you would have poke sallet growing at the fence line.

We picked those greens for food, but also for medicine. Those were the days when most doctors did not take blacks as patients. So we had to make do. If you were sick, your neighbor might walk a mile or more to pick something green to bring to your bedside, and then sit by the bed to feed and comfort you.

Those greens were like black folks' health food. They followed us wherever we went. After people had gone off up north, we would send a big box of ingredients up to New York or Pittsburgh, a big cardboard box full of fresh ground cornmeal with eggs submerged in the middle, so that when they opened it up, they could have country eggs and cornbread. After I moved north, my sister would can watercress and then put it in a box full of cornmeal with maybe some ham and farm-fresh eggs and ship it to me in New York City. I'd open it up and have a whole Southern meal. I remember that as the next best thing to going home.

Edna Lewis, a native of Freetown, Virginia, is one of the grand doyennes of African American cooking. Among her cookbooks are The Taste of Country Cooking *and* In Pursuit of Flavor.

DANDELION SALAD

Best in the spring when the leaves are tender and tasty.

YIELD: 4 SERVINGS

1 pint fresh white dandelion
1 clove garlic, cut in half
Plain French Dressing (see page 77)
2 hard-cooked eggs, sliced, or 2 medium-size
*   beets, sliced (optional)*

Cut off the roots of the dandelions and the green portion of leaves. Wash and steep in salt and water until crisp. When crisp, drain and press dry. Rub a salad bowl with the garlic, add the dandelions, and season them with the French dressing. Top with the egg slices or beet slices, if desired.

The Picayune's Creole Cookbook
The Times Picayune Publishing Corporation
New Orleans, Louisiana

McINNIS SALAD

This salad needs to be made two days ahead.

YIELD: 10 TO 12 SERVINGS

1 head lettuce, cored and chilled
1 cup finely chopped celery
½ cup finely chopped onion
1 green bell pepper, finely chopped
1½ cups cooked English peas
2 cups mayonnaise

1 pound bacon, fried, drained, and crumbled
1 cup grated medium cheddar cheese

Break the lettuce into bite-sized pieces. Toss with the celery, onion, and green pepper in a large bowl. Place in an oblong glass dish. Sprinkle the peas on top. Cover with mayonnaise, and seal the edges well. Top with the bacon and cheese. Seal with foil and refrigerate. Do not open for 2 days. Cut into squares to serve.

Southern Sideboards
Junior League of Jackson
Jackson, Mississippi

WILTED LETTUCE

Under a blanket of bacon fat, even the most tired lettuce comes alive.

YIELD: 6 SERVINGS

½ cup sliced green onions (including tops)
8 cups leaf lettuce, torn into bite-sized
*   pieces*
6 slices bacon
¼ cup vinegar
¼ cup water
1 tablespoon sugar
½ teaspoon salt
Black pepper to taste
2 to 3 hard-cooked eggs

In a large bowl, toss the sliced green onion with the lettuce and refrigerate until ready to serve.

Fry the bacon until crisp. Drain, reserving the drippings, and crumble. Add the vinegar, water, sugar, salt, and pepper to the bacon drippings in the pan. Cook and stir until boiling.

When ready to serve, slice the eggs over the lettuce. Pour the hot dressing over all. Sprinkle the crumbled bacon over the top. Should be eaten immediately.

One of a Kind
Junior League of Mobile
Mobile, Alabama

RAW HOT SPINACH SALAD

Olive oil pinch-hits for bacon fat in this modern adaptation of the wilted salad.

YIELD: 6 TO 8 SERVINGS

2 pounds fresh spinach leaves, washed and trimmed
6 tablespoons olive oil
3 tablespoons red wine vinegar
2 cloves garlic, crushed
1 tablespoon dry mustard
Salt to taste
¼ teaspoon freshly ground pepper
1½ cups thinly sliced mushrooms
6 slices bacon, fried and crumbled
¼ cup minced fresh parsley

Break up the spinach in a large bowl. Heat the remaining ingredients in a large skillet until just warm. Pour the warm mixture over the spinach and serve at once.

1982 Official World's Fair Cookbook
Phila Hach
Knoxville, Tennessee

CUCUMBERS WITH DILL DRESSING

YIELD: 4 SERVINGS

2 to 3 medium cucumbers, peeled and sliced
½ cup sour cream
1 teaspoon salt
1 tablespoon vinegar
1 or 2 drops Tabasco
2 tablespoons snipped chives or finely chopped green onions
1 teaspoon snipped dillweed
Dash of black pepper

Soak the cucumbers in salted ice water for 30 minutes. Drain well. In a medium bowl, blend the sour cream, salt, vinegar, Tabasco, chives, dillweed, and pepper. When ready to serve, combine the sour cream mixture with the cucumbers.

Second Round
Junior League of Augusta
Augusta, Georgia

HEARTS OF PALM SALAD

The cabbage palm tree, native to Florida, has an edible inner portion that makes a fine salad. Some Floridians know it as swamp cabbage.

YIELD: 6 SERVINGS

1 egg
1½ teaspoons sugar

1 teaspoon salt

¼ teaspoon paprika

1½ tablespoons brown spicy prepared
   mustard

1 teaspoon Worcestershire sauce

1 clove garlic, crushed

¼ cup water

½ cup wine vinegar

1 cup vegetable oil

2 heads Bibb lettuce

4 cups cooked hearts of palm, or 2
   14-ounce cans hearts of palm

1 pound mushrooms, sliced

1 cup chopped walnuts

In a medium bowl, combine the egg, sugar, salt, paprika, mustard, Worcestershire, garlic, water, and vinegar. Slowly add the oil, beating constantly. Chill the dressing.

Rinse and drain the lettuce leaves; tear into bite-sized pieces. Arrange on 6 salad plates. Arrange the hearts of palm in spoke formation on the lettuce. Sprinkle each salad evenly with mushrooms and nuts. Spoon the desired amount of dressing over the salads.

Thymes Remembered
Junior League of Tallahassee
Tallahassee, Florida

POTATO SALAD

3 cups diced warm boiled potatoes
2 tablespoons grated onion
1 tablespoon minced green bell pepper
¾ cup finely diced celery
¼ cup minced parsley
1 hard-cooked egg
1 tablespoon chow-chow
5 tablespoons mayonnaise
2 tablespoons white vinegar
1 teaspoon salt
¼ teaspoon black pepper
Lettuce, for garnish

Combine all the ingredients except the lettuce in a large bowl while the potatoes are still warm. Chill and serve with a garnish of lettuce.

Global Feasting, Tennessee Style
Phila Hach
Knoxville, Tennessee

HOT POTATO SALAD WITH BACON

A variation on a German theme from Texas, once rife with German immigrants, now home to Germanic Southerners.

YIELD: 6 TO 8 SERVINGS

9 potatoes, well scrubbed
8 ounces bacon, diced
½ cup diced onion

Our Southern Receipt

Cold Potato Salad with Bacon

YIELD: 6 TO 8 SERVINGS

1 quart sliced potatoes (cooked)
6 pieces crisp bacon, chopped
3 chopped hard-boiled eggs
1 large green pepper, minced
2 pimientos, minced
4 tablespoons mayonnaise
2 tablespoons prepared mustard
Salt and pepper to taste

Combine all ingredients in a large bowl. Serve with quartered tomatoes, sliced dill pickles, mixed sweet pickles, and quartered onions.

Hotel Vicksburg in Mississippi
Collected by Eudora Welty for the Federal Writers Project
"America Eats"

¼ cup white wine or apple cider vinegar
¼ cup water
½ teaspoon salt
¼ teaspoon black pepper
2 tablespoons chopped parsley

Drop the unpeeled potatoes into a large saucepan of boiling water. Cover and boil until there is a slight resistance to a knife point. Drain, peel, and cut into ¼-inch slices. Set aside, tightly covered.

In a medium skillet, fry the bacon until crisp; drain on paper towels, reserving the drippings. Sauté the onion in the drippings until tender; drain. Add white wine and the remaining ingredients. Pour the hot sauce over the potatoes, turning gently with a fork to coat evenly. Gently stir the bacon into the salad. Serve immediately.

Calf Fries to Caviar
Janel Franklin and Sue Vaughn
Tahoka, Texas

CORNBREAD SALAD

A Southern variation on Italian bread salad

Y I E L D : 1 0 S E R V I N G S

1 pan Cornbread from Georgetown, Arkansas
   (page 39)
8 slices bacon, fried and crumbled
1 onion, chopped
1 green bell pepper, chopped
2 hard-cooked eggs, chopped
2 tomatoes, chopped
1 cup mayonnaise

Prepare the cornbread. Let cool, then crumble into a bowl. Add the crumbled bacon, onion, bell pepper, and eggs. Add the tomatoes and stir in the mayonnaise. Chill until served.

Note: If you like it hot, add a small amount of cayenne pepper.

From Rose Budd's Kitchen
Rose Budd Stevens
Amite County, Mississippi

CHICKEN SALAD

Y I E L D : 4 T O 6 S E R V I N G S

4 cups diced, cooked chicken
1 cup diced celery
¼ cup toasted pecans
1 cup mayonnaise
1 cup sour cream
Salt to taste
2 tablespoons fresh lemon juice (optional)
½ cup sliced mushrooms, optional

Combine all the ingredients in a large bowl. Chill until ready to serve.

Candlelight and Wisteria
Lee-Scott Academy
Auburn, Alabama

WEST INDIES SALAD

The bounty of the Mobile Bay makes this salad everyday fare.

Y I E L D : 2 T O 4 S E R V I N G S

1 medium onion, chopped fine
1 pound fresh lump crab meat
Salt and pepper
½ cup vegetable oil
6 tablespoons apple cider vinegar
½ cup ice water

Spread half of the onion over the bottom of a large bowl. Cover with separated crab lumps and then the remaining onion. Add salt and pepper to taste. Pour the oil, vinegar, and ice water over all. Toss. Cover and marinate for 2 to 12 hours. Toss lightly before serving.

Recipe Jubilee!
Junior League of Mobile
Mobile, Alabama

FLORIDA LOBSTER SALAD

The spiny lobsters of Florida offer sweet meat, well featured in this salad.

YIELD: 2 SERVINGS

1 clove garlic, cut in half
1 cup cooked lobster meat
2 tablespoons Plain French Dressing
*   (see page 77)*
1 tablespoon finely chopped onion
1 chopped cup celery
¼ cup chopped green bell pepper
3 slices pimiento, cut up
1 cup mayonnaise
1 hard-cooked egg, chopped
Fresh lemon juice
½ teaspoon salt
½ teaspoon black pepper
½ teaspoon Tabasco

Rub a salad bowl with the garlic halves. Cut the cooked lobster meat with scissors into ¼-inch cubes; place in the bowl. Combine the French dressing and the onion. Pour over the lobster; allow the lobster to marinate. Add the celery, bell pepper, and pimiento; mix together well. Add the

mayonnaise and egg. Add plenty of lemon juice, and the salt, pepper, and Tabasco.

The Gasparilla Cookbook
Junior League of Tampa
Tampa, Florida

BOILED DRESSING

YIELD: ABOUT 1¼ CUPS

4 eggs, well beaten
⅔ cup white vinegar
4 teaspoons sugar
½ teaspoon dry mustard
2 teaspoons prepared mustard
Dash of cayenne pepper
Dash of black pepper
2 tablespoons unsalted butter

Combine all the ingredients except the butter in a saucepan. Cook over low heat, stirring constantly, until the mixture thickens. Stir in the butter. Pour over salad.

1982 Official World's Fair Cookbook
Phila Hach
Knoxville, Tennessee

BUTTERMILK-GARLIC DRESSING

Buttermilk, whether fresh from the churn or straight from the fridge, gives a tangy zip to this salad dressing.

YIELD: 4 CUPS

2 cups mayonnaise
⅓ cup buttermilk
⅓ cup vegetable oil
¼ cup water
1½ tablespoons garlic powder
2 tablespoons white vinegar
1½ teaspoons fresh lemon juice
1½ teaspoons honey
¾ teaspoon dry mustard
½ teaspoon salt
¼ teaspoon white pepper

Whisk together the mayonnaise and buttermilk in a bowl; stir in the remaining ingredients. Refrigerate, covered, at least 8 hours.

Peachtree Bouquet
Junior League of DeKalb County
Decatur, Georgia

PLAIN FRENCH DRESSING

YIELD: ABOUT ¼ CUP

3 tablespoons olive oil
¼ teaspoon salt
¼ teaspoon black pepper
1 tablespoon white vinegar

Place the oil in a small bowl. Gradually add the salt and pepper; mix well. Gradually add the vinegar, stirring continuously for 1 minute.

New Orleans Cookbook
Rima Collin and Richard Collin
New Orleans, Louisiana

MUSTARD-POPPY SEED DRESSING

YIELD: ABOUT ¾ CUP

1 tablespoon sugar
2 tablespoons white wine vinegar
Salt
Freshly ground white pepper
1 teaspoon Dijon mustard
6 tablespoons olive oil
1 teaspoon poppy seeds

Combine the sugar, vinegar, salt, pepper, and mustard in a small bowl; whisk until well blended. Gradually whisk in the olive oil. Stir in the poppy seeds. Chill before serving.

Concerts from the Kitchen
Arkansas Symphony Orchestra Society Guild
Little Rock, Arkansas

SIDES & VEGETABLES

....

IN PRAISE OF POTLIKKER

Each night the hunchback came down the stairs with the air of one who has a grand opinion of himself. He always smelled slightly of turnip greens, as Miss Amelia rubbed him night and morning with pot liquor to give him strength.

CARSON McCULLERS, *BALLAD OF THE SAD CAFÉ*

In Praise of Potlikker

....

For readers in need of a definition, potlikker (or in more rarefied circles pot liquor) is the liquid essence of a vegetable (most often turnip, mustard, or collard greens, but sometimes other greens, black-eyed peas, or butter beans), braised at a low simmer for hours in a stock rich with the taste of pork hock, maw, or some other sufficiently fatty swine product.

Potlikker is more than the sum of the juices at the bottom of a bowl of greens. It may well be one of the more plebeian of Southern culinary indulgences, but never let it be said that potlikker is without import.

Enshrined early in the pantheon of Southern folk belief, potlikker has been prescribed by many a mother for ailments as varied as the croup and colic, rabies and fatigue. And though the bathing of hunchbacks in potlikker may be a bit of literary invention, it was not too long ago that puny children were said to grow strong after a quick dip in the soupy leavings from a pot of greens.

Though claims of its curative qualities may be far-fetched, potlikker is indeed packed with nutrients. During the cooking process, vitamins and minerals leach out of the greens, leaving the collards or turnips, mustards or cresses comparatively bereft of nutrients, while the potlikker itself is enriched with vitamins A and C as well as potassium.

Nutritive claims and folk beliefs aside, potlikker is, for many Southerners, a food invested with meaning beyond the mere sustenant. For some, the swampy elixir is a reminder of a time when making dinner meant making do. For others, it harks back to a simpler past, when not only did you eat "every part of the hog but the squeal," you also ate every bit of the vegetable in the pot. For others still, it is a taste of the past, a dish inextricably linked to a simpler South.

Such sentiments reached the dizziest of heights back in the spring of 1931, when Huey Long, senator-elect from Louisiana, engaged the editors of the Atlanta *Constitution* in a debate on the proper consumption of potlikker. Long asserted it was best enjoyed by dunking corn pone into the liquid. The *Constitution* countered that corn pone should be crumbled into potlikker.

On March 8, after three and a half weeks, the editors of the *Constitution* pulled the plug on the debate, announcing, "Crumblers' Victory Complete, Curtain Falls on Potlikker Discussion Which Rocked World." The article in the *Constitution* read:

> *Leaving a mark upon the culinary life of this and other continents, the great potlikker and cornpone, or "crumbling-dunking" war comes to a close today with the laurels of victory crowning the brow of the leaders of the crumbling crusade. . . .*
>
> *Governors of 14 states, mayors of as many towns, perhaps, noted American writers, scientists, public figures of the radio and moving picture fields, took part in the raging discussion . . . between February 13 and Saturday, at which time the Potlikker and Cornpone Editor reached the decision to terminate the controversy.*
>
> *Here today the curtain falls on this most widely published of all stories within the first 30 years of the century; and with it come poems in praise of potlikker and cornpone and a final word from the editor of The*

Constitution's Potlikker and Cornpone Department, who has laid aside the glittering mantle of patriotic "crumbling" leadership:

> *"The spread of this superficially fantastic but fundamentally salutary discussion was even greater than had been anticipated. It reverberated in the press of the nation, seeped into the national weeklies, blossomed in feature articles, won its way into notable broadcasts, and finally reached the movies. It is to be hoped that a good time was had by all."*

That final dispatch included this poem, penned by Elder George King of Atlanta. It is a fitting, if facetious, tribute to the virtues of crumbling pone in potlikker:

Ode to a Crumbled Pone

I've eaten many luscious fruits,
I've tasted many sweets;
I've been in many hot disputes
About the choicest eats,
I've dined on tongue of nightingale,
At manus I'm some picker;
But how I wish I were a whale
Facing cornpone and potlikker.

Hog and hominy are hard to head,
Rabbit Roast is fare;
Country ham with gravy red
Is in the race for rare.
I like rich, juicy chicken pie
With dumplings rich and slicker,
But, bless your heart, this gets my eye;
Crumbled cornpone and potlikker.

Reprinted with permission from The Atlanta Journal *and* The Atlanta Constitution.

CURRIED FRUIT

When paired with a pork loin, this sweet and savory dish satisfies.

YIELD: 10 TO 12 SERVINGS

1 (1-pound) can each sliced peaches, apricots,
　　chunk pineapple, and sliced pears
1 can mandarin oranges
1 small bottle maraschino cherries
½ stick unsalted butter
¾ cup firmly packed dark brown sugar
¾ cup chopped pecans
4 teaspoons curry powder

Preheat the oven to 325°. Drain the fruit and pat it dry. Melt the butter in a small skillet; stir in the brown sugar, pecans, and curry powder. Pour over the fruit and bake for 1 hour. Serve hot or cold.

The Best of the Bushel
Junior League of Charlottesville
Charlottesville, Virginia

HAM BONE AND SNAP BEANS

A recipe from the files of Sook Faulk, cook and matriarch of the Monroeville, Alabama, family that reared young Truman Capote.

YIELD: 6 TO 8 SERVINGS

3 pounds fresh snap beans
1 bone from cooked ham
Salt to taste

Our Southern Receipt

Jellied Apples

YIELD: 12 SERVINGS

12 Winesap or Jonathan apples
2½ cups sugar
Juice of ½ lemon
Chopped raisins
Chopped pecans
Crystallized ginger
Sugar

Pare and core apples. Moisten the 2½ cups sugar in a saucepan; boil for 5 minutes. Immerse apples in the syrup, allowing plenty of room for each apple. Add the lemon juice, cover tightly, and allow to cook slowly until apples appear somewhat clear. (Watch closely and turn frequently to prevent them from falling apart.) Remove from stove. Combine the raisins, pecans, and ginger in a small bowl. Fill apple centers. Sprinkle each apple with sugar and baste several times with the thickening syrup. Place apples in a baking dish and bake, uncovered, at 350°. Baste several times during this last process.

Mrs. Herschel D. Brownlee
Port Gibson, Mississippi
Collected by Eudora Welty for the Federal Writers
Project "America Eats"

Small amount of cayenne pepper
1 teaspoon summer savory, chopped fine

Wash, snap, and string the beans. Place the ham bone in a large iron kettle, cover well with water, and let simmer for 1 hour. Add the snap beans, salt, and cayenne and cook until the beans are tender and the meat from the ham bone has flavored them. Sprinkle the fresh savory over the top of the cooked beans just before serving them. Serve with homemade cornbread.

Sook's Cookbook
Marie Rudisill
Monroeville, Alabama

LEATHER BRITCHES BEANS (FODDER BEANS)

Named for the coarse, almost leathery consistency these fodder beans take on after a few weeks drying on a string, this dish is a favorite of the Appalachian South.

YIELD: 6 TO 8 SERVINGS

2 pounds green beans
½ cup coarse salt
1 gallon water
Salt and black pepper to taste
Lard or bacon grease

String very full beans as you would for cooking, but do not break them. Thread beans on twine, using just enough beans on each string for one or two meals. Then drop them into a brine of ½ cup coarse salt and water for 15 minutes. Drain

on newspaper. The brine will keep bugs away from your beans. Hang the strings of beans on wire or rope in a dry place for at least three weeks. Make sure they are completely dry or they will mold.

Prior to cooking the dried beans, pour lots of boiling water over the beans and soak overnight. In the morning, wash the beans well and cover with water in a pan. Cook for 2 hours; then add salt, pepper, and lard. Finish cooking about 2 hours more, adding water as needed.

Mountain Measures
Junior League of Charleston
Charleston, West Virginia

GREEN BEANS

YIELD: 6 TO 8 SERVINGS

2 pounds string beans
½ cup coarsely chopped onion
¼ cup vegetable oil

String the beans and cut into desired lengths. Wash the beans and leave them in a bowl of water. Sauté the onions in the oil until golden brown. Lift the beans from the water and add to the onions. Stir occasionally to keep the beans from sticking. Steam until tender. Add extra water if needed. (There should be enough water on the beans to keep them from sticking, since they have soaked in the water.)

Waddad's Kitchen
Waddad Habeeb Buttross
Natchez, Mississippi

Green Bean Casserole

Many a green bean casserole is bound together by that ubiquitous duct tape of culinary creation—cream of mushroom soup—but not this version from the ladies of DeKalb County.

YIELD: 12 SERVINGS

1 stick (¼ pound) unsalted butter
1 large onion, chopped
¼ cup flour
1½ cups milk
3 cups grated cheddar cheese
⅛ teaspoon Tabasco
2 teaspoons soy sauce
½ teaspoon black pepper
1 teaspoon salt
2 pounds fresh green beans or 3 (10-ounce) packages frozen French-style green beans, cooked and drained
4 ounces canned sliced mushrooms
1 (8-ounce) can sliced water chestnuts, drained
½ cup chopped almonds

Preheat the oven to 350°. Heat the butter in a large skillet. Sauté the onion in the butter. Stir in the flour and gradually stir in the milk. Mix in cheese, Tabasco, soy sauce, black pepper, and salt. Add the green beans, mushrooms, and water chestnuts. Pour into a baking dish; sprinkle with the chopped almonds. Bake for 25 to 30 minutes, or until thoroughly heated through.

Peachtree Bouquet
Junior League of DeKalb County
Decatur, Georgia

Pinto Beans "From the Pot"

Pinto beans are poor man's food all around the South, but this version, with its flavor of the Southwest, ups the ante in terms of taste and sophistication.

YIELD: 8 SERVINGS

2 pounds (4 cups) dried pinto beans
1 (4-ounce) piece of salt pork or bacon (optional)
2 white onions, one halved and one chopped fine
1 garlic head, halved
1 tablespoon plus ½ teaspoon salt
3 large ripe tomatoes, chopped fine
1 bunch cilantro, cleaned and chopped
2 to 4 serrano chiles, minced
Juice of 1 lime

Sort the beans through your hands to pick out any small stones and odd-looking beans. Rinse and place in a 6-quart pot. Add 4 quarts of water, the pork if desired, the onion halves, and the garlic (the water should come at least 3 inches above the level of the beans). Discard any beans that float. Slowly bring to a rapid simmer over medium heat, about 30 minutes. Lower the heat, cover, and continue simmering for about 2 hours, until the skins of the beans are soft.

Stir in the 1 tablespoon salt and continue cooking for 30 minutes. (At this point, the beans, when pressed between your fingers, should be creamy and the cooking liquid should be slightly thickened. The bean broth should be about 2 inches above the cooked bean level.) During the cooking process, stir the beans occasionally, adding hot water if needed.

Make a salsa: Thoroughly mix the tomatoes, chopped onion, cilantro, chiles, and lime juice and the remaining ½ teaspoon salt in a small bowl. Season to taste. Ladle the beans and broth into shallow bowls; top with salsa.

Celebración
National Council of La Raza
Washington, D.C.

BUTTER BEANS

North of the Mason-Dixon line, these meaty little pillows are known as lima beans.

YIELD: 4 TO 6 SERVINGS

2 pounds fresh small butter beans, shelled
2 tablespoons bacon drippings
1 teaspoon seasoning salt
1 onion, halved
1 teaspoon salt, plus additional to taste
Black pepper to taste
1 clove garlic (optional)
2 tablespoons unsalted butter
6 green onions, chopped
1 tablespoon flour
4 teaspoons paprika

Cook the fresh beans with the drippings, seasoning salt, onion, 1 teaspoon salt, black pepper, and garlic in a small amount of water until tender. Remove the onion and garlic; drain the beans, reserving 1 cup of the cooking liquid.

Melt the butter in a saucepan and sauté the green onions briefly. Stir in the flour until smooth and add the reserved cooking liquid. Stir until thickened. Add the beans and paprika and more salt and pepper to taste.

If dried beans are used, double the amount of sauce. Frozen baby limas can also be used, but be sure to cook in the seasoned water for the amount of time specified on the package.

Cotton Country Collection
Junior League of Monroe
Monroe, Louisiana

SUCCOTASH

A Southern dish of Native American origins, this is one that tastes as good on *the tongue as it sounds rolling* off *it.*

YIELD: 4 TO 6 SERVINGS

1 pound fresh butter beans, shelled
Salt pork
1 cup chopped onion
1 clove garlic, minced
4 to 6 ears sweet corn
½ stick unsalted butter
Heavy cream
Salt and black pepper
Tabasco

Cook the beans in water seasoned with salt pork, onion, and garlic until done. The water should cover the beans by about 2 to 3 inches. Cut the corn off cob. Heat the butter in a heavy skillet, and sauté the corn. Drain the beans, reserving the cooking water. Add the beans to the corn and

NATHALIE DUPREE

CELEBRATE THE SOUTHERN VEGETABLES

When I return home after traveling—after eating all that rich food, after eating so many hot dogs and pizza on the run between planes—I like to sit down to a Southern vegetarian meal. I want turnip greens, baby butter beans, maybe some green beans, even cabbage. I don't think one bit about meat; it's the vegetables I crave.

The Southern meals I most remember are the ones where the focus was on the fresh vegetables. They just resonate so with me. They are the music of the meal, they carry the melody. They have staying power and beauty.

I crave tender, tiny pigeon peas, so delicate, so full of flavor and texture. They're not much bigger than the iris in your eye. Little pearls, so much smaller and more delicate than black-eyed peas, they hardly need cooking. My mother-in-law always serves them with a bit of sweet tomato conserve on top. And while I do like tomato conserve, they can be at their best when they're swimming in just a bit of buttery liquid.

And butter beans, I love the tiny ones, the baby ones. Sometimes I split a slice of cornbread open and ladle them on top. It's like eating a butter bean sandwich. To come home to a butter bean sandwich, when I've been traveling, well, that just makes my day. That means I'm home; that tastes like home.

Cookbook author and television personality Nathalie Dupree lives in Social Circle, Georgia. She is the author of Nathalie Dupree's Comfortable Entertaining, *among other works, and is the host of a companion television series.*

add enough cream and bean liquid to cover the corn and beans. Season with salt, black pepper, and Tabasco. Simmer for an additional 15 to 20 minutes.

Cook with a Natchez Native
Bethany Ewald Bultman
Natchez, Mississippi

WHITE BEANS

The River Road, as defined by a famous series of cookbooks by that title, is the area on both sides of the Mississippi River between New Orleans and Baton Rouge. That definition creates the perception of uniform cooking, but the following recipe demonstrates the fact that cooking on the River Road often varied from family to family so that, at least in the past, subtle but significant differences in cuisine occurred every mile or two on that part of the Mississippi.

YIELD: 8 TO 10 SERVINGS

2 pounds navy beans, soaked overnight in cold
   water to cover
1 cup chopped onion
2 cloves garlic, chopped
1 large ham bone, with some meat on it (optional)
2 quarts cold water, or more as needed
¼ cup flour
½ cup oil
1 teaspoon cayenne pepper, or more or less to
   taste
2 teaspoons salt, or more or less to taste
2 cups chopped green onion tops
5 to 6 cups cooked rice, for serving

Drain the soaked beans in a colander. Combine the beans, onion, garlic, and ham bone if using in a heavy 8- to 10-quart pot, adding enough water to cover. Bring to a boil over high heat; lower the heat, cover, and simmer over low heat for 2 to 2½ hours, or until the beans are tender and a thick gravy has formed. Add hot water as needed during the cooking process. Stir occasionally to prevent scorching.

Remove the ham bone and mash the beans when they are tender. Using the flour and oil, make a light-brown roux and add it to the beans with the cayenne and salt. Continue to cook the beans slowly on low heat for 15 to 20 minutes. Remove the pot from the heat, add the chopped green onion tops, cover, and let stand for 5 minutes. Serve over rice.

Family Collection
Mona Roussel Abadie
Edgard, Louisiana

WHITE BEANS, RICE, AND SMOKED SAUSAGE

The classic New Orleans version of white beans, slow-cooked with plenty of seasoning meat and slices of smoked sausage.

YIELD: 8 SERVINGS

2 pounds dried white (navy) beans, soaked
   overnight in cold water to cover
2 cups chopped onion
½ cup chopped green bell pepper
½ cup thinly sliced green onion tops
1½ teaspoons finely minced garlic

1 pound baked ham, cut into 1-inch cubes

1 large ham bone with some meat on it, sawed
   into 4- to 5-inch lengths

1 teaspoon salt

½ teaspoon freshly ground black pepper

⅛ teaspoon cayenne pepper

⅛ teaspoon dried hot red pepper flakes

2 whole bay leaves, crushed

½ teaspoon dried thyme

¼ teaspoon dried basil

3 quarts cold water

6 Creole, Polish, or French smoked garlic
   sausages

Boiled rice, for serving

Drain the soaked beans in a colander and put them, along with all the other ingredients except the sausages, in a heavy 8- to 10-quart pot or kettle. Bring to a boil over high heat, then lower the heat and simmer for 2 to 2½ hours, or until the beans are tender. Stir from time to time and scrape the sides and bottom of the pot to prevent scorching. Add more water toward the end of the cooking if the mixture begins to appear too dry.

While the beans are cooking, pan-grill the sausages in a heavy skillet for about 12 to 15 minutes, turning them frequently, until they are well browned on all sides. Drain on paper towels, then cut them into slices ½ inch thick. Add them to the beans about 1¾ hours after the simmering begins. Serve over boiled rice.

New Orleans Cookbook
Rima Collin and Richard Collin
New Orleans, Louisiana

FRIED CABBAGE

Cabbage, derived from the French colloquial term for head, caboche, *takes well to a skilletful of bacon grease.*

YIELD: 2 SERVINGS

3 slices bacon, chopped
½ medium onion, chopped
½ medium cabbage, chopped
1 ounce pimiento, sliced or chopped
Pinch of salt
Pinch of pepper
2 tablespoons sugar (optional)
3 to 4 tablespoons water

Fry the bacon with the onion in a large skillet. Add the cabbage and the remaining ingredients. Cook, covered, about 18 to 20 minutes, or until the cabbage is tender.

Wild About Turkey
National Wild Turkey Federation
Edgefield, South Carolina

RED CABBAGE CASSEROLE

YIELD: 6 SERVINGS

1 medium red cabbage, shredded
1 small onion, chopped
3 medium apples, peeled, cored, and
  chopped
¼ cup red wine vinegar
¼ cup water
2 tablespoons firmly packed dark brown sugar

Freshly ground black pepper to taste
2 tablespoons unsalted butter

Preheat the oven to 300°. Grease a large casserole dish. In a large bowl, combine all the ingredients except the butter. Place in the casserole. Dot with the butter. Cover and bake for 2 hours.

Ambrosia
Junior Auxiliary of Vicksburg
Vicksburg, Mississippi

SCALLOPED CABBAGE

YIELD: 4 SERVINGS

3 tablespoons unsalted butter
1 medium head green cabbage, sliced
3 cloves garlic, minced
Salt and black pepper to taste
1 cup heavy cream
Paprika

Preheat the oven to 325°. Heat the butter in a large skillet that has a cover and sauté the cabbage and garlic until tender and slightly brown. Add salt and pepper to taste and then the cream. Place in a buttered 2-quart casserole and bake for 25 minutes. Sprinkle with paprika.

Virginia Celebrates
Council of the Virginia Museum of Fine Arts
Richmond, Virginia

Green Corn

The best way to cook roasting ears is to boil them tender in a big pot of salted water, and serve with slathers of golden butter and a sprinkle of black pepper. Some people, however, seem to have a delicacy about getting buttered from ear to ear, which is almost necessary if one is to eat corn on the cob. To please these strange people, the Southern cook prepares the juicy and delectable dish that we call fried corn.

Collected by Kate C. Hubbard in Possum & Pomegranate *for the Federal Writers Project "America Eats"*

CABBAGE WITH PORK

This unusual recipe demonstrates how one family on the River Road, drawing on their French background and Southern circumstances, used patient and imaginative cooking to turn ordinary cabbage into a rare and elegant dish.

YIELD: 4 TO 6 SERVINGS

2 large heads cabbage
2 tablespoons oil
2 pounds pork chops or other cut of pork
2 teaspoons salt, or more or less to taste
1 teaspoon cayenne, or more or less to taste
1 medium onion, chopped fine
2 to 4 cloves garlic, minced
4 to 6 cups cooked rice, for serving

Cut the cabbage into wedges, remove the veins, put into a large pot with ½ cup water, and cook until tender. Drain, saving the juice for vegetable stock or soup.

Put the oil in a heavy pot, add the cabbage, cover, and smother while cooking the pork.

Season the pork with salt and cayenne; brown in a skillet on low heat. When the cabbage is a light-brown hashlike substance, add the onion and garlic. Combine the cabbage, pork, and drippings. Cook, uncovered, until dark brown (about 1 hour). Stir frequently to prevent sticking. Serve over the rice.

Family Collection
Mona Roussel Abadie
Edgard, Louisiana

COPPER PENNIES

Orange carrots turn a burnished copper color when glazed with this marinade.

YIELD: 8 TO 10 SERVINGS

2 pounds carrots, sliced
1 small green bell pepper, sliced
1 medium onion, sliced
½ cup salad oil
1 (10¾ ounce) can tomato soup
¾ cup white vinegar
1 cup sugar
1 teaspoon prepared mustard
1 teaspoon Worcestershire sauce

Boil the carrots in salted water until tender. Drain and let cool. Alternate layers of carrot,

Fried Corn

The ears must be carefully freed of cling-ing corn silks first of all. Then the cook stands the ear on end and slices the very outer tip of the grain off with a thin keen knife. Then she scrapes boldly down the ear with the back of the blade so as to bring out the rich, delicious, milky center of the corn, leaving the tougher outside of the grain still attached to the cob. It will take a goodly number of ears for the family so don't stop too soon. Fry two or three slices of sweet bacon in the skillet until the grease is extracted. Remove the slices and pour in the corn. Season with salt and black pepper. Add a cupful of water, cover tightly and weight the lid—a flat iron will serve for that. Simmer gently until most of the water is gone and the corn is thoroughly done. Stir occasionally to prevent scorching.

Collected by Kate C. Hubbard in Possum & Pomegranate
for the Federal Writers Project "America Eats"

pepper, and onion slices in a 2-quart dish. Beat the remaining ingredients together in a mixer un-til completely blended. Pour the marinade over vegetables. Refrigerate. The dish can be prepared several days ahead.

Possum on the Half-Shell
Possum Kingdom Chamber of Commerce
Possum Kingdom, Texas

BUTTER-ROASTED CORN

This Southern staple feeds hogs and humans alike, but it tastes best straight from the field, steamed in a faux husk of aluminum foil.

YIELD: 6 SERVINGS

6 tablespoons unsalted butter, at room
  temperature
3 tablespoons minced parsley
1½ teaspoons salt
Pinch of paprika
6 ears corn, husked and cleaned

Combine the butter, parsley, salt, and paprika in a small bowl. Spread on corn. Loosely wrap each ear in foil, sealing tightly. Grill over hot coals for about 15 minutes, turning frequently. Partially unwrap and serve in foil.

Outdoor Tables and Tales
Southeastern Outdoor Writers Association
Memphis, Tennessee

SOUTHERN-FRIED CORN

Some call this creamed corn, but all Southerners agree you had best scrape the cut kernels with the back of your knife to extract the milky pulp that remains.

YIELD: 6 TO 8 SERVINGS

8 tender ears of corn
2 tablespoons sugar
1 tablespoon salt

1 tablespoon flour
1 teaspoon black pepper
½ cup cold water or part milk
2 tablespoons bacon drippings

Cut the corn from the cob and place in a bowl. (Cut the top grain, then scrape the cob with the back of a knife.) Combine the sugar, salt, flour, and pepper; add to the corn, mixing well. Add the water and/or milk. Melt the bacon drippings in a skillet over medium to low heat. Add the corn mixture; cook slowly, stirring constantly, about 30 minutes or until creamy. Remove from the heat and serve immediately.

Southern Accent
Junior League of Pine Bluff
Pine Bluff, Arkansas

CORN PUDDING

The little soufflé that couldn't . . . rise, that is. We prefer it dense and just a tad soupy.

YIELD: 4 SERVINGS

2 eggs, separated
1 cup milk
1½ tablespoons flour
½ teaspoon salt
1 heaping tablespoon sugar
1 good pinch black pepper
1 pint scraped corn, with juices
1 tablespoon unsalted butter, melted

Preheat the oven to 400°. Beat the egg yolks in a large bowl. Add the milk. Combine the flour, salt,

sugar, and pepper in a bowl; add to the egg mixture. Add the corn and butter. Beat the egg whites in a large bowl; fold into the yolk mixture. Pour into a buttered baking dish. Bake for 30 minutes, or until set in the center.

Smoky Mountain Magic
Junior League of Johnson City
Johnson City, Tennessee

CORN FRITTERS

Known by some as mock fried oysters, these fritters are first cousins to the hush puppy.

YIELD: 2 DOZEN SMALL FRITTERS

1 egg
A little less than ¼ cup milk
1¼ cups flour
1 teaspoon baking powder
½ teaspoon salt
1 tablespoon unsalted butter, melted
1 cup cream-style corn
Oil, for deep frying

Combine all the ingredients except the oil. Drop by tablespoonfuls into deep oil and fry until golden brown.

Woman's Exchange Cookbook II
Woman's Exchange
Memphis, Tennessee

Maque Choux

Some Cajuns say this dish is a mock cabbage.
Believe what you will, it's tasty nonetheless.

YIELD: 4 TO 6 SERVINGS

8 ears tender corn
2 tablespoons cooking oil
1 teaspoon salt
½ cup water
½ green bell pepper, chopped
Cayenne and black pepper to taste
3½ cups canned tomatoes, drained and
*   chopped*
½ cup milk

Shave off the top of kernels with sharp knife, then scrape the milky substance with the back of the knife. Place all the ingredients except the milk in a heavy aluminum skillet and cook on low heat for 15 minutes, stirring frequently. Add the milk and cook 5 minutes longer.

Recipes and Reminiscences of New Orleans II
Parents Club of Ursuline Academy
New Orleans, Louisiana

Hominy Casserole

Time was when hominy was loosened from the
dried corn kernel by a bath in lye. Today, we're
more likely to find hominy in the Hispanic section
of the grocery store.

YIELD: 6 TO 8 SERVINGS

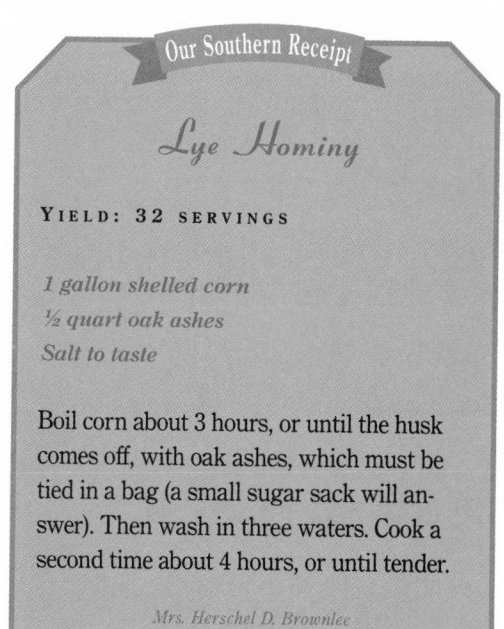

Our Southern Receipt

Lye Hominy

YIELD: 32 SERVINGS

1 gallon shelled corn
½ quart oak ashes
Salt to taste

Boil corn about 3 hours, or until the husk comes off, with oak ashes, which must be tied in a bag (a small sugar sack will answer). Then wash in three waters. Cook a second time about 4 hours, or until tender.

Mrs. Herschel D. Brownlee
Port Gibson, Mississippi
Collected by Eudora Welty for the Federal Writers
Project "America Eats"

2 slices bacon, chopped
1 small onion, chopped
¼ green bell pepper, chopped
1 (15-ounce) can tomatoes
1 (29-ounce) can hominy
4 ounces cheddar cheese, grated, or 4 slices
*   American cheese*
Parmesan cheese, grated

Preheat the oven to 350°. Cook the bacon, onion, green pepper, and tomatoes in a skillet for 5 minutes. Place the hominy in a baking dish; cover with the tomato mixture. Top with the grated cheddar and Parmesan cheese. Bake until hot and bubbly and the cheese is melted.

Variations: You may want to vary this according to your taste by using stewed canned tomatoes—such as Mexican-, Cajun-, or Italian-style—and topping with shredded jalapeño or Monterey Jack cheese.

Stoney Creek Recipe Collection
Independent Presbyterian Church
McPhersonville, South Carolina

NEW ORLEANS EGGPLANT

YIELD: 6 TO 8 SERVINGS

2 medium eggplants
Bacon drippings
1 large onion
½ green bell pepper
½ bunch green onions
2 cloves garlic
2 tablespoons minced parsley

3 to 4 slices of bread, soaked in water
1 pound shrimp, boiled, peeled, and chopped
1 small piece of ham, ground
1 to 2 eggs
2 teaspoons sugar
Salt and black pepper to taste
Bread crumbs
Unsalted butter

Boil the eggplants until fork-tender. Let cool. Chop the onion, bell pepper, and green onions finely. Heat the in bacon drippings in a skillet and sauté the vegetables in bacon drippings with the garlic (do not brown). Scoop out the eggplant pulp carefully so as not to damage skin. Add the pulp to the skillet and simmer 20 minutes. Preheat the oven to 350°. Stir in the minced parsley and simmer about 5 minutes. Take off the heat. Squeeze the bread dry and mix in well. Add the chopped shrimp and ground ham. Blend in 1 or 2 eggs, the sugar, and salt and pepper to taste. Stir in a few bread crumbs if needed. Stuff the eggplant shells, sprinkle with bread crumbs, and dot with butter. Bake for 15 minutes.

Cotton Country Collection
Junior League of Monroe
Monroe, Louisiana

FRENCH-FRIED EGGPLANT

YIELD: 4 TO 6 SERVINGS

1 medium eggplant
Oil for deep frying
Salt and pepper
Flour

1 egg, lightly beaten
Fine, dry bread crumbs

Peel the eggplant and cut it lengthwise into finger-size strips. Soak 1 hour in cold salted water. Drain and soak in plain cold water 30 minutes. Drain again and dry well. Heat the oil just to the smoking point. Sprinkle the strips lightly with salt and pepper. Dredge each strip in flour, then in the lightly beaten egg, then in the bread crumbs. Fry until a golden brown. Drain on paper towels.

Cross Creek Cookery
Marjorie Kinnan Rawlings
Cross Creek, Florida

FRIED OKRA

According to Jessica Harris, preeminent scholar of the foodways of the African Diaspora, the word okra *comes from* nkruma, *the term for the vegetable in the Twi language of Ghana.*

YIELD: 4 SERVINGS

½ cup cornmeal
Salt, pepper, and garlic salt to taste
1 pound okra, washed, trimmed, and cut into
   ¾-inch slices
Oil for frying

Mix the cornmeal, salt, pepper, and garlic salt in a zip-top bag. Soak the okra in water for 1 to 3 minutes. Drain, leaving the okra wet. Shake gently in the bag.

Cover the bottom of a skillet with less than ¼ inch oil. Add the okra to the hot oil, spreading the slices out evenly, and cover. After 2 to 3 minutes, turn the okra and cover again. Do this several times for 6 to 7 more minutes, always replacing the lid. Stab or gouge the okra with the edge of a metal spatula to eliminate excess coating. In the perfect dish, the slices should be partly crispy and party semi-chewy, some pieces still intact and some pieces a little smashed up.

Apron Strings
Junior League of Little Rock
Little Rock, Arkansas

OKRA FRITTERS

Okra may be African in origin, but Southerners of all hues and hometowns love it.

YIELD: 2 SERVINGS

1 cup steamed sliced okra
1 egg, lightly beaten
¼ cup diced onion
¾ to 1 cup self-rising cornmeal
½ teaspoon sugar
½ teaspoon salt
⅛ teaspoon black pepper
Vegetable oil, for deep frying
Ketchup, tomato sauce, or melted cheese,
*   for serving*

Combine the okra, egg, and onion in a large bowl. Gradually add the cornmeal until the mixture is batter consistency. Season with the sugar, salt, and pepper. Deep-fry in oil until golden brown. Serve hot with ketchup, tomato sauce, or melted cheese.

Among the Lilies
Women in Missions
First Baptist Church of Atlanta
Atlanta, Georgia

ONIONS, OKRA, CORN, AND TOMATOES

The green pods of the okra plant are native to Africa, and wherever they turn up, Africa has had some influence on the cooking. In many parts of the African American South, okra is mixed with corn, one of the staples of the New World larder. In others, it is mixed with both tomatoes and corn. Most of the combinations are hot and spicy with chiles or hot sauce; some are seasoned with a smoky piece of bacon or a ham hock.

YIELD: 10 SERVINGS

8 ounces bacon
1 large onion, sliced
3 large tomatoes, sliced
4 cups whole-kernel corn or 2 (16-ounce) cans,
*   drained*
1½ cups fresh okra, washed and trimmed, or
*   1 (10-ounce) package frozen cut okra*
¾ teaspoon salt
¼ teaspoon black pepper

Fry the bacon in a large, heavy saucepan over medium heat until crisp, turning frequently. Drain, reserving 2 tablespoons of drippings in

RICHARD HOWORTH

GETTING A TASTE FOR OKRA

Growing up in a large family of five brothers, I always had a lot of competition. We all became very fast eaters, racing through our first helpings so that we might be assured a second.

There was also a lot of competition for attention. One way I learned to get attention was by becoming known as a courageous eater, an eater of basically any kind of food. Anything like squash or okra or turnips or brussels sprouts—anything children were typically finicky about—I would eat and pretend to relish, though I may have been choking it down, gagging on the inside. My mother would always point me out to my older brothers, saying what a mature person I was for eating those things. She would ask my brothers, "Why don't y'all follow your little brother's example?" Deep down I think my brothers knew I was choking these things down, and resented me all the more for it. Of course, that made me even happier.

That's how I came to like a wide variety of foods, how I came to acquire a taste for things like okra. In retrospect, I'm astonished, but I ate it boiled and unadorned as early as five or six. The amazing, science-fiction quality of the slime of okra, which children almost universally find appalling, I pretended was ordinary, perfectly tasty. When we were all sitting at the table, my brothers and I would do things—slide food over onto one another's plates, "show your food," send various signals across the table, or kick one another underneath the table—things we thought were undetectable by grown-ups.

But Eudora Welty, who was a friend of my aunt's and a person with world-class powers of observation, once caught me showing my food to my brothers, and I don't think I've tried that trick since.

Richard Howorth, owner of Square Books in Oxford, Mississippi, is president of the American Booksellers Association.

the saucepan. Heat the reserved drippings in the saucepan on medium heat. Add the onion and cook, stirring, until tender. Add the tomatoes, corn, okra, salt, and pepper. Cover and simmer 30 minutes, stirring occasionally. Crumble the bacon and sprinkle over the top just before serving.

Celebrating Our Mothers' Kitchens
National Council of Negro Women
Washington, D.C.

HOPPIN' JOHN

Culinary scholar Karen Hess asserts that Hoppin' John is a corruption of pois à pigeon, *a French term for pigeon peas, a dish enjoyed in the Caribbean, where many slaves were sent for seasoning before they reached the Southern shores. Hoppin' John is also the nickname for Low-country cooking master John Martin Taylor, whose meal memory is on page 221.*

YIELD: 12 SERVINGS

1 pound dry field peas
2 cups raw rice
3 bacon slices, chopped
1 medium onion, chopped
3¼ cups broth from peas
Salt and pepper to taste
1 teaspoon sugar (optional)

Wash and cull the peas. Place the peas in a pot, cover with water, and soak overnight. Drain the peas.

In a pot of fresh water, bring the peas to a boil; reduce the heat and cook until tender.

Wash the rice thoroughly.

In a 2-quart saucepan, fry the bacon. Add the onion and sauté until tender. Add the broth (if you do not have enough from the peas, add water), raw rice, and peas; season to taste. Bring to a boil, lower the heat, cover, and simmer 20 minutes without stirring. Add the 1 teaspoon sugar, if using, to the peas after cooking. Stir well before serving.

Uptown Down South
Junior League of Greenville
Greenville, South Carolina

LIMPIN' SUSAN

Sister to the more well-known Hoppin' John, Limpin' Susan gets its savor from okra instead of black-eyed peas.

YIELD: 4 TO 6 SERVINGS

3 to 4 slices bacon, chopped
1 pint okra, washed, dried, trimmed,
*   and cut into rings*
1 cup washed raw rice
1 cup water
Salt and black pepper to taste

Fry the bacon and okra in a skillet. When the okra is tender, add the rice, water, salt, and pepper. Put in a rice steamer and cook until dry, about 1½ hours.

Charleston Receipts
Junior League of Charleston
Charleston, South Carolina

Potlikker

In the beginning let it be understood that there must be a black pot—no other kind will exactly do. The pot must be more than half filled with boiling water. Into this water goes a sizable slice of smoke-cured pork, a piece with streaks of lean untainted bacon. Let this boil while the turnip greens or mustard are being washed and washed until they are free of even one lingering grain of sand. Let the clean leaves freshen in cold water for an hour or so, then put them gently into the pot with the meat. When the water begins to bubble again, season with salt, black pepper, and a very small pod of red pepper. Move the pot to the back of the stove or turn down the heat; cover, and let simmer until the greens are tender and the meat is perfectly done. If it takes two hours, then it is still worth all the time it takes, for a cupful of steaming potlikker and a slice of golden egg-bread dripping with melted butter will put a rosy glow on a hungry world. If a lingering desire for food remains, take a big helping of greens, chop into it a couple of shallots and sprinkle with pungent pepper sauce. Then butter a new slice of egg bread and go right ahead.

Collected by Kate C. Hubbard in Possum & Pomegranate *for the Federal Writers Project "America Eats"*

BLACK-EYED PEAS

Black-eyed peas, those harbingers of good luck, are a Southern staple on New Year's Day. For an eye-opening variation, add a sliced jalapeño pepper to the cooking water.

YIELD: 6 SERVINGS

1 pound fresh black-eyed peas
2 tablespoons cooking oil
Salt to taste
½ cup chopped ham, chopped bacon, or chopped onion (optional)
Chopped onion, for serving

In a 3-quart saucepan, cover the peas with water. Stir in the oil and salt. Add the ham, if desired. Bring to a boil, reduce the heat, cover, and simmer about 30 minutes, or until tender. Pass the chopped onion for topping.

Heart and Soul
Junior League of Memphis
Memphis, Tennessee

BAKED VIDALIA ONIONS IN SHERRY CREAM SAUCE

YIELD: 6 SERVINGS

3 cups precooked thick-sliced Vidalia onions, or other sweet onions
⅓ cup dry sherry
1 cup light cream or sour cream
½ teaspoon salt

½ teaspoon black pepper

2 eggs, lightly beaten

2 tablespoons chopped pimientos

4 ounces mushrooms, sliced

3 tablespoons unsalted butter

⅓ cup grated sharp cheddar cheese

Preheat the oven to 350°. Drain the onion and arrange in a shallow baking dish. Combine the sherry, cream, salt, pepper, eggs, pimientos, and mushrooms in a bowl and pour over the onion. Dot with the butter and sprinkle with the cheese. Bake, covered, for 20 minutes.

Savannah Style
Junior League of Savannah
Savannah, Georgia

SPINACH MADELEINE

From the best-selling River Road *series of community cookbooks, which are as much social documents as they are recipe collections.*

YIELD: 6 SERVINGS

3 cups chopped spinach

2 tablespoons unsalted margarine

2 tablespoons plus 1 teaspoon flour

3 tablespoons chopped onion

⅔ cup reserved spinach cooking water

¾ cup evaporated skim milk

2 teaspoons minced jalapeños

1 teaspoon Worcestershire sauce

½ teaspoon black pepper

½ teaspoon garlic powder

½ teaspoon ground celery seed

Cayenne pepper to taste

4 ounces cheese, cubed

Buttered bread crumbs, for topping (optional)

Cook the spinach in 1½ cups water until tender. Drain, reserving ⅔ cup of the cooking water. Melt the margarine in a heavy saucepan over low heat. Add the flour and cook, stirring, until blended but not brown. Add the onion and cook until soft but not brown. The mixture will be coarse-looking at this point. While stirring constantly, slowly add the reserved spinach cooking water. To avoid lumps be sure to stir constantly until smooth. Gradually add the evaporated milk. Continue to cook, stirring, until smooth and thick. Add the jalapeños, Worcestershire sauce, black pepper, garlic powder, celery seed, and cayenne. Add the cheese and stir until melted. Combine with the cooked spinach.

This dish can be served immediately or put into a casserole and topped with buttered bread crumbs. The flavor is improved if the latter is done and the dish is kept in the refrigerator overnight. It can also be frozen.

River Road Recipes III
Junior League of Baton Rouge
Baton Rouge, Louisiana

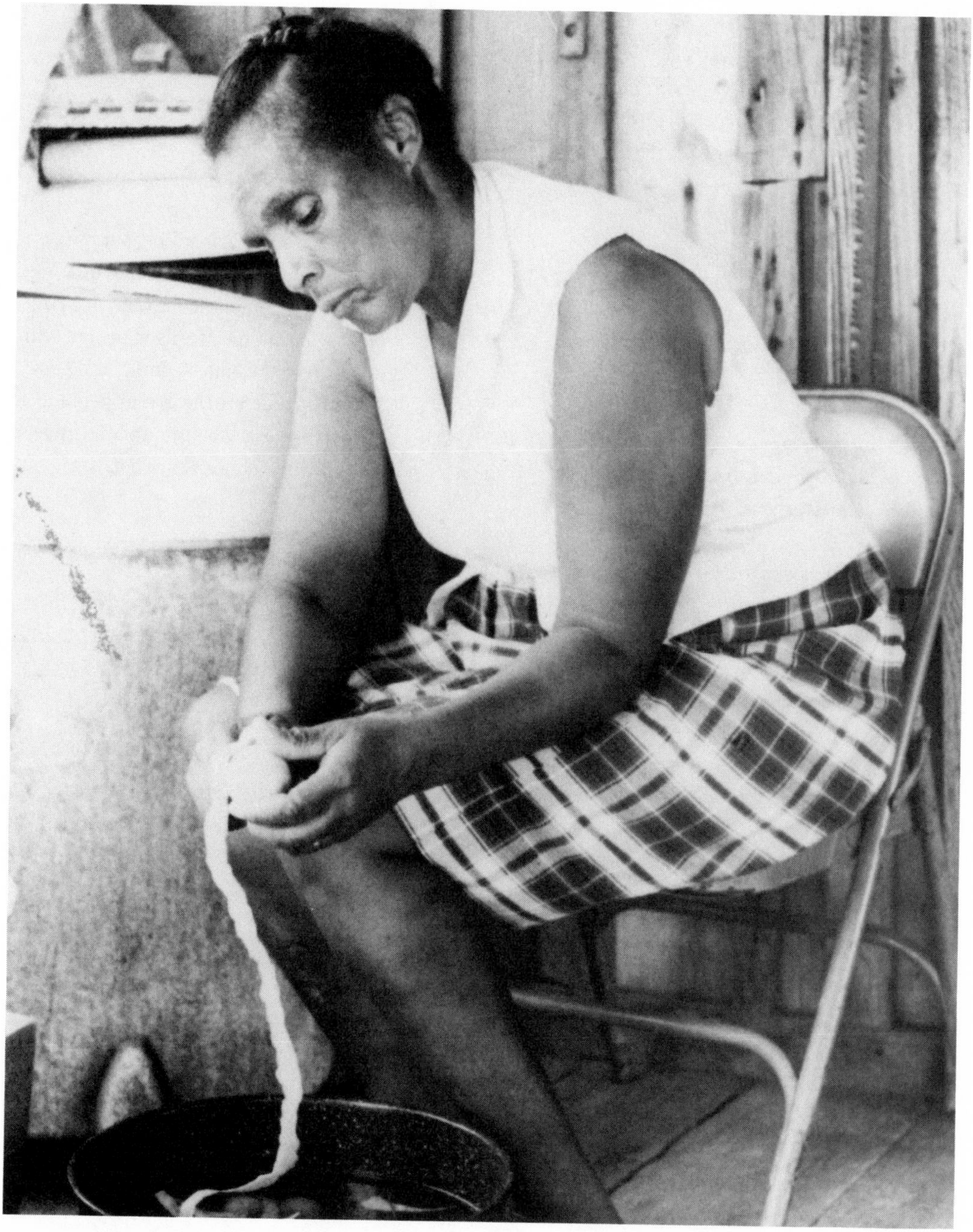

Miss Daisy's Southern Greens

You can use whatever proportion of greens for this recipe you want, but make sure you use a total of 2 pounds.

YIELD: 6 TO 8 SERVINGS

8 ounces ham hocks
2 tablespoons cooking oil
4 cups water
1 cup chopped onion
1 pound mustard greens, washed and drained
8 ounces turnip greens, washed and drained
8 ounces collard greens, washed and drained

Brown the ham hocks in the oil in a large, heavy stockpot. Add the water and onion and bring to a boil. Add the greens and return the liquid to a boil. Reduce the heat, cover, and simmer 2 hours. Drain, remove the ham hocks, and cut the meat into bite-sized pieces. Add the meat to the greens.

Miss Daisy Celebrates Tennessee
Daisy King
Nashville, Tennessee

Collard Greens with Ham Hocks

Southern food goes west to California without a hitch. Greens are greens no matter where they're cooked.

YIELD: 8 TO 10 SERVINGS

4 bunches collard greens
4 ham hocks, precooked
2 medium onions, chopped
3 cloves garlic
½ green bell pepper, chopped
Salt and pepper

Wash the greens leaf by leaf, taking out the large stems and breaking each leaf into quarters. Cook the precooked ham hocks in water for 30 minutes before putting the greens in the pot with the ham hocks. Add the onions, garlic, bell pepper, salt, and pepper before the greens begin to cook. Cook, stirring occasionally, until the greens are well done, about 2 hours. Serve hot.

Soul Food
Albert Ikner
San Jose, California

Mary Joe's Turnip Greens

As a general rule, turnip greens are favored in the Upper South, collards in the Deep South.

YIELD: 6 SERVINGS

3 thick slices salt pork
6 cups water
3 pounds turnip greens

Rinse the salt pork and place in a 3-quart saucepan. Add the water, bring to a boil, and reduce the heat. Cook, uncovered, over medium heat, for 45 to 60 minutes, or until the water is reduced to 1 cup.

Twist the leaves from the stems of the greens and the discard the stems. Wash the greens thoroughly. Add the greens to the salt pork and water in the saucepan. Bring to a boil, reduce the heat to low, cover, and cook, stirring occasionally, about 1 hour, or until tender.

Heart and Soul
Junior League of Memphis
Memphis, Tennessee

TURNIP GRATIN

We're known to love our turnip greens, stewed long and slow, but we Southerners have a taste for the bulbous root, too.

YIELD: 6 SERVINGS

1½ pounds turnips, peeled and cut into
⅛-inch slices
1 clove garlic, cut in half
3 tablespoons unsalted butter, divided
½ cup grated Gruyère cheese
½ cup grated Parmesan cheese
1 teaspoon minced parsley
1 teaspoon dried tarragon
1 teaspoon dried thyme
1 teaspoon dried oregano
Salt and white pepper to taste
½ cup light cream
¼ cup bread crumbs

Preheat the oven to 400°. Parboil the turnips for 2 to 3 minutes; drain. Rub a gratin dish with the garlic halves. Butter the dish well with 2 tablespoons of the butter and arrange one-third of the turnip slices in a layer. In a small bowl, mix the Gruyère, Parmesan, parsley, tarragon, thyme, and oregano. Add salt and pepper to taste. Sprinkle a third of this mixture over the turnip layer. Repeat the layers twice, ending with the cheese mixture. Pour the cream over the turnips; sprinkle with the crumbs and dot with the remaining tablespoon of butter. Bake for 45 minutes.

Standing Room Only
New Stage Theatre
Jackson, Mississippi

YELLOW SQUASH

A staple of the Native American diet, squash owes its name to the Narragansett Indian word asquatasquash.

YIELD: 6 TO 8 SERVINGS

6 small tender squash, sliced
1 stick (¼ pound) unsalted butter
1 medium onion, chopped
(optional)
3 eggs, well beaten
3 tablespoons heavy cream
2 tablespoons sugar
1 tablespoon flour
Salt and black pepper to taste

Cook the squash in a small amount of water until tender; drain. Melt the butter in a large skillet; sauté the onion, if using, until tender. Add the drained squash and continue to cook very slowly, stirring often, until all the liquid has evaporated.

Add the eggs, cream, sugar, and flour. Keep cooking until very dry.

The Southern Gourmet
Virginia Clower Robbins
St. Louis, Missouri

SQUASH CASSEROLE

YIELD: 4 TO 6 SERVINGS

6 to 8 medium yellow squash
1 medium onion, chopped
2 tablespoons unsalted butter
2 eggs, well beaten
½ teaspoon salt
¼ teaspoon black pepper
2 tablespoons minced parsley
3 tablespoons diced pimiento
½ cup grated cheese
¼ cup bread crumbs

Preheat the oven to 375°. Slice the squash and cook it in a small amount of water with the onion until tender; drain and mash. Add the butter. When the butter is melted, add the eggs, salt, pepper, parsley, pimiento, cheese, and bread crumbs. Mix well and pour into a greased casserole. Bake for 30 minutes. (If desired, more grated cheese can be added on top for the last 15 minutes of baking time.)

Woman's Exchange Cookbook II
Woman's Exchange
Memphis, Tennessee

BAKED STUFFED SQUASH

YIELD: 6 SERVINGS

6 small yellow squash
½ stick unsalted butter
½ cup fine, dry bread crumbs
2 tablespoons minced onion
½ teaspoon salt
1 tablespoon minced parsley
⅛ teaspoon black pepper
Pinch of sage
Dash of thyme

Drop the whole, unpeeled squashes in boiling salted water. Boil for about 10 minutes, or until tender but not soft. Remove from the heat, drain, and let cool. Preheat the oven to 375°. Slice a portion from the top and scoop out the pulp and seeds to make a cavity, reserving the pulp. Melt the butter in a saucepan; add the remaining ingredients to the butter. Stir until the bread crumbs are browned. Add the chopped squash removed from the cavity. Pack the mixture into the squash cavities. Place in a baking dish. Bake for 20 to 25 minutes.

North Carolina and Old Salem Cookery
Elizabeth Sparks
Kernersville, North Carolina

Zucchini Stuffed with Cheese

We are not just a region of Africans and Anglo-Saxons, as evidenced by this Greek-derived dish from North Carolina.

YIELD: 6 SERVINGS

6 medium zucchini
¾ cup crumbled feta cheese
⅔ cup small-curd cottage cheese
2 eggs
¼ cup grated Parmesan cheese
1 tablespoon minced parsley
Dash of pepper
½ bunch snipped dill
½ cup grated Parmesan cheese, plus extra for
   sprinkling on the zucchini

Preheat the oven to 425°. Cut the zucchini in half lengthwise. Scoop the pulp out carefully with a vegetable corer; reserve the pulp for later use in a soup or vegetable dish. Parboil the zucchini 5 minutes to tenderize; drain. Combine the feta, cottage cheese, eggs, Parmesan, parsley, and pepper. Stuff the zucchini with the cheese mixture.

Bake in a shallow baking pan for 10 minutes. Remove from the oven; sprinkle with the dill and the additional Parmesan cheese. Place under the broiler to brown briefly. Serve warm. Cut into bite-sized pieces if serving as an appetizer.

The Grecian Plate
The Hellenic Ladies Society
Durham, North Carolina

Mirlitons Stuffed with Shrimp

Mam Papaul says, "We like these cooked with tiny river shrimp . . . the tails of the bigger ones were about a half inch long. During the river shrimp season, just about everything from okra to eggplant was cooked with them. River shrimp are hard to come by now, so we use lake shrimp."

YIELD: 6 TO 8 SERVINGS

6 medium mirlitons (also called chayotes)
⅔ cup finely chopped onion
6 tablespoons unsalted butter
2 cups medium shrimp, peeled and
   deveined
3 slices bread, soaked in water and squeezed
¼ cup finely chopped shallots
¼ cup chopped parsley
1 teaspoon salt
¼ teaspoon black pepper
3 tablespoons melted butter
¼ cup plain dried bread crumbs

Cut the mirlitons in half lengthwise and place in boiling water. Cover and boil for 25 to 30 minutes, or until tender. Preheat the oven to 350°. When the mirlitons are cool enough to handle, remove the seeds and scoop out and reserve the pulp and shells. Heat 3 tablespoons of the butter in a large skillet and sauté the onion for 5 minutes. Add the shrimp and cook for about 8 minutes. Add the mirliton pulp, bread, shallots, parsley, salt, and pepper; mix well. Cook for 10 minutes, stirring constantly. Pile into the mirliton shells. Top with buttered bread crumbs made with the remaining 3 tablespoons butter. Bake for 20 minutes.

Mam Papaul's Country Creole Basket
Nancy Tregre Wilson
Baton Rouge, Louisiana

FRIED PLANTAINS

Native to Africa, the plantain, called a cooking banana by many, is not as sweet as the banana we use for puddings and the like.

YIELD: 8 TO 10 SERVINGS

5 ripe plantains
Salt
Palm oil or peanut oil for deep frying

To peel the plantains, slice off the tips at both ends. Make a lengthwise slit through the peel. Pry off the skin by inserting your fingers between the palm and plantain. Slice the plantains diagonally ½ inch thick; sprinkle with salt. Cover and refrigerate until ready to fry.

In a deep fryer or heavy skillet, heat the oil to 380°. Carefully drop in enough plantain slices to cover the bottom of the skillet. Fry until golden, turning once. Using a slotted spoon, lift the plantain slices out of the skillet and drain on paper towels.

Mother Africa's Table
National Council of Negro Women
Washington, D.C.

SCALLOPED TOMATOES

A good way to gussy up those cans of tomatoes that are collecting dust at the back of the cupboard.

YIELD: 6 SERVINGS

1½ cups stale bread, torn in coarse pieces
½ stick unsalted butter, melted
2 cups canned tomatoes
1 teaspoon salt
6 tablespoons firmly packed dark brown sugar

Preheat the oven to 425°. Distribute the bread evenly on the bottom of a 9-inch baking dish 2 inches deep; pour the melted butter over the bread and stir to coat the pieces. Heat the tomatoes, salt, and brown sugar in a saucepan; bring to a boil. Pour over the bread. Bake for 25 minutes, or until well browned.

Miss Lillian and Friends
Beth Tartan and Rudy Hayes
Plains, Georgia

STUFFED TOMATOES

YIELD: 6 SERVINGS

6 large tomatoes
½ teaspoon salt
2 cups fresh chopped spinach, cooked, or 1 (10-ounce) package frozen chopped spinach, cooked
1 large onion, chopped
3 stalks celery, chopped
1 cup chopped green bell pepper
2 carrots, chopped
2 teaspoons chopped parsley
2 tablespoons unsalted butter
¾ cup seasoned fine, dry bread crumbs
⅓ cup milk
1 egg, lightly beaten
1 tablespoon grated Parmesan cheese

Preheat the oven to 400°. Cut a ¼-inch slice from the tops of the tomatoes. Scoop out the pulp and seeds, reserving the pulp and discarding the seeds. Sprinkle salt inside the tomato shells and invert to drain. Press all the moisture out of the spinach. Heat the butter in a large skillet and sauté the onion, celery, bell pepper, carrots, and parsley until tender. Combine the sautéed vegetables and the spinach, bread crumbs, milk, and egg in a large bowl. Mix well. Spoon the vegetable mixture into the tomatoes; place on a lightly greased 8-inch square baking dish. Sprinkle the cheese over the filled tomatoes. Bake for 15 minutes.

Treasures of the Smokies
Junior League of Johnson City
Johnson City, Tennessee

FRIED GREEN TOMATOES

Long before the movie, or the book, Southerners were rolling tomatoes in cornmeal and frying them up for a tasty treat.

YIELD: 6 SERVINGS

4 large green tomatoes
½ cup cornmeal
1 teaspoon salt
¼ teaspoon black pepper
Bacon fat

Slice the tomatoes ¼ inch thick. Mix the cornmeal with the salt and pepper. Dip each slice into the seasoned meal mixture. Place the seasoned vegetable in a heavy skillet containing melted bacon fat. Fry slowly until brown, turning once.

Bayou Cuisine
St. Stephen's Episcopal Church
Indianola, Mississippi

JOHN ALEX FLOYD, JR.

THE FIRST TOMATO

When I was a little boy I thought it would be fun to see how many tomatoes I could produce (I don't know if I ever liked tomatoes then). It wasn't about size; it was about number. As I got older it got to be about taste.

One of the things I relish most in life is the first tomato of the summer, sliced and sprinkled with salt and pepper. For years, the kinds you get in the supermarket have sort of tasted like cardboard.

The last frost date in the Birmingham area is right around Easter, and I will do anything to bring in a crop early. I've tried early fruiting selections. I've been given bigger plants. I've even tried little insulators for the plants. But for years, the first week I could count on tomatoes fresh from the garden was the week of July 4. So the last few years I've cheated.

I have a great friend in Kosciusko, Mississippi, named Paul Newell, and he has been growing tomatoes religiously in his little homemade greenhouse for years. Now he's sending the plants to me by way of his son, David. And I'm putting them out in my garden to grow. This year, I am happy to report that my first tomato came in during the second week of May—and it was damn good!

Now, to ensure that the *first* taste of that *first* tomato is absolutely perfect, here's what my wife, Pam, and I do. First we get water rolling to a nice boil on the stove. Then we drop the tomatoes in the water for a few seconds, maybe thirty. When we pull them out, we run a bit of cold water over them until they cool. Then we gingerly peel off the skin, and nicely slice the tomato, placing it on a clear glass plate to show off the color, adding a bit of salt and pepper.

Usually we divide it piece by piece, maybe giving our two boys one slice apiece. It is a treat we enjoy with great delight. And from that point on through the end of August, we have tomatoes for at least one meal each day we are at home.

But you should know that I'm not satisfied to get just one crop of tomatoes. No, I want to beat the odds. So during the week of the Fourth of July, I always plant a second crop. Just as my summer crop is coming in, I plant my fall crop, so that when late-October frost comes, I'm still picking green tomatoes. My goal is to have a tomato from my garden ripening on the windowsill come Christmas morning.

John Alex Floyd, Jr., editor of Southern Living *magazine, tends his tomatoes in Birmingham.*

Green Tomato Pie

A specialty of the Bluegrass State.

YIELD: 8 SERVINGS

3 large green tomatoes, sliced
½ cup water
½ cup seedless raisins
Pastry for 2 (9-inch) layers
1 cup sugar
2 tablespoons flour
¾ teaspoon cinnamon
½ teaspoon ginger
¼ teaspoon nutmeg
2 tablespoons unsalted butter
Grated zest of 1 lemon
1½ tablespoons fresh lemon juice
¼ cup brandy or whiskey

Preheat the oven to 450°. Select firm green tomatoes, about 8 ounces each. Pour the water over the tomatoes in a skillet and simmer 5 minutes or until they have absorbed most of the water and seem tender. Add the raisins and cook a little longer. Drain the skillet, reserving the liquor, and place the tomatoes and raisins in a 9-inch pie pan lined with uncooked pie dough. Mix the sugar and flour together and sprinkle over the tomatoes. Sprinkle with the cinnamon, ginger, and nutmeg. Dot the surface with the butter. Add the grated zest and lemon juice. Pour the brandy over the top. If there is room, add a few tablespoons of the reserved tomato liquor. Top with a slashed solid crust or with strips of dough. Bake for 15 minutes. Reduce the heat to 375° and bake 30 minutes longer, or until the crust is golden brown.

Out of Kentucky Kitchens
Marion Flexner
Lexington, Kentucky

Tex-Mex Enchiladas

Where Texas meets Mexico, great tastes collide.

YIELD: 12 SERVINGS

¾ cup cooking oil
2 cups finely chopped onion
2 cloves garlic, minced
2 tablespoons flour
2½ cups chopped tomatoes, or 2½ cups tomato juice
2 cups water
2 tablespoons chili powder, or more to taste
1 teaspoon cumin seed
1 tablespoon salt
12 tortillas
1½ pounds grated American cheese

Heat ¼ cup of the oil in a skillet and sauté ¼ cup of the onion until soft but not brown. Add the garlic and flour; blend well. Combine the tomatoes and the 2 cups water; add to the skillet. Add the chili powder, cumin seed, and salt. Simmer for about 1 hour. (If sauce gets too thick, add a little water. It should be the consistency of cream.)

Preheat the oven to 400°. Heat the remaining ½ cup cooking oil. Dip the tortillas, one at a time, in the hot oil, then in the sauce. Spread each dipped tortilla with about 2 teaspoons of the grated cheese and 1 teaspoon chopped onion. Roll and fasten with a toothpick. Place the enchiladas side by side in a shallow baking dish or enchilada dish. Sprinkle with the remaining onion and cheese; pour the remaining sauce over all. Heat in the oven for 10 minutes, or until the cheese is melted.

Houston Junior League Cookbook
Junior League of Houston
Houston, Texas

CHILES RELLENOS

From Central Texas, where the Hill Country meets the arid plains . . . at Possum Kingdom Lake.

YIELD: 10 SERVINGS

10 Anaheim or poblano chiles
1 pound Monterey Jack cheese, cut into 3x1-inch
sticks
1 to 2 cups flour
Salt and black pepper
4 eggs
Pinch of salt
Corn oil or peanut oil
Red Chile Sauce, for serving (recipe follows)

Char the chiles over a gas flame or under the broiler, turning to blacken all over. Place in a paper bag, close the bag, and let the chiles steam for 15 minutes. Rub the skin off the chiles. Cut a slit lengthwise in each chile, stopping about ½ inch from the tip. Remove the seeds and veins.

Stuff each chile with a stick of cheese. Season the flour with salt and pepper to taste. Dredge the chiles in the flour mixture. Separate the eggs. Beat the whites until foamy; add a pinch of salt and beat until stiff. Beat the yolks; then fold them into whites. Working quickly, dip the chiles in the egg to coat. Fry the chiles in 1 inch hot oil in a large skillet, turning to brown evenly. Drain on paper towels. Serve with Red Chile Sauce.

RED CHILE SAUCE

20 dried red chiles
2 cloves garlic, peeled and crushed
1 small yellow onion, peeled and quartered
1 teaspoon ground cumin
Salt
1 teaspoon sugar (optional)

Wash the chiles and remove the stems, seeds, and veins. Add the chiles to a pot of boiling water; cover the pot and immediately remove from the heat. Let the chiles soak until soft, about 1 hour. Drain, reserving the soaking water. Place the chiles, garlic, and onion and 2 cups of the reserved soaking water in a blender and purée until smooth. Thin the purée with more soaking water if the sauce is too thick. Strain the sauce and add the cumin. Season with salt to taste. Add sugar, if desired.

Possum on the Half-Shell
Possum Kingdom Chamber of Commerce
Possum Kingdom, Texas

REAL MASHED POTATOES

Southerners, weaned on sweet potatoes, know the white version as Irish potatoes.

Y I E L D : 6 S E R V I N G S

6 medium potatoes, peeled and quartered
Salted water
½ stick unsalted butter
Salt and black pepper to taste
½ cup milk

Place the potatoes in salted water in a saucepan. Cook, covered, until tender; drain. Place in a large mixing bowl. Mash with a potato masher or on the low speed of an electric mixer. Add the butter, salt, pepper, and milk. Whip until fluffy. (Add more milk as needed to make potatoes smooth.)

More Calf Fries to Caviar
Janel Franklin and Sue Vaughn
Tahoka, Texas

GARLIC MASHED POTATOES

Y I E L D : 6 S E R V I N G S

3 pounds potatoes, peeled and cubed
1 large head garlic
5 tablespoons heavy cream
½ stick unsalted butter
¼ cup roasted-garlic olive oil
1 egg yolk
Salt and pepper

Place the potatoes in a large pot, cover with cold water, and bring to a boil. Reduce the heat slightly and cook until tender, about 20 minutes.

While the potatoes are cooking, peel the paper skin from the garlic and separate cloves. Place the garlic cloves in a small pot, cover with water, and bring to a boil. Lower the heat and simmer until the garlic is very soft, about 15 minutes. Drain and allow to cool.

Drain the potatoes and return them to the pot. Shake over medium heat to remove the remaining moisture, 10 to 15 seconds. Set the potatoes aside.

Slip the skins from the garlic cloves and purée the garlic cloves and the heavy cream in a food processor.

Put the potatoes through a potato ricer or use an electric mixer (do not beat long or the potatoes will be gluey). Mix in the garlic purée, butter, roasted-garlic olive oil, and egg yolk. Season with salt and pepper.

A Taste of Memphis
Share Our Strength
Memphis, Tennessee

SWEET POTATO CASSEROLE

Y I E L D : 4 T O 6 S E R V I N G S

1½ sticks unsalted margarine, plus extra for
   greasing the baking dish
2 cups mashed cooked sweet potatoes
1¼ cups granulated sugar
2 eggs, lightly beaten
1 cup milk

ROBERT KHAYAT

A PLACE FOR MORE THAN EATING

The only time we came together as a family was at mealtime. We didn't have a car, so we didn't go for rides in the country. We didn't take vacations. Usually, we all seemed to be headed in different directions at once. Even on Sunday, we went to different Sunday school classes. But when it came time for dinner or supper, my mother, father, two sisters, and brother and I all gathered around the small white table in the kitchen of our house in Moss Point, Mississippi.

What I see in my mind's eye most clearly is the butter dish that sat in the middle of the table. (I recall that the butter had been churned over at Mrs. Spann's house, which was about three blocks from us. Milking her cow was one of our chores.) The butter always seemed to be sort of melted. We didn't have air conditioning, and no matter the season, it seemed like it was always 85 or 90 degrees in that little kitchen.

Fried chicken, mashed potatoes, English peas, and plain white bread: we ate on crockery plates, not china, and the cutlery was always stainless steel. There was always music at the meal table. We had either a radio or a phonograph playing all the time, because my mother loved music so much.

The table was the place for family business and for family quarrels as much as a place for eating. But most important, it was where we shared stories and learned lessons. I remember one night when the subject of managing money came up. Daddy took ten dimes out of his pocket and laid them out on the tablecloth. He said, You give the first dime to the church. The second dime goes in your savings account. And you live on the rest. That, he said, was called tithing, and is how we should manage our money, and our lives.

At that small white table in our hot kitchen, we learned the values and traditions that I later tried to teach—to recommend to—my own children.

A native of Moss Point, Mississippi, Robert Khayat is chancellor of the University of Mississippi, home of The Center for the Study of Southern Culture.

¼ teaspoon nutmeg
½ teaspoon cinnamon
¾ cup corn flakes
½ cup chopped pecans
½ cup firmly packed dark brown sugar

Preheat the oven to 400°. Melt 6 tablespoons (¾ stick) of the margarine and combine in a large bowl with the sweet potatoes, granulated sugar, eggs, milk, nutmeg, and cinnamon; blend well. Pour into a greased baking dish and bake for 20 minutes. Mix the corn flakes, pecans, and brown sugar and the 6 tablespoons remaining margarine in small bowl. Spread evenly over the baked casserole. Return the casserole to the oven and bake for 10 minutes longer.

Bless Us Cooks
Grace–St. Luke's Episcopal Church
Memphis, Tennessee

GLAZED SWEET POTATOES

As if they weren't sweet enough!

YIELD: 6 SERVINGS

6 medium sweet potatoes
¾ stick unsalted butter
½ teaspoon salt
Dash of paprika
¼ cup firmly packed light brown sugar
¼ cup chopped pecans

Preheat the oven to 350°. Wash the sweet potatoes and bake them until tender. Cut into halves and scoop out the pulp. Place the pulp in a bowl.

Our Southern Receipt

Sweet Potatoes Baked in Ashes

Born in 1864, at the close of the slavery era, George Washington Carver won international fame for his experiments with peanuts and sweet potatoes, research that continues today under the auspices of the National Aeronautics and Space Administration.

In this method, the sweetness and piquancy of the potato is brought out in a manner hardly obtainable in any other way. Cover the sweet potatoes with warm ashes to a depth of 4 inches. Place live coals and hot cinders over them. Bake slowly for at least 2 hours. Remove the ashes with a soft brush. Serve with butter while hot.

How the Farmer Can Save His Sweet Potatoes
(Bulletin #38, 1936)
George Washington Carver
Tuskegee Institute, Tuskegee, Alabama

Melt 2 tablespoons of the butter and add it to the pulp, along with the salt and paprika; beat until light and fluffy. Return this mixture to the shells.

Combine the brown sugar, the remaining ½ stick butter, and the pecans in a saucepan. Cook for 3 minutes, then spread on the potato halves.

Bake the sweet potatoes for 20 minutes longer.

A Cook's Tour of the Azalea Coast
Auxiliary to the New Hanover–Pender County
   Medical Society
Wilmington, North Carolina

GRITS

According to Marjorie Kinnan Rawlings, "Grits are the Deep South member of the hominy family. What the North knows as hominy, we call 'big hominy.' This is the whole grains of white corn treated, amazingly, with lye, and boiled. Grits are hominy dried and ground fine. They are a staple food in Florida."

YIELD: 3 TO 4 SERVINGS

1 cup grits, washed
4 cups boiling water
1 teaspoon salt

Stir the grits slowly into the boiling water. Cover and let cook slowly, about 30 to 40 minutes, stirring often.

Cross Creek Cooking
Marjorie Kinnan Rawlings
Cross Creek, Florida

GARLIC CHEESE GRITS

YIELD: 6 TO 8 SERVINGS

1 cup regular grits, uncooked
4 cups water
1½ teaspoons salt
1 stick (¼ pound) unsalted butter
1 cup (4 ounces) grated sharp cheese, such as cheddar
1 teaspoon dried minced garlic or garlic powder
2 tablespoons Worcestershire sauce
Paprika

Preheat the oven to 350°. Prepare the grits according to the package directions, using 4 cups water and 1½ teaspoons salt. Add the butter, cheese, garlic, and Worcestershire to the cooked grits; stir until the butter and cheese are melted. Spoon the grits mixture into a greased 1½-quart casserole. Sprinkle with paprika. Bake for 15 to 20 minutes.

Among the Lilies
Women in Missions
First Baptist Church of Atlanta
Atlanta, Georgia

NASSAU GRITS

Are grits singular or plural? According to Bill Neal, the late Southern food authority, "'Grits' comes from the Old English grytt, which even in its earliest forms most often appeared in the plural, grytta."

YIELD: 8 SERVINGS

8 slices bacon
1 medium onion, chopped
2 small green bell peppers, finely chopped
2 cups chopped tomatoes
¼ teaspoon sugar
6 cups water
1 teaspoon salt
1½ cups regular grits, uncooked

Fry the bacon in a skillet until crisp. Drain the bacon, crumble, and set aside. Pour off all but 2 tablespoons drippings. Sauté the onion and bell pepper in the skillet; stir in the tomatoes and sugar. Bring to a boil, reduce the heat, and simmer 30 minutes, stirring occasionally. Bring the 6 cups of water to a boil. Add salt and the grits. Cook 20 minutes, stirring frequently, until the grits have thickened. Remove from the heat and stir in the tomato mixture. Sprinkle the bacon on top.

A Taste of South Carolina
Orangeburg, South Carolina

FRIED GRITS

A great use for day-old grits

YIELD: 8 SERVINGS

4 cups water
1 cup regular grits, uncooked
2 teaspoons salt
1 cup flour
1 egg, lightly beaten with 1 tablespoon
  water
About ½ cup bacon drippings
Fresh tomato sauce, for serving

Bring the 4 cups of water to a boil in a large pot; pour the grits into the pot and add the salt. Lower the heat and simmer for 10 minutes; stir frequently. While the grits are still warm, fill 8 tall, slender glasses with grits. Chill overnight. When ready to fry, unmold and cut into ½-inch-thick slices. Dip into flour, then into egg mixture. Place enough bacon drippings in a large skillet to brown the circles of grits. Brown on

Our Southern Receipt

Aberdeen Spanish Rice

YIELD: 6 SERVINGS

4 tablespoons oil
1 cup rice
1 onion, sliced
1 green pepper, chopped
1 quart canned tomatoes
2 teaspoons salt
⅛ teaspoon pepper

Heat 2 tablespoons of the oil in a large frying pan and add the rice. Cook until brown, stirring constantly. Heat the remaining 2 tablespoons oil and cook the onion and green pepper until onion is yellow and tender. Combine with rice. Add tomatoes and let simmer until the rice is tender, stirring constantly Add a little hot tomato juice if the rice seems dry. Season with salt and pepper.

Mrs. Bicknell T. Eubanks
Aberdeen, Mississippi
Collected by Eudora Welty for the Federal Writers
Project "America Eats"

both sides. Serve warm with a fresh tomato sauce.

Miss Daisy Celebrates Tennessee
Daisy King
Nashville, Tennessee

SAVANNAH RED RICE

According to Damon Fowler, keeper of the Classical Southern Cooking flame, "Savannah's name has only been associated with the dish in this century. Old Savannahians knew it as 'mulatto rice,' [a reference to] the lovely ruddy skin tone of the people that mulatto originally described, those of mixed African and Native American blood."

YIELD: 12 TO 14 SERVINGS

4 ounces bacon
½ cup chopped onion
2 cups raw rice
2 cups tomatoes
½ teaspoon salt
¼ teaspoon black pepper
1 teaspoon sugar
⅛ teaspoon Tabasco

In a large skillet, fry the bacon until crisp; remove from the drippings and drain. Preheat the oven to 350°. Cook the onion in the bacon drippings until tender. Wash the rice and add it to the skillet with the tomatoes, salt, pepper, sugar, Tabasco, and crumbled bacon. Cook on low for 10 minutes. Pour into a greased 1-quart baking dish. Cover tightly and bake for 1 hour.

Little Bit Different
St. John's Episcopal Church
Moultrie, Georgia

DIRTY RICE

A Cajun dish of rice flavored with gizzards and such that's gone upriver to Shreveport.

YIELD: 6 TO 8 SERVINGS

1 cup ground beef
1 cup ground chicken livers and gizzards,
combined
½ cup ground onion and parsley
2 tablespoons unsalted butter or
margarine
2 cups cooked rice
Salt and pepper to taste

Sauté the beef, liver mixture, and onion mixture in the butter in a large skillet until onion is golden brown. Add the rice and season with salt and pepper.

A Cook's Tour of Shreveport
Junior League of Shreveport
Shreveport, Louisiana

RED BEANS AND RICE

Louis Armstrong loved this traditional New Orleans washerwoman's dish so much that he signed his letters, "Red Beans and Ricely, Yours, Louis."

YIELD: 4 TO 6 SERVINGS

8 ounces red beans
1 cup raw rice

10 to 12 slices fat meat or salt meat
1 onion, chopped
1 clove garlic, chopped

Cover the beans with water in a large saucepan. Simmer, covered, for 4 to 5 hours, adding water as needed to make a thick juice. Put the rice on to cook. While it is cooking, fry fat meat in a hot skillet, then add to the beans, reserving the drippings. Sauté the onion and garlic in the reserved drippings, then add to beans. Continue cooking until the rice is tender. Serve the beans over the rice.

Bayou Cuisine
St. Stephen's Episcopal Church
Indianola, Mississippi

SUNSET FARMS OKRA

Some folks dote on okra. Others find its mucilaginous quality off-putting. In this recipe, it's the slime that binds.

YIELD: 6 TO 8 SERVINGS

6 slices bacon
2 medium onions, chopped
2 green bell peppers, chopped
6 cups (½-inch-thick) okra slices
4 medium tomatoes, peeled and chopped
Salt and pepper
1 tablespoon minced parsley

Fry the bacon until crisp; drain, reserving the drippings, and crumble. Cook the onion and

DAMON LEE FOWLER

DINNERS ON THE GROUNDS

I remember well dinners on the grounds at the Grassy Pond Baptist Church in Gafney, South Carolina, and at the First Baptist Church in Clover. My dad was the pastor, and I grew up eating at the church.

In Clover, there was a vacant lot, shaded with big trees, next door to the church, where they put up folding tables to hold the food, six or more tables set in a straight line, with maybe a separate table for the desserts if need be. The line of tables stretched as long as the church building itself.

Nobody—and I do mean nobody—could eat before my father said grace. Though there was a bit of a pecking order established as to who could go down the table first, for the most part it was very democratic, touched with a great corporate spirit, a spirit that harks back to the days of the early Christian rituals. It may well have been unconscious, but for me, the sharing of the food had a deep, understated religious significance.

You could hover at the edge of the line, peering over shoulders to survey the tables, but you always had to start at the back of the line. If nothing else, you could always count on there being five or six different kinds of macaroni pie. And I loved macaroni pie. No two cooks made it the same, just like no two pots of baked beans were the same. There was everything from custardy, almost soupy pies to the kind that was real set, with a consistency similar to the Italian dish *pasta al forno*. And you could always count on loads of fried chicken, with subtle but real variations, for there are as many ways to fry chicken as there are cooks in the South. There were always slow-cooked green beans, with variations dependent on what variety of beans the cook was growing and whether they cured their own salt pork for seasoning.

And then there were the desserts. With desserts, the women really put themselves out. There were lemon meringue pies, pecan pies, and chocolate cream pies, coconut cake and always, always pound cake.

At those dinners on the grounds our church functioned like a family. We loved and prayed. We had our ups and downs. But no matter what, we ate well.

Savannah resident Damon Lee Fowler is the author of, among other works on Southern cookery, Classical Southern Cooking *and* Fried Chicken: The World's Best Recipes from Memphis to Milan, from Buffalo to Bangkok.

green pepper in the drippings until golden; drain. Add the okra; cook until golden. Add the tomatoes and season with salt and pepper. Cover and simmer for 20 minutes. Add the crumbled bacon and the parsley just before removing from heat.

North Carolina and Old Salem Cookery
Elizabeth Hedgecock Sparks
Kernersville, North Carolina

OKRA AND CORN PILAU

YIELD: 8 SERVINGS

1 tablespoon shortening or oil
2 cups sliced okra
1 cup chopped onion
¼ cup chopped green bell pepper
2 cups low-sodium chicken broth
1½ cups canned corn, drained
1 cup uncooked long-grain rice
1 teaspoon salt
2 cups canned tomatoes, drained
3 slices bacon, fried and crumbled

Heat the shortening in a Dutch oven over medium heat. Add the okra, onion, and green pepper. Cook until tender. Add the broth, corn, rice, and salt. Bring to a boil. Stir once. Simmer, uncovered, 20 minutes, or until rice is done. Stir in the tomatoes and bacon. Heat through. Serve immediately.

The Black Family Dinner Quilt Cookbook
National Council of Negro Women
Washington, D.C.

CREAMY MACARONI AND CHEESE

Sure, macaroni has its ties to Italy, but the popularity of this Southern starch owes more to the folks at Kraft.

YIELD: 6 SERVINGS

2 tablespoons vegetable oil
½ cup chopped green onions
1 clove garlic, minced
2 tablespoons flour
¼ teaspoon dried basil
¼ teaspoon dry mustard
⅛ teaspoon black pepper
1 teaspoon Worcestershire sauce
Dash of hot pepper sauce
2 cups skim milk
½ cup sour cream
4 ounces reduced-fat (⅓ less fat) sharp cheddar cheese, shredded
1½ cups uncooked small elbow macaroni, cooked without salt or fat, well drained
1 tablespoon unseasoned fine, dry bread crumbs

Preheat the oven to 350°. Grease a 2-quart casserole. Set aside. Heat the oil in a large skillet over medium heat. Add the onions and garlic. Sauté until tender. Stir in the flour, basil, dry mustard, black pepper, Worcestershire, and hot pepper sauce. Stir until well blended. Stir in the milk. Cook and stir on medium heat until mixture thickens and gradually bubbles. Add the sour cream and cheese. Stir until smooth. Add the sauce to the macaroni. Toss to mix. Pour into the greased casserole. Sprinkle with the bread crumbs. Bake for 25 minutes.

The Black Family Dinner Quilt Cookbook
National Council of Negro Women
Washington, D.C.

NEWBERRY MACARONI CASSEROLE SPECIALTY

You can add ground beef to this casserole to make a one-dish meal.

YIELD: 10 TO 12 SERVINGS

4 large onions, chopped
3 cups water
2 (16-ounce) cans tomatoes, mashed
1½ cups raw elbow macaroni, cooked and
*   drained*
12 ounces cheddar cheese, shredded
4 tablespoons unsalted margarine
Salt and pepper to taste

Preheat the oven to 350°. Cook the onion in a large saucepan in the 3 cups water until tender. Add the mashed tomatoes. Boil about 10 minutes; remove from the heat. Add the macaroni, cheese, margarine, salt, and pepper; mix well. Place in a greased baking dish. Bake for 30 to 40 minutes, or until lightly browned and bubbly.

Stoney Creek Recipe Collection
Independent Presbyterian Church
McPhersonville, South Carolina

CORNBREAD DRESSING

Did somebody say "stuffing"? That's a sure way of spotting a Yankee in the woodpile. Down South we call it dressing—and it never sees the inside of a turkey.

YIELD: 8 TO 10 SERVINGS

1 cup chopped onion
1 cup chopped celery
1 clove garlic
4 cups chicken stock or turkey stock
4 cups cornbread, dried and crumbled
2 cups fine, dry bread crumbs
3 eggs, lightly beaten
1 cup milk
2 teaspoons salt
½ teaspoon black pepper

Preheat the oven to 375°. Grease well a 9x13-inch casserole.

Simmer the onion, celery, and garlic in the stock until the celery is soft. Discard the garlic. In a bowl, mix the cornbread and bread crumbs; pour the stock, with the onion and celery, over the cornbread mixture. Add the remaining ingredients; mix well. Bake in the prepared casserole for 30 to 40 minutes.

Upper Crust
Junior League of Johnson City
Johnson City, Tennessee

ANDOUILLE SAUSAGE CORNBREAD DRESSING

A bit of smoked andouille makes this Southern favorite distinctly Cajun.

YIELD: 4 TO 6 SERVINGS

2 tablespoons unsalted butter
1 medium yellow onion, chopped
2 large stalks celery, chopped
3 cups crumbled cornbread
3 small biscuits, crumbled
¼ teaspoon dried sage
¼ teaspoon dried thyme
Salt and freshly ground black pepper to taste
1 large egg
3¾ cups chicken stock
8 ounces cooked andouille or hot Italian sausage, sliced or chopped

Preheat the oven to 400°. Grease a casserole. Heat the butter in a skillet and sauté the onion and celery until tender. Combine the onion mixture with the cornbread, biscuits, sage, thyme, salt, pepper, egg, and stock in the prepared casserole. Bake for 45 minutes. Stir in the sausage and cook 15 minutes longer.

Come On In!
Junior League of Jackson
Jackson, Mississippi

FRENCH BREAD DRESSING

YIELD: 8 SERVINGS

8 ounces chicken livers
1 pound chicken gizzards (also liver and gizzard from the fowl you are cooking)
3 sticks (¾ pound) unsalted butter
1 bunch green onions, chopped
1 large onion, chopped
2 cloves garlic, minced
1 stalk celery, chopped
1 bunch parsley, chopped
1½ loaves stale French bread
2 eggs
Salt and pepper to taste

Preheat the oven to 350°. Boil the livers and gizzards in a large saucepan until tender; drain, reserving the stock. Let cool and then chop. Heat the butter in a skillet and sauté the green onions, onion, garlic, celery, and parsley. Put this mixture through a vegetable grinder. Put the chopped livers and gizzards through a meat grinder. Soften the bread in the reserved stock and put through the vegetable grinder. Combine the vegetables, gizzards, and bread in a large bowl. Add the eggs, salt, and pepper. Spoon into a baking dish. Bake for 30 minutes. If the dressing seems dry, it can be softened with drippings from the fowl before baking. When combining ingredients, you should have one-third seasoning, one-third bread, and one-third meat.

Note: This dressing can be made ahead of time and frozen. Be sure to thaw before baking.

A Cook's Tour of Shreveport
Junior League of Shreveport
Shreveport, Louisiana

OYSTER DRESSING

Camille Roussel LeBoeuf, Mona Roussel Abadie's maternal grandmother, was a creative cook who made a rich dressing of pork, beef, and six dozen oysters for holiday meals, but during the Civil War she often served her family a gumbo made with one egg.

YIELD: ENOUGH DRESSING FOR 1
TURKEY OR 2 HENS

3 pounds lean ground pork
2 pounds lean ground beef (round or other lean cut)
3 to 4 teaspoons salt, or to taste
2 teaspoons black pepper, or to taste
2 cups chopped onion
4 cloves garlic, chopped
6 dozen oysters, with their liquid
1 large loaf French bread, with the crusts removed
2 cups finely chopped green onion tops
1 cup finely chopped parsley
2 tablespoons freshly ground allspice

Season the meat with salt and pepper, mixing the salt and pepper into the meat. Brown the meat, with the chopped onions and garlic, in a large heavy skillet on medium heat. Drain the meat as it cooks. Reserving the oyster liquid, cut up the oysters and add to the meat. Soak the bread in the oyster liquid and break it into the skillet as the mixture cooks. Add the green onion tops and parsley. Cook 2 to 3 hours, until very brown. Stir often (almost constantly) to prevent scorching. Add the freshly ground allspice at end.

Note: Save a small amount (about 1 cup) to serve with crackers or toast as hors d'oeuvres. Oyster dressing can also be served in pie shells.

Family Collection
Mona Roussel Abadie
Edgard, Louisiana

SOUPS & STEWS

IT'S THE OLD POT THAT MAKES THE GOOD SOUP

*What kind of pots are you using? Throw out all of them except
the black ones. The cast-iron ones like your mother used to use.
Can't no Teflon fry no fried chicken.*

VERTAMAE GROSVENOR, *VIBRATION COOKING,*
OR THE TRAVEL NOTES OF A GEECHEE GIRL

It's the Old Pot That Makes the Good Soup

····················

Each time a Southern cook hefts a skillet to the stovetop, he or she is not alone. Trapped within the iron confines of these skillets and stewpots are the scents and secrets of a family's culinary history. Burnished black by countless batches of fried chicken and catfish, embossed an inky ebony by the crusts of cracklin' cornbread past, cast-iron cooking utensils are meal memories in and of themselves.

Chances are that the great taste of Grandmother's fried chicken owed as much to the skillet in which it was cooked as to her secret marinade. Accordingly, most Southerners would not dream of frying a chicken or making a roux without their trusty skillet. Though some may dismiss this as quaint affectation, the truth is that cast-iron cooking utensils retain more than memories of meals gone by.

As porous as they are heavy, cast-iron skillets absorb and impart flavor with each dish prepared. Maybe it is because of our long, culinary love affair with the pig, but many a Southerner claims that an evanescent hint of cured pork wafts their way with the first lick of flame from the burner. And whether they choose to acknowledge it or not, the oils from country sausages and bacon that seasoned their grandmother's skillet long ago, when loosed from within the skillet's porous iron walls, now flavor each helping of sautéed squash prepared by a new generation of health-conscious Southern cooks.

Layer upon layer, meal after meal, oils coat the skillets with a carbonized, nonstick film, far superior to anything ever conceived by a cookware chemist. By way of this strange and thoroughly Southern alchemy of seasoning, the basest of metals is transformed into a treasure rivaled only by the fabled

Southern family silver. Like a good country ham or a single-barrel bourbon, cast iron only improves with age. That is, if you take care of it.

Have you ever noticed that Southerners rarely accept a guest's offer to help out in the kitchen? Though some may attribute this to Southern hospitality, the real reason is they are afraid that some well-meaning outlander will "scrub out Momma's skillet in the sink." For at the moment that soap meets cast iron, the non-stick surface so prized by the Southern cook, that same surface charred a beautiful black by generations of gustatory successes—*and failures*—vanishes down the drain.

So that such food *faux pas* might be prevented, aspiring Southern cooks are lectured early and often on the proper care and cleaning of cast-iron cookware. By the time they are able to lug a 5-pound skillet from the stove to the sink for cleaning, they know to reach for only coarse salt and a rag.

Despite today's proliferation of newer, lighter, and less troublesome cookware, cast iron endures. Now Southern cooks heft these heavy relics to the stovetop for reasons often more sentimental than practical. So why do these old black skillets remain so dear? Perhaps it is because we could not dream of making Grandmother's fried chicken without Grandmother at our side. Failing that, we reach for her skillet and trust that the scents and secrets called forth will work their magic.

CUCUMBER SOUP

YIELD: 4 SERVINGS

2 tablespoons unsalted butter
3 green onions, chopped
1 small white onion, finely chopped
4 cups chicken broth
3 cups boiling water
½ cup chopped parsley
½ cup finely chopped celery
3 medium potatoes, peeled and quartered
½ teaspoon thyme
Dash of Tabasco
2 cups sour cream
1 teaspoon salt
1 large cucumber, peeled, seeded, and finely grated

Melt the butter in a small skillet and sauté 2 of the green onions and the white onion for 5 minutes. Bring the chicken broth and water to a boil in a medium saucepan. Add the onions, parsley, celery, and potatoes. Return to a boil. Cook over low heat 20 minutes. Place the cooked ingredients in a blender, one-third at a time, and blend until smooth. Stir in the thyme, Tabasco, sour cream, salt, and cucumber. Chill. Serve chilled, using the remaining finely chopped green onion as a garnish.

From the Kitchen Door
Nashville, Tennessee

Iced Cucumber Soup

Served cold on a hot summer day, this soup envelops the tongue, if not the soul, in a bath of creamy cucumbery coolness.

YIELD: ABOUT 2½ QUARTS

4 cucumbers, peeled and sliced into ½-inch
  slices
2 shallots or 1 medium onion, finely
  chopped
7 cups chicken stock
½ stick unsalted butter
2 tablespoons flour
Salt and black pepper
3 egg yolks
¾ cup heavy cream
Green food coloring (optional)
1 tablespoon chopped mint or chives

Combine the cucumber, shallots, and stock in a saucepan. Simmer until the cucumbers are tender, about 15 to 20 minutes. Purée the mixture in a food processor or blender.

Melt the butter in a kettle. Stir in the flour and cook the mixture until it is straw-colored. Stir in the puréed cucumber mixture gradually and bring the soup to a boil. Season with salt and pepper to taste. Simmer for 2 to 3 minutes.

Mix the yolks and ½ cup of the cream in a bowl. Add a little hot soup, stirring constantly. Remove the soup from the heat; gradually stir in the egg mixture. Allow to cool slightly. Gently reheat the soup until it thickens slightly; do not boil. Add the food coloring, if desired. Chill the soup. Whip the remaining ¼ cup cream. Place the chilled soup in bowls and stir a spoonful of whipped cream into each bowl. Sprinkle each serving with chopped mint or chives.

Concerts from the Kitchen
Arkansas Symphony Orchestra Society Guild
Little Rock, Arkansas

Black Bean Soup

Called turtle beans by some Southerners, black beans are best known as the bean most favored where the South meets the West.

YIELD: 8 SERVINGS

2 cups dried black beans
5 cups water
1 onion, chopped
1 stalk celery, thinly sliced
8 ounces smoked ham, diced
2 cloves garlic, pressed
¼ cup chopped fresh cilantro
⅛ teaspoon dry mustard
Salt and pepper to taste
½ cup dry sherry
Dollop of sour cream, for garnish
Crumbled bacon, for garnish
Finely minced green onions, for
  garnish
Crispy croutons, for garnish

Cover the beans with water and soak overnight; drain. Add the 5 cups of water and the onion, celery, ham, garlic, cilantro, mustard, salt, and pepper. Bring to a boil. Simmer, covered, 3½ to 4 hours, or until the beans are tender. Add the sherry the last 15 minutes of cooking. Pour the soup into a warmed tureen or cups. Garnish with sour cream, bacon, green onions, or croutons.

Necessities and Temptations
Junior League of Austin
Austin, Texas

VEGETABLE SOUP

In tribute to his mother, Mrs. Walter Tillman, whose determination and delicious cooking stayed him through studies at Harvard, Oscar Rogers, a native of Natchez, Mississippi, captured Creole recipes like this one for posterity.

YIELD: 4 TO 6 SERVINGS

1 soup bone
1 pound beef shank
2 cups canned tomatoes, chopped
2 large white potatoes, diced
2 medium onions, chopped
4 ounces tomato sauce
1 teaspoon sugar
1 teaspoon black pepper
Salt
1 green bell pepper, chopped
2 green onions, chopped
2 stalks celery, diced
1 cup shredded white cabbage
1 turnip, diced
2 teaspoons Worcestershire sauce
2 carrots, diced
Corn, green peas, snap beans

Cover the soup bone with water in a large, heavy pot. Bring to a boil and simmer 30 minutes. Add the meat and cook until tender; skim off the scum and discard. Add the remaining ingredients. Bring to a boil, reduce the heat, and simmer until all the vegetables are cooked. Add more water as needed.

My Mother Cooked My Way Through Harvard with These Creole Recipes
Oscar Rogers
Natchez, Mississippi

CREAM OF CARROT SOUP

YIELD: 4 SERVINGS

½ stick unsalted butter
1 cup finely chopped yellow onion
2 pounds carrots, chopped
6 cups chicken stock
½ cup fresh orange juice
¼ teaspoon cayenne pepper
1 teaspoon salt
½ teaspoon black pepper
2 to 3 tablespoons sherry, or to taste

Melt the butter in a soup pot. Add the onion and sauté until tender, about 20 minutes. Add the carrots and 4 cups of the chicken stock. Bring to a boil. Reduce the heat, cover, and simmer until the carrots are tender, about 30 minutes. Pour the soup through a strainer, reserving the liquid and solids separately, and return the liquid to the soup pot. Transfer the solids to the bowl of a food processor and process until smooth. Return the purée to the pot and add the orange juice, cayenne, salt, black pepper, and sherry. Add additional stock, up to 2 cups, until the soup is the

desired consistency. Simmer until heated through. Serve immediately.

Ambrosia
Junior Auxiliary of Vicksburg
Vicksburg, Mississippi

CREAM OF PEANUT SOUP

YIELD: 8 SERVINGS

½ stick unsalted butter
2 stalks celery, chopped
1 small onion, chopped
2 tablespoons flour
2 cups chicken broth
1 cup milk
1 cup light cream
1 cup creamy peanut butter
Salt and pepper, to taste
Chopped peanuts, for garnish
Watercress, for garnish

Heat the butter in a large skillet and brown the celery and onion. Stir in the flour and gradually add the chicken broth. Add the milk and cream. Strain the soup. Stir in the peanut butter and simmer for 5 minutes. Season with salt and pepper. Garnish with chopped peanuts and a sprig of watercress.

Savannah Style
Junior League of Savannah
Savannah, Georgia

Our Southern Receipt

Peanut Soup

Take roasted peanuts; grind or mash real fine. To every half pint, add a quart of milk, half a teaspoon salt, 1 saltspoon pepper, 1 small onion minced very fine, 1 bay leaf, 1 stalk celery chopped very fine or a saltspoon celery seed. Cook for 15 minutes. Great care must be exercised to keep from burning. Moisten 1 tablespoon of cornstarch in a quarter cup of cold milk; add to the soup. Stir until thick and smooth. Strain through a fine sieve, and serve with peanut wafers.

How to Grow the Peanut and 105 Ways of Preparing It
for Human Consumption (Bulletin 31, June 1925)
George Washington Carver
Tuskegee Institute
Tuskegee, Alabama

OYSTER SOUP

In purchasing oysters for soup, always ask the vendor to add the oyster liquor. In making good oyster soup, the Creoles never use water, only the liquor from the oysters.

YIELD: 4 SERVINGS

4 dozen large fresh oysters, with their
*   liquor*
3 sprigs parsley, chopped fine
1 dozen black peppercorns

1 quart milk
1 tablespoon unsalted butter
Salt and pepper to taste
Slices of lemon, for serving
Oyster crackers, for serving

Drain the oysters, reserving the liquor. Keep the oysters cold. Strain the liquor into a soup kettle. Add the parsley and peppercorns and bring to a boil. Boil the milk in a separate saucepan, then add to the oyster liquor. Add the butter. (You can thicken the soup with cornstarch, if desired.) Stir constantly, and add the oysters. Continue to stir until the soup comes to a boil. Season to taste with salt and pepper. Serve immediately with slices of lemon and oyster crackers.

Note: Some add a little nutmeg and mace, and some Creoles place chopped celery in small quantities, and an herb bouquet, in the oyster juice, being careful to allow it to give just the desired flavor, and taking it out before adding the milk. But this, too, is a matter of taste. Made according to the above formula, oyster soup is a most delightful dish and can be eaten and relished by the most delicate stomachs.

The Picayune's Creole Cookbook
New Orleans, Louisiana

CREAM OF CRAB SOUP

YIELD: ABOUT 2½ QUARTS

1 tablespoon flour
2 tablespoons unsalted butter
2 quarts milk

½ onion, chopped
Chopped parsley, celery, onion salt, salt, and
  white pepper, to taste
1 pint crab meat
1 cup heavy cream, whipped

Cream the flour and butter together. Put the milk in a double boiler and stir in the creamed butter mixture. Add the onion. Add the parsley, celery, onion salt, salt, and white pepper to taste. Simmer until the soup thickens a little, then add the crab meat. Serve with a dollop of whipped cream.

Mirations and Miracles of Mandy
Natalie Scott
New Orleans, Louisiana

SHE-CRAB SOUP

*A soup to remember! The feminine gender
of crabs is expedient—the secret ingredient.
The flavor essential, makes men reverential,
who taste this collation, and cry acclamation.*

She-crab is much more of a delicacy than he-crab, as the crab eggs add a special flavor to the soup. Vendors make a point of calling "she-crab" loudly and of charging extra for them.

YIELD: 4 SERVINGS

1 tablespoon unsalted butter
1 teaspoon flour
1 quart milk
2 cups white crab meat and crab eggs
A few drops onion juice

½ teaspoon Worcestershire sauce
½ teaspoon salt
⅛ teaspoon mace
⅛ teaspoon pepper
¼ cup dry sherry
½ cup heavy cream, whipped
Paprika and finely chopped parsley, for garnish

Melt the butter in the top of a double boiler and blend with the flour until smooth. Add the milk gradually, stirring constantly. Add the crab meat and crab eggs. Stir in the onion juice, Worcestershire sauce, salt, mace, and pepper. Cook slowly over hot water for 20 minutes. To serve, place 1 tablespoon warmed sherry in each bowl. Add the soup and top with whipped cream. Sprinkle with paprika and parsley.

Charleston Receipts
Junior League of Charleston
Charleston, South Carolina

Basic Gumbo Filé

Gumbos are thickened by the addition of either okra or filé but never both. Here, filé, the ground leaves from the sassafras tree (the same tree whose roots once flavored root beer), does the thickening, imparting an herbaceous muskiness in the process.

Yield: 4 servings

1 onion, quartered
3 cloves garlic
½ green bell pepper

3 quarts water
3 tablespoons oil or bacon drippings
3 tablespoons flour
1½ teaspoons salt
Black pepper
Shrimp (⅔ pound or more)
Oysters (½ pint or more)
1 teaspoon filé

Let the onion, garlic, and bell pepper simmer in 3 quarts water in a large stockpot until they fall apart. Remove to a plate, reserving the cooking water, and mash, discarding the pepper skin. Return the pulp to the water. Make a dark roux of the oil and flour, stirring constantly. Slowly stir the roux into the seasoned water, then add salt and pepper. Cook 5 minutes. Add the shrimp and cook 15 minutes; then add the oysters and simmer 5 more minutes. The filé should be added after the gumbo is removed from the heat, just before serving. Allow to stand 5 minutes after stirring in the filé.

Note: The roux should be thicker for an oyster gumbo than one without, because of the water exuded by oysters.

River Road Recipes
Junior League of Baton Rouge
Baton Rouge, Louisiana

Gumbo z'Herbes

Traditionally a Lenten dish served when meat was not eaten by Catholics, this stew of greens is no longer strictly vegetarian today.

*1 bunch each of greens in any combination, but
use at least five (spinach, collard greens, mustard greens, turnip greens, watercress,
chicory, beet tops, carrot tops, pepper grass,
radish tops)*

1 bunch parsley, chopped

½ bunch green onions, chopped

1 small green cabbage, chopped

1 gallon water

4 tablespoons flour

4 tablespoons vegetable shortening

1 pound boiled ham, diced

1 large white onion, diced

2 bay leaves

2 sprigs thyme

¼ teaspoon ground allspice

Salt

Black pepper

Cayenne pepper

1 pint oysters, with their liquor

Rice, for serving

Wash the greens thoroughly; remove the stems
and hard centers. Boil the greens, parsley, green
onions, and cabbage in 1 gallon water for about 2
hours. Strain the greens, reserving the water.
Chop the greens finely.

Make a brown roux of the flour and shortening in a large cast-iron pot. Add the ham and
onion and sauté 5 minutes, or until soft. Add
greens mixture and simmer 15 minutes. Add the
reserved cooking water and the bay leaves,
thyme, allspice, salt, black pepper, and cayenne.
Simmer for 1 hour. About 15 minutes before
serving, add the oysters and any available oyster

Our Southern Receipt

Okra Gumbo

A valuable gumbo recipe from Biloxi.

2 to 3 onions

½ bunch parsley

5 to 6 stalks celery

1 clove garlic

*1 dozen fresh okra pods, washed and
trimmed*

1 pound tomatoes

*1 pound veal stew meat or 4 slices
raw ham*

2 tablespoons vegetable oil

Cut all the ingredients into small pieces
and brown in oil in a large skillet. Add as
much water as desired. Let simmer for 40
to 45 minutes.

Note: If shrimp are desired, pickle and
parboil them and add the shrimp and the
water in which they were boiled to the
gumbo. If oysters or crab meat is desired,
add to gumbo about 20 minutes before
done.

*Collected by Eudora Welty
for the Federal Writers Project "America Eats"*

water. Remove the bay leaves. Adjust the seasoning to taste. Serve over rice.

Recipes and Reminiscences of New Orleans
Parents Club of Ursuline Academy
New Orleans, Louisiana

LOUISIANA SEAFOOD GUMBO

Here, okra, with its mucilaginous qualities (the impolite say it's slimy), thickens a rich kitchen-sink conglomeration of seafood.

YIELD: 4 TO 6 SERVINGS

5 tablespoons oil
3 tablespoons flour
2 pounds peeled fresh shrimp
2 large onions, chopped
3 cups okra, washed, trimmed, and chopped
2 cups tomatoes
3 cloves garlic, minced
2 quarts water
Salt, black pepper, and cayenne pepper
½ pint oysters, with their liquor
1 cup crab meat
Several whole crabs, cleaned, with their claws
½ cup finely chopped parsley
½ cup finely chopped green onion tops
Rice, for serving
Fresh filé, for serving

Make a roux with 3 tablespoons of the oil and the 3 tablespoons flour in a large skillet, stirring constantly until dark brown. Add the shrimp and cook for a few minutes; set the skillet aside. Cook the onion and okra in another skillet in the remaining 2 tablespoons oil. Add the tomatoes and garlic when the okra is almost done; cook a few minutes longer. Add the 2 quarts water and the salt, black pepper, and cayenne. Combine the shrimp mixture with the okra mixture and simmer for about 30 minutes. Add the oysters, with liquor, crab meat, and whole crabs. Simmer until the crabs are cooked. Add the parsley and green onions; simmer for 15 to 20 minutes. Serve over rice, and let each person add fresh filé.

Louisiana Wildlife Magazine
Baton Rouge, Louisiana

ANDOUILLE AND CHICKEN GUMBO FILÉ

Says Nancy Tregre Wilson, "This was always a Sunday dinner dish. When all the andouille from the boucherie *was used, we made chicken gumbo filé. Ask any Louisiana cook how to prepare a gumbo and chances are she will begin by saying, "First you make a roux." The brown roux, which is frequently used in Louisiana dishes, is made by browning flour in hot oil. This is a slow process usually done in a black cast-iron skillet. Because the roux burns easily, it must be cooked over low heat and stirred constantly. The success of many sauces depends on cooking the roux to the proper golden-brown or dark-brown stage.*

YIELD: 12 SERVINGS

6 quarts water
1 (4- to 6-pound) hen
4 teaspoons salt

ALBERT MURRAY

GET YOUR SMIDGENS STRAIGHT

This very simple okra-and-sausage dish is not mentioned in either *South to a Very Old Place* or *Train Whistle Guitar,* but it used to be standard midweek fare among people in both books. It makes a fine main course for luncheon and is great for a Saturday night beer supper.

There are down-home cuisine classics that you don't mess around with once you get your smidgens straight (usually after years of apprenticeship). But this is not one. Chez me and Mozelle these days, it is used in somewhat the same manner as the traditional twelve-bar blues chorus stanza is used by the great jazz performer composer: as a basis for improvisation and orchestration. In other words, we play riffs on it as in a jam session.

The traditional folk street-corner guitar (plus train whistle harmonica) version consists of okra, onion, and old-fashioned down-home country-style smoked hot or sweet link sausages. But in most supermarkets these days there are spicy Italian sweet arid hot links, garlicky Polish kielbasa, and sweet and hot Spanish chorizo.

1 pound sausage	*Smidgen of salt*
1 pound fresh okra	*Smidgen of black pepper*
1 medium or large red or yellow onion	*Smidgen of oregano (optional)*

Cut the sausages and okra into ½-inch-thick medallions. Chop the onion medium to fine. Sauté the sausages until a brown crust forms on both sides. Discard the excess fat, if any, or add cooking oil if needed. Sauté onions. Add the okra and onions and stir-fry until done but still bright green and not very slippery.

Serve on a bed of rice cooked so that each grain stands free, as down-home housewives used to require. (Down-home girls whose rice came out as sticky as it must in the best Chinese restaurants used to be told that they would never be able to hold a husband!)

The version using Italian sweet sausage without rice goes very well with pasta on the side, say fettuccine Alfredo or linguine with pesto Genovese. The chorizo version with rice is enhanced by taco chips in spite of the extra starch and calories. After all, authentic taco chips (not Fritos) are the nearest thing to good old golden-crusted corners of thin cornbread.

Author Albert Murray was born in Nokomis, Alabama. This selection originally appeared in The Great American Writers' Cookbook.

1 teaspoon black pepper
½ cup oil
¾ cup flour
2½ cups chopped onion
1½ cups chopped celery
1 pound andouille or smoked sausage
¾ cup chopped shallots
¾ cup chopped parsley
Filé
Rice, for serving

Heat the water in a large pot. Cut the hen into serving pieces. Season with 2 teaspoons of the salt and ½ teaspoon of the black pepper. Heat the oil in a large, heavy skillet and brown the chicken; remove the chicken from the skillet and set aside. Add the flour to the pan drippings. Scrape the bottom of the skillet to loosen the brown bits. Make a medium-brown roux. Add the onion and celery. Cook for 10 minutes, stirring constantly. Add the roux and vegetables to the hot water in the pot. Stir until dissolved. Add the hen pieces, andouille, and remaining salt and pepper; simmer. Remove the andouille when tender. Cut into serving pieces and set aside. Cook the chicken until tender, about 2 hours. Return the andouille to the pot and add the shallots and parsley. Adjust the seasoning if necessary. Cook 15 minutes longer. Remove the portions to be served to a small pot and add the filé, allowing at least ¼ teaspoon per serving. Heat 3 minutes; do not boil. Serve over rice.

Mam Papaul's Country Creole Basket
Nancy Tregre Wilson
Baton Rouge, Louisiana

DUCK GUMBO

Gumbos are not precious meals but hearty stews of whatever one has on hand. This gumbo owes its success to the prowess of the duck hunter.

YIELD: 12 SERVINGS

2 pounds wild duck, skinned with meat cut off
  bones
1 pound turkey sausage
½ cup roux (recipe on page 140)
3 quarts water
2 bay leaves
1 teaspoon thyme
1 tablespoon Worcestershire sauce
¼ teaspoon salt
Black pepper to taste
1 cup chopped celery
1 cup chopped onion
½ cup chopped green bell pepper
1 tablespoon gumbo filé
Rice, for serving

Cook the duck in boiling water until done. Let cool and cut into cubes. Brown the turkey sausage in a large, heavy skillet until done. Remove from the skillet and drain well. Add the roux to the skillet. Add the water, bay leaves, thyme, Worcestershire sauce, salt, and black pepper. Mix well. Add the celery, onion, and bell pepper and simmer 1 hour, stirring occasionally. Add the duck and sausage. Simmer 45 minutes. Stir in filé. Serve over rice.

Southern But Lite
Jen Avis and Kathy Ward
West Monroe, Louisiana

GRANDMOTHER CRUMP'S CLEAR TOMATO SOUP

A generations-spanning soup that is still a family favorite. Especially good with a slice of French bread toasted with butter and Parmesan cheese.

YIELD: 4 SERVINGS

4 cups tomatoes
2 stalks celery, chopped
2 tablespoons chopped onion
4 whole cloves
Dash of salt
Dash of cayenne pepper
1 tablespoon apple cider vinegar
Lemon slices and parsley sprigs, for garnish

Combine the tomatoes, celery, onion, and cloves in a saucepan. Cook, covered over low heat until the tomatoes are soft. Remove from the heat and add the salt, cayenne, and vinegar. Pour the mixture through a sieve into a second saucepan, mashing the tomatoes against the sieve for juice. Serve hot with a lemon slice afloat in the center of each serving. Garnish with parsley.

Gracious Goodness
Memphis Symphony League
Memphis, Tennessee

TOMATO BISQUE

Pale, creamy, and tinged a delicate pink, this bisque deserves to be served in the finest of bone china, but it tastes just as good from a clunky coffee mug.

YIELD: 6 SERVINGS

1 tablespoon unsalted butter
1 medium onion, thinly sliced
2 pounds ripe tomatoes (6 or 7), peeled and
  chopped
1 bay leaf
1 heaping tablespoon firmly packed light brown
  sugar
2 whole cloves
1 teaspoon salt
¼ teaspoon black pepper
2 teaspoons finely chopped fresh basil
2 cups light cream
1 cup milk
Butter, croutons, and chives, for garnish

Heat the butter in a large skillet and sauté the onion until tender. Add the tomatoes, bay leaf, brown sugar, cloves, salt, pepper, and basil. Simmer, stirring occasionally, until the tomatoes are thoroughly cooked, about 25 minutes. Remove the bay leaf and cloves and transfer the mixture to a blender to purée. Add the cream and milk; heat well but do not let boil. Serve topped with the butter, croutons, and chives.

Charlotte Cooks Again
Junior League of Charlotte
Charlotte, North Carolina

SHRIMP BISQUE

YIELD: 4 SERVINGS

1 pound shrimp
1 quart milk
4 tablespoons (½ stick) unsalted butter
Heaping ¼ cup flour
1 teaspoon Worcestershire sauce
1 teaspoon Tabasco
Dash of nutmeg
Salt to taste
3 twists of lemon zest
½ cup sherry

Cook the shrimp in boiling, salted water. Peel and remove the veins. Run the shrimp through a coarse food grinder. Make a rich sauce in the top of a double boiler with the milk, butter, flour, Worcestershire, Tabasco, nutmeg, salt, and lemon zest. Add the shrimp and sherry; cook just long enough to heat through.

The Charlotte Cookbook
Junior League of Charlotte
Charlotte, North Carolina

OYSTER BISQUE

YIELD: 6 SERVINGS

6 tablespoons unsalted margarine
4 stalks celery, chopped
4 carrots, chopped
2 tablespoons flour
1 pint half-and-half
2 dozen oysters, shucked
2 cups milk
Parsley, salt, pepper, and Worcestershire sauce
   to taste

Heat 2 tablespoons of the margarine in a small skillet and sauté the celery and carrots until tender; set aside. Melt 2 tablespoons of the remaining margarine in a large saucepan; add the flour and mix well. Add the half-and-half and stir until thickened. Stir the vegetables into the sauce. Cook the oysters in the remaining 2 tablespoons margarine in a small skillet until the edges curl. Add to the sauce. Stir in the milk and season to taste with parsley, salt, pepper, and Worcestershire. Simmer until hot.

Family Secrets
Lee Academy
Clarksdale, Mississippi

CRAWFISH BISQUE

Less delicate than the shrimp or oyster bisques, this crawfish concoction packs a Louisiana wallop.

YIELD: 16 TO 20 SERVINGS

40 to 50 pounds fresh live crawfish
Baking soda
2 green bell peppers
7 stalks celery
1 cup chopped fresh parsley
3 large onions, quartered
1 cup shallots
4 slices stale French bread
4 eggs, lightly beaten
1 tablespoon garlic powder

Salt to taste

Cayenne to taste

Black pepper to taste

Flour

Vegetable oil, for frying

2 quarts boiling water

Roux (recipe follows)

Parsley

Scald the live crawfish in water in a large stock-pot. Peel and save the tails, the fat, and at least 300 large heads. Clean the heads by soaking outside the shell in water. Remove the eyes, feelers, etc., and discard. Keep the point. Soak and clean the heads again. Soak overnight in a solution of water and baking soda.

Grind the cleaned crawfish tails, bell peppers, celery, parsley, onions, shallots, and bread in a food grinder. Add the eggs, garlic powder, salt, cayenne, and black pepper. Stuff the drained crawfish heads with the meat mixture. Coat the heads with flour. Fry the outsides to a golden brown in vegetable oil.

Place the browned stuffed heads in a large Dutch oven. Cover with the 2 quarts boiling water or enough to cover the heads completely. Add the dissolved roux from the roux recipe. Bring to a boil, reduce the heat, and simmer. Taste after 15 minutes; season to taste with salt, black pepper, and cayenne. Simmer for 1 hour, or until the bisque reaches the desired thickness. Add the parsley 10 minutes before serving. Stir occasionally before serving.

Roux

2 cups flour

2 cups vegetable oil

Reserved crawfish fat from bisque recipe

1 large onion, chopped

1 cup chopped shallots

½ cup chopped green bell pepper

2 quarts boiling water

Salt, black pepper, and cayenne pepper
   to taste

½ cup chopped parsley

Brown the flour in the oil to peanut butter color over low heat in a large skillet. Add the crawfish fat, onion, shallots, and bell pepper. Cook over low heat until the grease rises. Add 2 quarts boiling water, stirring constantly until roux is dissolved.

Foods à la Louisiane
Louisiana Farm Bureau Women
Baton Rouge, Louisiana

Burgoo

This Kentucky dish—first cousin to the Brunswick stews of Georgia, Virginia, and North Carolina—is usually cooked all day outside in a huge pot over a low fire. Someone must be standing by tending the fire and stirring very often with a large wooden paddle to prevent scorching on the bottom. The meat and vegetables are all precooked the day before, or all night, then combined in the pot on the day it will be served and cooked together.

YIELD: 50 SERVINGS

10 pounds round steak, trimmed and cubed

10 pounds lean pork, trimmed and cubed

1 (3- to 4-pound) chicken, skinned and cut up

1 squirrel, skinned and cut up, or 2 pounds venison

4 to 5 pounds potatoes, peeled and diced

2 to 4 large heads cabbage, shredded

2 pounds fresh or frozen corn

2 pounds fresh carrots, diced

2 pounds onions, chopped

2 pounds green beans

6 (No. 2½) cans tomatoes, cut into small pieces

1 pound jowl bacon, whole (for seasoning)

½ cup sugar

¾ cup salt

1 cup Worcestershire sauce (optional)

4 tablespoons hot sauce (optional)

Fresh-baked cornbread, for serving

Cover the beef and pork with water in a large pot and cook until falling apart; do not drain. In another pot, cover the chicken and squirrel with water. Cook until falling apart. Remove the bones, cut up the meat, and return it to its broth. Refrigerate all the meat and broth until ready to prepare the burgoo.

Place the potatoes, cabbage, corn, carrots, onion, and green beans in a large kettle. (Most home cooks may not have a kettle large enough to accommodate all the ingredients, so several separate kettles may be used.) Cover with water and cook until done; do not drain. Refrigerate until ready to use.

On the day of serving, combine the meats and vegetables and their broths in a huge kettle. Add the tomatoes, bacon, sugar, and salt; add the Worcestershire and hot sauce, if desired. Simmer all the ingredients for 8 or 9 hours in a huge cooking kettle outdoors (as described in the introduction to this recipe). The longer it cooks, the better. Stir often. Cook until the meat is in shreds and the burgoo is very thick. During cooking it may be necessary to add water. Toward the end of the cooking time, adjust the salt to taste. Do not oversalt. Serve in very large mugs or cups with plenty of fresh-baked cornbread on the side. Keep the burgoo simmering until all is served. Never allow it to stand at room temperature, as it spoils quickly. Remove what is left over from the simmering pot, let it cool slightly, and refrigerate or freeze immediately. It is delicious when reheated.

What's Cooking in Kentucky
Irene Hayes
Hueysville, Kentucky

FISH MUDDLE

YIELD: 6 SERVINGS

6 pieces rockfish or any meaty fish

3 cups tomatoes

6 slices bacon

6 tablespoons chopped onion

Salt and black pepper to taste

Hot sauce to taste

Steam the fish in salted water. When done, remove from the water, reserving the cooking water, and remove all the bones. Put the fish in a heavy pot with the water that the fish was cooked in, adding more water, if necessary. Add the tomatoes. Fry the bacon in a skillet until crisp; remove from the drippings, drain, and crumble. Sauté the onion in the bacon drippings. Add the crumbled bacon and onions to the muddle. Season with salt, pepper, and hot sauce. Cook slowly for 3 hours, or until the consistency of thick soup.

The Smithfield Cookbook
Junior Woman's Club of Smithfield
Smithfield, Virginia

1927 VIRGINIA OKRA STEW

YIELD: 8 SERVINGS

1 gallon water
½ beef shin or equivalent amount of other bony
  meat
1 quart fresh tomatoes, cut into pieces
4 small onions, thinly sliced
2 green bell peppers, thinly sliced
1 pint fresh okra, trimmed and thinly sliced
½ rutabaga (also known as yellow turnip), diced
Salt and black pepper to taste
Boiled rice, for serving
Lemon slices, for garnish (optional)

Pour the water in a large stockpot; add the beef and simmer until the liquid is reduced in half, about 3 hours. Add the tomatoes, onions, and green peppers. Now add the okra and rutabaga. Cover and cook slowly until the mixture becomes nice and thick. This should take about 4 hours. Season to your taste with salt and black pepper. Serve hot with boiled rice. You might add a slice of lemon to each plate as a garnish, if desired. The total time in cooking this is about 7 hours.

Forgotten Recipes
Jane Rodack
Memphis, Tennessee

SHRIMP STEW

YIELD: 6 TO 8 SERVINGS

3 pounds shrimp
¾ cup diced salt pork
1 tablespoon flour
¼ cup diced onion
1 cup diced cooked potatoes
1 teaspoon salt
½ teaspoon pepper
2 cups water

Shell and devein the shrimp. Fry the salt pork in a saucepan until brown. Add the flour and brown slightly. Add the onion, shrimp, potatoes, salt, pepper, and water. Cook, covered, until shrimp are tender.

Southern Sportsman Cookbook
Franc White
Greenville, North Carolina

FROGMORE STEW

Named for the village of Frogmore, South Carolina, an early African American settlement at St. Helena in the Lowcountry, this stew is now sweeping the South.

YIELD: 8 SERVINGS

Salt
Chopped celery
Seafood seasonings
2 pounds smoked link sausage, cut into 2-inch
  pieces

16 ears corn, shucked
4 pounds shrimp

Bring a large stockpot of water to a boil. Add ¼ cup salt for each gallon of water. Add the celery and seafood seasonings. Add the sausage and boil for 7 minutes. Add the corn and boil for 7 minutes. Add the shrimp and cook for 4 minutes. Drain and serve in a large bowl or tub.

Variation: Raw cleaned crabs can be added at the same time as the corn.

Charleston Receipts Repeats
Junior League of Charleston
Charleston, South Carolina

SOUTHERN CATFISH STEW

YIELD: 6 SERVINGS

1 pound catfish fillets
3 slices bacon, chopped
1 cup chopped onion
½ cup chopped green bell pepper
1 (28-ounce) can tomatoes
2 cups peeled and diced potatoes
1 cup water
¼ cup ketchup
2 tablespoons Worcestershire sauce
1 teaspoon salt
½ teaspoon pepper
½ teaspoon thyme
Cornbread, for serving

Wash the catfish fillets and cut them into 1-inch pieces. Fry the bacon for 2 to 3 minutes in a large heavy saucepan. Add the onion and bell pepper and cook until tender. Add the remaining ingredients and bring to a simmer. Cook, covered, for 30 minutes. Add the fish and cook for another 20 minutes. Correct the seasonings if necessary and serve hot with cornbread.

Classic Catfish
Evelyn and Tony Roughton
Indianola, Mississippi

JEANNE VOLTZ

BARBECUE, BRUNSWICK STEW, AND POLITICKIN'

One day back in 1930 or 1931, when I was nine or ten, my mother was sick and in the hospital, so my uncle took me with him to a political rally in Birmingham. My uncle was a doctor, but he loved politics. He loved it so, like it was a big game to be played. I think the rally was for Cooper Green, a man of the same ilk as the infamous Bull Conner. But this was long before they brought out the fire hoses.

It was a hot summertime day. The primary was coming up soon, in the early fall, and everyone had turned out to hear the speeches, that wonderful mellifluous Southern oratory. It was really something quite special. The speakers' platform was draped in red, white, and blue bunting. People were milling about, the air was thick with dust, and the men were drinking lemonade and such, while the children drank water from the faucet.

I remember the barbecue smelled so good. They had dug a big pit, laying an old set of mattress springs across it. I was absolutely enthralled by the African American men standing over that split, whole hog, moving the coals this way and that with a rake. That barbecue looked so good. And I wanted a sandwich. But my uncle thought it would be too spicy for me. He didn't want to risk me getting an upset stomach, so he bought me a bowl of Brunswick stew instead. At the time, I thought that was the best Brunswick stew that I would ever have.

In fact, through the years, I've attended many a political rally and eaten many a plate of barbecue, many a bowl of Brunswick stew. And I've had some fine Brunswick stew—stew that was far better than what I had that day. But I will always remember the barbecue at that political rally on that summer day. I can still smell it now.

Jeanne Voltz, a native of Collinsville, Alabama, is the author of numerous cookbooks, including Barbecued Ribs, Smoked Butts, and Other Great Feeds.

Oyster Stew

Yield: 4 servings

½ stick unsalted butter

3 to 4 tablespoons minced green onions or onion juice

1 pint oysters, drained, juice reserved

Oyster liquid and enough milk to make 3 cups

Herbs: garlic powder, oregano, marjoram, basil, thyme, parsley flakes (or chopped fresh), celery salt, rosemary, paprika, salt and pepper

In a skillet, melt the butter and sauté the green onions, if using, until tender. Add the oysters and cook until the edges curl, being careful not to overcook. Remove from the heat. In the top of a large double boiler, heat the oyster liquid and milk and the onion juice, if using, with a dash of each of the seasonings. Add the oysters and sautéed onions; heat thoroughly, but do not boil. (If using onion juice, add it when adding the oysters to the milk.)

Great Performances
Symphony League of Tupelo
Tupelo, Mississippi

Mrs. Habersham's Terrapin Stew

Yield: 12 servings

6 hard-cooked eggs, separated into yolks and whites

2 sticks (½ pound) unsalted butter, at room temperature

3 tablespoons flour

Turtle or chicken stock

Juice and zest of 1 lemon

½ nutmeg, grated

Meat and eggs from 3 terrapin

1 onion, chopped

Salt to taste

Cayenne pepper to taste

1 tablespoon Worcestershire sauce

2 cups heavy cream

1 cup good wine or sherry

Hot milk, as needed

Rub yolks of eggs, butter, and flour together in a bowl. Bring the stock to a boil; add the egg mixture, lemon juice and zest, and nutmeg. Stir in the terrapin meat, terrapin eggs, and onion. Season with salt, cayenne, and Worcestershire sauce. Then add the cream and wine; do not allow to curdle. Add chopped whites of eggs. Have hot milk ready to thin the soup, if needed.

Savannah Cook Book
Harriet Ross Colquitt
Savannah, Georgia

Chicken Stew

Yield: 4 to 6 servings

2 tablespoons unsalted butter

½ cup flour

1 onion, chopped

1 green bell pepper, chopped

1 stalk celery, chopped

½ cup chopped parsley

2 cups water

1 chicken, cut up
Salt and pepper to taste
1 teaspoon garlic salt

In a large, heavy stockpot, make a roux with the butter and flour. Add the onion, bell pepper, celery, and parsley; cook until wilted. Add the water, chicken, salt, pepper, and garlic salt. Cook about 25 minutes, or until chicken is done.

Cajun Cooking
Lafayette, Louisiana

BRUNSWICK STEW

This version includes squirrel, a legacy of the day when this was a huntsman's stew, cooked beneath the stars after a day in the woods.

Y I E L D : 4 Q U A R T S

2 squirrels
4 ounces bacon or side meat, cut in small
   pieces
Water
4 cups butter beans (lima beans)
2 cups corn
4 cups peeled, quartered tomatoes

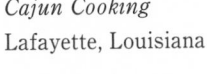

2 cups diced potatoes
Small piece of red pepper or cayenne pepper to
    taste
Salt
Pepper
2 tablespoons sugar (optional)
2 tablespoons unsalted butter

In a large stockpot, cover the squirrel and bacon with water and simmer until the squirrel falls apart. Remove the squirrel, debone, cut the meat into small pieces, and return it to the stock. Add the butter beans and cook over moderate heat for 1 hour. Add the remaining ingredients, except the butter, and simmer until well done and thickened, at least 2 hours. Add butter and serve.

Note: Refrigerating and reheating the next day improves the flavor. Leftovers can be frozen.

Variation: One stewing chicken can be used instead of the 2 squirrels.

The Smithfield Cookbook
Junior Woman's Club of Smithfield
Smithfield, Virginia

MAMA'S BRUNSWICK STEW

"As there are usually fifty people at least at our pig-pickin' parties," writes Betty Talmadge, "Mama's recipe is multiplied several times. This is what we cook on the kitchen stove for the crowd, keeping it hot in the old iron washpot over a wood fire. The guests have fun serving themselves from the pot with a long-handled soup dipper."

YIELD: 50 SERVINGS

3 (5-pound) hens
1 hog's head
1 (28-ounce) bottle ketchup
4 pounds okra, trimmed and washed
2 gallons canned tomatoes
2 onions, grated
5 unpeeled lemons, cut into pieces
2 tablespoons sugar
2 tablespoons Tabasco
½ cup apple cider vinegar
3 tablespoons Worcestershire sauce
1 gallon white cream-style corn

Boil the hens in water to cover; save the broth. Bone the hens and cut into serving pieces. Boil and bone the hog's head; drain. Discard this broth. Add the chicken pieces, the hog's head pieces, and all the remaining ingredients except the corn to the broth from the hens. Cook at least 3 hours over very low heat. Add the corn 1 hour before serving.

How to Cook a Pig and Other
Back-to-the-Farm Recipes
Betty Talmadge
Lovejoy, Georgia

BRUNSWICK STEW WITH CHICKEN

Brunswick County, Virginia; Brunswick County, North Carolina; and the city of Brunswick, Georgia, all claim to be the origin point of this rich stew. This version, from Virginia, is emblematic of a gentler stew, far from its frontier origins.

1 whole chicken, cut up

1 onion, quartered

2 stalks celery, diced

1 teaspoon salt

¼ teaspoon pepper

2 cups white shoepeg corn

1½ cups small butter beans

1 pound canned tomatoes

2 small potatoes, cubed

⅓ cup ketchup

2 to 3 tablespoons vinegar

1 tablespoon firmly packed dark brown sugar

1 teaspoon Worcestershire sauce

½ teaspoon Tabasco

¼ teaspoon marjoram

2 to 3 tablespoons unsalted butter

Place the chicken in a Dutch oven and add enough water to cover well. Add the onion, celery, salt, and pepper. Boil until the chicken is ready to come off the bones easily. Remove the chicken pieces and let cool. Add the corn, butter beans, tomatoes, potatoes, ketchup, vinegar, and brown sugar to the broth; cook 2 hours, or until tender. Remove the chicken from the bones and add it to the vegetables, along with the Worcestershire, Tabasco, marjoram, and butter.

Note: For a soupier stew, add up to 1 cup of chicken broth.

Virginia Hospitality
Junior League of Hampton Roads
Newport News, Virginia

VENISON STEW

2 pounds cubed venison (from shoulder or ham)

3 tablespoons vegetable shortening

½ teaspoon salt

¼ teaspoon pepper

Dash of cayenne pepper

1 bay leaf

2½ cups beef stock

1 cup red wine

12 small onions, peeled

6 carrots, peeled and sliced

6 medium potatoes, quartered

Flour, for thickening (optional)

Brown the meat in the shortening. Add the salt, pepper, bay leaf, stock, and wine. Cover and simmer for 2 hours. Add the onions, carrots, and potatoes and cook until the vegetables are fork-tender, about 30 minutes. You can thicken the stew with a little flour and cook a bit longer. Remove bay leaf before serving. Delicious served with cornbread or French rolls and your favorite red wine.

Hospitality
Harvey Woman's Club
Palestine, Texas

MEATS

....

PIG PICKIN' AND POLITICKIN'

Southern political personalities, like sweet corn, travel badly.
They lose flavor with every hundred yards away from the patch.

A. J. LIEBLING, *THE EARL OF LOUISIANA*

Pig Pickin' and Politickin'

....

Through much of our region's history there was only one political party of import, the Democratic Party. That is not to say that Southern political contests lacked spirited rivalry. Far from it. Without the partisan bickering that defined political races in other regions, Southerners sought differentiation based on matters more sonorous and savory.

Though fish fries and oyster roasts have earned their share of voters teetering on the fence, it was the barbecue that candidates most often called upon when the race was tight, the outcome uncertain. It was a time when stump speeches were still given on the stumps of newly felled trees, and when barbecue meant pork that had been slow-smoked over hardwood coals and doused with a sauce tasting of vinegar and maybe a bit of tomato, perhaps a pinch or two of pepper.

Often, the setting was the grounds of the county courthouse, though a clearing in the woods worked just as well. Days before, a pit had been dug in the ground, cord after cord of oak or hickory wood stacked nearby, and plywood-topped sawhorses set out as makeshift serving tables. Lured by the promise of bombast and barbecue, families journeyed from the far reaches of the county, intent upon making a day of picnicking and politicking. Though political barbecues might be staged at any time, the prime season was in late summer, as the Democratic primary drew near. By August, seemingly every courthouse square was awash in a porcine fog, every voter attuned to the burgeoning opportunities for free food and riotous debate.

Southern politicians from George Washington to George Wallace have relied on the political barbecue as a means of shoring up the vote, but perhaps the most accomplished practitioner of pork and politics was Eugene Talmadge, four-time governor of Georgia in the twenties and thirties. With his thumbs hooked in a pair of red suspenders, his brogans planted on a makeshift stage, and his political opponent flailing on the ropes, Talmadge entertained crowds as large as 20,000 at campaign rallies throughout rural Georgia. Though there was no denying the grandiloquence of his speech, neither Talmadge nor his supporters would deny that the size of the crowds had as much to do with the reputation of the local pitmaster in charge as with their loyalty to the man everyone called Farmer Gene.

The next week you might be just as likely to find the same crowd at a rival candidate's rally, ears open to invective, stomachs rumbling with the promise of slow-smoked pork. To all but the most loyal of supporters, barbecue was the prime draw. And even then a clean plate did not always translate into a vote.

It should come as no surprise to learn that many a politician awoke the morning after an unsuccessful primary campaign to a case of indigestion and a realization that though it seemed that everyone in the state was eating his barbecue, they voted for someone else.

POT ROAST WITH VEGETABLES

Valued as much for its deep, rich gravy as for its tender meat, pot roast is a wintertime favorite 'round these parts.

Y I E L D : 6 S E R V I N G S

1 (3-pound) chuck roast
¼ teaspoon pepper
1 teaspoon crushed rosemary
1 large onion, sliced
1 celery stalk, sliced
½ cup soy sauce
1½ cups water
6 medium potatoes, cut into wedges
6 medium carrots, cut into thirds
2 to 3 tablespoons cornstarch or flour

Preheat the oven to 325°. Place the roast in a 3-quart casserole and season with the pepper and rosemary. Cover the roast with the onion, celery, and soy sauce. Add the water and bake, covered, for 1½ hours. Add the potatoes and carrots and continue cooking for 1½ to 2½ hours more, or until the roast is tender. Drain the juice into a small skillet. Make a gravy by adding 2 to 3 tablespoons of cornstarch to the hot pan juices, and cooking briefly. Serve immediately.

A Southern Collection Then and Now
Junior League of Columbus
Columbus, Georgia

PASSOVER BRISKET STUFFED WITH SPINACH AND CARROTS

YIELD: 8 TO 10 SERVINGS

4 pounds beef brisket

2 tablespoons oil

2 cloves garlic, minced

6 green onions, chopped

1¾ pounds fresh spinach, well washed and
   stemmed

1 egg

1 cup matzo farfel

1 teaspoon salt

¾ teaspoon freshly ground black pepper

6 medium carrots, peeled

2 large onions, sliced

¾ cup dry red wine

¾ cup beef stock or canned beef broth

Have the butcher cut a pocket horizontally along one side of the brisket, leaving a ½-inch border around three sides. In a large skillet, heat the oil. Add the garlic and cook over moderate heat for 30 seconds. Add the green onions and cook 2 minutes longer. Transfer the garlic and scallions to a large bowl. Add the spinach to the same skillet and cook until barely wilted and still bright green (about 2 minutes). Set aside to cool slightly, then squeeze dry. Chop the spinach coarsely and squeeze out any remaining liquid. Place the spinach in the bowl with the scallions and garlic. Stir in the egg, farfel, salt, and pepper.

Preheat the oven to 425°. Place 4 yards of kitchen string in a small bowl of water to soak. Cut 2 carrots lengthwise into thin slices. Slice the remaining carrots into ½-inch rounds and set aside. Place one half of the thin-sliced carrots in the brisket pocket in a layer going against the grain of the meat. Spread the spinach stuffing on top of the carrots and arrange the remaining thin carrot slices on top of the stuffing.

Using the kitchen string, tie the brisket at 1-inch intervals to secure the stuffing. Scatter the sliced onions and carrot rounds over the bottom of the pan. Place the brisket on top of the vegetables. Season the brisket with salt and pepper. Cook in the oven, uncovered, for 15 minutes.

Pour the wine and stock into the roasting pan and cover tightly with foil. Reduce the oven to 325° and cook until the meat is fork tender (3½ to 5 hours). Remove from the oven, loosen the foil, and let the brisket rest for 30 minutes. Meanwhile, strain the liquid from the pan, remove any fat, and strain again. If there is less than ¾ cup liquid, add more stock or water. Place the carrots and onions in a food processor, add the liquid, and purée. Reheat in a small pan. Season to taste.

Slice the brisket against the grain in thick slices and serve with the sauce on the side.

The brisket can be made one day ahead and reheated and sliced before serving.

From Generation to Generation
Sisterhood of Temple Emanu-El
Dallas, Texas

ELI EVANS

THE SECRET OF "ATLANTA BRISKET"

My mother, Sara, never really had the patience to cook. Besides, she had a business to run and, like all eight Nachamson girls, she was a great manager. Brisket was a weekly occasion, a marvelous, succulent, gravy-laden triumph that took hours to marinate and simmer and baste. Lifting the lid of the Dutch oven to savor the aroma and taste a sliver was as heady as a first kiss.

When I was a kid, Ethel Benjamin and Zola Hargrave and Roady Adams, our family cooks . . . used to let me help. And as the official family taster, I got to crunch the crispy ends that had burned a little as the rest of it finished cooking.

I once heard someone mysteriously refer to it as "Atlanta Brisket," but I never knew why or what its secret was until I moved to New York. Each time I would leave home in Durham to go back to the City, Mom would hand me a large, ice-cold package—an already sliced brisket, each portion wrapped in foil with the gravy frozen in. Back in my bachelor apartment, I could take it out of the freezer one serving at a time and "eat great" in what she viewed as the barren canyons of Manhattan. Like magic, I could produce Southern Jewish home cookin'—in the Big Apple.

One day, after consulting Zola and Roady, I decided to try cooking it myself. I bought fresh onions, plus onion-soup mix, bay leaves, and paprika. But before I browned the meat in oil (to retain the juices), they told me the "secret" ingredient. It was so Southern, really. Fundamentally and soul-deep Atlanta bubbled up from its epicenter. . . . The secret was not fine wine, not Heineken's, not a special marinade handed down for generations. The secret was—dare I reveal it?—Coca-Cola! or rather, marinating the meat overnight in the dark epicurean liquid, which has so much fizzy potency, it breaks down the fibers and transforms this brisket into the tenderest softest delicacy you ever put in your mouth. . . .

So try it. Just soak three pounds of meat in Coca-Cola overnight. Remove it and let it drain. Brown it in oil, then put it in a Dutch oven with sliced onions and onion-soup mix and bay leaves in an inch or so of water. Cook about two hours on low, basting and checking it every so often, and adding boiling water when needed (cold water spatters). Slice and serve with the onion mixture as gravy. It's great cold or reheated. And you can eat it for a week in sandwiches.

Eli Evans, a native of Durham, North Carolina, now lives in New York City. This selection originally appeared in his book The Provincials.

GRILLED BRISKET

In a pinch, we Southerners have been known to give up the barbecue pit for the oven, even in Texas where smoke-suffused barbecued beef is sacrosanct.

YIELD: 10 TO 12 SERVINGS

1 (32-ounce) bottle of ketchup
5 tablespoons Worcestershire sauce
1 tablespoon Tabasco
Salt and lemon pepper to taste
Juice of ½ lemon
1 stick (¼ pound) unsalted butter, melted
1 small onion, finely chopped
1 (6- to 8-pound) brisket of beef

Prepare the grill. In a bowl, combine all the ingredients except the brisket. Baste the brisket with the marinade, grilling over low flames. Use the marinade to keep the meat moist throughout the grilling process, about 30 to 45 minutes, or until the brisket is browned. Wrap the brisket in foil and continue basting and cooking slowly over low heat (about 1 hour per pound). When the brisket is done, preheat the oven to 275° or 300°. Slice the meat, place it in a baking pan, and pour the marinade over the top. Heat, covered, in the oven for 1 hour.

Some Like It Hot
Junior League of McAllen
McAllen, Texas

COUNTRY-FRIED STEAK WITH CREAM GRAVY

We Southerners would eat shoe leather battered and fried. Traditionally this dish relied on cuts of meat that had the texture and chew of a brogan, but this updated version benefits from tender sirloin.

YIELD: 8 TO 10 SERVINGS

1 (3-pound) sirloin tip roast,
    sliced into 1½-inch-thick slices
1 to 2 tablespoons salt
1 tablespoon white vinegar
3 cups flour
2 tablespoons freshly ground black pepper
Vegetable oil for deep frying
Cream Gravy (recipe follows)

Pound the meat with a spiked meat mallet to tenderize. Cut each slice crosswise into 3 pieces. Place in a large bowl and cover with water. Mix in the salt and vinegar and let marinate for 2 hours.

Combine the flour and pepper in a plastic bag. Add meat (do not pat dry), one piece at a time, and shake to coat. Heat the oil in a deep fryer or deep large skillet over medium-high heat to 350°. Add the meat in batches (do not crowd) and fry until light brown, about 30 seconds per side. Drain on paper towels. Reserve 2 tablespoons pan drippings for the gravy. Place the meat on a warm platter. Tent with foil. Serve with Cream Gravy.

CREAM GRAVY

2 tablespoons pan drippings
2 tablespoons flour
2 to 3 cups milk
¼ teaspoon salt
¼ teaspoon pepper
Parsley sprigs

Heat the pan drippings over medium heat. Stir in the flour and cook, stirring constantly, for 3 minutes. Remove from the heat and gradually whisk in the milk. Stir in the salt and pepper. Whisk over medium heat until thickened, about 1 minute. Spoon over the steaks. Garnish with the parsley and serve.

Augusta Cooks for Company
Augusta Council of the Georgia Association for
Children and Adults with Learning Disabilities
Augusta, Georgia

CHICKEN-FRIED STEAK

From a cook in Ville Platte on the western plains of Louisiana comes this battered and fried taste of the West.

YIELD: 6 TO 8 SERVINGS

2 pounds round steak, tenderized
Seasoned salt and pepper
2 eggs
½ cup milk
Flour
Vegetable oil

Trim all fat and gristle from the meat. Cut the meat into pieces about the size of your hand. Season with salt and pepper on both sides. Beat the eggs and milk together lightly. Dip the steak pieces in the flour, then in the egg mixture, then in the flour again. For a thicker crust, repeat procedure.

Heat the oil, ¼ inch deep, to about 400° in an electric skillet or to very hot in a regular skillet. Place the steaks in the hot oil, then turn heat to low. Cook 15 to 20 minutes on first side, or until golden brown. Turn without puncturing the crust, and cook 10 minutes on the second side. Drain on paper towels and keep warm in the oven while making gravy with the drippings (see Cream Gravy, this page).

Foods à la Louisiane
Louisiana Farm Bureau Women's Committee
Baton Rouge, Louisiana

GRILLADES AND GRITS

From down Louisiana way comes this Creole favorite, transported from the French-Catholic land of south Louisiana to the Baptist belt of the north.

YIELD: 6 SERVINGS

2½ pounds beef or veal round
2 teaspoons salt, plus additional for seasoning
    the meat before dredging
1 teaspoon black pepper, plus additional for sea-
    soning the meat before dredging
½ cup flour
3 tablespoons vegetable oil

2 tablespoons unsalted butter
2 large onions, coarsely chopped
1 large green bell pepper, coarsely chopped
½ cup coarsely chopped celery
3 cloves garlic, minced
2 cups chicken stock
2 tomatoes, chopped
1 bay leaf
6 servings grits, uncooked

Pound the beef or veal rounds to flatten; cut into 2x3-inch pieces and season with salt and pepper. Dredge the meat in the flour and shake off the excess.

In a heavy skillet, heat the oil and brown the meat. Remove the meat from the skillet and set aside. Pour off the remaining fat in the skillet. Add the butter and melt over moderate heat. When the foam begins to subside, add the onion, bell pepper, celery, and garlic. Cook, stirring frequently, for about 5 minutes, or until the vegetables are tender. Stir in the stock, tomatoes, bay leaf, 2 teaspoons salt, and 1 teaspoon pepper and bring to a boil. Reduce heat to low, partially cover the skillet, and simmer for 20 minutes.

Return the meat and accumulated liquid to the skillet, stirring well. Simmer partly covered for about 1 hour, or until the meat is tender and the sauce is thickened. Adjust the seasonings.

Thirty minutes before the grillades are done, cook the grits according to the package directions. Mound the grits on warm plates and ladle the grillades over the grits.

Celebrations on the Bayou
Junior League of Monroe
Monroe, Louisiana

KIBBEE

Bubba Mohamed, son of acclaimed stitchery artist Ethel Wright Mohamed (1906–1992), shares a favorite recipe of his Lebanese father, who ran a mercantile store in the Mississippi Delta.

YIELD: 2 TO 3 SERVINGS

1 cup cracked wheat (bulghur)
1 pound lean round steak, ground twice
1 onion, puréed
½ cup vegetable oil
Salt and pepper to taste
Parsley, olives, or mint, for garnish

Soak the wheat in cold water for 45 minutes (it must swell). Squeeze the water out with your hands. Place the wheat in a bowl and add the meat, onion, oil, salt, and pepper; mix well. Form into patties or balls, and fry or bake. Or mold on a platter and eat uncooked. Garnish with parsley, olives, or mint.

The Share-Cropper
Central Delta Academy
    Parent-Teacher Organization
Inverness, Mississippi

Jimmy's Meat Loaf

Pray for leftovers. Slice a meaty hunk. Spread with a bit of mayo, a touch of ketchup, and a slice of onion. Place between two slices of white bread, and enjoy!

YIELD: 6 SERVINGS

1 pound ground round
4 ounces sausage meat
2 medium onions, minced
2 cloves garlic, chopped
2 celery stalks, chopped
1 egg, lightly beaten
¼ cup milk
½ cup ketchup
2 teaspoons salt
½ teaspoon black pepper
1½ cups bread crumbs
1 cup tomato sauce

Preheat the oven to 350°. In a bowl, mix all the ingredients except the tomato sauce and shape into a loaf. Place in a baking dish and top with the tomato sauce. Bake for 1 hour.

Upper Crust
Junior League of Johnson City
Johnson City, Tennessee

Chili

A pot of chili is the traditional favorite when the first cold front blows through in the fall.

YIELD: 6 TO 8 SERVINGS

1 pound kidney beans
6 cups warm water
3 teaspoons salt
¼ cup oil or bacon fat
1½ cups diced onion
1 pound ground beef
2 cloves garlic, minced
3 to 4 tablespoons flour
¼ teaspoon black pepper
1 cup tomato sauce
1 cup water
1 tablespoon chili powder
2 teaspoons ground cumin

Wash the beans and add to the 6 cups warm water in a casserole or heavy pot. Let the beans soak several hours.

Add 2 teaspoons of the salt to the beans and the water in which they soaked; cover and place over low heat to simmer gently. While the beans cook, heat the oil in a skillet, add the onion, and cook 5 minutes over low heat. Add the meat and garlic and cook until the meat browns. Mix in the flour. Immediately add the remaining teaspoon salt and the pepper, tomato sauce, 1 cup water, chili powder, and cumin. Stir the meat mixture into the beans. Cover and simmer for 2 hours, or until the beans are tender and the sauce is thick and rich.

Pearls of the Concho
Junior League of San Angelo
San Angelo, Texas

Natchitoches Meat Pies

Once sold by street corner vendors, these meaty turnovers are an integral part of the culture and cuisine of Cane River country.

Yield: 26 to 28 pies

1½ pounds ground beef
1½ pounds ground pork
1 cup chopped green onions (white and green parts)
1 tablespoon salt
1 teaspoon coarsely ground black pepper
1 teaspoon dried hot red pepper flakes
½ teaspoon cayenne pepper
⅓ cup all-purpose flour
2 cups self-rising flour
Heaping ⅓ cup shortening, not melted
1 egg, lightly beaten
¾ cup milk
Fat for deep frying

Combine the beef, pork, onions, salt, black pepper, red pepper flakes, and cayenne in a large Dutch oven. Cook over medium heat, stirring often, until the meat loses its red color (do not overcook). Sift the all-purpose flour over the meat mixture, stirring often, until well combined with meat. Remove from heat and let cool to room temperature. Drain meat in a large colander.

Sift the self-rising flour; cut the shortening into the flour. Add the egg and milk. Form the dough into a ball. Roll about one-third of the dough at a time on a lightly floured board. Cut the dough into 5- to 5½-inch circles. Place a heaping tablespoon of filling on one side of the pastry round. Dampen the edge of the pie with your fingertips, fold the top over the meat, and crimp with a fork dipped in water. Prick with the fork twice on top.

Fry in a deep-fat fryer at 350° until golden brown. These can be frozen, if desired, before frying. Do not thaw before frying.

Cane River Cuisine
Service League of Natchitoches
Natchitoches, Louisiana

Moussaka

Rather than a land of Anglo-Saxons and Africans, the South is a stew of many hues and nations, as evidenced by this contribution from the Hellenic Ladies Society in Durham, North Carolina.

Yield: 30 pieces

3 medium eggplants
Salt
1 cup olive oil
2½ sticks unsalted butter
1½ cups all-purpose flour
2 large onions, minced
2 pounds lean ground beef
2 cups tomato sauce
½ cup red wine
Salt and pepper to taste
¼ cup chopped fresh parsley
⅛ teaspoon ground cinnamon
Dash of sugar
6 tablespoons plain bread crumbs
1 cup grated Parmesan cheese
Cream Sauce (recipe follows)

Slice the eggplants lengthwise ¼ inch thick. Sprinkle with salt; let stand 15 minutes in a colander. Heat the oil and 2 sticks of the butter in a large skillet. Rinse the eggplant well in cold water and pat dry. Dredge in the flour. Fry the eggplant slices in the oil and butter until golden on both sides. Drain on paper towels.

In a large skillet, heat the remaining ½ stick butter and sauté the onion until tender. Crumble the beef into the pan and brown. Add the tomato sauce, wine, salt, pepper, parsley, cinnamon, and sugar; mix well. Simmer, uncovered, for 30 minutes, or until the juice is absorbed. Remove from the heat and let cool. Drain the excess oil.

Preheat the oven to 350°. Stir 3 tablespoons of the bread crumbs and ½ cup of the Parmesan into the meat mixture. Sprinkle the remaining bread crumbs on the bottom of a greased 17x11-inch baking pan. Place a layer of eggplant slices on top of the bread crumbs and cover with a layer of meat mixture. Repeat the layers, ending with eggplant. Pour the Cream Sauce over all. Sprinkle with the remaining cheese. Bake for 50 minutes, or until golden brown. Remove from the oven; let cool 15 minutes. Cut into squares.

CREAM SAUCE

6 tablespoons unsalted butter

6 tablespoons flour

3 cups warm milk

4 egg yolks, lightly beaten

Salt and pepper

¼ teaspoon nutmeg

Melt the butter in the top of a double boiler over hot water; blend in the flour, stirring constantly with a wire whisk. Slowly add the warm milk, stirring constantly until slightly thickened. Slowly add ½ cup of the cream mixture to the egg yolks, then pour the yolks into the sauce. Cook over low heat until thickened, about 6 minutes. Add salt, pepper, and nutmeg.

The Grecian Plate
Hellenic Ladies Society
St. Barbara Greek Orthodox Church
Durham, North Carolina

HOT TAMALES

What's a tamale recipe doing in a Southern cookbook? When Mexican migrant workers came to work the Mississippi Delta's cotton fields in the early 1900s, they brought with them a taste for tamales. Though the workers were here only on a seasonal basis, their culinary legacy endures, as tamale stands are now a fixture on the Delta roadsides. 'Most every family knows a maker willing to sell a few dozen, but few know of the Mexican connection.

YIELD: ABOUT 200 LARGE TAMALES

10 to 12 pounds chopped beef (top round)

3 pounds suet (fat)

Salt to taste

12 to 15 medium onions

3 heads garlic

12 (6-ounce) cans tomato paste

½ cup black pepper

Cayenne pepper to taste

2 ounces chili powder

10 pounds white cornmeal
Tamale shucks

Boil the beef and suet in water to cover until tender. Add salt to taste, and save the broth for mush. Then take the meat out and let cool. Grind the meat with the onion and garlic. Mix with 8 cans of tomato paste and the black pepper, the cayenne, 1 ounce chili powder, and salt to taste. Mix well.

For the cornmeal mush, bring the reserved broth to a boil. Place the cornmeal in a large stockpot and add the hot broth to the cornmeal. Season with salt, black pepper, and cayenne. Add the remaining 1 ounce of chili powder and the remaining 4 cans of tomato paste. Mix well. Add the cornmeal mixture to the meat mixture until there are equal amounts of meat mixture and mush mixture.

Roll in the shucks. (If you can have shucks already trimmed, all you do is soak in boiling water until the shucks are soft enough to handle. If not, trim the stalk end off the point end. This makes a nice shuck for your filling.) Place the tamales on a rack and steam over hot water for 2 hours.

Festival Cookbook
Humphreys Academy Patrons
Belzoni, Mississippi

TAMALE CASSEROLE

YIELD: 6 SERVINGS

8 ounces ground pork sausage meat
1 cup minced onion
¾ cup diced green bell pepper
8 ounces ground beef
1½ cups whole-kernel corn, liquid reserved
⅓ cup sliced ripe olives, liquid reserved
1½ cups tomato sauce
1 to 1½ teaspoons salt
1 teaspoon chili powder
½ teaspoon garlic salt
1 dozen or more fresh tamales or 2 (15-ounce)
   cans tamales
⅓ cup tamale liquid
1½ cups grated cheddar cheese

Brown the sausage in a large skillet. Remove the sausage and drain. Spoon out all but 3 tablespoons drippings from the skillet. Add the onion and green pepper and sauté until tender. Stir in the ground beef and cook until browned. Drain the corn, reserving the liquid. Add the corn, 1 teaspoon corn liquid, the ripe olives, 1 teaspoon ripe olive liquid, and the sausage meat to the skillet. Mix in the tomato sauce, salt, chili powder, and garlic salt. Simmer gently for 15 minutes.

Preheat the oven to 350°. Drain the tamales; add ⅓ cup of the tamale liquid to the meat mixture. Remove the wrappings from the tamales and slice the tamales in half lengthwise. Spoon the meat mixture into a large, shallow casserole and arrange the tamales on top. Bake, uncovered, for 15 minutes. Sprinkle with the cheese and re-

SHELBY FOOTE

HOT TAMALE MAN

Most evenings before supper, sitting in the shade of the front porch of our home in Greenville, Mississippi, we waited on the hot tamale man to make his way through the neighborhood. You could hear him cry out, "Hot tamale man, hot tamales, get your mollies!" We would whistle him over and get, say, a dozen or so. They were a sort of hors d'oeuvre, I guess, though we didn't even know that word then.

Hot tamales became very much a Delta food. Hell, we were eating them before I ever recall seeing a Mexican. We were eating them all through the twenties. In fact, I was eating hot tamales long before I had ever heard of a hush puppy.

Tamales were sold off of a two-wheeled cart, loaded with 20-gallon brassy-looking lard buckets. When you placed your order—they were 15 cents a dozen—one of the salesmen would fish out a bundle of three or six tamales and wrap them in newspaper to keep the grease from dripping all over you. I remember those tamales as being just superb, with an awful lot of meat in them—not like the kind they make today, with a whole lot of cornmeal and a thin vein of meat.

Back then, anything the least bit hot would set my mouth aflame, and hot tamales were in that category. As I recall, the two vendors who worked our neighborhood were named Stanfield and Six Sixty-Six. Of course, Six Sixty-Six is the devil's number. Maybe that had something to do with them being so hot!

Shelby Foote, a native of Greenville, Mississippi, now living in Memphis, Tennessee, is perhaps best known for his three-volume history of the Civil War: Fort Sumter to Perryville, Fredericksburg to Meridian, *and* Red River to Appomattox.

turn to the oven until the cheese is melted, about 20 more minutes.

Houston Junior League Cookbook
Junior League of Houston
Houston, Texas

1846 FRIED SALT PORK WITH CREAM GRAVY

According to Marie Rudisill, old-time salt pork, fried, with cream gravy has a pull that does not lessen as the years go by.

Salt pork
Fine cornmeal
Flour
Oil for frying
Cream Gravy (recipe follows)

Slice the salt pork thin. Remove the rind and slash one edge of the slices so that they will not curl as they fry. Freshen the pork a little by soaking it in ice water or by parboiling it for a few minutes to remove the excess salt. Dry the slices thoroughly with a cloth. Mix equal amounts of cornmeal and flour in a bowl. Dip each slice in the meal mixture. Fry in hot oil in a skillet until brown and crisp. Serve with Cream Gravy.

CREAM GRAVY

Pork fat
2 tablespoons flour
½ cup milk
½ cup heavy cream
Salt and black pepper to taste

Blend the pork fat and the flour well. Add the milk and cream. Cook in a double-boiler, stirring constantly, until smooth and creamy. Season with a little salt and black pepper.

Sook's Cookbook
Marie Rudisill
Monroesville, Alabama

VEAL SCALOPPINE CHARLESTON

Charleston Receipts *is one of the standard-bearers of Southern cooking, long treasured by new brides and matrons alike. With* Charleston Receipts Repeats, *from which this recipe is drawn, we get a new taste of the Holy City.*

YIELD: 4 SERVINGS

8 (2-ounce) veal scaloppine, pounded flat
1 cup flour
Salt
Freshly ground black pepper
½ stick (4 tablespoons) butter, clarified
½ stick unsalted butter, at room
*   temperature*
Juice of ½ lemon
¼ teaspoon Worcestershire sauce
1 tablespoon chopped parsley
1 tablespoon dry white wine
½ teaspoon Dijon mustard
1 cup crab meat
2 ounces prosciutto, cut into thin julienne
*   strips*
Hollandaise or béarnaise sauce, for serving
*   (optional)*

PAUL McILHENNY

FOR THE LOVE OF GAME

I'm an avid hunter. And I pride myself on cooking whatever I shoot for whomever I'm feeding. Over the years, my wife and now my daughters have developed a real love of game—of ducks, and doves, and quail. Even my eight-year-old grandson has developed an affinity for doves and ducks. He likes to go hunting with us, though of course he doesn't shoot.

This past Thanksgiving my family went down to my hunting club for the holiday. The club is in a lovely spot, about forty miles southwest of our home here in Avery Island, Louisiana, in the coastal marsh. I hunted with my wife, Judy, and my daughters hunted with their husbands and husbands-to-be. We all shot ducks. And we all got our limits.

For supper late that afternoon, we cooked a beautiful speckle-bellied goose, a white-fronted goose. We had deboned it and then stuffed it with boudin, a pork and rice dressing.

We love to eat oysters as well, especially the ones from Abbeville, just down the road. It's one of the oyster capitals of the Deep South. So we bought a gallon, ate some of those raw, fried a few and then put them atop a green salad like the French do, and then the rest—along with all the oyster liquor—went into the gumbo. I made a wild duck, andouille sausage, and fresh oyster gumbo, which my family really enjoys. My daughters tell me that they would rather have this dish than turkey or ham for Thanksgiving. And my wife certainly loves it, if for no other reason than that I'm the one doing the cooking. It's just a wonderful dish that brings together the oyster liquor, the smoked sausage, and the wild duck that we hunted as a family.

We hunt from September through January for doves, and ducks, and geese. And now with my grandson along, it's a three-generation family affair. So when it comes time to eat on Thanksgiving Day, it's my great pleasure to celebrate the grand finale of the hunt at the table with my entire family gathered around, knowing that we've all participated from beginning to end.

Paul McIlhenny, of New Iberia, Louisiana, is president of the McIlhenny Company, makers of Tabasco hot pepper sauce.

Dredge the veal in the flour. Season lightly with salt and pepper. Heat the clarified butter in a sauté pan until it just starts to smoke. Sauté the veal quickly in batches until light brown on both sides. Arrange on a platter. Pour off the excess butter from the pan.

In a bowl, knead together the ½ stick of room-temperature butter and the lemon juice, Worcestershire, parsley, wine, and mustard. Add the kneaded butter mixture to the sauté pan. When the mixture is hot, add the crab meat and the prosciutto. Toss until all is heated through. Serve over the scaloppine. You can serve this with hollandaise or béarnaise sauce.

Note: To clarify butter, melt over low heat until the solids separate from the clear yellow liquid. Pour off or spoon off solids and discard, reserving the liquid—the clarified butter.

Charleston Receipts Repeats
Junior League of Charleston
Charleston, South Carolina

MAMIE'S LAMB WITH RED GRAVY

Mamie is Mamie Sikes, cook for "Sweetie" (Mrs. Charles Cohn) and then for her daughter, Marion Cohn Bradley, whose husband was mayor of Invernes, Mississippi, from 1948 to 1972.

YIELD: 4 TO 6 SERVINGS

1 (6- to 8-pound) leg of lamb
½ cup vinegar
1 cup water

Salt, pepper, and garlic powder to taste
½ cup flour
2 (6-ounce) cans tomato paste
Hot, cooked rice, for serving

Preheat the oven to 350°. Wash the leg of lamb and place it in a roasting pan. Mix the vinegar with the water and pour over the lamb. Sprinkle with the salt, pepper, and garlic powder. Roast, covered, for 30 minutes per pound. Remove from the oven 45 minutes prior to finish. Make a paste with the flour and tomato paste and spread over the lamb. Place some paste in with the drippings to make the gravy. Continue cooking, uncovered. Serve with rice.

The Share-Cropper
Central Delta Academy
    Parent-Teacher Organization
Inverness, Mississippi

LAMB CHOPS WITH HERBS AND ANCHOVIES

YIELD: 4 SERVINGS

3 cloves garlic, peeled
3 anchovy fillets
2 tablespoons fresh rosemary leaves
1 teaspoon freshly ground pepper
½ teaspoon salt
¼ cup chopped fresh parsley
½ teaspoon dried thyme
3 tablespoons olive oil
2 tablespoons dry red wine
8 thick lamb loin chops, trimmed of fat
8 fresh rosemary sprigs

Place the garlic, anchovies, rosemary leaves, pepper, salt, parsley, thyme, oil, and wine in a food processor fitted with a steel blade and process until smooth. Using a small, sharp knife, make several shallow incisions in both sides of the lamb chops. Rub the anchovy marinade generously over both sides and press into incisions. Marinate 1 to 2 hours at room temperature.

Prepare charcoal for grilling. For medium-rare, grill the chops about 4 inches from hot coals, 5 to 6 minutes per side. Serve garnished with the fresh rosemary sprigs.

The Artful Table
Dallas Museum of Art League
Dallas, Texas

Breakfast Sausage Casserole

Look in many a Southern freezer and you will find two or three casseroles of this brunchtime favorite lying in repose, awaiting a crowd. It needs to be made at least the night before.

Yield: 10 to 12 servings

1 pound medium or hot sausage meat
1 large onion, chopped
12 slices white bread, cut into quarters
10 ounces sharp cheddar cheese, grated
8 eggs, well beaten
4 cups milk
1½ teaspoons salt
¼ teaspoon pepper
½ teaspoon dry mustard

Cook the sausage meat until browned; drain all the drippings except 2 tablespoons. Sauté the onion in the reserved drippings until tender. In a greased 9x13-inch baking dish, layer the ingredients. Begin with half the bread, then half the sausage, half the onion, and half the cheese; repeat layers. Beat together the eggs, milk, salt, pepper, and mustard; then pour over the layers. Cover and refrigerate at least overnight before cooking. When ready to bake, remove the baking dish from the refrigerator 1 hour before baking to bring to room temperature; then bake at 350° for 50 minutes.

The Magnolia Collection
Gene Westbrook
Millbrook, Alabama

Boudin

Boudin comes in two varieties, blanc et rouge, *with the latter colored by hog's blood. This is the* blanc *version for those who blanch at the thought of* rouge.

Yield: 12 to 14 pounds sausage

1 large hog's head
2 pounds mixed variety meats (heart, kidneys, etc.)
3 pounds lean pork
2 pounds pork liver
3 medium onions
2 cups chopped green onion tops
20 sprigs fresh parsley
2 gallons cooked rice

Salt and pepper to taste
Sausage casings

Boil the hog's head until tender; let cool. Remove the meat from the bones. Grind the hog's head meat, variety meats, lean pork, and pork liver with the onions in a meat grinder. Combine the meat mixture with the chopped green onions, parsley, and rice, adding salt and pepper as desired; mix well. Stuff the meat mixture into sausage casings. Boil for 5 minutes, or until the meat is done.

Foods à la Louisiane
Louisiana Farm Bureau Women
Baton Rouge, Louisiana

JAMBALAYA

Etymologists tell us that the word jambalaya *comes from the Spanish word for ham,* jamón, *a legacy of the onetime Spanish ownership of what is now Louisiana.*

YIELD: 6 TO 8 SERVINGS

1½ pounds sausage or cubed beef
3 tablespoons bacon drippings (if beef is used)
3 tablespoons flour
2 medium onions, chopped
1 bunch green onions, chopped
2 tablespoons chopped parsley

2 cloves garlic, minced

2 cups uncooked rice

2½ cups water

2 teaspoons salt

Black pepper to taste

¾ teaspoon cayenne pepper

In a heavy black pot, brown the sausage. (If using beef, brown in the bacon drippings.) Remove the meat. Add the flour to the pot and brown it to a dark roux. Add the onions, green onions, parsley, and garlic. Cook until soft, then add the rice, water, salt, black pepper, cayenne pepper, and browned meat. When the mixture comes to a boil, lower the heat to the lowest point and cook, covered tightly, for about 1 hour. When the rice is done, remove the lid and let cook for a few minutes until the rice dries a little.

River Road Recipes
Junior League of Baton Rouge
Baton Rouge, Louisiana

LOUISIANA RED BEANS WITH RICE

YIELD: 6 TO 8 SERVINGS

1 pound red beans, washed, drained, soaked in
    water overnight, and drained

3 cups cold water

2 cloves garlic, chopped

½ cup chopped celery

1 large bay leaf, crushed

1 medium onion, chopped

½ cup cooking oil

Salt and black pepper

1 pound smoked sausage, sliced

2 tablespoons chopped parsley

Steaming rice, for serving

Place the beans in the 3 cups cold water in a 4-quart pot. Add the garlic, celery, bay leaf, onion, and oil and bring to a boil. Reduce the heat and simmer for about 2 hours. Add water as needed, stirring occasionally. Add salt and pepper to taste and the sausage and parsley and continue cooking over low heat for about 1 hour. Serve over a mound of steaming rice.

Louisiana Legacy
Thibodaux Service League
Thibodaux, Louisiana

PORK TENDERLOIN

YIELD: 2 TO 4 SERVINGS

¼ cup soy sauce

1 tablespoon firmly packed dark brown
    sugar

¼ cup bourbon

1 clove garlic, minced

1 (2- to 3-pound) pork tenderloin

⅓ cup commercial sour cream

1 tablespoon dry mustard

½ teaspoon vinegar

Salt to taste

⅓ cup mayonnaise

1 tablespoon finely chopped green onion

Mix the soy sauce, brown sugar, bourbon, and garlic thoroughly in a bowl. Add the tenderloin and marinate overnight. Combine the sour cream and the remaining ingredients together in a small bowl and refrigerate until ready to use.

Preheat the oven to 325°. Drain the tenderloin, reserving marinade. Bake covered for 1 to 1¼ hours. Check after 45 minutes. Baste occasionally with marinade while cooking. Remove the cover during the last few minutes of cooking. Slice diagonally and spoon sour cream sauce at room temperature over the top.

Almost Heaven
Junior League of Huntington
Huntington, West Virginia

BARBECUED RIBS

YIELD: 4 TO 6 SERVINGS

6 pounds spareribs
1½ cups water
3 tablespoons firmly packed dark brown sugar
½ teaspoon chili powder
½ teaspoon dry mustard
1 teaspoon onion salt
Dash of Tabasco
1 teaspoon fresh lemon juice
3 tablespoons vinegar
¾ cup ketchup
⅓ cup Worcestershire sauce
1 (12-ounce) can beer

Preheat the oven to 425°. Place the spareribs in a shallow pan and bake for 1 hour. Skim off the fat. Combine the water, brown sugar, chili powder, mustard, onion salt, Tabasco, lemon juice, vinegar, ketchup, Worcestershire sauce, and beer. Pour the sauce over the ribs. Reduce the oven temperature to 325° and bake for 2 hours, basting occasionally.

A Cookbook of Pinehurst Courses
Moore Regional Hospital Auxiliary
Pinehurst, North Carolina

CARTER HILL BARBECUE RIBS

YIELD: 4 SERVINGS

4 pounds fresh spareribs, cut into pieces
1 quart apple cider vinegar
1 cup firmly packed dark brown sugar
1 tablespoon coarsely ground black pepper
½ teaspoon salt
¼ teaspoon cayenne pepper
¼ teaspoon paprika
2 large cloves garlic, crushed

Cut the ribs into 3- or 4-inch pieces. Rinse in cold water. Drain. Pour the vinegar into a large glass dish. Add the brown sugar, black pepper, salt, cayenne, paprika, and garlic. Mix well. Place ribs in mixture to marinate overnight in refrigerator.

Preheat oven to 450°. Place the ribs in a baking pan. Pour 1 cup of the marinade over the top. Bake, basting occasionally with the sauce, for 30 minutes, or until the ribs are brown on both sides. Reduce the heat to 350° and continue to baste while cooking another 1½ hours, or until done.

Black Family Reunion Cookbook
National Council of Negro Women
Washington, D.C.

LAWRENCE CRAIG

WHY I AM A COOK

Folks always talk about how black folks are good cooks. There's a reason for that. Back when I was growing up there were two kinds of jobs black folks could get without being challenged by white folks: cooking and heavy lifting.

For instance, back before I started cooking, I worked for the U.S. Corps of Engineers on the Mississippi River, first on a snag boat and then on a dredge boat. Now, when I first started out, coal and wood fueled the boat. And it was a black man's job to do the heavy, dirty work of feeding the fire. But when they started using oil, when all you had to do was turn a knob, well, they got a white man to sit down and turn that knob, and that became a white man's job.

So I chose cooking. I figured that no one else wanted to stay in that hot kitchen all day. I figured I had the green light. My mother had been a cook in white folks' homes and gotten along just fine. So I chose cooking. Back then that was acceptable. Folks thought black folks could cook—same as they thought black folks could sing and dance, that we had rhythm and could play musical instruments. They thought we could barbecue better. So black folks cooked. I cooked.

When I started out on the boat in 1933, I was seventeen, working as a mess attendant. That means you do what they tell you to do. But the cook started letting me experiment, and soon I was doing most of the cooking. And then in the off season, when I was back home in Devall's Bluff, I started doing a little bit of barbecuing. We'd dig a pit in the ground and lay an old bedspring across it, fill the pit with coals, slap the meat on the springs, and lay a piece of tin across the top to conserve heat and concentrate the smoke. You had to stay by the fire all night and all day.

By 1947, I had opened my own barbecue place right down the road. I guess I was pretty good at it. It's still there—Craig's Barbecue. Maybe the white folks were right. Maybe black folks are better at cooking. Maybe we are better at barbecuing. In 1997, the Smithsonian Institution invited me to cook up in Washington, D.C. You figure the folks at the Smithsonian know something about cooking, don't you?

Lawrence Craig is a native of Devall's Bluff, Arkansas, where he opened Craig's Barbecue in 1947.

DRY BARBECUE RIBS

Memphis, Tennessee, along with Lexington, North Carolina, and Owensboro, Kentucky, lays claim to the title "Barbecue Capital of the South." Dry ribs and barbecue spaghetti are the defining dishes of the Memphis school.

YIELD: 4 TO 5 SERVINGS

4 to 5 pounds pork loin back ribs
  (2 slabs)
1 cup fresh lemon juice
4 tablespoons ground cumin
8 teaspoons chili powder
4 teaspoons seasoned salt
½ teaspoon cayenne pepper
2½ cups white vinegar
¾ cup cooking oil

Lay the ribs on a piece of heavy foil that is large enough to wrap the meat. Rub the meaty side of each slab of ribs with 1½ tablespoons of the lemon juice. Sprinkle each slab with 1 tablespoon of the cumin, 2 teaspoons of the chili powder, 1 teaspoon of the seasoned salt, and ¼ teaspoon of the cayenne. Wrap the ribs and refrigerate overnight.

For the basting sauce, combine in a bowl the vinegar, the oil, the remaining lemon juice, the 3 tablespoons of remaining cumin, 6 teaspoons remaining chili powder, and 3 teaspoons remaining seasoned salt. Stir well.

In a covered grill, arrange preheated coals in a circle or on the sides, leaving a hole in the center. Test for medium-slow heat over the center. Place the ribs in the center of the cooking grid or on a rib rack. Grill, covered, for 5 to 6 hours, or until tender, turning and basting with sauce every 30 minutes. Add coals every 45 to 60 minutes to maintain the grilling temperature.

Heart and Soul
Junior League of Memphis
Memphis, Tennessee

BATTER-FRIED PORK CHOPS

As some Southerners are wont to say, "Pigs plump up quick." And we love them for it. Long valued for their affinity for grazing on wild nuts and such, and their propensity to take on weight quickly, they are the South's favorite livestock.

YIELD: 6 SERVINGS

1 cup flour
½ cup plain bread crumbs
1 cup milk
1 egg, lightly beaten
1 teaspoon salt
½ teaspoon paprika
¼ teaspoon oregano
¼ cup vegetable oil
6 (½-inch-thick) loin pork chops

Combine the flour, bread crumbs, milk, egg, salt, paprika, and oregano. Heat the vegetable oil to 350° in a large, heavy skillet. Dip each chop into the batter and brown on both sides in the heated oil. Drain well on paper towels.

Food for Body and Soul
Highway 5 Church of God
Nauvoo, Alabama

COUNTRY-STYLE PORK CHOPS WITH PAN GRAVY

YIELD: 4 TO 6 SERVINGS

3 tablespoons flour
Salt and black pepper to taste
6 pork chops
2 tablespoons fat
½ teaspoon salt
2 cups cold water

Preheat the oven to 325°. Put 2 tablespoons of the flour in a shallow dish and mix in salt and pepper to taste. Roll the chops in the flour. Heat a large, heavy skillet and put the fat in the skillet when the skillet is hot. Brown the chops quickly on both sides. Remove from pan. Add the remaining 1 tablespoon flour to the hot grease; brown the flour, and mix in the ½ teaspoon salt and 2 cups cold water. Add the chops to the gravy and bake for 1 hour.

Variation: Steak is delicious cooked by the same recipe.

Favorite Recipes Old and New
North Carolina Federation
    of Home Demonstration Clubs
Raleigh, North Carolina

LIVER PUDDIN'

Down Charleston way, pâtés are passé, but liver puddin' goes great with grits.

YIELD: 16 TO 20 SERVINGS

1 pound pork end loin pieces with bone
    and fat
3 pounds pork liver
2 teaspoons salt
1 teaspoon pepper
2 tablespoons cornmeal
1 envelope gelatin, dissolved in ¼ cup cold
    water

Boil the pork and the pork liver with salt and pepper in water to cover for 45 minutes. Let cool. Reserve broth. Remove from the pot, reserving the stock. Remove the bones and grind the meat. Mix the ground mixture, broth, cornmeal, and gelatin. Put in a loaf pan or several small containers and chill.

Charleston Receipts Repeats
Junior League of Charleston
Charleston, South Carolina

BAKED HAM

YIELD: 12 TO 15 SERVINGS

1 (10- to 12-pound) ham
About 1½ cups prepared mustard
¼ teaspoon ground cloves
1 cup finely packed dark brown sugar
1 cup sherry

Preheat the oven to 300°. Rub the surface of the ham with about ¼ cup of the prepared mustard. Cover the ham with foil and place it in a roasting pan. Bake for 20 minutes per pound.

One hour before ham is done, remove it from the oven. Cover the ham again with a light coating of mustard, about ¼ cup, and sprinkle with ground cloves. Combine 1 cup each of prepared mustard, brown sugar, and sherry in a small bowl. Baste the ham with the mustard mixture and cover with foil. Continue cooking for the remaining hour.

A Southern Collection—Then and Now
Junior League of Columbus
Columbus, Georgia

COUNTRY-CURED HAM

According to Betty Talmadge, "There are no two people who cook country-cured ham the same way. There are no two hams that will come out looking and tasting exactly the same, no matter how similarly they are cooked. But I do have three ways to cook our country-cured hams, and I've never had a guest who didn't exclaim and usually ask that I record the steps from the ham house to the table. This puts me on the spot, because sometimes I soak them overnight, and sometimes I don't. Sometimes I bake them in the oven, and sometimes I boil them on top of the stove. Often, I just shave off a ¼-inch slice and fry it quickly and serve it with red-eye gravy." Here are the three methods for cooking ham, Talmadge-style.

OVEN-BAKING METHOD

Wash the ham thoroughly. Place it in a large container filled with warm water and soak overnight. Drain. Place it in a roaster. Pour 2 pints of cola or fruit juice and an equal amount of water over ham. Cover with lid or foil. Bake in a 350° oven 20 minutes to the pound (approximately 4 hours for a 12-pound ham). Remove the outer skin and cut off the excess fat. Score the remaining fat; insert cloves. Cover with brown sugar or a fruit glaze. Bake in a hot oven (450°) for 20 minutes, or until glazed or brown.

STOVETOP METHOD

Wash the ham thoroughly, soak overnight, and drain. Place the ham in a roasting pan in water to cover, along with 6 onions, 2 cups brown sugar, 1 pint vinegar, 2 bay leaves, and 24 cloves. Cover and simmer (do not boil) 20 minutes to the pound. The ham is done when the small bone at the hock end can be twisted out. Let the ham cool in the liquid. Then remove the skin and cut off the excess fat. Score and insert whole cloves. Glaze with a mixture of 1 cup brown sugar and 2 teaspoons dry mustard. Bake 20 minutes at 450° to glaze.

COUNTRY-FRYING METHOD

Cut slices ¼ inch thick (very important). Lightly grease pan with bacon fat or lard. Fry on each side and remove from pan immediately. To the hot fat remaining, add ¼ teaspoon sugar and 4 tablespoons water (or coffee). Cover the pan and simmer a few more minutes to make red-eye gravy, adding paprika to make gravy redder, if desired. Pour the gravy over the ham slices to serve.

Note: Serve any of the above with Sweet-and-Sour Mustard Sauce (page 236).

*How to Cook a Pig
and Other Back-to-the-Farm Recipes*
Betty Talmadge
Lovejoy, Georgia

JOHN EGERTON

THE PLEASURES OF THE SMOKEHOUSE

My grandfather on my mother's side was a miller. He had a flour and grist mill in Cadiz, Kentucky, where he made and marketed cornmeal and flour. When I was a boy, growing up around there in the thirties and forties, I used to hang out at the mill, a big old, tall, poured-concrete building. My grandfather was almost stone deaf, but it never came across as a handicap. He was a little bitty guy, slender and short. To look at him, you would think he couldn't do much. But in my country-boy eyes, he could do anything.

He lived on the edge of Cadiz, in a big brick house that he had built himself, sometime in the early part of the century. Back behind the house he had built a brick smokehouse, a really wonderful one, with a dirt floor and lots of cracks up around the eaves for the smoke to escape. In one corner there was a trough made from a big old hollow log, where he salted the hams. He designed that smokehouse right. It was tall and skinny, and had rafters where he would hang the hams and sausages so that all the grease dripped out onto that dirt floor.

I grew up with that smell, that wonderful aroma of smokehouse ham. I guarantee that if you found me such a place today and led me there blindfolded, I would start salivating the moment I walked in the door. The smell still drives me wild.

Now, if you walked across some flagstone steps and up a stairway to an enclosed porch, you would come upon my grandmother's biscuit brake. It looked like a Singer sewing machine with a marble top and a washing-machine wringer mounted on it. It was nickel-plated, and really quite a lovely contraption.

Biscuit making was my grandmother's department. Like my grandfather, she was small-framed—a short, birdlike little lady. She loved to make all kinds of biscuits, but she loved beaten biscuits best—especially when there was a country ham in the house.

So from the time my brother and I got to be strong enough to turn the crank on that biscuit brake, she would plop us down there and we would take turns cranking while she rolled the dough through. Nowadays, when I make beaten biscuits—which I do on ceremonial occasions—I get one of my sons to turn the crank, and I roll the dough through there. It requires a certain dexterity, a certain strength, and I think of that little woman, my grandmother, doing that, and I marvel at how she was able to control the dough, but she was really good at it. And she made superb beaten biscuits.

From the time I was seven or eight or so, I knew what an extraordinary culinary combination that was: to take a boiled or baked country ham—coated with my grandmother's special crust of bread crumbs, brown sugar, and black pepper—and slice it paper-thin so that you got a cross section with red ham meat, a little strip of fat, and finally the brown coating. That ham on a beaten biscuit is just about as near to a perfect comestible as I have ever tasted.

I've been eating country ham and beaten biscuits for at least fifty-five years. Tradition means a lot to me. It means almost as much as the flavor does. So I still go back to Cadiz, back to Trigg County, Kentucky, every year, to get my hams. There aren't many people who cure hams the old-fashioned way anymore.

But the tradition is not dying out on its own. It is being strangled to death by United States Department of Agriculture regulations that say unless you can document the temperature of the meat and other factors at every step along the way, the meat is unsafe. It is dangerous. Never mind that these hams have been made this way for a couple of hundred years, and as far as anyone knows, no one has ever died of food poisoning from eating a traditionally cured ham. The USDA has decreed that these hams are dangerous. And dangerous means that you can't send them through the mail, but if somebody wants to drive to your house and pick one up, that's okay. That won't make you sick.

There are a lot of mysteries in life. And that's one I've never been able to figure out. But it saddens me to know that something as old and rich and vital as this—a true culinary art, like winemaking—may soon be lost forever.

John Egerton is the author of Southern Food, Speak Now Against the Day, *and numerous other works. He lives in Nashville, Tennessee.*

COUNTRY HAM AND RED-EYE GRAVY

Made from ham drippings, a bit of water, and a dash of coffee, this gravy gets its name from the appearance of a red eye at the center of the reduced gravy.

YIELD: 6 SERVINGS

Sugar
6 (¼-inch-thick) slices of ham,
  with fat
½ cup cold water
2 tablespoons brewed coffee

Sprinkle sugar lightly on each side of the ham before cooking (this really does bring out flavor), then fry. Remove from the pan when done; pour off the grease. Put ½ cup cold water in the skillet and allow it to boil; add the brewed coffee and 1 teaspoon sugar to make the gravy.

Huntsville Entertains
Huntsville Historic Foundation
Huntsville, Alabama

HAM LOAF

Kissing cousin to the meat loaf, this Sunday dinner staple puts the pig at center stage.

YIELD: 20 SERVINGS

2 pounds ground smoked ham
2 pounds ground fresh uncooked pork
1½ cups fresh cracker crumbs

½ cup chopped onion
4 eggs, well beaten
1¼ teaspoons salt
2 cups milk
2 tablespoons finely chopped fresh
  parsley
Glaze (recipe follows)
Mustard Sauce (recipe follows)

Preheat the oven to 350°. Combine the ham and pork; set aside. Combine the cracker crumbs, onion, eggs, salt, milk and parsley in a large bowl. Add the meat mixture and mix thoroughly. Shape into 2 loaves and put into two 9x5x3-inch loaf pans. Bake 30 minutes. Remove the loaves from the oven, baste with glaze, and bake 1 hour longer. Remove the loaves from the pans. Serve 1 tablespoon Mustard Sauce on each slice of ham loaf. Serve the remaining sauce at the table.

GLAZE

8 ounces (1 cup plus 2 tablespoons) firmly
  packed brown sugar
½ cup apple cider vinegar
1½ tablespoons dry mustard

Combine all the ingredients in a saucepan; boil for 1 minute before using to baste ham loaves.

MUSTARD SAUCE

½ cup mayonnaise
½ cup sour cream
¼ cup prepared mustard
1 tablespoon minced chives
2 tablespoons or more horseradish

Combine all the ingredients in a small bowl; mix well before serving.

Virginia Celebrates
Council of the Virginia Museum of Fine Arts
Richmond, Virginia

PIGS' FEET

Known to many as trotters, pigs' feet are as favored in France as they are in Dixie. They call them pieds à porc. *We call them good eating.*

YIELD: 4 TO 6 SERVINGS

6 pigs' feet
2 cups apple cider vinegar
3 blades of mace
1 dozen whole cloves
2 bay leaves
1 red pepper pod
Salt, black pepper, and cayenne to taste

Select young and tender pigs' feet. Clean and scrape well and soak in cold water several hours. Split and crack the feet in several places and put them in a stewpot. Cover with cold water and simmer until tender. When done, lay in a crock. Boil the vinegar, mace, cloves, bay leaves, and pepper pod together for 2 or 3 minutes. Season the feet to taste with salt, black pepper, and cayenne. Pour the spiced vinegar over the feet while boiling. Cover the crock and set aside to let cool. The feet will be ready in 24 hours.

The Picayune's Creole Cookbook
New Orleans, Louisiana

OVEN-BAKED PIGS' FEET

YIELD: 4 TO 6 SERVINGS

6 pigs' feet
1 large onion, sliced
1 clove garlic
1 teaspoon vinegar
3 or 4 whole black peppercorns
1 teaspoon salt
6 whole cloves
Melted butter or bacon fat
Bread crumbs or cornmeal

Wash the pigs' feet. Cover with water in a saucepan. Bring to a boil. Reduce the heat and simmer, covered, for 3 hours. Add the onion, garlic, vinegar, peppercorns, salt, and cloves. Simmer 30 minutes longer. Let cool in the cooking water.

Preheat the oven to 450°. Remove the pigs' feet, let drain, and dry or pat dry with a folded clean dish towel or paper towels. Split each foot in two lengthwise. Roll in melted butter or bacon fat, then in bread crumbs or cornmeal. Place in a shallow baking pan. Bake for about 15 minutes, or until nicely browned.

From Rose Budd's Kitchen
Rose Budd Stevens
Amite County, Mississippi

ROY BLOUNT, JR.

MY MOTHER'S GRAVIES

There's a Memphis Minnie song called "Selling My Pork Chops." The refrain is "I'm selling my pork chops, but I'm giving my gravy away." Gravy is a personal expression of the soul. You can't sell gravy.

My mother tended to make thinnish gravy, thin in terms of physical bulk and globbiness. Her gravy was never globby. You had no notion you were getting fat from it. But I guess you were.

I remember my mother's giblet gravy. Just thick enough. Just loose enough. For Thanksgiving and Christmas she would make cornbread dressing as opposed to stuffing, which you run into in the North. (I feel a little strange about eating something out of the inside of a turkey. Of course, giblets have been in there, but that's different.) My mother made it gritty but also moist. The things that are great are fusions of opposites: gritty and moist, thick and thin, chunky and runny. And you got all those things combined when you put some of my mother's giblet gravy on top of my mother's cornbread dressing. It had savor. It had texture.

She also made wonderful beef stew with onions and potatoes and carrots. When she finished cooking it, little glistening, round grease circles floated on top of the gravy. Now, that might sound off-putting, but I remember those glistening gravy circles as if they were little halos. The gravy somehow managed to be greasy yet light.

Of course, she also made red-eye gravy. You wouldn't think that a mixture of coffee and grease would be good. In fact, it doesn't even seem like it would mix. It didn't. What you got was coffee suspended in ham juice or vice versa. The coffee gave it a bit of bitterness that cut the grease. And it was wonderful with grits.

But there's a sad side to gravy. The terrible thing about gravy is it's so hard to get at all of it. It slips off into the corners. You can't get it with a spoon or a fork, so you've got to have something to sop it with. That's what white bread and cornbread were made for—sopping. But even then you can't quite get it all.

Roy Blount, Jr., a native of Decatur, Georgia, is the author of, among other works, Be Sweet, *a memoir, and editor of* Roy Blount's Book of Southern Humor.

Chittlins

It has been said that hog meat, in one form or another, is the Mississippian's staple diet. Considering how we eat it fresh in winter, cured in spring, and salted in summer, and how we use the belly fat with vegetables the year round, we have to admit that pork is certainly our dish.

We favor the small intestines for our chittlin feast, but the small ones come in right handy for casing the sausage meat, so the large intestines will do. It takes a keen knife to split them from end to end, then they must be scraped and washed until they are good and white. They have to soak overnight in salted water, but since we ourselves are too tired from hog sticking to do the dish justice, we can it.

By sunup Ma has drained the chittlins and put them to boil in fresh salted water. She does this outdoors, since boiling chittlins have a right high stench and she won't have them smelling up her kitchen. After they boil tender, Ma takes them out and cuts them into pieces two or three inches long. She says you can meal them or flour them according to your fancy, but she always meals hers and fries them crisp in deep fat. Those that like 'em extra hot put red pepper and sage in the boiling water, and everybody sees that there's plenty of catsup and salt and pepper on the table.

Collected by Kate C. Hubbard in Possum & Pomegranate *for the Federal Writers Project "America Eats"*

CHITTLINS

Chitterlings—or chittlins, as we really call them—are the pig's innards. Like so many elements of African American cooking, these unwanted parts were taken, scrupulously cleaned, seasoned, cooked, and transformed into a delicacy with loving attention.

YIELD: 12 SERVINGS

10 pounds frozen chittlins, thawed
¼ cup vinegar
1 large potato, cut in half
2 medium onions, quartered
1 stalk celery, cut into thirds
2 cloves garlic
1 tablespoon salt
2 bay leaves
½ teaspoon crushed red pepper
Hot cooked rice, for serving
Hot pepper sauce, for serving

To clean the chittlins, wash and scrub, using a small brush, in warm water in a sink. Rub to remove excess fat and residue. Wash and rinse several times until water runs clear; drain. Place chittlins, cold water to cover, vinegar, potato, onions, celery, garlic, salt, bay leaves, and crushed red pepper in a large saucepan. Boil on high heat. Reduce the heat to medium, cover, and simmer 1½ to 2 hours, or until tender. Discard the potato. Remove the chittlins from the saucepan and let cool slightly. Cut into pieces. Serve over rice with pepper sauce.

Celebrating Our Mothers' Kitchens
National Council of Negro Women
Washington, D.C.

TOM RANKIN

THE HUNTER

One weekend in early December a couple of years ago, I headed down to our deer camp in Copiah County, Mississippi, with Larry Brown, a good friend and a great novelist, for what was Larry's first hunt in many, many years. We hunt on about 600 acres down there, mostly white oak bottoms and pine ridges.

I put Larry up in a stand at about four forty-five on that Friday afternoon, and by five-fifteen he had killed a nice buck. By five-thirty, I was standing by his side. The first thing he said to me was, "I hate that I killed your buck, bro. But now the pressure's off." Larry didn't know if he could go back home if he missed his first shot at a deer in nearly eighteen years.

We cleaned it that night, and when I asked him if he was going to hunt with us the next morning, he said, "No, I got my deer. I'm just going to enjoy myself." I think he stayed up half the night reading.

That next morning, the rest of us headed out at five-thirty or so to hunt, returning to camp at around ten to find that Larry had been up since eight cooking—like a housewife waiting for the hunters to return. He had taken the backstrap and tenderloin from the deer and sliced them, like he describes in his novel *Joe*.

He had them turn the deer on its side and then he tested the edge of the blade against his thumb.

"This is the best meat on it right there," he said, and he put the tip of the knife just behind the shoulder and sank it into the meat.

"Just hold it steady now," he said. He pushed the knife down until he felt it stop against the first rib and drew it down, slicing the backstrap away from the vertebrae all the way down to the hip.

"Where did y'all get this deer?"

"It was hung up in a fence up at Mr. Lee's old house a while ago," Stacy said. "He and Henry was comin back from town and seen it. I come home and got George's pistol and shot it."

He cut deeply just behind the shoulder and just ahead of the hip, then took the knife forward under the meat and sliced toward his belly with the tip until he could grasp a corner of the loin and pull it up. He worked the blade back and forth against the ribs, pulling the meat up in a single strip and

*keeping the blade close against the bone. It came up smoothly, the white
sinew wrinkling over the dark burgundy flesh until he passed the knife all the
way down the ribs and held in his hand a thick strip of meat almost two feet
long. He laid it on the table.*

"That's some good stuff there," he said. "Look here."

*He placed the top side down and cut and squared off the end and pushed
the scrap aside with the knife. He cut off a loin steak two inches thick, then
cut halfway through it again, so that when he spread it with his fingers it had
doubled in size.*

"That's how you do it. Butterfly steak. That's the best meat on it."

After butterflying, Larry had rolled the steaks in flour and pepper and fried
them, making a gravy with the pan juices and oil. He had also made about two dozen
biscuits, a big pot of grits, scrambled eggs, coffee, and a bunch of Bloody Marys.

So when we got back to the hunt camp—there were five or six of us all together—we walked in the door to find this incredible feast. We split the biscuits open,
poured the venison gravy on top, and cut into the meat. The meat was wonderful, tender and delicate. Only twelve hours had passed since Larry shot the buck.

It had been more than a decade and a half since Larry had been hunting. And at
this point in the trip, no one else had killed a deer. That meal was Larry's way of
sharing his largesse—and of affirming what he had done. He was the hunter. It was
his meat, and he was going to share it with us.

*A native of Louisville, Kentucky, photographer and folklorist Tom Rankin is the author
of* Sacred Space *and other books. He is the executive director of the Center for Documentary
Studies at Duke University. Larry Brown is the author of, among other works,* Joe *and*
Father and Son. *He lives out from Yocona in rural Lafayette County, Mississippi.*

BURGUNDY ROAST VENISON

By early winter, freezers are full of venison, the huntsman's prize for an eternity spent in a tree stand, rifle sighted on the deer that darts out from cover of the woods. Here's a roast recipe suited for the hunt camp or home.

YIELD: 6 TO 8 SERVINGS

2½ *pounds boneless venison roast*
  or loin
½ *cup meat marinade or teriyaki sauce*
¼ *cup butter or margarine*
1 *large onion, sliced*
8 *ounces white mushrooms, sliced*
1 *teaspoon salt*
1 *teaspoon black pepper*
1 *teaspoon garlic powder*
1 *cup burgundy wine*

Slice the meat into serving-size pieces. Place in a large zip-top plastic bag. Add the marinade. Seal the bag and marinate in the refrigerator for 1 hour, turning occasionally.

Remove the meat. Grill on a preheated gas or electric grill, turning to thoroughly brown the meat on both sides. While the meat is grilling, melt the butter in a pressure cooker pan and sauté the onion and mushrooms for 12 to 15 minutes. Add the salt, black pepper, and garlic powder to the vegetables. Place the browned meat in the pressure cooker with the vegetables. Pour the wine over meat. Close the pressure cooker and cook at 15 pounds pressure for 15 minutes, or until meat is tender.

Note: This roast can also be cooked in the oven at 325° or in a slow-cooker, with cooking time lengthened accordingly.

Campsite to Kitchen
Outdoor Writers Association of America
Memphis, Tennessee

FRIED CHITTERLINGS

YIELD: 4 TO 6 SERVINGS

2 *pounds chitterlings*
1 *tablespoon whole cloves*
1 *red bell pepper, chopped*
Fat for deep frying
1 *tablespoon water*
1 *egg, lightly beaten*
Cracker crumbs

Wash the chitterlings thoroughly. Remove the membrane and cover with boiling salted water. Add the cloves and bell pepper. Simmer at least 1 hour, or until tender; drain.

Heat the fat to 370°. Add the 1 tablespoon of water to the egg and beat in lightly. Cut the chitterlings into pieces the size of oysters. Dip each piece in the egg mixture, then in the cracker crumbs. Deep-fry in the fat until brown.

Soul Food
Albert Ikner
San Jose, California

Venison Roast

Yield: 16 to 20 servings

1 quart vinegar
1 quart water
1 tablespoon salt
1 tablespoon dried hot red pepper flakes
1 tablespoon black pepper
3 cloves garlic, minced, plus more for inserting
   in roast
3 bay leaves
1 teaspoon cloves
1 teaspoon allspice
1 teaspoon thyme
1 (8- to 10-pound) venison roast
8 ounces salt pork, cut into strips
1 cup currant jelly
Flour for gravy
1 tablespoon brandy

In a bowl, combine the vinegar, water, salt, red pepper flakes, black pepper, garlic, bay leaves, cloves, allspice, and thyme. Place the roast in a roasting pan and pour the marinade over it. Let stand in the refrigerator for 6 to 8 hours, turning several times.

Preheat the oven to 325° or 350°. Before roasting, punch several holes in the roast with a sharp knife. Insert the salt pork with the additional garlic cloves. Bake for 20 to 25 minutes per pound, basting frequently with the drippings and the marinade. When the meat is tender, remove it from the pan and keep it warm while making the gravy.

In the pan, slowly melt the jelly with the drippings and the marinade. Measure the liquid and allow 2 tablespoons of flour for each cup.

Mix the flour with a little water and add to the pan to thicken the gravy. When the gravy is the desired consistency, add the brandy. Stir well and serve.

Louisiana Wildlife Magazine
Baton Rouge, Louisiana

Casserole of Possum

According to Jessica Harris, author of The Welcome Table *and authority on the foodways of the African Diaspora, possums "were the creatures most likely to be about after dark, when slaves were able to go hunting, so they were a frequent catch." Though this dish is rarely served in the urban South, it is still a favorite where tall trees outnumber tall buildings.*

Yield: 4 servings

1 (2-pound) dressed, washed possum
1 tablespoon salt
2 pods red pepper, divided
2 tablespoons flour
1½ pounds sweet potatoes, peeled and
   halved

Place the possum in a 3-quart saucepan. Add 5 cups cold water, the salt, and 1 pod red pepper. Heat to boiling; reduce heat, cover, and simmer for 1½ hours.

Preheat the oven to 350°. Drain the broth, reserving 1 cup. Place the possum in a baking dish. Sprinkle with the flour and the remaining pod of crushed red pepper. Put two halves of sweet potato inside the body. Arrange the remaining

B. B. KING

THE SUNDAY FEAST

Usually, we sharecroppers would get an advance around the first of March, with the money given out according to the size of the family. That was supposed to last until July, but a lot of times it ran out long before July came. So we would fill up on whatever we could. Some folks would hunt rabbits or possums or coons, and then we would hang them up and smoke them. And we grew white potatoes to use as a substitute when we ran out of cornmeal.

But one day a week, we feasted. Sunday was a special day for food, my special day for food. It was a joy to have dinner on Sunday. (Back then we didn't use the words for meals that we do now. Back then we had breakfast, dinner, and supper. Nowadays, we have breakfast, lunch, and dinner, which still throws me off a bit.) And breakfast was special too. If we were lucky, we might have a fried T-bone steak in the morning before heading off for church. And biscuits, we always had buttered biscuits on Sunday mornings, with preserves that we put up ourselves.

At dinner, we really ate. We would have greens—mustards, turnips, collards, maybe cabbage. And lima beans, crowder peas, black-eyed peas—not all at the same time but they all showed up. And sweet yams, I still love them today.

We usually had pork of some kind, maybe ham hocks or fried ham. And we loved chicken, either baked or fried. For dessert, there would always be a cake or two, maybe chocolate or coconut. But my favorites were sweet potato pies and custards. I loved those soupy pies with the dough crust on top.

On that one day we feasted. It was just family (we would have been happy to have guests, but I don't remember many), and that was our day for eating. Everybody looked forward to Sunday dinner.

Today I have to watch my diet. I am a diabetic so I have to watch out for sugar. And I no longer eat meat. But I still love some of the same foods. I still love yams. I travel a lot now, but I'm kind of like the tortoise, I carry my house with me. I carry my yams with me.

B. B. King, born near Itta Bena, Mississippi, out from Indianola, is perhaps the most revered bluesman of the modern era.

potatoes around the body. Pour the reserved broth around the possum. Bake, covered, until the meat and potatoes are tender. Remove the cover and bake until golden brown.

A Good Heart and a Light Hand
Ruth L. Gaskins
Alexandria, Virginia

RABBIT PIE

Rabbits have long been a favorite of the hunter, and now farm-raised rabbits are coming to the fore, as a new generation of cooks discovers the dark, delicate taste of this meat.

YIELD: 4 TO 6 SERVINGS

1 rabbit
Vinegar
Salt and pepper to taste
Flour
2 onions, chopped
2 medium carrots, chopped
2 to 3 potatoes, cut up
Biscuit dough

Rabbit should be decapitated and dressed immediately after shooting. After skinning, wipe the carcass with a cloth dipped in scalding water to remove loose hair. Alternatively, dressed rabbit can be purchased at many grocery stores.

Cut the rabbit into serving pieces. Soak in equal parts vinegar and water for 12 to 24 hours.

Drain and wipe dry. Sprinkle with salt and pepper and dredge with flour. Sear quickly in a skillet. Place in a pot, add water to cover, cover

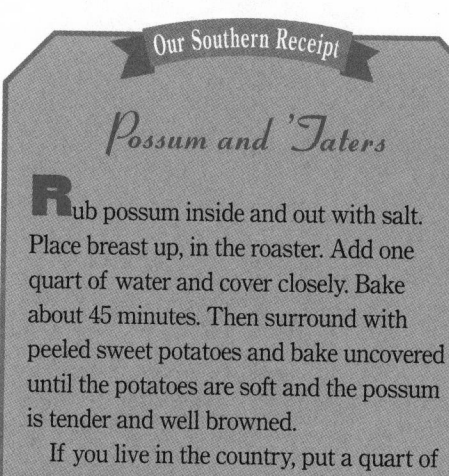

Our Southern Receipt

Possum and 'Taters

Rub possum inside and out with salt. Place breast up, in the roaster. Add one quart of water and cover closely. Bake about 45 minutes. Then surround with peeled sweet potatoes and bake uncovered until the potatoes are soft and the possum is tender and well browned.

If you live in the country, put a quart of hardwood ashes in a pot of boiling water and scald possum in that. If you live in town, you'll just have to put a tablespoon of lye in the pot of water. Scrape the possum carefully so as not to break the skin.

Collected by Kate C. Hubbard in Possum & Pomegranate *for the Federal Writers Project "America Eats"*

the pot, and simmer slowly for 1½ hours. Add the onion, carrot, and potato. Cook until the vegetables are done. Thicken with flour. Cook in a greased baking dish in a 425° oven until bubbling. Cover with biscuit dough and return to the oven to bake until the dough is done.

Charleston Receipts
Junior League of Charleston
Charleston, South Carolina

POULTRY

....

A SOUTHERN WAY OF CARING

Somehow in rural Southern culture, food is always the first thought of neighbors when there is trouble. . . . "Here I brought you some fresh eggs for breakfast. And here's a cake and some potato salad." It means "I love you. And I am sorry for what you are going through and I will share as much of the burden as I can." And maybe potato salad is a better way of saying it.

WILL D. CAMPBELL, *BROTHER TO A DRAGONFLY*

A Southern Way of Caring

························

When a death occurs in the South, news spreads quickly. Chalk it up to our celebrated sense of community or good, old-fashioned gossip, but nevertheless, little time elapses between the passing of the loved one and the passing of the potato salad. Like some maternal, military task force trained in the ways and means of aggressive Southern hospitality, they descend upon the home of the closest living relation. Each ring of the doorbell, each rap on the screen door signals the arrival of another relative, neighbor, Bible school classmate, coworker, club member, or friend. They need not knock; we were expecting them. For in the South, fried chicken follows a funeral as sure as grits follow scrambled eggs.

Granted, in times of trouble, folks up North and out West have been known to bake a cake or boil up a pot of beef stew. Yet Southerners, ever inclined toward exaggeration in both word and deed, are in a league all their own when it comes to sharing a soul's burden through the sharing of food.

In the South, if your second cousin, whom you have not seen since she moved away three years ago, calls to express her sorrow upon learning of the "passing of your momma," and promises to "be over directly with a little somethin'," you had best retrieve the card tables from the cellar: three casseroles of macaroni and cheese will soon be arriving at your front door.

Filled to overflowing with simple foods that hark back to simpler times, the casserole is a leitmotif of the Southern funeral food tradition. Corn pudding, cheese grits, Hoppin' John, and Limpin' Susan; sweet potato souffle, squash casserole, spinach pie, and maquechou: these one-pot, covered-dish meals are remnants of a shared culinary past, when cooks, black and white, native born and émigré, sated both creative impulse and economic necessity by making do with whatever was on hand.

Though we Southerners have since begun to cook in a more health-conscious fashion, in years past, these dishes did not want for butter, sugar, and pork. One more stick of butter, an extra cup of sugar, or another link of sausage was often added to the pot as a sort of gastronomic rebuke of the Grim Reaper.

Tales of the excesses of the Southern table are legend. Yet mere extravagance was not the motivation for the largesse of the Southern funeral food tradition. And despite delicious claims to the contrary, the primary impetus was not symbolic. Rural isolation and the scarcity of hotels and restaurants were more likely reasons.

In times past, much of the activity centered on the family home instead of the funeral home. After the body had been prepared for burial and laid out on the cooling board, mourners began to gather at the house of the bereaved to pay their respects. Neighbors and friends alike opened their homes and hearts to these weary pilgrims. Couches were folded out into beds, children were encouraged to stay over with friends, and pallets were laid out on the floor.

Lodging thus secured, the women of the community went to work in the kitchen. Their efforts were nothing less than awe-inspiring. Charged with feeding any and all who graced their threshold or that of the bereaved, they fried chicken, baked cakes, and chopped coleslaw with abandon. No matter the sheer quantity of their output, nothing went to waste, for Southern communities, ever fond of ceremony and circum-

stance, turned out for funerals en masse. And everybody turned out hungry.

Some things never change. Though fast-food restaurants and economy motels now dot the Southern landscape, and strip malls have replaced courthouse squares as community centers, Southern funeral food traditions endure. Neighbors still welcome distant relatives into their homes; pound cakes, potato salad, and sweet potato casserole still vie for space on hurriedly erected card tables; and home-cooked foods still mean, "I love you. And I am sorry for what you are going through and I will share as much of the burden as I can."

FRIED CHICKEN

There is no such thing as Southern fried chicken. Instead, there is chicken fried in the South, and the variations are as myriad as the cooks. This version relies on a covered skillet for juiciness.

YIELD: 6 SERVINGS

3 cups vegetable oil
1½ cups flour
¼ teaspoon salt
¼ teaspoon pepper
¼ teaspoon paprika
1 chicken, fat and skin removed, cut into pieces
¾ cup buttermilk

Heat the oil in large cast-iron skillet on medium heat until hot. Combine the flour, salt, pepper, and paprika. Dip each chicken part in the buttermilk, then in the flour mixture. Be sure the oil is very hot before putting the chicken pieces in;

otherwise, chicken will be greasy. Brown chicken about 10 minutes on each side with the skillet covered. Remove the cover and turn up the heat to medium-high; cook the chicken 5 minutes longer on each side or until crisp. Remove and drain well on paper towels. Serve hot or cold.

Impressions
Auxiliary to the Memphis Dental Society
Memphis, Tennessee

BUTTERMILK FRIED CHICKEN

An uncovered version of the classic.

YIELD: 4 SERVINGS

1 (3- to 3½-pound) chicken, cut into serving pieces
1½ teaspoons salt
⅞ teaspoon black pepper
1½ cups flour
½ teaspoon cayenne pepper
¼ teaspoon paprika
1 large egg, lightly beaten
½ cup buttermilk
Vegetable oil

Season chicken with ½ teaspoon of the salt and ⅛ teaspoon of the black pepper. In a small bowl, combine the flour with the remaining 1 teaspoon salt, the remaining ¾ teaspoon black pepper, the cayenne, and the paprika; stir well. Mix the egg and the buttermilk together. Dip each piece of chicken in the egg mixture, then dredge in the flour mixture, coating well. Pour oil 1 inch deep in a large skillet; heat to 350°. Add the chicken

and fry 20 to 25 minutes, or until golden, turning to brown on all sides. Drain well on paper towels.

Very Virginia
Junior League of Hampton Roads
Newport News, Virginia

SPICY FRIED CHICKEN

A spicier version of that old Southern favorite.

YIELD: 4 SERVINGS

1 (3-pound) broiler-fryer, cut into 8 pieces
Milk to cover
1½ teaspoons garlic powder
2 teaspoons seasoning salt
1 tablespoon ground black pepper
2 teaspoons cayenne pepper
1 cup flour
2 cups vegetable oil

Put the chicken pieces in a large bowl and cover with milk. Refrigerate for 1 hour or longer. Drain the chicken and shake off the excess liquid. Mix the garlic powder, seasoning salt, black pepper, and cayenne; sprinkle the spices over the chicken so that the pieces are evenly coated.

Pour the flour into a large plastic bag and add the chicken pieces, a few at a time, shaking gently. As the pieces are floured, transfer them to a wire rack or a sheet of waxed paper, placing them well apart from one another. Let stand for 20 to 25 minutes.

Heat the oil in a large, heavy skillet over high heat until it is nearly smoking. Add the chicken pieces in one layer; the fat should come halfway up the pieces. Cover and cook 10 to 12 minutes, or until golden brown on one side; turn the pieces and reduce the heat to medium-low. Continue cooking, covered, until evenly browned on both sides, turning as needed. Total cooking time should be 20 to 25 minutes. As the pieces are cooked through, remove them to a rack to drain.

Mother Africa's Table
National Council of Negro Women
Washington, D.C.

GEORGIA SMOTHERED CHICKEN

Kissin' cousin to the étouffées *of Louisiana, this smothered chicken dish is an after-church favorite.*

YIELD: 4 TO 6 SERVINGS

1 medium fryer, cut into serving pieces
Salt and pepper to taste
½ stick (4 tablespoons) unsalted margarine
¼ cup flour

Juice of ½ lemon

2 tablespoons Worcestershire sauce

1½ cups water

Season the chicken with salt and pepper. Let stand 1 hour. Preheat the oven to 500°. Place the chicken in a 9x13-inch baking dish: dot with the margarine. Sprinkle with the flour. Bake until brown; reduce the heat to 350°. Add the lemon juice, Worcestershire sauce, and water. Cover tightly with foil. Continue baking for 1 to 1½ hours, basting occasionally. Gravy may be thickened, if desired.

The Pastors Wives
Memphis, Tennessee

OVEN-BAKED CHICKEN WITH LEMON BARBECUE SAUCE

Though we love our chicken smoked in the back-yard pit, we Southerners are not averse to cheating . . . just a bit.

YIELD: 8 SERVINGS

¼ cup salad oil

¼ cup fresh lemon juice

2 tablespoons finely chopped onion

½ teaspoon thyme

1 cup flour

½ teaspoon salt

¼ teaspoon pepper

¼ teaspoon paprika

1 (3½-pound) fryer, cut up

¼ cup butter or margarine

Preheat the oven to 350°. In a small bowl, combine the oil, lemon juice, onion, and thyme. Sift together the flour, salt, pepper, and paprika. Coat the chicken well with the flour mixture. Melt the butter in a shallow baking pan; add chicken and coat on all sides with butter. Place chicken skin side down in baking pan. Bake for 30 minutes. Turn the chicken; pour the lemon barbecue sauce over the top. Continue baking for 20 minutes. Serve hot.

Favorite Recipes of the Deep South
Montgomery, Alabama

HERB-ROASTED CHICKEN

Granted, we have a love of things fried, and there are arguments that Southerners will eat even shoe leather too if it's battered and cooked in hot oil, but we do roast a chicken every once in a while!

YIELD: 4 SERVINGS

1 medium roasting hen

½ cup chopped fresh basil, or other fresh herbs

Salt and pepper

1 medium orange, quartered

½ cup dry white wine

5 to 8 cloves garlic, peeled

10 shallots

Preheat the broiler. Rinse the hen and pat dry. Loosen the skin over the breast and thighs and stuff the basil between the skin and the meat. Rub the cavity of the hen with salt and pepper.

Place the hen, breast side down, in a roasting pan and brown under the broiler, turning to brown on all sides. Remove from oven.

Lower the oven to 350°. Drain the grease from the pan. Squeeze the juice from the orange quarters over the hen, then place the used orange quarters inside the hen. Pour the wine over the hen and place the shallots and garlic around it. Roast, uncovered, for 20 minutes per pound, basting frequently. The hen is done if juices run clear when thigh is pierced with a fork. Transfer the hen to a serving platter and tent with foil to keep warm. Skim the fat from the pan juices. Bring to a boil and reduce to desired consistency. Slice the hen and serve with the pan juices.

The Artful Table
Dallas Museum of Art League
Dallas, Texas

CHICKEN AND RICE (ARROZ CON POLLO)

Pilau, purloo, and purlow are Southern varia-tions of the theme of chicken and rice. Count this Cuban version in their number.

YIELD: 6 TO 8 SERVINGS

2 slices of bacon, chopped
4 tablespoons olive oil
8 pieces of chicken (3 pounds)
3 cloves garlic, pressed
1 bell pepper, chopped fine
1 cup minced onion
1 cup peeled and seeded tomatoes
1 (2-ounce) jar diced pimientos
1 can petits pois, drained
½ teaspoon white pepper
¼ teaspoon cayenne pepper
⅛ teaspoon ground nutmeg
5 cups water
2 cups white rice
½ cup cognac
2 small bay leaves
½ teaspoon saffron
1 tablespoon salt

Heat a pressure cooker on a high burner for about 5 minutes. Place the bacon in the food processor and pulse two or three times before re-moving it to fry in the pressure cooker. Fry the bacon until it is almost crisp. Add the oil and fry the chicken lightly. Add the garlic, bell pepper, onion, tomatoes, pimientos, peas, white pepper, cayenne, and nutmeg and fry for about 5 min-utes; add the water and let it come to a boil. Add the rice, cognac, bay leaves, saffron, and salt; cover the cooker until steam escapes, then set the escape valve and bring to 15 pounds pressure. Set the burner on low setting and allow to cook for 10 minutes. (If your cooker has a gauge, cook at 10 pounds of pressure for 10 minutes.)

Remove the pressure cooker from the burner; allow it to cool on its own. Remove the bay leaves before serving. Transfer to a heated casserole for serving.

La Cocina Cubana Sencilla
Paul L. Adams
Louisville, Kentucky

CRAIG CLAIBORNE

THANKSGIVING SPAGHETTI

There is one aroma that, more than any other, rekindles concrete thoughts of my mother in the kitchen. This is the smell of chopped onions, chopped celery, chopped green pepper, and a generous amount of finely minced garlic. This was the basis for, it seems to me in recollection, at least half of the hundreds of dishes that she prepared, and it is a distinctly Southern smell.

And there is one dish, her own creation, and using this base, that I recall most vividly. This was chicken spaghetti, which she almost invariably made for special occasions—birthdays, holidays, Sundays. The boarders and her own family loved it, and it has remained throughout my many years in the world of food a special favorite.

There were two holidays each year—Christmas and Thanksgiving—when my mother stipulated that meals would not be served to boarders, all of whom went to visit relatives or friends anyway. I remember one nonturkey Thanksgiving that came about because the three children in the family announced that they were bored with a daily diet of poultry. A vote was taken. Almost in unison we asked for Mother's baked spaghetti. On that day we had it fresh from the oven for the midday Thanksgiving dinner, and reheated for supper.

When the vegetables were cooked (they always remained al dente), a little ground beef was added and a tomato sauce containing cream, Worcestershire sauce, and Tabasco. Worcestershire sauce and Tabasco were primary ingredients in my mother's kitchen. Once the meat and tomato sauce were finished, the time came for the assembly of the dish. A layer of sauce was topped with a layer of cooked spaghetti or vermicelli, a layer of shredded chicken, and a layer of grated cheddar cheese. The layers were repeated to the brim of an enormous roasting pan, ending with a layer of cheese. The pan was placed in the oven and baked until it was bubbling throughout and golden brown on top. The spaghetti was served in soup bowls with grated Parmesan cheese and two curious but oddly complimentary side dishes—sliced garlic pickles and potato chips.

MY MOTHER'S CHICKEN SPAGHETTI

YIELDS: 12 OR MORE SERVINGS

1 (3½-pound) chicken with giblets
Fresh or canned chicken broth to cover
Salt
3 cups imported Italian peeled tomatoes
7 tablespoons unsalted butter
3 tablespoons flour
½ cup heavy cream
⅛ teaspoon grated nutmeg
Freshly ground black pepper
8 ounces fresh mushrooms
2 cups finely chopped onion

1½ cups finely chopped celery
1½ cups chopped seeded green pepper
1 tablespoon or more finely minced garlic
¼ pound ground beef
¼ pound ground pork
1 bay leaf
½ teaspoon hot red pepper flakes (optional)
1 pound spaghetti or spaghettini
½ pound cheddar cheese, grated (about
  2 to 2½ cups)
Freshly grated Parmesan cheese, for serving

1. Place the chicken with neck, gizzard, heart, and liver in a kettle and add chicken broth to cover and salt to taste. Partially cover. Bring to a boil and simmer until the chicken is tender without being dry, 35 to 45 minutes. Let cool.

2. Remove the chicken and take the meat from the bones. Shred the meat, cover, and set aside. Return the skin and bones to the kettle and cook the stock down for 30 minutes or longer. There should be 4 to 6 cups of broth. Strain and reserve the broth. Discard the skin and bones.

3. Meanwhile, put the tomatoes in a saucepan and cook down to half the original volume, stirring.

4. Melt 3 tablespoons of the butter in a saucepan and add the flour, stirring to blend with a wire whisk. When blended and smooth, add 1 cup of the reserved hot broth and the cream, stirring rapidly with the whisk. When thickened and smooth, add the nutmeg and salt and pepper to taste. Continue cooking, stirring occasionally, for about 10 minutes. Set aside.

5. If the mushrooms are very small, leave them whole. Otherwise, cut them in half or quarter them. Heat 1 tablespoon of the remaining butter in a small skillet and add the mushrooms. Cook, shaking the skillet occasionally and stirring, until the mushrooms are golden brown. Set aside.

6. Heat the remaining 3 tablespoons of butter in a deep skillet and add the onion. Cook, stirring, until wilted. Add the celery and green pepper and cook, stirring, for about 5 minutes. Do not overcook. The vegetables should remain crisp-tender.

7. Add the garlic, beef, and pork and cook, stirring and chopping down with the edge of a large metal spoon to break up the meat. Cook just until the meat loses its red color. Add the bay leaf, and red pepper flakes if desired. Add the tomatoes and the white sauce made with the chicken broth. Add the mushrooms.

8. Cook the spaghetti in 3 or 4 quarts of boiling salted water until it is just tender. Do not overcook. Remember that it will cook again when blended with the chicken and meat sauce. Drain the spaghetti and run under cold running water.

9. Spoon enough of the meat sauce over the bottom of a 5- or 6-quart casserole to cover it lightly. Add about one-third of the spaghetti. Add about one-third of the shredded chicken, a layer of meat sauce, and a layer of grated cheddar cheese. Continue making layers, ending with a layer of spaghetti topped with a thin layer of meat sauce and grated cheddar cheese.

10. Pour in up to 2 cups of the reserved chicken broth or enough to almost but not quite cover the top layer of spaghetti. At this point the dish may be left to stand, covered, for up to an hour. If the liquid is absorbed as the dish stands, add a little more chicken broth. Remember that when this dish is baked and served, the sauce will be just a bit soupy rather than thick and clinging.

11. When ready to bake, preheat the oven to 350°.

12. Place the spaghetti casserole on top of the stove and bring it just to the boil. Cover and place it in the oven. Bake for 15 minutes and uncover. Bake for 15 minutes longer, or until the casserole is hot and bubbling throughout and starting to brown on top. Serve immediately with grated Parmesan cheese on the side.

A native of Sunflower, Mississippi, Craig Claiborne was the long-serving food editor of The New York Times. *This excerpt is from his 1982 memoir* A Feast Made for Laughter.

COUNTRY CAPTAIN CHICKEN

One theory for the presence of curry in this recipe is that it came to Georgia from India by way of British sea captains.

YIELD: 8 TO 10 SERVINGS

1½ cups flour
Salt
Freshly ground black pepper
Paprika
2 frying chickens, cut into pieces
6 tablespoons unsalted margarine
6 tablespoons vegetable oil
2 large onions, chopped
1 cup chopped green bell pepper
2 cloves garlic, minced
1 tablespoon curry powder
2½ cups stewed tomatoes with liquid
1 cup golden raisins
4 cups steamed rice, for serving
1 cup chopped peanuts or 8 ounces toasted
   almonds, for topping

Combine the flour, salt, black pepper, and paprika in a paper bag. Shake the chicken pieces in the flour mixture until coated. Shake off the excess flour.

Combine the margarine and oil in a large skillet; heat until sizzling. Brown the chicken on all sides over medium-high heat. Remove the chicken pieces, reduce the heat to medium-low, and allow the fat to cool a little. Add the onion, bell pepper, and garlic to the pan and stir until soft but not browned. Add the curry powder and tomatoes; stir until blended. Return the chicken to the pan, cover, and cook over low heat for 25 to 30 minutes, or until the chicken is tender. Remove the chicken pieces to a platter and keep warm.

Turn the heat to high and reduce the liquid until thickened, stirring frequently. Taste and correct the seasonings. Stir in the raisins. Spoon the sauce over the chicken and serve with rice. Top with the peanuts or toasted almonds.

Augusta Cooks for Company
Augusta Council of the Georgia Association for
   Children and Adults with Learning Disabilities
Augusta, Georgia

CHICKEN AND DUMPLINGS

Some folks call dumplings wet biscuits. Down South, we know them as ballast in a bowl of chicken, broth, and vegetables.

YIELD: 4 SERVINGS

1 (3-pound) chicken
1 small onion, sliced
1 carrot, sliced
1 stalk celery, including leaves
6 black peppercorns
1 teaspoon salt
3 tablespoons unsalted butter
3 tablespoons flour
⅛ teaspoon paprika
½ cup half-and-half
White pepper to taste
Dumplings (recipe follows)

Place the chicken, onion, carrot, celery, peppercorns, and salt in a pot and add water to cover. Simmer 1 hour, or until tender. Remove from the broth; when cool, remove the meat from the bones and cut the meat into 1-inch cubes. Strain the stock; add water if needed to make 2½ cups.

Melt the butter in a Dutch oven; mix the flour with the paprika and stir into the butter. Add the chicken stock gradually, stirring until slightly thickened. Add the half-and-half; season with white pepper to taste. Add the chicken and heat until the mixture is slowly bubbling.

Prepare the dumpling dough according to the recipe that follows.

Dip a teaspoon into cold water, then into the dumpling dough. Spoon the dough onto the chicken mixture about ½ teaspoon at a time, pressing some of the dumplings down into the pot with the back of a spoon. Cook, covered, over medium-low heat for 15 minutes without lifting the lid. The correct cooking temperature is critical at this point. It should be high enough to just bubble gently; if too high, chicken will stick and burn on the bottom.

Dumplings

1 cup all-purpose flour
½ teaspoon salt
2 teaspoons baking powder
½ tablespoon shortening
⅓ cup milk

Sift together the flour, salt, and baking powder into a large bowl. Blend in the shortening until the mixture resembles coarse crumbs. Add the milk; mix well. If too dry, add 1 teaspoon more milk. Mixture should be the consistency of biscuit dough.

Peachtree Bouquet
The Junior League of DeKalb County
Decatur, Georgia

Mother's Hot Browns

Created in the late 1920s or the early 1930s by Fred Schmidt of the Brown Hotel in Louisville, this open-face sandwich remains a Kentucky favorite.

Yield: 8 servings

12 to 16 chicken or turkey slices
⅓ cup unsalted butter
½ medium onion, minced
⅓ cup flour
3 cups hot milk
2 sprigs chopped parsley (optional)
Dash of nutmeg
1 teaspoon salt
Dash of cayenne pepper
8 ounces bacon
8 slices bread
Grated cheddar cheese

Cook the chicken ahead; cut into slices. Melt the butter in a skillet over low heat. Add the onion and cook until light brown in color, about 15 to 20 minutes. Remove from the heat. Add the flour and stir in until well blended. Whisk in the milk. Add the parsley, if using, and the nutmeg, salt, and cayenne pepper. Blend thoroughly. Return

sauce to the heat and cook 25 to 30 minutes, stirring constantly, until thick and smooth. Strain the sauce.

Fry the bacon slices and set aside. Remove the crusts from the bread and toast the slices. Place a slice of toast in each of 4 individual ovenproof dishes (or 1 very large dish). Place 3 to 4 chicken slices on each piece of toast. Cut remaining 4 slices of toast diagonally. Place the halves to bracket each of the open sandwiches. Pour a generous amount of sauce over the sandwiches. Set 4 to 5 inches below preheated broiler and broil until lightly browned. Place ½ strip of the bacon, whole or crumbled, on each sandwich and broil again just to heat the bacon. Sprinkle with grated cheese. Serve at once.

What's Cooking in Kentucky
Irene Hayes
Hueysville, Kentucky

NORTH CAROLINA CHICKEN PIE

Y I E L D : 6 S E R V I N G S

1 (3- to 4-pound) chicken
1 carrot, sliced
1 stalk celery, chopped
1 sprig parsley
1 onion, sliced
Salt and pepper to taste
Enough pastry for 3 8-inch layers
¼ cup flour

Dress and singe the chicken. Put in a saucepan with boiling water to cover. Add the carrot, cel-

Our Southern Receipt

Chicken Pie

Cut chicken into serving pieces, salt and pepper to taste and parboil until tender. Line sides of a deep baking dish with pastry cut in strips. Put in a layer of chicken, then a layer of dough. Fill nearly to the top of the dish. Put a solid piece of the dough rolled very thin over the top for the crust. Press down edges and make a hole in the center. Pour stock in which chicken was boiled through the hole. Bake in hot oven until brown. When crust is delicately brown, dot all over with butter and pour in a cup of rich milk or thin cream. Let it boil up once and then serve. If one chicken is not enough to make a big pie, chop off another's head, but don't fill your chicken pie with extraneous materials such as carrots, potatoes, green peas, or anything else until it becomes a stew. Or, at least, if you do that, do not call the result a chicken pie.

Collected by Kate C. Hubbard in Possum & Pomegranate *for the Federal Writers Project "America Eats"*

ery, parsley, and onion. Bring to a boil, cover, and simmer until the chicken is tender, about 30 minutes per pound. When half done, season with salt and pepper. When done, remove the chicken from the broth, debone, and cut up meat.

Preheat the oven to 350°. Line a shallow baking dish with pastry. Add a layer of half the chicken, then another layer of pastry. Top with the remaining chicken. Boil the chicken stock down to 3 cups; strain and skim off most of the fat. Combine the flour with cold water and mix into a smooth paste. Add to the stock. Bring to a boil, stirring constantly.

Add stock over the second layer of chicken in the baking dish and bake until the bottom crust is almost done. Add the remainder of the stock, if any, and cover with pastry. Cook slowly until the crust is brown.

North Carolina and Old Salem Cookery
Elizabeth Hedgecock Sparks
Kernersville, North Carolina

SOUTHWESTERN WHITE CHILI

The beans may be Northern, but the taste is Southern.

YIELD: 6 TO 8 SERVINGS

1 pound dry white Great Northern beans
7 cups chicken broth
2 cloves garlic, minced
1 large white onion, chopped
1 tablespoon ground white pepper
1 teaspoon salt
1 teaspoon dried oregano
1 tablespoon ground cumin
½ teaspoon ground cloves
1 (7-ounce) can diced green chiles
3 cups cooked chicken breast, diced
1 tablespoon diced jalapeño pepper
Flour tortillas or rice
Monterey Jack cheese, shredded (optional)

Black olives, sliced (optional)
Avocado, diced (optional)
Salsa (optional)

Soak the beans in water to cover for 24 hours.

Drain the beans and place in a large pot. Add 5 ¼ cups of the broth and the garlic, onion, white pepper, salt, oregano, cumin, and cloves.

Simmer, covered, for about 3 ½ hours, or until the beans are tender, stirring occasionally. Stir in the green chiles, the chicken, the remaining 1 ¾ cups of broth, and the jalapeño. Simmer, covered, for 1 hour.

To serve, line each bowl with 1 flour tortilla or spoon some rice into each bowl. Spoon in the chili and garnish with the cheese, black olives, avocado, and/or salsa, if desired.

And Roses for the Table
Junior League of Tyler
Tyler, Texas

OLD-FASHIONED ROAST TURKEY

Wild turkeys still roam the Southern woods, but these days we are more likely to get our turkeys from the freezer case at the grocery store.

YIELD: 14 SERVINGS

1 (14- to 16-pound) turkey
4 teaspoons unsalted butter or margarine,
  melted
1 tablespoon salt
2 teaspoons seasoned salt

1 teaspoon ground poultry seasoning or sage

1 teaspoon garlic powder

1 teaspoon ground ginger

1 teaspoon paprika

½ teaspoon black pepper

½ teaspoon cayenne pepper

¼ teaspoon dried basil

1 large onion, quartered

4 stalks celery, including leaves

1¼ cups water

3 tablespoons flour

Preheat the oven to 350°. Clean and dry the turkey. Chop up the neck and giblets; set aside. Brush the turkey with the melted butter. In a measuring cup or small bowl, mix the salt, seasoned salt, poultry seasoning, garlic powder, ground ginger, paprika, black pepper, cayenne, and basil. Rub thoroughly over the inside and outside of the bird. Put the onion and celery inside the cavity. Truss and tie securely. Place breast side up in a roaster. Add 1 cup water and the reserved giblets; cover. Bake until tender, about 3 to 4 hours. Uncover for the last 30 minutes and lower the temperature to 300° to brown evenly. Combine the pan juices, the giblets and neck meat, flour, and ¼ cup water in the roaster pan. Stir constantly until thickened. Serve with the turkey.

Wild About Texas
Cypress-Woodlands Junior Forum
Spring, Texas

FRIED WHOLE TURKEY

Though more often associated with the cooking of Louisiana, deep-fried turkeys have taken the South by storm in the past few years.

YIELD: 12 TO 14 SERVINGS

1 (12-pound) whole turkey

Salt, as needed

Pepper, as needed

Paprika, as needed

5 gallons peanut oil

Thaw the turkey and remove the giblets. Sprinkle the bird generously with salt, pepper, and paprika. Remove excess skin from around neck and cavity opening. In a pot large enough to submerge the turkey, heat the peanut oil to 375°. Tie the legs together, and tie the wings to the body with heavy-duty string. Cook the turkey 3½ to 4 minutes per pound, or until it floats, shifting it frequently to prevent burning.

Wild About Turkey
National Wild Turkey Federation
Edgefield, South Carolina

WILD DUCK COOKED WITH TURNIPS

The rice fields of Arkansas and Mississippi are the setting for many of our region's fabled hunting camps. Each fall, ducks by the thousands are plucked from the air by Southern sharpshooters.

YIELD: 6 SERVINGS

2 ½ tablespoons bacon drippings
3 wild ducks, cleaned, dried, and cut into pieces
1 ½ tablespoons flour
1 medium white onion, chopped
20 young white turnips, peeled and halved
2 cups hot water
1 tablespoon minced parsley
2 teaspoons finely minced garlic
½ teaspoon dried thyme
Cayenne pepper to taste
1 ½ teaspoons salt
½ teaspoon freshly ground black pepper
Cooked rice, for serving

Heat the bacon drippings over medium heat in a heavy 6- to 8-quart saucepan. Brown the duck pieces in the hot drippings, turning them frequently to brown evenly. Remove the duck pieces and set aside.

Reduce the heat to very low and gradually stir the flour into the drippings to make a roux. Cook 2 minutes, stirring constantly, and add the onion. Continue cooking and stirring until the onion is browned and the roux is dark brown in color, about 15 to 20 minutes more. Add the turnips and cook in the roux for 2 minutes, turning several times. Gradually add the hot water, stirring constantly. Add the parsley, garlic, thyme, cayenne, salt, and pepper and mix well. Bring the mixture to a boil. Add the browned duck pieces. Reduce heat and simmer 1 ¼ hours or until duck is tender when pierced with fork.

Serve with rice, about ½ cup of pan gravy, and several pieces of turnip ladled over each portion.

Gracious Goodness
Memphis Symphony League
Memphis, Tennessee

BETSY'S SHERRIED DOVES

YIELD: 6 SERVINGS

12 dove breasts
¼ teaspoon salt
¼ teaspoon pepper
¼ cup unsalted butter or margarine
2 cups sherry
2 tablespoons cornstarch
¼ cup water
Hot cooked rice, for serving

Preheat the oven to 400°. Sprinkle the dove breasts with salt and pepper. Melt the butter in a 10-inch cast-iron skillet. Place the dove breasts meaty side up in the skillet and cover with sherry. Bake, covered, for 35 to 40 minutes. Remove the dove breasts and keep warm; reserve 2 cups of the pan drippings (add enough water to make 2 cups, if necessary). Combine the cornstarch with the ¼ cup water, stirring well; then stir into the pan drippings. Bring to a boil over medium heat; boil for 1 minute. Serve gravy and doves over rice.

Outdoor Tables and Tales
Southeastern Outdoor Press Association
Leland, Mississippi

SMOTHERED DOVES

Tiny but tasty, doves are prized for their dark meat by Southern huntsmen and cooks.

YIELD: 4 TO 6 SERVINGS

½ cup olive oil
¼ cup flour
½ teaspoon salt
¼ teaspoon pepper
10 dove breasts
2 cloves garlic
1 cup dry red wine

Heat the oil to 350° in an electric skillet. Season the flour with the salt and pepper and coat the dove breasts. Reserve the flour mixture. Add the garlic and doves to the skillet and brown the breasts. Remove the garlic; add the wine and enough water to almost cover the breasts. Lower the heat to 300° and simmer for 1½ hours. Thicken the pan juices with some of the remaining seasoned flour. Cook until smooth; pour over the breasts to serve.

The Southern Sportsman Cookbook
Franc White
Greenville, North Carolina

DOVE AND OYSTER PIE

YIELD: 8 TO 10 SERVINGS

16 doves
2 cups chopped celery
1 cup chopped onions
3 slices bacon, chopped
Salt and cayenne pepper to taste
1 quart water
4 dozen oysters
¼ cup flour
¼ cup water
Enough flaky pastry for two 9-inch layers

Place the cleaned and drawn whole doves in a heavy pot. Add the celery, onions, bacon, salt, and cayenne. Cover with the 1 quart water. Bring the water to a boil, reduce the heat, and simmer until the doves are tender. Remove from the heat. Place the doves on a flat pan until cool enough to handle. Drain the oysters, then stuff as many as possible into each dove.

Preheat the oven to 350°. Mix the flour with the ¼ cup water to make a paste, then add enough liquid from the pot to blend well. Add this to the pot in which the doves were cooked, place over low heat, and stir constantly until thickened to about the consistency of cream. Add the remaining oysters, and remove from the heat.

Line a deep baking dish with a layer of pastry and bake for 10 minutes, or until the pastry is set. Remove from the oven and let cool. Add a layer of doves and a layer of liquid with oysters. Repeat until the layers are within ½ inch of the top. Cover with another layer of pastry, rolled thin. Prick the top of the pastry and bake for 45 minutes.

Louisiana Wildlife Magazine
Baton Rouge, Louisiana

SOUTHERN QUAIL

Known to many as bobwhites for their cry that sounds something akin to "Bob, Bob White," these birds were in years past only available to hunters. Today, they are widely available from commercial farms.

YIELD: 4 SERVINGS

8 quail
Salt and pepper to taste
Unsalted butter, melted
2 cups cooked brown and wild rice mixture
½ cup chopped walnuts
½ cup chopped apples
8 strips bacon

Preheat the oven to 350°. Sprinkle the quail with salt and pepper and brush with butter. Mix the rice with the walnuts and apples and stuff the quail with some of the rice mixture. Wrap each quail with strips of bacon. Bake, covered, for 1 hour. Remove cover and bake 15 to 20 minutes longer, or until browned. Serve on top of additional rice mixture.

Gracious Goodness
Memphis Symphony League
Memphis, Tennessee

FRIED FROG LEGS

Known by the old French name of grenouilles frites *in Creole country.*

YIELD: 4 SERVINGS

½ cup fresh lemon juice
1 teaspoon salt
1 dozen frog legs
Salt and pepper to taste
Hot lard for deep frying
1 cup fine, dry bread crumbs
2 eggs, well beaten
Fried parsley, sliced lemon, and radishes for
  garnish (optional)

Place enough water to cover the frog legs in a saucepan and add the lemon juice and salt. Bring to a boil, add the frog legs, and scald for 3 minutes. Remove from the water and dry. Season with salt and pepper to taste. Heat the lard to the boiling point in a deep fryer or deep, heavy skillet. Add the bread crumbs to the eggs to make a batter. Dip the frog legs in the batter. Pat the legs well and drop into the boiling lard. Fry until golden brown; drain well. Garnish with fried parsley, lemon slices, and radishes, as desired.

The Picayune's Creole Cookbook
New Orleans, Louisiana

FISH & SEAFOOD

THE SOUTHERN KITCHEN IN BLACK AND WHITE

The needs of a society determine its ethics, and in the Black American ghettos the hero is that man who is offered only the crumbs from his country's table but by ingenuity and courage is able to take for himself a Lucullan feast.

MAYA ANGELOU

I was raised Southern-style— by the maid. No one can understand the mystery of the South without delving into this murmuring undertone— a relationship primordial, like parent and child, of discipline and need, shadowing every white Southerner throughout the rest of his life.

ELI EVANS

The Southern Kitchen in Black and White

....

The question is often asked: What is the difference between soul food and country cooking, between the foods of Southern blacks and whites? Answers are as numerous, and as various, as recipes for fried chicken. Some allow that the foods of black Southerners tend to be a bit sweeter, maybe a touch hotter. Others argue that the pig tells all, that a propensity toward using pork offal marks the foods of African Americans. Others still look for the telltale turnip among the collards as proof positive of European influence or suggest that the green tip of the okra pod points the way to Africa.

The wisest among us look not for differences but similarities. Such Southern standards as okra, black-eyed peas, collards, and benne seeds may well have made the passage from Africa to the Americas in the hold of a ship filled with human cargo. The journey was arduous, the aftermath, slavery, incomprehensibly cruel. The legacy of inhumanity will not soon be wiped clean from the historical slate. And yet, today, okra pods are okra pods, whether called gumbs by the Gullahs in Lowcountry, South Carolina, or ladyfingers by the Ladies Who Lunch in Tidewater, Virginia. And greens are greens, with most Southerners caring less about whether they are of European or African origin and more about whether there is a cruet of pepper sauce close by.

Foremost among the similarities may be that, through the years, there always seemed to be a black hand on the Southern skillet. Granted, there were exceptions, homes where the meal made it from field to table by dint of sweat from a white brow. But more commonly, in columned homes of pretense and dogtrot cabins alike, black backs bent to heft the kettle from the stove, black arms flexed to beat the biscuit dough on the stump, black fingers plucked the feathers from the chickens. Never mind that the only hint at mealtime may have been the rattle of pots and pans in the kitchen—the black presence, if it was at times out of sight, was never out of mind.

Jim Crow laws may have dictated where blacks could go to school and with whom they could consort, but in the kitchen the black cook was able to express a sort of subversive creativity, slipping in a pepper pod here, an okra pod there. In the kitchen, freedom of expression was tolerated, even encouraged. As a result, the foods of the South were reinterpreted, in an Africanized manner, by African American cooks.

Today, the legacy of African American contributions to our culinary experience lives on in, among many others, dishes like New Orleans's pralines, Savannah's red rice, and Memphis's barbecue ribs. But the legacy is more than the sum of the recipes, the influence more than can be captured in the pages of this cookbook, the tastes as much a part of country cooking as of soul food.

FRIED SOFT-SHELL CRABS

When the crabs have molted and these crustaceans teem in Gulf waters, it's soft-shell crab season, and we eat these delicate little spiders in sandwiches or on a bed of rice—in short, any way we can.

YIELD: 6 SERVINGS

6 soft-shell crabs
1 egg
1 cup buttermilk
Salt and pepper to taste
¾ cup self-rising flour
¼ cup yellow cornmeal
Shortening for deep frying
Lemon slices and fresh minced parsley,
  for garnish
Tartar sauce, for serving

Clean the crabs and pat dry. Beat the egg, buttermilk, salt, and pepper in a large bowl. Soak the crabs for two hours in this mixture. Heat the shortening to 375°. Combine the flour and cornmeal and dredge the crabs in it. Fry in the shortening until golden brown; drain. Garnish with lemon slices and parsley. Serve with tartar sauce.

Recipes and Reminiscences of New Orleans II
Parents Club of Ursuline Academy
New Orleans, Louisiana

DEVILED CRAB

Casserole dishes are as common as cast-iron skillets in Southern kitchens. And this recipe, though it comes from a cookbook entitled The Share-Cropper, *is about as highfalutin as casseroles come.*

YIELD: 2 TO 3 SERVINGS

1 pound fresh lump crab meat
3 tablespoons unsalted butter, plus extra for
*   greasing casserole*
3 tablespoons cornstarch
2 cups milk
Salt to taste
1 medium green bell pepper, finely chopped
Several sprigs of parsley, finely chopped
3 eggs, well beaten
Bread crumbs
Worcestershire sauce

Pick over the crab meat and remove any shell or cartilage and set aside. Melt the butter in the top of a double boiler, blend in the cornstarch, then blend in the milk. Cook over hot water until thickened, adding salt to taste. Let cool.

Preheat the oven to 400°. Add the crab meat, bell pepper, parsley, and eggs to the milk mixture; mix well. Grease a 2-quart casserole liberally with butter (not margarine). Turn the crab mixture into the casserole and cover with bread crumbs. Bake casserole 10 minutes, then reduce heat to 350° and bake 30 minutes longer, or until well browned on top. Before serving, sprinkle top of casserole lightly with Worcestershire sauce.

This recipe can be prepared a day in advance and refrigerated until baking time, but re-

move from the refrigerator and bring to room temperature before adding the eggs (eggs in the chilled mixture can cause curdling).

The Share-Cropper
Central Delta Academy
    Parent-Teacher Organization
Inverness, Mississippi

CRAB CAKES

Crab cakes, with the slightest of ballast, are a brunch favorite down Florida way.

YIELD: 4 SERVINGS

1 pound crab meat
1 egg, lightly beaten
2 teaspoons prepared mustard
2 tablespoons mayonnaise
Salt and pepper to taste
6 tablespoons unsalted butter, melted, plus extra
*   butter for greasing cookie sheet*
Cracker meal

Preheat the oven to 450°. Combine the crab meat, egg, mustard, mayonnaise, salt, pepper, and butter in a bowl. Add just enough cracker meal to hold the mixture together. Shape into patties and place on a lightly greased cookie sheet. Bake for 20 minutes, or until golden brown. Serve immediately.

Fare by the Sea
Junior League of Sarasota
Sarasota, Florida

CRAB MEAT RAMEKINS

From Patti Carr Black, former director of the Old Capitol Museum in Jackson and author of several works, the latest being Art in Mississippi, *come these crab meat soufflés.*

YIELD: 8 SERVINGS

7 tablespoons unsalted butter
6 tablespoons flour
1½ cups milk, heated
½ cup cream, heated
2 eggs, well beaten
1 tablespoon white wine
1 bell pepper, chopped fine
2 ounces pimientos, drained and chopped
3 green onions, chopped
1 clove garlic, minced
1 pound fresh crab meat
2 tablespoons fresh lemon juice
Salt to taste
Dash of cayenne pepper
Plain bread crumbs

Preheat the oven to 350°. In a saucepan, melt 4 tablespoons of the butter; stir in the flour and cook. Whisk in the warmed milk and cream and cook until thick. Pour a little of the hot sauce into the eggs; mix well, then return the mixture to the saucepan. Add the wine, bell pepper, and pimiento.

In a large skillet, melt 2 tablespoons of the remaining butter and lightly sauté the onion, garlic, and crab meat. Add the lemon juice, salt to taste, and the cayenne. Combine the two mixtures, put in 8 individual ramekins, top with bread crumbs, and dot with the remaining tablespoon of butter. Bake at 350° for 20 minutes.

Standing Room Only
New Stage Theatre
Jackson, Mississippi

FRIED OYSTERS OR SHRIMP

YIELD: 1 DOZEN

Fat for deep frying
¼ cup flour
¼ teaspoon baking powder
1 egg, lightly beaten
4 drops Tabasco
1 dozen oysters or shrimp
Cracker crumbs, fine, dry bread crumbs, or
*   cornmeal*

Heat the oil for deep frying. Combine the flour and baking powder in a bowl. Mix the egg and Tabasco in another bowl. Roll the oysters or shrimp in the flour mixture. Dip them in the egg mixture and then roll them in the cracker crumbs. Deep-fry in hot grease until golden brown.

Acadian Bi-Centennial Cookbook
Louisiana Acadian Handicraft Museum
Jennings, Louisiana

OYSTER PO'BOY LOAF

Po'boys are to New Orleans what hoagies are to Philadelphia. The name is a tip of the hat to the socioeconomic status of those who most enjoyed these sandwiches, or perhaps it is an elided version of the French term for a restaurant gratuity, pourboire.

YIELD: 4 SERVINGS

1 unsliced loaf French bread
Unsalted butter
2 dozen oysters, fried in one cup of cornmeal
*   with ¼ teaspoon salt, ¼ teaspoon cayenne*
*   pepper, and 1 teaspoon baking powder added*
Pickle slices, dill or sour

Slice the French bread in two lengthwise. Scoop out the inside of the bottom half and toast the shell. Butter inside generously and keep warm. Fry oysters as directed in recipe on this page; drain. Place in the bread shell. Top with the pickle slices. Place the top back on the loaf and warm the loaf in the oven. Slice into 4 servings.

Acadian Bi-Centennial Cookbook
Louisiana Acadian Handicraft Museum
Jennings, Louisiana

BARBARA ENSRUD

THE JEFFERSONIAN LEGACY

In 1993, I went to a celebration of Thomas Jefferson's 250th birthday at the Willow Grove Inn, an old coach stop in Orange, Virginia. On April 13, his birthday, we enjoyed lunch and dinner featuring Jefferson's favorite foods and a variety of Virginia wines. Jefferson would have been wonderfully proud of the wines especially, for he made tremendous efforts to grow wine grapes at Monticello. He believed that a wine industry would be a great endeavor for the new republic.

For lunch, Edna Lewis cooked many of Jefferson's favorite dishes and talked about Jefferson's love of those foods—oyster pie, corn pudding, green beans and ham hock, guinea hens, and especially, macaroni and cheese. Jefferson may well have introduced macaroni and cheese to the United States by way of his Italian friend Filippo Mazzei, with whom he worked to grow wine at Monticello.

It was a lovely, sunny day. The azaleas were blooming, as were the cherry trees. Edna Lewis's food was, as always, perfectly seasoned, full of flavor and real savor. It was a meal to be proud of, one that would have pleased Jefferson himself.

I consider him our first true gastronome, a man who understood fine dining and good wine. Of course, he was our minister to France. And as he traveled to wine regions in France, the Rhine and Moselle valleys in Germany, and Italy, he tasted some of the world's great wines, bringing that appreciation back to the States.

Perhaps there is something about the legacy of Jefferson at Monticello that is felt even today. For dinner that same night of his birthday, we had wines from Barboursville Winery in Virginia. Governor James Barbour was a contemporary and good friend of Jefferson's. And appropriately enough, an Italian family, the Zonins, bought out Barboursville in the late 1970s, proving that the Italian–Virginian connection still resonates in the modern-day South. Barboursville makes an outstanding Pinot Grigio, as well as good Merlots, Chardonnays, and Sauvignon Blancs—as do a number of other wineries from Virginia, through North Carolina, northern Georgia, and westward into the Hill Country of Texas. True, there was a time—not too long ago—that Southern wines lacked the richness and ripeness of fruit of wines from California, but the quality of the best wines has improved greatly over the past two decades. Today I am genuinely pleased and proud of our Southern wines. And I think Thomas Jefferson would share my enthusiasm.

Barbara Ensrud, a native of Arkansas, is the author of, among other works, American Vineyards *and* Wine with Food.

OVEN-FRIED OYSTERS

Not as crisp as the previous version but a darn sight less messy.

YIELD: 4 SERVINGS

1 stick (¼ pound) unsalted butter, melted
Dash of Worcestershire sauce
Dash of Tabasco
Salt and pepper to taste
1 pint oysters, drained
1 cup fine, dry bread crumbs

Mix the melted butter, Worcestershire sauce, Tabasco, salt, and pepper. Dip the oysters in the mixture; then roll them in the crumbs. Place close together in a 10x7-inch pan. Pour any remaining butter sauce over the oysters. Refrigerate 3 to 4 hours or overnight. Refrigeration is important. Preheat the oven to 350° and bake for 15 to 20 minutes, or until the crumbs are golden brown and the oysters begin to release their juice.

Southern Sideboards
Junior League of Jackson
Jackson, Mississippi

BAKED OYSTERS

YIELD: 4 TO 6 SERVINGS

3 dozen oysters, drained
⅔ cup chopped parsley
⅔ cup chopped green onions
1 cup cracker crumbs, rolled fine
Juice of 1 small lemon

½ teaspoon dry mustard
2 teaspoons Worcestershire sauce
1 stick (¼ pound) unsalted butter, melted

Preheat the oven to 450°. Place the oysters in a shallow baking dish. Sprinkle with the parsley and green onions. Sprinkle the cracker crumbs on top. Add the lemon juice, mustard, and Worcestershire sauce to the melted butter. Pour over the crumbs. Bake for 10 to 15 minutes, or until the oysters curl and the crumbs are brown.

Delta Dining, Too
Delta Academy Mothers Club
Marks, Mississippi

SCALLOPED OYSTERS

YIELD: 6 SERVINGS

4 dozen oysters
Tabasco to taste
Salt and pepper to taste
1½ cups finely chopped celery tops
Small bunch parsley, chopped fine
1 bunch green onions, chopped fine
1 stick (¼ pound) unsalted butter or margarine, melted, plus extra butter for dotting the oysters before baking
Oyster liquid
Cracker crumbs

Place an oven rack in the center position in the oven and preheat the oven to 350°. Drain the oysters, reserving all the liquid. Season the oysters with Tabasco, salt, and pepper. Sauté the celery, parsley, and green onions in the melted butter until tender. Layer the seasoned oysters, then the sautéed ingredients in a shallow baking dish. Pour the oyster liquid over all; cover with cracker crumbs and dot with butter. Bake for 30 minutes.

Standing Room Only
New Stage Theatre
Jackson, Mississippi

OYSTER PIE

YIELD: 6 TO 8 SERVINGS

2 rounded tablespoons flour
2 tablespoons vegetable shortening or bacon
* drippings*
½ cup chopped onion
1 pint oysters
½ cup chopped celery
¼ cup chopped green bell pepper
1 tablespoon Worcestershire sauce
Salt and pepper to taste
Enough pastry for two 9-inch layers

Make a roux by browning the flour in the shortening. Add the onion and brown. Add enough water to make a gravy. Cover and simmer for 10 minutes. Add the oysters, celery, bell pepper, Worcestershire, salt, and pepper. Cook 5 to 10 minutes, until gravy is thickened; let cool. Preheat the oven to 400°. Pour the oyster mixture into an unbaked pie shell and cover with the top layer of pastry. Make slits in the top to allow steam to escape. Bake for 30 minutes, or until brown.

Acadian Bi-Centennial Cookbook
Louisiana Acadian Handicraft Museum
Jennings, Louisiana

BRAVO OYSTER LINGUINE

YIELD: 6 SERVINGS

1 stick (¼ pound) salted butter
½ cup plus 3 tablespoons olive oil
8 large cloves garlic, peeled and cut into
* ⅓-inch-thick pieces*
3 teaspoons dried basil, or ½ cup fresh
3 tablespoons finely minced fresh parsley
1 teaspoon freshly ground pepper
6½ teaspoons salt
2 pints freshly shucked oysters (about 4 dozen
* medium-size), drained*
6 quarts cold water
24 ounces linguine

In a heavy cast-iron skillet, melt the butter over low heat; add the ½ cup olive oil, mixing thoroughly. Heat 4 minutes. Add the garlic and cook over medium heat just until it begins to brown, about 5 minutes. Remove immediately with a slotted spoon. Add the basil, parsley, pepper, and ½ teaspoon of the salt; simmer for 4 minutes. Add the oysters and warm for 5 minutes over low heat. Remove the skillet from the heat, cover, and set aside.

Place the 6 quarts cold water, the remaining 6 teaspoons salt, and the remaining 3 teaspoons olive oil in a 6- to 8-quart saucepan. Bring to a fast boil. Add the linguine; cook for 7 minutes after the water comes to a second boil. Drain well and place back in saucepan. Add the oyster mixture and blend gently. Cover the pot and keep warm for 10 minutes before serving.

Standing Room Only
New State Theatre
Jackson, Mississippi

LES ECREVISSES
A CRAWFISH BOIL

CRAWFISH FOR SALE. This announcement chalked on blackboards in front of seafood shops is as true a harbinger of spring in south Louisiana as is the first robin elsewhere. Restaurants proudly proclaim that crawfish étoufée or crawfish bisque is available, and the thoughts of informal party givers turn to crawfish boils.

A crawfish boil is an unbeatable kind of get-together. Men get their chance to prove their cooking skill, and the cooking and eating are done outdoors. First, the crustaceans are hosed down and washed. Then they are placed in an enormous pot filled with water and an unbelievable amount of salt and red pepper. About three boxes of salt and two bottles of red pepper are right for 50 pounds, which is enough for ten to twelve people.

A boil doesn't call for damask napkins and the family Spode. Instead, the outdoor table is spread with newspapers. Running down the center is a steaming line of red crawfish. Everyone reaches for his own, and a man's best friends are his fingers. Good accompaniments to crawfish are potato salad, garlic bread, an iced drink, and a sweet dessert. You don't have to worry about cooking too many crawfish. There are all sorts of ways of using up the extras—in bisques, in croquettes, in cocktails or salads.

Acadian Bi-Centennial Cookbook
Louisiana Acadian Handicraft Museum
Jennings, Louisiana

CRAWFISH ÉTOUFFÉE

Étouffée means smothered, as this crawfish is smothered beneath a beatific gravy.

YIELD: 6 TO 8 SERVINGS

½ cup butter
1 cup chopped green onions
¼ cup chopped parsley
2 pounds crawfish tails
1 cup crawfish fat, if available, or 1 cup un-
    salted butter
Salt and pepper to taste
1 teaspoon cornstarch (optional)
Steamed rice, for serving
Lemon slices, for garnish (optional)

Melt the butter in a large, heavy skillet or Dutch oven and sauté the green onions until tender, about 10 to 15 minutes. Add the parsley, crawfish tails, and crawfish fat (or butter) and salt and pepper to taste. Cook over medium heat 15 to 20 minutes. If a thicker gravy is desired, dissolve the cornstarch in a small amount of water and add to the sauce. Serve over steamed rice and garnish with lemon slices, if desired.

Louisiana Legacy
Thibodaux Service League
Thibodaux, Louisiana

CRAWFISH JAMBALAYA

Call 'em mud bugs if you like. Just don't call them crayfish, else you'll brand yourself an interloper down Louisiana way.

YIELD: 4 TO 5 SERVINGS

1 tablespoon flour
2 tablespoons oil
1 cup chopped onion
1 pound (2½ cups) crawfish tails
¼ cup crawfish fat or unsalted butter
1⅛ cups raw long-grain rice
½ cup chopped parsley
½ cup chopped green onions
½ cup chopped celery
½ cup chopped green bell pepper
2½ teaspoons salt
½ teaspoon black pepper
⅛ teaspoon cayenne pepper

Make a roux with the flour and oil in a large skillet; add the onion, and cook, stirring, until almost tender. Add 1½ cups cold water; simmer 30 minutes. Add the crawfish tails and fat; cook until crawfish turn pink, about 10 to 15 minutes. Add 2 cups less 2 tablespoons water and bring to a boil. Add the remaining ingredients; stir to blend. Cook, covered, on low heat for about 30 minutes, or until rice is tender. Five minutes before serving, fluff up with a two-pronged fork.

Cajun Cooking
Lafayette, Louisiana

Crawfish Pies

*When Hank Williams sang of jambalaya, craw-
fish pie, filé gumbo, he sang a paean to the foods
of Cajun Louisiana, among which was this
favorite from Iberia Parish.*

YIELD: 4 INDIVIDUAL PIES

Crust

2¾ cups flour
1½ teaspoons salt
1 cup shortening
1 egg

Sift together the flour and salt. Cut in the shortening with a fork or pastry blender until the mixture resembles crumbs. Beat the egg well; add
enough water to the egg to make ¼ cup liquid.
Add the egg mixture to the flour mixture; mix
well. Roll the dough out on a lightly floured
board to make 4 individual double pie crusts; set
aside.

Filling

1 cup ground celery
1 cup ground green pepper
2 cups chopped onions
¼ cup vegetable oil
2 tablespoons crawfish fat or butter
4 cups water
2 pounds peeled raw crawfish
1 heaping tablespoon prepared roux
2 tablespoons chopped green onions
2 tablespoons minced parsley
Salt to taste

Pepper to taste
Garlic powder to taste
Cornstarch (optional)
Water (optional)

Combine the celery, green pepper, and onion in a
large pot. Add the oil, the crawfish fat, and 4
cups water. Cook over medium heat until tender.
Add the crawfish, roux, green onions, parsley,
salt, pepper, and garlic powder. Cook for 20 minutes. If not thick enough, add enough cornstarch,
mixed in a small amount of water, to thicken.
Preheat oven to 350°. Pour into individual unbaked pie shells. Cover with the top pie crust.
Make 4 slits in the top crust. Bake until brown.

Foods à la Louisiane
Louisiana Farm Bureau Women
Baton Rouge, Louisiana

Bar-B-Q Shrimp

YIELD: 8 TO 10 SERVINGS

8 pounds large shrimp, unpeeled
2 sticks (½ pound) unsalted butter
1 cup olive oil
8 ounces chili sauce
3 tablespoons Worcestershire sauce
2 lemons, sliced
4 cloves garlic, chopped
3 tablespoons fresh lemon juice
1 tablespoon chopped parsley
2 teaspoons paprika
2 teaspoons oregano
2 teaspoons cayenne pepper
1 teaspoon Tabasco

3 tablespoons Liquid Smoke

Salt and pepper to taste

French bread, for serving

Wash the shrimp and spread them out in shallow pans. Combine the remaining ingredients in a saucepan over low heat and pour over shrimp. Refrigerate for several hours, basting and turning the shrimp every 30 minutes. Preheat the oven to 300° and bake for 30 minutes, turning shrimp at 10-minute intervals. Serve in soup bowls with French bread to dip in the sauce.

Recipes and Reminiscences of New Orleans
Parents Club of Ursuline Academy
New Orleans, Louisiana

SHRIMP CREOLE

Smothered in a piquant red gravy, this shrimp dish owes its origins to the Creoles of New Orleans.

YIELD: 6 SERVINGS

2 tablespoons unsalted butter

½ teaspoon paprika

1 cup chopped onion

1 cup chopped green bell pepper

½ clove garlic, chopped

2 cups stewed tomatoes

Salt to taste

Pepper to taste

1 cup peeled and deveined raw shrimp

Fluffy rice, for serving

Melt the butter in a skillet over low heat; add the paprika and stir thoroughly. Add the onion, bell pepper, and garlic; simmer on low heat until tender. Add the tomatoes, salt, and pepper. Boil 5 minutes. Add the shrimp and boil 10 minutes. Serve hot over fluffy rice.

Foods à la Louisiane
Louisiana Farm Bureau Women
Baton Rouge, Louisiana

BREAKFAST SHRIMP

Long before shrimp and grits became a restaurant menu mainstay in the South, it was a favorite breakfast among fishermen. While the simplest way to prepare this dish is to sauté the shrimp in melted butter and serve hot, this variation is sure to please.

YIELD: 4 SERVINGS

3 tablespoons bacon drippings
2 tablespoons chopped onion
2 teaspoons chopped green bell pepper
1½ cups small, peeled raw shrimp
1 cup water or more
1½ tablespoons flour
Salt and pepper to taste
1 teaspoon Worcestershire sauce
1 tablespoon ketchup
Hominy, for serving

In a large, heavy skillet, heat the bacon drippings and add the onion and green pepper. When the onion is golden, add the shrimp; turn these several times with the onion and pepper. Add enough water to make a sauce—about 1 cup. Do not cover the shrimp with water or your sauce will be tasteless. Simmer 2 to 3 minutes and thicken with flour and a little water made into a paste. Add salt and pepper, the Worcestershire sauce, and the ketchup. Cook slowly until the sauce thickens. Serve with what the dear ladies of Charleston call hominy, known beyond the holy city as grits.

Charleston Receipts
Junior League of Charleston
Charleston, South Carolina

SALMON CROQUETTES

YIELD: 6 TO 8 SERVINGS

Oil for deep frying
2 (16-ounce) cans salmon
2 eggs
1 teaspoon salt
½ teaspoon black pepper
1 teaspoon fresh lemon juice
2 tablespoons minced onion
1 cup fine, dry bread crumbs

Heat the oil gradually to 365°. Meanwhile, drain the salmon. Remove the skin and bones and mash the salmon in a bowl. Beat one of the eggs and add the salt, pepper, lemon juice, and onion and half the bread crumbs to the beaten egg. Add this mixture to the salmon and mix thoroughly with your hands. Shape the salmon mixture into patties, balls, or cones. Beat the remaining egg.

John Martin Taylor

In My Mama's Floating Kitchen

I can't deny that my taste in food is a legacy of the rural South. For my Mama, and now for me, fresh and local are everything. I grew up spending weekends at Hilton Head Island. For twenty-plus years, we were one of three families with a sailboat down there. I still remember riding in the car with the windows rolled down. When we first smelled the marsh, first smelled the pluff mud, we knew we were deep in the Lowcountry.

I learned a lot about cooking on that boat with my mother. Mama would say, "Go get lunch," and she meant just that. Go check the crab trap, throw the shrimp net, go get oysters off the bank. I didn't even know you paid for seafood until I went away to college. I didn't even know you paid for watermelons; they came from the field.

My mother was a phenomenal cook. But she wasn't what we think of as a traditional Southern cook. She loved to experiment. Did you ever see the Hitchcock movie, the really good, really sick one, the one where this guy murders women by strangling them with a necktie? There's this character—the police inspector's wife—that's my mother. The police inspector would come home from a long day at work, and she would say something like, "Tonight, we go to Czechoslovakia!" That's my mother; she would make some fantastic dish, some terrine of some sort, from an obscure cookbook she had. And we would say something like, "Aw, Mama, can't we have fried chicken?"

If she was cooking some dish that required an ingredient she couldn't get from a local grower, she would make the grocery store order it. Mama would go to her bridge club and say, "Now wouldn't y'all really like some broccoli? Let's make them get some. Y'all can split a flat with me."

She was a great cook, and I think I learned more from her in that little kitchen on our sailboat than I've learned from anyone since.

John Martin Taylor, of Charleston, South Carolina, is the proprietor of Hoppin' John's culinary website and the author of a number of cookbooks, including Fearless Frying.

Dip the croquettes in the remaining bread crumbs, then in the egg, and then in the bread crumbs again. Fry in the oil until golden brown; drain.

Waddad's Kitchen
Waddad Habeeb Buttross
Natchez, Mississippi

SEAFOOD MEDLEY

YIELD: 16 TO 18 SERVINGS

¾ cup flour
1½ sticks butter, melted, plus extra butter for
    buttering baking dishes
3 cups half-and-half
1½ teaspoons salt
½ teaspoon cayenne pepper
2 cups sharp cheddar cheese, grated
3 teaspoons onion juice
½ cup sherry
⅔ cup water or milk
1 pound crab meat
1 pound shrimp, cooked, peeled, and deveined
1 pound scallops, steamed 2 to 3 minutes
2 (8½-ounce) cans water chestnuts, drained
2 (14-ounce) cans artichoke hearts, halved
1 cup slivered almonds
Parmesan cheese, grated

Preheat the oven to 325°. Add the flour to the butter in a large skillet. Stir over low heat 3 minutes. Add half-and-half, salt, and cayenne pepper. Continue cooking, stirring constantly, until thickened. Add the cheddar cheese and stir until the cheese melts. Add the onion juice, sherry, and

water; mix well. Butter two 6x12-inch baking dishes and line them with crab meat, shrimp, scallops, water chestnuts, and artichoke hearts. Add the cream sauce. Sprinkle with the almonds and Parmesan cheese. Bake for 30 minutes.

Fare by the Sea
Junior League of Sarasota
Sarasota, Florida

ROYAL COURT BOUILLON

YIELD: 6 TO 8 SERVINGS

2 to 2½ pounds cleaned fish
¼ cup olive oil
2 cups chopped yellow onions
2 cloves garlic, minced, or ¼ teaspoon instant
    minced garlic
½ cup diced green bell peppers
3½ cups Italian-style plum tomatoes or 1 (28-
    ounce) can, undrained
1 tablespoon salt
½ teaspoon black pepper
4 whole bay leaves
½ lemon, seeds removed, cut into 3 round slices
Steamed rice, for serving
Hot French or Italian bread, for serving

Cut the cleaned fish crosswise into pieces about 1½ inches wide. Keep refrigerated until ready to use.

Put the olive oil, onion, and garlic in a fryer or Dutch oven. Fry slowly until the onions are soft and golden, stirring frequently. Add the diced green pepper and stir; fry about 3 minutes longer. Remove from the heat.

Fish Courtboullion

This recipe comes from Biloxi, on the Mississippi coast, where seafood is king. Biloxi began in 1669, and even today, the blessing of the fleet during the opening of shrimp season is observed.

YIELD: 8 TO 10 SERVINGS

5 to 6 onions, finely chopped
1 bunch parsley, finely chopped
2 to 4 stalks celery, finely chopped
4 cloves garlic, finely chopped
6 small cans tomatoes
1 to 2 bay leaves
Hot peppers to taste
8 to 10 fish fillets
Cooking oil

Brown the onion, parsley, celery, and garlic in a skillet. Add the tomatoes, bay leaves, and hot peppers. Let simmer for about 1 hour. Fry the fish in cooking oil in another skillet. Cover with a portion of the gravy. Cook until fish is done. Pour the rest of the gravy over the fish before serving.

Collected by Eudora Welty for the Federal Writers Project "America Eats"

Place the tomatoes one at a time on a small dish and mash well with a fork, using the edge of the fork to cut through the long fibers. Add the mashed tomatoes and all the tomato liquid to the onions and garlic in the fryer. Stir in the salt and pepper. Add the bay leaves and return to the heat. Cook gently over low heat, uncovered, about 5 minutes.

Dry the fish and arrange in the sauce. Spoon the sauce over the pieces of fish. Slip the lemon slices into the sauce. Bring back to a simmer, cover, and cook gently for about 20 minutes, or until the fish is cooked. Baste occasionally with the sauce, but do not stir or turn the fish. Remove the lemon slices and bay leaves. Serve with steamed rice and hot French or Italian bread.

Marie's Melting Pot
Marie Lupo Tusa
New Orleans, Louisiana

SAUTÉED SHAD ROE

Roe, or eggs, from shad are an Atlantic Coast favorite, often enjoyed with grits as a breakfast treat.

YIELD: 2 SERVINGS

2 sets shad roe
1 quart salted water
Waxed paper
2 teaspoons fresh lemon juice
Salt and black pepper to taste
2 tablespoons bacon drippings
Lemon wedges, for serving

Soak the shad roe in the salted water for 15 minutes. Drain. Place each set of shad roe on a square of waxed paper. Season each with 1 teaspoon of the lemon juice, salt, pepper, and 1 teaspoon of the bacon drippings. Wrap sandwich-style in the waxed paper. Keep the folded ends tucked underneath. Grease a heavy skillet with the remaining fat. Place the wrapped roe in the skillet, edges tucked under; fry over medium heat 10 to 15 minutes on each side, until the roe browns (browning can be seen through paper). Unwrap and serve with lemon wedges.

Virginia Hospitality
Junior League of Hampton Roads
Newport News, Virginia

FILLET OF RED SNAPPER AMANDINE

YIELD: 6 SERVINGS

6 red snapper fillets
Salt and pepper
Flour for dredging
3 sticks (¾ pound) unsalted butter
1 cup sliced almonds
Juice of 1 lemon

Preheat the oven to 375°. Wipe the fillets with a damp cloth. Sprinkle with salt and pepper and dredge in a little flour. Melt 1 stick of the butter and sauté the fillets until done but not too brown. Place the fillets in a baking pan. Melt the remaining cup of butter. Mix the almonds and the melted butter in a skillet and cook until the almonds are light brown. Pour the almond mixture

over the fillets and sprinkle with the lemon juice. Bake for 3 to 5 minutes, or until nicely browned.

Note: This amandine sauce is excellent with other fish.

The Gasparilla Cookbook
Junior League of Tampa
Tampa, Florida

SHRIMP-AND-MUSHROOM STUFFED SNAPPER

YIELD: 4 TO 6 SERVINGS

1 (4-pound) red snapper fillet
1 clove garlic, crushed
1 stick (¼ pound) unsalted butter or margarine,
  at room temperature
1 teaspoon salt
⅛ teaspoon black pepper
½ teaspoon dried thyme
1 teaspoon flour
8 ounces large shrimp, shelled and deveined
8 ounces fresh mushrooms, sliced
3 tablespoons fresh lemon juice
½ cup dry white wine
1 teaspoon grated lemon zest
¼ cup chopped fresh parsley
Lemon slices, for garnish

Preheat the oven to 375°. Slit the fillet lengthwise to form a cavity. Rinse inside and out, and dry well. Combine the garlic, butter, salt, pepper, thyme, and flour in a small bowl; mix well. Place the fish on double heavy-duty foil. In the cavity, place 1 tablespoon of the garlic mixture, 4 shrimp, and ½ cup mushrooms. Sprinkle with 1 tablespoon of the lemon juice and ¼ cup of the wine. Dot the top with the remaining garlic mixture.

Arrange the remaining shrimp and mushrooms over the top; sprinkle with the remaining lemon juice, the remaining wine, and the lemon zest. Bring the long sides of the foil together over the fish; secure with a double fold. Fold both ends of the foil upward several times; place on a cookie sheet. Bake for 40 minutes, or until the fish flakes easily with a fork. Open the foil; spoon the juices over the fish and sprinkle with the parsley. Serve with lemon slices.

Tampa Treasures
Junior League of Tampa
Tampa, Florida

HERB-GRILLED CATFISH FILLETS

YIELD: 6 TO 8 SERVINGS

6 to 8 catfish fillets
3 to 4 tablespoons fresh lemon juice
2 tablespoons cayenne pepper
2 tablespoons garlic powder
2 teaspoons dried parsley
2 teaspoons ground thyme
2 teaspoons basil
2 teaspoons black pepper
2 teaspoons onion powder
2 teaspoons sage
2 teaspoons marjoram

Wash the catfish fillets and pat dry. Place in a glass dish and sprinkle the lemon juice over the fillets. Place the remaining ingredients in a jar and combine well. The herb mixture can be stored, tightly covered, for several months. Shake the herbs over the fillets, covering both sides of the fish. Allow the fillets to marinate, refrigerated, in the herb-and-lemon mixture for at least 24 hours.

When ready to serve, grill over a medium-hot fire for 4 to 5 minutes per side, basting with any juices. Serve immediately. (Or place under a hot broiler in a pan that will collect the juices and cook for 3 to 4 minutes without turning the fish. Serve immediately with any accumulated juices.)

Classic Catfish
Evelyn and Tony Roughton
Indianola, Mississippi

FRIED CATFISH

Once a whiskered bottom dweller, the catfish has gone uptown, thanks to the efforts of aquaculturists, feeding on grain at the top of the water, rather than muck at the bottom.

YIELD: 6 SERVINGS

2 pounds catfish fillets (6 large or 12 small)
2 eggs
¼ cup milk
1½ cups white cornmeal
½ cup flour
2 teaspoons salt
1 teaspoon black pepper
½ teaspoon cayenne pepper
Solid vegetable shortening or oil
Tartar sauce, for serving

Fried Fish

Clean the fish and wipe perfectly dry, then dip in beaten egg and afterwards in bread crumbs or corn meal, but preferably in the crumbs, patting these on well that no loose ones may fall off and burn in the fat, then plunge the fish, a few pieces at a time, in the fat which must be smoking hot and of which there must be sufficient in the pan to completely cover the fish. Cook golden brown, and drain well before serving.

Collected by Kate C. Hubbard in Possum & Pomegranate *for the Federal Writers Project "America Eats"*

Rinse the catfish and dry with paper towels. Beat the eggs and milk together in a large flat dish. Combine the cornmeal, flour, salt, black pepper, and cayenne in another flat dish. Heat ¼ inch shortening or oil in a skillet. Dip the catfish into the egg mixture and then into the cornmeal mixture, coating well on both sides. Fry for about 2 minutes on each side. Serve with tartar sauce.

Cookin' Up a Storm
Jane Lee Rankin
Louisville, Kentucky

PAN-FRIED NATIVE TROUT CAMPFIRE-STYLE

YIELD: 4 SERVINGS

4 fresh trout, cleaned and scaled
Salt and pepper to taste
8 slices bacon
⅔ to 1 cup yellow cornmeal
¼ cup cooking oil or bacon
  drippings
1 small onion, thinly sliced (optional)

Season the fish inside and out with salt and pepper. Secure the end of a slice of bacon in a gill of a fish and wrap it around the fish. Start a second slice of bacon where the first slice ends and continue wrapping, ending at the tail of the fish. Secure with a toothpick in the tail. Repeat with each fish. Roll the fish in cornmeal, coating fully.

Heat the oil in a large skillet until very hot. Add the trout. Pan-fry 4 minutes on each side until firm to the touch and golden brown. Remove. Sauté the onion slices in the pan and spoon them over the fish, if desired.

A Second Serving
Junior League of Charleston
Charleston, West Virginia

TROUT AMANDINE

YIELD: 4 SERVINGS

4 fillets of trout
1 cup milk
1 teaspoon salt
⅛ teaspoon black pepper
½ cup flour
2 sticks (½ pound) unsalted butter
½ cup chopped almonds
Lemon wedges and parsley,
   for garnish

Dip the fillets in the milk; season with salt and pepper, then coat with flour. Melt the butter in a skillet and cook the fillets, browning evenly on both sides. Remove the fish from the skillet. Add the almonds to the skillet and sauté. Serve over the fillets. Garnish with lemon wedges and parsley.

Louisiana Wildlife Magazine
Baton Rouge, Louisiana

GRILLED REDFISH

YIELD: 4 SERVINGS

4 (6-ounce) redfish with skin
½ stick unsalted butter or margarine
⅓ cup white wine
1 tablespoon Worcestershire sauce
1 tablespoon garlic powder
1 tablespoon purchased Creole seasoning
2 lemons

Our Southern Receipt

Vicksburg Fried Catfish

In the old steamboat days, Vicksburg—Mississippi's wicked, wide-open town—lived high with all the trimmings. Perched on the bluffs overlooking the Mississippi, it is still famous for its excellent catfish. This old, disarmingly simple recipe comes from that city.

YIELD: 2 SERVINGS

1 pound catfish
Salt and black pepper
Cornmeal
Fat for deep frying

Season the catfish well with salt and pepper. Roll in cornmeal. Use a pot of deep fat with temperature at 360°. Place the fish in the pot and fry until done. Serve very hot.

Collected by Eudora Welty for the Federal Writers Project "America Eats"

Fillet fish, leaving skin on each half. Melt the butter in a skillet and add the wine, Worcestershire sauce, and garlic powder. Pour half of this liquid over the redfish (with skin side down). Generously sprinkle Creole seasoning over the redfish. Slice 1 of the lemons and place the slices on the redfish. Place redfish directly on a medium grill. Cook for 20 to 25 minutes, basting

ED SCOTT

DOWN FREEDOM HIGHWAY

Back during the sixties, when the Freedom Riders came through Mississippi, I would load up the back of my pickup with food—fried chicken, collards, pole beans, potato salad, cornbread, whatever my wife cooked that night—and drive it down to where they camped out. I wanted to help out, do what I could to show support.

That was a crazy time around here. Folks were coming to Mississippi to help with voter registration. And local folks like Fannie Lou Hamer were in the thick of it. Me and my wife helped out how we could. We were a farming family. Rice and soybeans mostly. Just like our fathers before us.

My father moved to the Delta in 1919. He started out with row crops, corn and cotton, and beans. By 1929 he had his own land, and by 1948 he had put in 800 acres of rice when he didn't even have a well to water them with. He was the first black man to grow rice in the Delta. You know, we used to laugh about him splashing water out of a ditch onto that rice, thinking that would do some good.

But the sixties was a rough time. It got to be that even the churches were feeling the pressure. When our church over in Mound Bayou tried to get a building loan, the bankers told 'em, "No, y'all likely to get involved in that Civil Rights Movement mess."

So when the Freedom Riders came through, camping down in Glendora and down near Scott, we would bring them some food. It's the least we could do. And after a while I would be driving up and down that highway so much—the bed of my pickup filled with food—that every patrolman in the state knew my tag number by heart.

Ed Scott, a native of Drew, Mississippi, was the first African American catfish farmer in the Mississippi Delta.

occasionally with the butter liquid. After cooking, squeeze the remaining lemon over the top before serving.

River Road Recipes III
Junior League of Baton Rouge
Baton Rouge, Louisiana

POMPANO EN PAPILLOTE

When the Brazilian aviation pioneer Alberto Santos-Dumont visited New Orleans in 1901, Antoine's honored him with a dish made to look like a turn-of-the-century flying balloon—a dish that became one of Antoine's most famous creations. The fish is poached in a very rich sauce inside a closed envelope made of baking parchment. A marvelous aroma fills the room when the papillote (paper bag) is cut open at the table. This dramatic dish tastes just as good with redfish, trout, or red snapper. Prepare the boiled shrimp ahead of time.

YIELD: 4 SERVINGS

4 (12-inch) squares of baking parchment
6 tablespoons unsalted butter, plus extra for
  basting the insides of the papillotes
¼ cup flour
⅔ cup finely minced shallots
1 tablespoon finely minced fresh parsley
1 tablespoon dry white wine
¼ teaspoon salt
½ teaspoon freshly ground white pepper
⅛ teaspoon cayenne pepper
2 large egg yolks, lightly beaten
6 tablespoons heavy cream
1 cup boiled fresh shrimp, broken into thirds

½ cup choice lump crab meat
½ cup freshly shucked small oysters (about 18),
  drained
2 small or 1 medium pompano, tenderloined
  (medium divided into 2 pieces)

Trim each square of parchment into the shape of a heart, and crease down the center.

Prepare the sauce in a large, heavy saucepan: Melt the 6 tablespoons butter over low heat, gradually add the flour, stirring constantly, and cook for 2 minutes. Add the shallots and parsley and cook 5 minutes longer, stirring frequently. Remove the pan from the heat. Add the wine, salt, pepper, cayenne, egg yolks, and cream; mix thoroughly. Return the pan to low heat and add the shrimp, crab meat, and oysters. Cook for 5 minutes, stirring gently. Remove the pan from the heat.

Preheat the oven to 425°. Butter the inside of each papillote; fold in half, buttered side in. Fold up the edge of the bottom half to form a lip about ¾ inch deep. Pour half the sauce in four equal quantities, on the bottom half of each papillote. Place a piece of fish on the sauce, then pour the remaining sauce over the fish. Fold down the top half of the papillote. Bring the top and bottom edges together, folding them over tightly several times. Be sure the pointed tip is tightly closed—fold the point over twice to make sure. Put the sealed papillotes in a large shallow baking dish; bake for about 18 to 20 minutes, or until the backing parchment begins to brown. Serve closed on individual plates; open at the table.

New Orleans Cookbook
Rima Collin and Richard Collin
New Orleans, Louisiana

SAUCES

....

THE TIES THAT BIND

I know dozens of Southerners who grew up hearing some version of the "He just up and died at the table" story. Given the typical Southern groaning board of three or four different kinds of meats, ten or twelve different kinds of vegetables, and mountains of hot bread dripping with butter, passing to one's reward while eating is to die in a perfect state of grace.

FLORENCE KING, *SOUTHÉRN LADIÉS AND GÉNTLÉMÉN*

The Ties That Bind

....

Time was when the infernal dog days of summer signaled the arrival of lay-by time, when thoughts turned from labor to luxury. With the cotton crop in the ground and the corn crop in the crib, our agrarian forebears settled in for a season of celebration.

From about the Fourth of July to Labor Day, Southerners of all hues and hometowns gathered for outdoor feasts. Whether it be a barbecue given to benefit of the local elementary school or an impromptu fish fry on the banks of a creek brimming with gasper goo and catfish, those in attendance were assured of three things: The food would be fresh, the tables would groan beneath the weight of their bounty, and a spot in the shade would be hard-won.

Though many of these lay-by feasts were community-wide events, the astute eater attempted to keep his appetite in check until time came for the annual family reunion and dinner on the grounds. Then and only then did Cousin Effie's buttermilk-dipped, corn flour–crusted fried chicken make an appearance. Then and only then did Aunt Ellen take the time to bake both a chess pie and a pecan pie, not to mention convince Uncle Jimmy to lug along the ice cream churn and a bushel of freshly picked peaches.

Many a reunion was staged on the grounds of the old family church, yet the preferred spot was beneath boughs of towering elm, live oak, or cedar trees that ringed the ancestral homeplace.

Early in the morning the men set to work, gathering tin tubs filled with ice for the watermelons and scavenging the surrounding countryside for sawhorses and plywood to be used as makeshift buffet tables. By midmorning the women have arrived. Soon the tables will be draped in white linens, and the spread will be spread.

The air is thick with the smells of squash casserole, spoonbread, fried chicken, black-eyed peas, and country ham; devil's food cake, chess pie, pound cake, and divinity. As each car pulls into the drive and each woman piles out, baskets in hand, children in tow, the bounty piles higher, the tension mounts.

In a clutch near the tallest tree stand the elder cooks, proud and haughty. As they unveil their specialties to the accustomed "oohs" and "ahhs" of the assembled throng, the younger women work the crowd, soliciting a promise to taste their sweet potato pie or take a nibble of their deviled eggs. And still the plates pile higher.

Sensing that the serving hour is drawing near, the men return, and soon thereafter the preacher steps forward to offer thanks. For the briefest of moments, all is still and quiet. But as soon as he utters amen, the rush is on. Savvy diners, secure in their knowledge of last year's best and worst, make a beeline for their favorites, while the cooks sit back to savor the praise and swap recipes. Not a few are soon embroiled in heated debate over the proper preparation of such Southern standbys as beaten biscuits and tomato aspic.

The eaters come in waves, first helpings followed by seconds and maybe thirds, with dessert a must no matter how many helpings have come before. As the platters of meats, breads, vegetables, and desserts dwindle, and the crowd dissipates, tribute is paid as the better cooks proudly bear their empty platters homeward.

TARTAR SAUCE

Kin to the French garlic-infused aïoli mayonnaise, this rich sauce suits shrimp especially well.

YIELD: 1½ CUPS

1 cup mayonnaise
1 tablespoon Creole mustard
¼ cup minced green onions, including tops
2 tablespoons minced parsley
1 teaspoon fresh lemon juice
Dash of Tabasco
Salt to taste

Combine all the ingredients in a small bowl; blend well. Serve with seafood.

Southern Accent
Junior League of Pine Bluff
Pine Bluff, Arkansas

RÉMOULADE SAUCE

New Orleans rémoulade sauce is highly seasoned and reddish in color. This version closely resembles the one served at Galatoire's and contains both puréed and minced fresh vegetables. The sauce can be prepared in advance and refrigerated, but don't sauce the shrimp until a few minutes before serving or they will get soggy.

YIELD: ABOUT 2 CUPS

1 bunch scallions, cut up
2 small stalks celery, cut up, plus 1 tablespoon chopped

2 sprigs fresh parsley, cut up, plus 2 teaspoons
   finely minced
3 tablespoons Creole mustard
5 teaspoons paprika
1¼ teaspoons salt
½ teaspoon freshly ground black pepper
¼ teaspoon cayenne pepper
6 tablespoons white wine vinegar
5 teaspoons fresh lemon juice
½ teaspoon dried basil
¾ cup olive oil
1 shallot, chopped
Chopped lettuce, for serving
Chilled shrimp, for serving

Process the scallions, cut-up celery, and cut-up
parsley in a food processor or reduce almost to a
purée in the blender. Place the purée in a china or
stainless steel bowl; then add the mustard, paprika, salt, pepper, and cayenne. Blend with a
wooden spoon. Add the vinegar, lemon juice, and
basil; blend again. Gradually add the oil, stirring
constantly. When well blended, add the chopped
scallions, chopped celery, and minced parsley;
blend thoroughly. Cover and refrigerate for at
least 3 hours.

Note: Serve over chopped lettuce and
chilled shrimp that have been peeled and
deveined.

New Orleans Cookbook
Rima Collin and Richard Collin
New Orleans, Louisiana

WALNUT KETCHUP

A derivative of Chinese fish sauces, catsup—or ketchup, as it is more commonly called—has long been made from substances other than the omnipresent tomato.

YIELD: 2 QUARTS

Young tender walnuts
1 handful salt for every 25 walnuts
Vinegar
For every 2 quarts liquid:
  2 ounces black pepper
  2 ounces ground ginger
  1 ounce ground cloves
  1 ounce ground nutmeg
  Large pinch of cayenne pepper
  1 shallot, minced fine
  Thimbleful celery seed

Bruise the walnuts with a wooden mallet and place in a large jar with sufficient water to cover them, adding a handful of salt for every 25 walnuts. Stir them twice a day for 14 days.
Drain off the liquor into a saucepan. Cover the walnuts with boiling vinegar, crush to a pulp, and strain through a colander into the liquor in the saucepan. For every 2 quarts, add above measures of spices tied up in a muslin bag. Boil for 1 hour, remove spices, and bottle. It is suggested you dribble melted beeswax around the top of the sealed bottles.

Rose Budd's Kitchen
Rose Budd Stevens
Amite County, Mississippi

COCKTAIL SAUCE

YIELD: ABOUT 1 CUP

½ cup tomato ketchup or chili
  sauce
3 tablespoons fresh lemon juice
Few drops Tabasco
¼ teaspoon salt
½ cup finely chopped celery
2 tablespoons Worcestershire sauce
Horseradish to taste

Combine the ingredients and store in a jar in the refrigerator. Use for oysters, clams, shrimp, crabmeat, or lobster.

The Memphis Cookbook
Junior League of Memphis
Memphis, Tennessee

HOMEMADE MAYONNAISE

There are those among us who would not dream of making a tomato sandwich without homemade mayonnaise.

YIELD: ABOUT 3 CUPS

3 egg yolks
1½ cups vegetable oil
1½ cups olive oil
Juice of 3 lemons
3 teaspoons salt
¾ teaspoon black pepper
¾ teaspoon dry mustard

Have all the ingredients at room temperature. Beat the egg yolks until thick and lemon-colored. Alternately add the oils and lemon juice, slowly at first. Add the salt, pepper, and mustard last (adding the seasonings last is the secret to perfect mayonnaise).

Cotton Country Collection
Junior League of Monroe
Monroe, Louisiana

SWEET-AND-SOUR MUSTARD

YIELD: 4 HALF-PINTS

½ cup dry mustard
1 cup tarragon vinegar
6 eggs
¾ cup sugar
1 stick (¼ pound) unsalted butter
1 teaspoon salt

Put the dry mustard in a mixing bowl and pour the vinegar over it but do not mix. Cover and let stand overnight or at least 3 hours. Put the mustard mixture in the top of a double boiler and mix with a wire whisk over hot water. Add the eggs, one at a time, whisking continuously until

thoroughly mixed. Add the sugar, butter, and salt; cook over hot water until the mixture thickens. (Do not overcook or the eggs will curdle.) Put into individual jars and refrigerate. This can be kept for several months in the refrigerator. Serve with any meat or cheese; perfect for gift giving.

Dinner on the Diner
Junior League of Chattanooga
Chattanooga, Tennessee

WILLOW LAKE FARM BARBECUE SAUCE

Barbecues were the favorite form of entertainment for the Jeter family at their farm in North Shelby County, Tennessee. Many friends from the cotton business on Memphis's Front Street fished at Willow Lake and feasted on barbecued pork— often a whole hog—which was marinated and then cooked on a grill over a pit dug beside one of the cabins at the farm. The meat was cooked from late afternoon all through the night. The sauce was made by Mrs. Jeter in quantities to last throughout the year—and in her words, made "by taste and smell and how it looks, and stored in a cool place." Here is a scaled-down version of her recipe, submitted by Mrs. J. Stovall Jeter.

YIELD: 4 CUPS

½ cup vegetable oil
2 tablespoons dry mustard
2 teaspoons allspice
2 teaspoons paprika
2 teaspoons cayenne pepper

JESSICA HARRIS

FINDING THE SOUTH IN THE NORTH

Though I've lived in Brooklyn most of my life, my grandparents on both sides are from the South: Virginia, Tennessee, North Carolina, and Alabama.

The South is very much with me. It may be sort of subcutaneous, but I tend to contend that if you scratch a black person pretty much anywhere, you will come up with some part of the South. Although I was reared in the North, I do know hog maws. I don't necessarily like to cook them or eat them, but my dad adored them.

The South is omnipresent in my part of the North. The people are here. The foods are here. I can get raw peanuts at the market. And black-eyed peas in the pod. And greens. I get collards. I get mustards. I get kale. And that's just the traditional Southern greens. I also get all the Caribbean greens: malanga, callaloo bush, you name it. They are all in the market, side by side. There is no segregation of greens. In my New York neighborhood, Southern sweet potatoes coexist with African yams.

On my street in Brooklyn, this little man used to set up shop selling fruits and vegetables from the trunk of his car. You could mark the changes in seasons by what emerged from his trunk. In the summer he had a little sign that said: "Watermelons, Sweet Like Your Woman." It was as if the South had been preserved in amber. The South found in the North is the South as remembered and maintained by folks who left the South twenty, thirty, fifty years ago.

My grandmother Jones made hot breads in industrial quantities once a week. My grandmother Harris grew collard greens in South Jamaica, Queens. And made lye soap to boot. That's not part of the urban experience. That's not something you do on the third floor of an apartment building. That is a habit that harks back to a rural Southern past. My grandmothers were stone-cold Southerners to the marrow of their bones.

Jessica Harris, a professor of English at Queens College, is the author of numerous works on the foods of the African Diaspora, including The Africa Cookbook.

2 teaspoons black pepper

1 cup white vinegar, or more to add later if a
    sharper, thinner sauce is desired

2 cups ketchup

½ cup Worcestershire sauce

7 tablespoons horseradish

½ cup firmly packed dark brown sugar

Put the oil in a small bowl and add the mustard, allspice, paprika, cayenne, and black pepper. Mix well. In another bowl, combine the vinegar, ketchup, Worcestershire, horseradish, and brown sugar; mix well. Stir the spice mixture into the ketchup mixture. Add more vinegar for a sharper, thinner sauce.

Gracious Goodness
Memphis Symphony League
Memphis, Tennessee

DR. BARBECUE'S CAROLINA MUSTARD SAUCE

The sauce around Columbia, South Carolina, has a mustard base. The professor got this recipe from his church, where they cook whole hogs at fundraisers. "I suppose the sauce will work on less than a hog," he says, "but it just isn't right!"

YIELD: 1¾ CUPS

¾ cup yellow mustard

¾ cup red wine vinegar

½ cup sugar

1½ tablespoons unsalted butter or margarine

2 teaspoons salt

½ tablespoon Worcestershire sauce

1¼ teaspoons ground black pepper

½ teaspoon Tabasco

Combine all the ingredients in a saucepan; mix well. Simmer over low heat for 30 minutes. Let stand at room temperature for 1 hour before using. The unused sauce can be kept, refrigerated, up to several weeks. Use as a basting sauce or table sauce with pork or chicken. Slap it on hot dogs, too.

The Ultimate Barbecue Sauce Cookbook
Jim Auchmutey and Susan Puckett
Atlanta, Georgia

LEXINGTON RED SPLASH

Lexington, North Carolina, home to some twenty barbecue restaurants, is the undisputed epicenter of this style of sauce making.

YIELD: ABOUT 2 CUPS

1½ cups white vinegar

⅔ cup ketchup

½ cup water

1 tablespoon sugar

½ teaspoon ground black pepper

½ teaspoon cayenne pepper

Pinch or two of red pepper flakes

Salt to taste

Combine all the ingredients in a small saucepan; simmer for 15 minutes. The unused sauce can be stored indefinitely in a cool dark place. It goes on right before serving and can also be used in coleslaw.

The Ultimate Barbecue Sauce Cookbook
Jim Auchmutey and Susan Puckett
Atlanta, Georgia

DEACON HUBBARD'S WHEAT STREET MOP

There is an unwritten Eleventh Commandment at the Wheat Street Baptist Church in Atlanta's Martin Luther King, Jr., historic district: Thou shalt not baste with barbecue sauce. That tomato stuff is fine for the table, but to see spareribs through fire and brimstone, you need to bless them with something thin and tart. Something like this mop that members Robert Hughey and James Rowland, Jr., use when they cook for the board of ushers. They actually brush it on with a short-handled mop. The recipe comes from the late Deacon Mark Hubbard, who had a standard response when people asked him why he didn't market his barbecue skills: "I'm rich when I make my friends happy."

YIELD: 2½ CUPS

1 cup Worcestershire sauce
1 tablespoon unsalted margarine
1 tablespoon ketchup
1 cup apple cider vinegar
¼ cup water
½ teaspoon ground black pepper
½ teaspoon paprika
Salt to taste

Combine the Worcestershire sauce and margarine in a small saucepan; simmer over medium-high heat until the margarine is melted. Add the remaining ingredients. Bring to a boil. Remove from the heat and use warm as a basting sauce. The sauce can be kept, refrigerated, for up to several weeks.

The Ultimate Barbecue Sauce Cookbook
Jim Auchmutey and Susan Puckett
Atlanta, Georgia

MY OLD KENTUCKY SAUCE

From John Egerton, author of Southern Food, *comes this complex tomato-and-vinegar number he adapted from Vince Leneave, a cook at a hunting lodge in his hometown of Cadiz, Kentucky.*

YIELD: ABOUT 1½ CUPS

1 cup apple cider vinegar
¼ cup water
¼ cup coarsely chopped onion
¼ cup coarsely chopped green bell pepper
¼ cup coarsely chopped celery
1 teaspoon minced garlic
2 teaspoons whole black peppercorns
1 bay leaf
1 cup ketchup
2 tablespoons unsalted butter or margarine
2 tablespoons fresh lemon juice
1 tablespoon sugar
1 tablespoon Worcestershire sauce
2½ teaspoons chili powder

2½ teaspoons paprika
½ teaspoon dry mustard
¼ teaspoon Tabasco
¼ teaspoon Liquid Smoke
¼ teaspoon cayenne

Combine the vinegar, water, onion, bell pepper, celery, garlic, peppercorns, and bay leaf in a large saucepan. Bring to a boil. Reduce the heat to low and simmer for 20 minutes. Strain and discard the solids. Return the liquid to the saucepan. Add the remaining ingredients; stir well over medium heat until the butter melts. Simmer 5 minutes longer. Serve warm as a finishing or table sauce on pork, chicken, and mutton. The unused sauce can be kept, refrigerated, for up to several weeks.

The Ultimate Barbecue Sauce Cookbook
Jim Auchmutey and Susan Puckett
Atlanta, Georgia

SWINE LAKE BALLET SAUCE

Dark as Mississippi mud, this sauce from the Swine Lake Ballet barbecue team of Corinth, Mississippi, is sneaky hot (mustard), a little sweet (brown sugar), and positively sinus-opening (vinegar, lots of vinegar).

1 cup yellow mustard
1 cup apple cider vinegar
⅔ cup firmly packed brown sugar
3 tablespoons paprika
1 heaping tablespoon chili powder
1 teaspoon cayenne pepper
1 teaspoon white pepper

Combine all the ingredients in a medium saucepan. Simmer over medium-low heat for 10 to 15 minutes. Serve warm as a marinade, basting sauce, or table sauce for pork or poultry. The unused sauce can be kept, refrigerated, for several weeks.

The Ultimate Barbecue Sauce Cookbook
Jim Auchmutey and Susan Puckett
Atlanta, Georgia

DADDY BOB'S SIT-DOWN CIDER SAUCE

From Charles Robert Auchmutey, Sr., grandfather of Jim Auchmutey, comes this vinegar-based barbecue sauce.

YIELD: 1½ CUPS

½ cup ketchup
1 tablespoon yellow mustard
1 cup apple cider vinegar
1 teaspoon ground black pepper
Salt to taste

Whisk together the ketchup and mustard in a medium saucepan. Stir in the vinegar, pepper, and salt. Simmer over medium-low heat for 15 minutes. Use on pork or any other meat that needs a wake-up call. The unused sauce can be stored indefinitely in a cool, dark place.

The Ultimate Barbecue Sauce Cookbook
Jim Auchmutey and Susan Puckett
Atlanta, Georgia

TOMATO GRAVY

Among the Italians in New Orleans, a tomato sauce and a tomato gravy are one and the same.

YIELD: ABOUT 4 CUPS

1 tablespoon vegetable shortening
2 tablespoons flour
1½ cups water
1 (10-ounce) can stewed tomatoes or 9 ripe
   tomatoes, chopped
Salt and pepper to taste
Biscuits, for serving

Melt the shortening in a 10-inch cast-iron skillet. Add the flour and stir until thickened and browned. Mix ¾ cup of the water with the tomatoes and add the mixture to the flour, stirring constantly. Add enough of the remaining water to make the mixture medium-thick. Add salt and pepper to taste. Serve over biscuits.

Family Secrets
Lee Academy
Clarksdale, Mississippi

GIBLET GRAVY

YIELD: ABOUT 2 TO 3 CUPS

Turkey or chicken giblets (neck, liver, gizzard, heart)
1 medium onion, chopped
3 stalks celery, chopped
1 quart water
½ teaspoon salt
¼ teaspoon black pepper
½ stick unsalted butter
¼ cup flour
2 hard-cooked eggs, chopped

Bring the first 6 ingredients to a boil in a 2-quart saucepan. Reduce the heat to low and cook until tender, about 1 to 2 hours. Remove the neck, liver, gizzard, and heart from the saucepan, reserving the broth. Remove the meat from the neck and chop the liver, gizzard, and heart. Set aside.

In a saucepan, melt the butter over medium heat; add the flour, stirring constantly for 2 minutes. Add the broth from giblets and cook until thickened. Add the meat, chopped giblets, and eggs.

Serve with turkey or chicken and cornbread dressing. (The giblets can be cooked the day before serving and the giblets and broth refrigerated.)

Impressions
Auxiliary to the Memphis Dental Society
Memphis, Tennessee

RED-EYE GRAVY

Cut ham slices ¼ inch thick. Lightly grease pan (bacon fat or lard). Fry ham on each side and remove from pan immediately. To hot fat remaining, add ¼ teaspoon sugar and 4 tablespoons water (or coffee). Cover pan and simmer a few more minutes to make gravy, adding paprika to make gravy redder if desired. Pour over ham slices to serve.

How to Cook a Pig
and Other Back-to-the Farm Recipes
Betty Talmadge
Lovejoy, Georgia

WHITE SAUCE

A blanket of white to envelop and bind.

YIELD: 1 CUP

2 tablespoons unsalted margarine
2 tablespoons flour
¼ teaspoon salt
Dash of white or black pepper
1 cup skim milk

Melt the margarine in a saucepan over low heat. Blend in the flour, the salt, and a dash of pepper. Add the milk. Cook quickly, stirring constantly, until the mixture thickens and bubbles.

Southern But Lite
Jen Avis and Kathy Ward
West Monroe, Louisiana

JALAPEÑO-CUMIN BUTTER

YIELD: ABOUT ½ CUP

2 pickled jalapeños, finely chopped
½ teaspoon ground cumin
1 stick (¼ pound) unsalted butter,
  at room temperature

In a bowl or food processor, beat the jalapeños and cumin into the room-temperature butter. Cover and refrigerate until ready to use. Serve at room temperature. Best if made at least 1 day in advance.

And Roses for the Table
Junior League of Tyler
Tyler, Texas

CHOCOLATE GRAVY

Chocolate gravy is a favorite in the Ozark Mountains of Arkansas and the hills of Mississippi. Should you pour this over your biscuits, it will be a favorite on your breakfast table as well.

YIELD: 10 TO 12 SERVINGS

2 cups sugar
¼ cup cocoa powder
1 stick (¼ pound) unsalted butter or
  margarine
3 cups milk
Hot homemade biscuits, for serving

Mix the sugar, cocoa, and butter in a large saucepan over medium heat. Add ½ cup of the milk. Let the mixture come to a boil, lower the heat, and simmer for 10 minutes. Add the remaining 2 cups of milk, raise the heat to medium, and cook, stirring constantly, until the mixture comes to a boil. Reduce the heat and simmer for 30 minutes. Serve over hot homemade biscuits.

Homemade Christmas
Memphis, Tennessee

PECAN PRALINE SAUCE

The street peddlers' treats of New Orleans liquefy and move up-South in this favorite topping for ice cream.

YIELD: 1¼ CUPS

½ cup light corn syrup
⅓ cup firmly packed light brown sugar
3 tablespoons unsalted butter
⅛ teaspoon salt
2 tablespoons evaporated milk
½ cup finely chopped pecans
Ice cream, for serving

Combine the syrup, brown sugar, butter, and salt in a microwave-safe bowl. Microwave on High for 2½ to 3 minutes or until thick and bubbly; do not overcook. Let cool for 5 minutes. Stir in the evaporated milk and pecans. Chill until ready to use. Serve over ice cream.

Children's Party Book
Junior League of Hampton Roads
Newport News, Virginia

PRESERVES, JELLIES, PICKLES

WOMEN'S WORK: LESSONS LEARNED
IN THE SOUTHERN KITCHEN

There is no spectacle on earth more appealing than that of a beautiful woman in the act of cooking dinner for someone she loves.

THOMAS WOLFE, *THÉ WÉB AND THÉ ROCK*

Women's Work:
Lessons Learned in the Southern Kitchen

···························

Long before there were chefs, the South was blessed with cooks—women, for the most part, who toiled over wood-fired stoves and sooty, infernal fireplaces, coaxing supper from the flames as black smoke belched forth. Such work was, ironically enough, dismissed as being beneath men, as being too delicate—too, well, womanly.

Truth be told, the work was nothing if not arduous, and the workplace, the kitchen, either too hot or too cold. In the dead of winter, drafts cut through the room like icepicks through butter. In the swelter of summer, rivulets of sweat ran down the cook's back, fused with steam from the stewpots, and formed a swampy cloud that hung heavy in the air, blanketing everyone, everything.

At the center of the kitchen was the stove, nexus of all activity, all exchange. Here was one of the few places in the home where women ruled the roost, where men were not welcome or at least were relegated to lesser roles by dint of their gender, their lack of culinary knowledge.

For Southern women the kitchen was a refuge unsuspected, a nurturing space where hard work and biting gossip were shared. Sure, men had their place, and young boys were known to spend hour upon hour prowling about, exploring the icebox and pantry, the smokehouse and root cellar, but for the most part, the kitchen was the province of the Southern woman, and her charge, the daughter, the heir apparent to the cookstove.

Here the generation gap was breached as mother taught daughter to put up peaches that tasted of clove and cinnamon yet retained their summer juiciness, their *peachiness,* when retrieved from the cup-

board months later for a wintertime treat. Here recipes were bequeathed like dowry, and privileges granted—the chance to roll a slice of green tomato in cornmeal and fry it in bacon fat before the whole bushel was chopped up for chow-chow, the privilege of plucking a pod of pickled okra from the brine before the mason jar lid was wrenched tight.

Most important, it was here in the kitchen, in that most female-centered of spaces, that children learned to value what was often derided as "women's work," giving credence to the task at hand, and paying homage to the cooks who went before.

Time and temperatures have to be worked out very carefully for canning. Too little time or too low a temperature means you are not protecting the food against bacteria, enzymes, molds, and yeasts. Too much time or too high a temperature may mean you are needlessly destroying nutrients in the food. Several different methods should be followed to the letter, such as *boiling water bath canning* or *steam pressure canning.* We suggest you use the professional guidance of *Mrs. Wages® New Home Canning Guide* or another reputable book in preparing the recipes in this section.

PEACH ORANGE MARMALADE

YIELD: 4 PINTS

12 medium peaches
3 medium oranges
Sugar

Wash and peel the peaches. Wash the oranges. Remove peel from 1½ of the oranges and discard. Grind the peeled and unpeeled oranges and the peaches in a food processor. Measure the fruit (should be about 6 cups). Put it into a large preserving kettle; add sugar to taste. Bring the mixture to a boil. Boil rapidly for 20 to 30 minutes, stirring occasionally to prevent burning. Pour into sterilized jars; seal.

Woman's Exchange Club Cookbook I
Woman's Exchange
Memphis, Tennessee

BLACKBERRY JELLY

Nancy Tregre Wilson says, "Memere was always in charge of the kitchen during jelly time. There never seemed to be enough blackberry jelly to last the year. For that reason it was rationed out and used for jellyrolls rather than put on the table every morning for breakfast. It was always my favorite. In later years, when I moved away from home, Mama would always sneak a jar into my suitcase as a 'surprise' for me when I reached my destination."

YIELD: 2 PINTS

3 quarts blackberries

3 cups sugar

Crush the berries; place in gauze jelly bags and squeeze out the juice, about 3½ cups. Place the juice and sugar in a large saucepan. Cook over medium heat to a rolling boil. When the jelly sheets from a spoon, remove from the heat and place in sterile jars. Seal.

Mam Papaul's Country Creole Basket
Nancy Tregre Wilson
Baton Rouge, Louisiana

FIG PRESERVES

There's more to figs than Newton would have you believe.

YIELD: ABOUT 4 PINTS

2 pounds figs

2 pounds sugar

1 cup water (1½ cups if using raw sugar)

1 lemon, thinly sliced

Wash and peel the figs. Make a syrup by boiling the sugar and water in a saucepan. Add the figs and lemon slices. Let stand 12 hours. Pour into cold sterile jars and seal.

A Cook's Tour of Shreveport
Junior League of Shreveport
Shreveport, Louisiana

Fig Preserves

Use measure for measure (volume): 1 cup figs to 1 cup sugar with ½ lemon sliced for quart of figs, but 1 lemon would be sufficient for 3 quarts cooked at once.

Wash figs, ripe but not mashed, leaving stems on. (Some use soda water; I prefer clear.) Do not let stand in water; take out immediately, drain (with hands or colander), put in heavy metal container large enough that liquid cannot boil over, twice as much space, at least. Cover figs with the sugar (layer or put all sugar on top), and let sit over 6 hours, or until all sugar is dissolved and juices are drawn from figs by sugar.

Cook slowly, without covering, at simmering temperature for 1½ hours. Syrup should be thick. When fig color and density are satisfactory, take off heat and set aside. This allows figs to soak up liquid back into cells (to "plump up"). Usually takes all day. Be sure to put where ants can't find it. Pack in jars, fig by fig with lemon slices against sides of jars (lemon needed to keep juices from crystallizing later). Cover figs with juice, leaving ¾-inch headspace. Tighten lids. I always process jars at 5 pounds pressure for 5 minutes (no higher, no longer). Lift jars (to hear pop seal) and cool. Store in dark place. Will keep indefinitely and can be eaten by stems of figs.

Sue Price Lipsey (1904–1997) was born in Louisiana, daughter of a Baptist preacher. She taught English at Mississippi College.

PLUM JELLY SAUCE

YIELD: ABOUT 1 CUP

¾ cup plum jelly

2 tablespoons fresh orange juice

Dash of mace

1 teaspoon flour

¼ teaspoon dry mustard

3 tablespoons pineapple juice

Melt the jelly in a saucepan; add the orange juice and mace. In a small bowl, blend the flour, mustard, and pineapple juice. Add to the jelly. Simmer 5 minutes. Serve with sliced lamb.

Treasures of the Smokies
Junior League of Johnson City
Johnson City, Tennessee

PEPPER JELLY

Jalapeño jelly spread over a block of cream cheese and served with crackers is a quick, delicious appetizer or snack.

YIELD: 4 PINTS

¼ to ½ cup chopped fresh jalapeño pepper
  (see Note)

1 cup chopped green bell pepper

1½ cups apple cider

1 cup apple cider vinegar

6½ cups sugar

6 ounces liquid pectin

Green food coloring (optional)

Bring all ingredients except pectin and food coloring to a hard, rolling boil in a large saucepan. Boil 1 minute. Remove from the heat. Let stand 5 minutes. Add pectin and stir well. Strain if clear jelly is desired. Food coloring can be added sparingly for a bright green color. Pour into hot, sterilized jars. Seal.

Note: Use caution when working with fresh jalapeños. Wearing rubber gloves is a good idea. Be careful not to rub your eyes or face until your hands are carefully washed.

Necessities and Temptations
Junior League of Austin
Austin, Texas

HOT PEPPER SAUCE

Piquant pepper sauces are a mainstay of the Southern table, deserving a place as prominent as that of salt and pepper.

YIELD: 4 (10-OUNCE) BOTTLES

8 cloves garlic

4 whole cloves

½ teaspoon salt

Hot green peppers, washed, dried, and stems removed

White vinegar

8 to 12 drops olive oil

Clean 4 (10-ounce) Worcestershire or similar bottles. In each bottle, place 2 cloves garlic, 1 whole clove, and ⅛ teaspoon salt. Fill each bottle with

hot green peppers. Boil the vinegar in a saucepan. Fill each bottle with vinegar. Add 2 to 3 drops of olive oil on top of the warm vinegar in each bottle. Store for 3 weeks before using.

Celebrations on the Bayou
Junior League of Monroe
Monroe, Louisiana

WATERMELON RIND PICKLES

After the last of the juicy red meat has been eaten, the rinds are savored as pickles. Pickling lime can be found in the canning section of your local supermarket.

Y I E L D : 3 P I N T S

3 quarts prepared watermelon rind
1½ tablespoons pickling lime
1 gallon water
A few drops of green food coloring (optional)
4 cups sugar
2 cups white vinegar
1 (2- to 3-inch) stick cinnamon
1 tablespoon whole cloves

Select a firm ripe watermelon. Remove the green skin and pink flesh from the rind; cut the rind into 1-inch pieces. Add the pickling lime to the water; mix well to dissolve. Pour over rind and soak overnight. It is important to drain and rinse carefully according to the lime package directions. Boil in water until tender, about 45 minutes. Add green coloring, if desired; drain. Mix the remaining ingredients and heat to the boiling

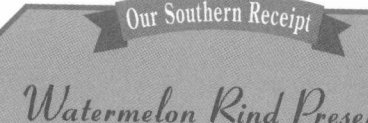

Our Southern Receipt

Watermelon Rind Preserves

Select watermelon with a thick rind, cut the rind in any shape desired, lay the pieces in strong salt water for two or three days; then soak them in alum water for an hour to harden them, to every pound of fruit use a pound of sugar. Make a syrup of a little water, sugar, and a few small pieces of white ginger root and one lemon, sliced. Take out the lemon and root, after the syrup has been boiled, and add the watermelon rind; let it boil until transparent. Carefully lift it and put it in the jars, pouring the syrup over it.

Collected by Kate C. Hubbard in Possum & Pomegranate
for the Federal Writers Project "America Eats"

point. Add the watermelon rind. Boil until the rind is transparent. Pack into hot sterilized jars with the syrup.

Favorite Recipes Old and New
North Carolina Federation of Home
    Demonstration Clubs
Raleigh, North Carolina

OKRA PICKLES

The perfect Southern counterpoint to the martini olive or cocktail onion, this pickled pod tastes great in an adult beverage or as a premeal nibble.

YIELD: ABOUT 34 OR 35 PINTS

½ bushel okra
Iced water
2 hot peppers per jar
1 sliced clove garlic per jar
6 quarts white vinegar
3 cups water
2 cups plain salt (not iodized)
8 tablespoons mustard seed
Pinch of powdered alum

Scrub and trim the okra; soak it in iced water overnight. Pack the okra firmly in hot sterile jars along with the hot peppers and sliced garlic. Combine the vinegar, water, salt, mustard seed, and alum in a saucepan; boil for 10 to 15 minutes. Pour the mixture over the okra in the jars until the jars are full. Let the mixture settle, then add more liquid, up to ¼ inch from top. Seal and store in a cool, dark place up to 6 to 8 weeks before using.

Bless Us Cooks
Grace–St. Luke's Episcopal Church
Memphis, Tennessee

JUGIE'S REFRIGERATOR PICKLES

YIELD: 12 PINTS

4 cups sugar
½ cup plain salt (not iodized)
4 cups apple cider vinegar
1½ teaspoons celery seed
1½ teaspoons turmeric
1½ teaspoons mustard seed
8 pounds cucumbers, thinly sliced
3 large white onions, thinly sliced

Combine sugar, salt, vinegar, celery seed, turmeric, and mustard seed in a medium bowl. Pour over cucumbers and onions in a large bowl; mix well. Let stand 2 hours. Put pickles into pint jars and refrigerate.

Good Cookin' from the Heart of Virginia
Junior League of Lynchburg
Lynchburg, Virginia

SQUASH PICKLES

YIELD: 6 PINTS

8 cups yellow squash, thinly sliced
⅔ cup pickling salt
3 cups sugar
2 cups white vinegar
2 tablespoons mustard seed
2 tablespoons celery seed
2 cups chopped green bell pepper
2 small white onions, thinly sliced
1 (4-ounce) jar pimientos

Soak the squash for 1 hour in 3 quarts water and the pickling salt. Drain the squash; rinse well. In a large stockpot, combine the sugar, vinegar, mustard seed, and celery seed. Bring to a boil. Add the squash, bell pepper, onion slices, and pimientos. Return to a boil for 1 minute. Spoon the squash mixture into hot sterilized pint jars and pour the hot syrup over the vegetables to cover. Seal. Process in a hot-water bath for 10 minutes.

Sensational Seasons
Junior League of Fort Smith
Fort Smith, Arkansas

Mustard Pickles

Murky, muddy, and tasty, these pickles pucker and satisfy.

Yield: 8 pints

1 quart roughly chopped celery
1 quart roughly chopped green tomatoes
1 pint roughly chopped green bell peppers
1 quart roughly chopped cabbage
1 pint roughly chopped white onions
1 pint small cauliflower buds
Salt
1 cup sifted flour
2 cups sugar
6 tablespoons dry mustard
1 tablespoon turmeric
1 tablespoon white celery seed
1 tablespoon mustard seed
3 pints vinegar

14-Day Sweet Pickles

There should be about two gallons of cucumbers. Place in a stone jar and pour over them two cups of salt and one gallon of boiling water. Let this stand for one week, skimming every day.

On the eighth day drain well and pour over the fruit one gallon of fresh boiling water. Let this stand for twenty-four hours.

On the ninth day drain again and pour over another gallon of boiling water and one tablespoon of powdered alum. Let this stand twenty-four hours.

On the tenth day drain liquid off and pour over one gallon of fresh boiling water. Let stand twenty-four hours.

On the eleventh day drain water off and put the fruit in a clean stone jar or a preserving kettle. Prepare a syrup of five pints of vinegar, ½ ounce of celery seed, six cups of sugar, and one ounce of stick cinnamon. When this is boiling hot pour it over the cucumbers. Let stand twenty-four hours.

On the twelfth, thirteenth, and fourteenth day drain and re-heat the syrup, adding one cup of sugar each day. On the last day pack the cucumbers in fruit jars, cover with the syrup. Put rubbers and tops on the jars and do not screw down tight. Heat these jars of sweet pickles to the scalding point and seal.

Collected by Kate C. Hubbard in Possum & Pomegranate
for the Federal Writers Project "America Eats"

Combine the celery, tomatoes, bell peppers, cabbage, onion, and cauliflower in a large mixing bowl. Sprinkle with salt and let stand for 1 hour; drain. In a large stockpot, combine the flour, sugar, mustard, turmeric, celery seed, and mustard seed. Add the vinegar gradually, stirring constantly. Bring to a boil. Add the vegetables and cook 5 minutes, stirring slowly. Put into sterilized pint jars and seal.

Woman's Exchange Club Cookbook I
Woman's Exchange
Memphis, Tennessee

DILLY BEANS

You will see the tips of these dill-infused beans poking out of the tops of many a Bloody Mary in the South.

YIELD: 4 PINTS

2 pounds small tender green beans
1 teaspoon cayenne pepper
4 cloves garlic
4 large heads dill
2 cups water
¼ cup pickling salt
2 cups white vinegar

Wash and string the green beans; pack uniformly in hot sterilized pint jars. To each pint, add ¼ teaspoon cayenne pepper, 1 clove garlic, and 1 head of dill. Heat together the water, salt, and vinegar. Bring to a boil and pour over the beans.

North Carolina and Old Salem Cookery
Elizabeth Sparks
Kernersville, North Carolina

PICKLED GREEN PEPPER STRIPS

Y IELD : 4 PINTS

4 cloves garlic
4 red chiles
4 teaspoons dill seed
Green bell peppers, cut into strips
3 cups water
1½ cups white vinegar
6 tablespoons salt (preferably pickling salt)
Green food coloring (optional)

In each of 4 pint jars, place 1 clove garlic, 1 red chile, and 1 teaspoon dill seed. Pack each jar with green pepper strips. Bring the remaining ingredients to a boil in a large saucepan; pour over the peppers. Seal and store in a cool, dry place. (They are better if not used before six weeks.)

La Piñata
Junior League of McAllen
McAllen, Texas

CHOW-CHOW

John Mariani, author of the Dictionary of American Food and Drink, *says that this dish may have its etymological origin in Mandarin Chinese. Though Mariani cites the influence of railroad workers in the American West, their impact was felt here as well—and earlier.*

Y IELD : 2 ½ GALLONS

1 gallon roughly chopped cabbage
1 gallon roughly chopped green tomatoes
1 quart roughly chopped onions
6 green bell peppers, roughly chopped
1 scant cup salt
2 bunches celery, roughly chopped
3 tablespoons mustard seed
¼ cup prepared mustard
2 tablespoons ground ginger
2 tablespoons ground cinnamon
1 tablespoon ground cloves
1 tablespoon ground nutmeg
4 tablespoons turmeric
2 hot peppers, diced (optional)
3 pounds sugar
2 quarts vinegar

Mix the cabbage, tomatoes, onion, and bell peppers in a large pan, sprinkle with salt, and let stand overnight. Drain the vegetables, squeezing out the surplus juice. Add the celery and place all the ingredients in a large saucepan; bring to a fast boil. Spoon into jars, seal, and process.

High Cotton Cookin'
Marvell Academy Mothers' Association
Marvell, Arkansas

WILLIAM FAULKNER

LIFE'S SIMPLE PLEASURES

The late Southern writer and raconteur Eugene Walter, author of *American Cooking: Southern Style,* was fond of telling this story about the favorite son of Oxford, Mississippi—William Faulkner:

> *On a summer afternoon some years ago, two of the South's most celebrated writers, William Faulkner and Katherine Anne Porter, were dining together at a plush restaurant in Paris. Everything had been laid on to perfection; a splendid meal had been consumed, a bottle of fine Burgundy emptied and thimble-sized glasses of an expensive liquor drained. The maître d' and an entourage of waiters hovered close by, ready to satisfy any final whim.*
>
> *"Back home, the butter beans are in," said Faulkner, peering into the distance, "the speckled ones."*
>
> *Miss Porter fiddled with her glass and stared into space. "Blackberries," she said, wistfully.*

As evidenced by Mr. Walter's story, Faulkner may well have had a taste for life's simple pleasures in the form of the South's staple foodstuffs, but that doesn't mean he didn't eat a bit higher on the hog every once in a while.

A case in point: Among the magazines found on the bottom shelf of his bedroom bookcase at Rowan Oak were a trio of *Gourmet* magazines from 1959—the March, April, and December issues, to be exact. Though no marginalia marks the pages, you can't help surmising that he perused, if only briefly, a discussion in the March issue over the correct preparation of "Oxford sausages." (For the record, they're heavy on beef suet, are sometimes laced with anchovies, and claim Oxford, England, as their point of origin.)

A peek into the Faulkner family spice cabinet yields other enticing clues, including a bottle of Escoffier brand "Sauce Diable," rich with tomatoes, tamarinds, dates, mangoes, and raisins. Could it be that the Faulkners were closeted epicures?

After a thorough accounting of the spice cabinet's contents, this theory loses some luster, for, exceptional of the aforementioned sauce, all else seems, well, rather Southern, even modestly Southern: two tins of sage, two bottles of filé, red food coloring, enough cloves to choke a horse, and enough dry mustard to sate a gaggle of deviled-egg-devouring Junior Leaguers. This is hardly the stuff of culinary invention.

And so the question remains. What did the greatest American writer of the twentieth century eat? If Mr. Walter's story is to be believed, you can bet he ate some butter beans. And if the following recipe, from Faulkner's wife, Estelle, is as appetizing as it seems, you can be assured that the butter beans shared space on the plate with a bit of iced green tomato pickles.

ICED GREEN TOMATO PICKLES

Wash and scrub green tomatoes. Do not peel. Slice thin and soak 24 hours in lime powder [mixed with] water . . . After soaking tomatoes, pour off water. Rinse well. For each seven pounds of green tomatoes, use the following:

5 pounds granulated sugar
1 tablespoon whole cloves
1 quart white vinegar
1 stick cinnamon
1 tablespoon whole allspice
2 teaspoons salt

Mix these and let syrup come to a boil. Add tomatoes, stirring occasionally. Test with straw. When straw pierces through easily, they are done.

William Faulkner lived most of his life in Oxford, Mississippi, working as a writer, attempting to give voice to his "postage stamp of native soil." He was awarded the Nobel Prize, among many other honors.

Green Tomato Relish

Green tomatoes have long been a favorite pickle product, firm, acid, and melding perfectly with spices.

YIELD: 6 PINTS

6 green bell peppers, chopped
1 fresh red or green chile, chopped
12 green tomatoes, chopped
6 onions, chopped
½ cup salt
3 cups sugar
1 quart white vinegar
1 tablespoon turmeric
¼ box whole mixed pickling spice

Soak the bell pepper, chile, tomatoes, onion, and salt overnight in water to cover. Drain and rinse. Place the sugar, vinegar, turmeric, and pickling spice tied in cheesecloth in a large saucepan. Bring to a boil. Add the drained vegetables. Return to a boil. Remove cheesecloth bag. Spoon into jars and seal.

Southern Sideboards
Junior League of Jackson
Jackson, Mississippi

Corn Relish

Time was that jar after jar of relish lined the cupboard of any industrious Southern cook—an attempt to capture the flavors of the harvest and stave off the winter doldrums.

YIELD: 7 OR 8 PINTS

4 cups chopped celery
3 cups chopped red or green bell pepper
1½ cups chopped onion
2 cups sugar
2 cups white vinegar
2 cups water
2 tablespoons plain salt (not iodized)
2 teaspoons celery seed
¼ cup flour
2 tablespoons dry mustard
1 teaspoon turmeric
½ cup cold water
8 cups corn (either frozen or fresh, cut from ears)
2 (4-ounce) cans pimientos, chopped

Combine the celery, bell pepper, onion, sugar, vinegar, water, salt, and celery seed in a large pot. Bring to a boil and boil 5 minutes, stirring occasionally. Combine the flour, mustard, turmeric, and ½ cup cold water. Mix to blend and stir into the boiling mixture along with the corn. Return to a boil; cook 3 minutes, stirring frequently. Add the pimiento and cook an additional 2 minutes. Seal the mixture immediately in hot, sterile pint jars.

Turnip Greens in the Bathtub
Genie Taylor Harrison
Baton Rouge, Louisiana

ELLEN DOUGLAS

PERFECT PRESERVES

My mother liked to cook preserves and jellies. It seems she always had a pantry lined with shelves, full of watermelon rind preserves and peach pickles, peach jam and strawberry sunshine, plum jelly and mayhaw jelly, blackberry jelly and blackberry jam—just about every kind of homemade preserve imaginable. She taught me how, though I have never been as completely successful as she was. I've had failures, jellies that were either too ropy or too runny.

I still make jellies today. In fact, I just finished making a batch of mayhaw jelly. Mayhaws are an oddity that no one seems to know about any more. They grow in the swamps, falling off trees and into the water, where they are retrieved with big nets. They look like smallish plums or haws; though, by the time they have been down in the water for some time, they look like rotten plums. But they make this beautiful, almost clear, red jelly that is just delicious on roast pork or with biscuits for breakfast.

When we lived in Arkansas, where the poor, sandy soil was perfect for growing strawberries, my mother often made what we called strawberry sunshine. She started out by bringing to boil on the stove the strawberries and a bit of sugar and water, measure for measure, stirring it until the sugar dissolved and the strawberries were cooked but not falling apart. Then she spread the mixture in a shallow pan and placed it in the sun for a few hours, where the berries continued to cook a bit, plumping up in the sun. It wan't a jam so much as whole strawberries in a thick syrup, and it looked beautiful in the jar. It put strawberry jam to shame.

I have a notebook full of notes on how to make jellies and jams and preserves, what to look for and what to listen for. I learned how to tell when a jelly had reached the right temperature by the bubbles. At first, when it starts to boil, the bubbles are really small, and then as it gets close to being done, it comes to a full, rolling boil, and when the large bubbles burst—you can hear them popping—you know it's almost there. Next, you test to see if it will stay between the tines of a fork. And the final test is to see if the jelly sheets off the spoon. When it is almost ready, it comes off the spoon in two heavy drops, but when the two drops join to form a sheet as it comes off the spoon, you know the jelly is done. Now, that's if you don't have a thermometer to test. Of course, I don't have one. And neither did my mother.

Ellen Douglas, a resident of Jackson, Mississippi, is the author of numerous novels, including Can't Quit You Baby, *and a memoir,* Truth: Four Stories I Am Finally Old Enough to Tell.

ARTICHOKE RELISH

These tubers are not from Jerusalem, nor are they artichokes, but they do make fine pickles.

Y I E L D : 1 7 O R 1 8 P I N T S

5 quarts Jerusalem artichokes, cleaned and
   chopped
2 gallons water
2 cups plain salt (not iodized)
3 pounds white cabbage, chopped
1½ pounds onions, chopped
6 large green and red bell peppers,
   chopped
¾ cup flour
1 (24-ounce) jar prepared mustard

2 quarts apple cider vinegar
3 pounds sugar
3 tablespoons mustard seed
2 tablespoons turmeric
2 tablespoons celery seed
1 tablespoon black pepper
1 tablespoon hot sauce, or more to taste

Soak the artichokes overnight in 1 gallon of the water and 1 cup of the salt. In a second container, soak the cabbage, onion, and bell peppers in the remaining 1 gallon of water and the remaining cup of salt.

The next day, drain the artichokes. Spread them on a large towel to drain thoroughly. Drain the vegetables. Spread them on a second large towel to drain thoroughly.

In a mixing bowl, combine the flour and prepared mustard carefully. Avoid lumping. Stir until the mixture is smooth.

In a large (at least 10-quart) kettle, mix the vinegar, sugar, mustard seed, turmeric, celery seed, and black pepper. Bring to a boil. Add the cabbage, onion, and bell peppers. Bring the mixture back to a boil and cook for 10 minutes over medium heat. Reduce to low heat. Dip out about a cup of the hot liquid and add to it the flour mixture. Mix well. Add the thinned flour mixture to the vinegar and vegetables. Stir thoroughly until well mixed. Add the hot sauce and the artichokes. Raise the heat and stir until the mixture is about to boil (about 5 minutes). Seal in sterilized jars.

Tea-Time at the Masters
Junior League of Augusta
Augusta, Georgia

PEACH PICKLE

Summer's development arrested.

Yield: 4 quarts

6 pounds firm peaches, peeled
Whole cloves
3 pounds sugar
2 cups white vinegar
2 cups water
Stick cinnamon (optional)
Fresh ginger (optional)

Stick each peach with 2 or 3 cloves. Make a syrup of the sugar, vinegar, and water and bring to a boil in a saucepan. Stick cinnamon and gin-

Our Southern Receipt

Brandied Peaches

4 pounds peaches, peeled
Cloves
4 pounds of sugar
3½ cups water
1 egg white
1 pint white brandy

Stick two cloves in each whole peach. Make a syrup of the sugar and water and add the egg white, beaten to a stiff froth. Skim carefully. Add the fruit one layer at a time and boil five minutes. Pack the peaches in sterilized jars. Boil the syrup about ten minutes longer, or until it thickens. Remove from the heat. Add the brandy and pour over the peaches. Seal at once. Aging for several months will improve the flavor, but it takes a hard heart, a watchful eye and a strong will to accomplish the aging.

Collected by Kate C. Hubbard in Possum & Pomegranate
for the Federal Writers Project "America Eats"

ger can be added to the syrup mixture if desired. Drop the peaches into the syrup and cook until they are clear and tender. Pack into hot jars, cover with syrup, and seal.

Puttin' on the Peachtree
Junior League of DeKalb County
Decatur, Georgia

APPLE CHUTNEY

Sweetness and heat coexist in this chutney, more often associated with Indian cuisine, but no less at home down South.

YIELD: 6 PINTS

10 medium Granny Smith apples, peeled and
   chopped
1 cup diced onion
1 cup diced red bell pepper
1 to 2 hot peppers
1½ pounds dark raisins
4 cups firmly packed light brown sugar
3 tablespoons ground ginger
3 tablespoons mustard seed
2 teaspoons allspice
2 teaspoons salt
1 clove garlic, crushed
1 quart apple cider vinegar

Combine all the ingredients in a large stockpot and bring to a boil. Reduce the heat and simmer 90 minutes. Stir frequently. Spoon the hot chutney into hot, sterilized jars. Leave ½-inch head-space. Wipe the rims and screw on the lids. Do not process. The heat from the chutney will seal the lids.

Dining by Fireflies
Junior League of Charlotte
Charlotte, North Carolina

THE COLONEL'S GREEN PEAR CHUTNEY

YIELD: 12 PINTS

¼ tablespoon Worcestershire sauce
1½ teaspoons ground black pepper
1 tablespoon whole cloves
1½ tablespoons ground cinnamon
Dash of cayenne pepper
4½ pounds green pears, sliced
4 lemons, peeled and sliced (cut the peels in
   strips)
12 ounces dark raisins
3 pounds dark brown sugar
8 cloves garlic
3 large onions, sliced
⅔ cup crystallized ginger, minced
7 cups canned pineapple chunks, drained
5 cups white vinegar
3 tablespoons mustard seeds
½ cup soy sauce

Mix all the ingredients. Bring to a boil, then lower heat. Simmer, covered, until the fruit is tender, 45 minutes to 1 hour after boiling. This does not spoil and does not need to be sealed. Serve with lamb, chicken, or roast beef.

Dinner on the Diner
Junior League of Chattanooga
Chattanooga, Tennessee

DESSERTS

....

SWEET AND SACRED

When one has tasted watermelons, he knows what angels eat. It was not a Southern watermelon that Eve took; we know it because she repented.

MARK TWAIN, *PUDD'NHÉAD WILSON*

Sweet and Sacred

························

The eating of vegetables is learned behavior. We do not spring perforce from the womb with a taste for things green. Many a Southern child came to love collards by dint of bribery. "If you want a slice of angel's food cake, you'll have to finish your greens," came the call from parents. But for a child reared south of the Mason and Dixon, a love of things sweet comes as naturally as an abhorrence of an early bedtime. Call it alimentary education if you like. Most Southerners call it a sweet tooth.

Pecan pie, chess pie, and meringue-crowned chocolate pie; sponge cake, pound cake, and teeth-shatteringly hard peanut brittle—these were the rewards for a plate cleaned, a yard raked, a messy bedroom made neat again. Lessons learned at the Sunday table complemented those taught at Sunday school: Eat right. Act right. And you will receive your reward in the hereafter—or at least after you have finished your liver.

Writer Flannery O'Connor once observed that the South was "Christ haunted." She was not speaking specifically of our eating habits, but she might just as well have been. A raft of Southern desserts owe their naming if not their inspiration to the deeply religious nature of our region: divinity, that saccharine-sweet, well-beaten, white nougat candy; heavenly hash, a kitchen-sink conglomeration of marshmallows, canned fruit, and heavy cream; angel food cake, light and airy as the egg whites in the batter; devil's food cake, rich with chocolate and as dark as Satan's own heart; and ambrosia, a jumble of fruits and grated coconut that owes its name to the Greek word *ambrotos,* meaning "immortal," the state induced by eating the food of the gods.

But perhaps the ultimate embodiment of this symbiosis of the sweet and the celestial came with the preparation of a scripture cake. Inspiration came from a tattered family receipt book. Guidance came from the pages of what Baptists call the Good Book. "In a large bowl mix six tablespoons First Samuel 14:25, one cup Judges 5:25, and two cups Jeremiah 6:20." So began the typical recipe of which a version is provided here (see page 287). For a cook of years past, these instructions were not a cryptic puzzle to be solved but an opportunity to prove one's knowledge of things both culinary and Christian.

A childhood of mornings spent in Sunday school and summers spent in Vacation Bible School aided the aspiring cook. And if her memory failed, a flip through the family Bible would reveal the secrets to this rich fruit-and-nut-studded treat. First Samuel 14:25 read, "And all the people came into the forest and there was honey on the ground." Judges 5:25 read, "He asked water and she gave him milk." Jeremiah 6:20 asked, "To what purpose does frankincense come to me from Sheba, or sweet cane from a distant land?" And thus honey was combined with butter and sugar as instructed. Next came eggs, flour, spices, salt, baking powder, milk, figs, raisins, and almonds. Before baking, some recipes advised cooks to follow Solomon's advice on the rearing of young boys as quoted in Proverbs 23:14, "Thou shalt beat him with a rod."

The resulting sweet was a reward for lessons learned—and for those lucky enough to partake of it, a reminder that we Southerners are a God-fearing, sugar-loving people.

GRANDMOTHER BESS'S APPLESAUCE CAKE

This Appalachian treat migrates southward to warmer climes.

Y I E L D : 1 2 T O 1 5 S E R V I N G S

3½ cups cake flour
2 teaspoons baking soda
½ teaspoon salt
3 teaspoons cinnamon
2 teaspoons ground allspice
2 teaspoons nutmeg
½ teaspoon cloves
1 cup black walnut pieces
½ to ¾ cup chopped raisins
1 cup vegetable shortening
2 cups sugar
2 eggs, lightly beaten
2 cups unsweetened applesauce

Preheat the oven to 350°. Grease and flour an angel food cake pan. Sift together twice the flour, baking soda, salt, cinnamon, allspice, nutmeg, and cloves. Stir ¼ cup of the flour mixture with the walnuts and raisins; set aside.

In a large bowl, cream the shortening. Add the sugar gradually and cream well. Add the beaten eggs; mix well. Add the flour mixture alternately with the applesauce. Stir in the nuts and raisins. Pour into the prepared pan. Bake about 1 hour 15 minutes. Let cool completely before removing from pan.

River Road Recipes II
Junior League of Baton Rouge
Baton Rouge, Louisiana

PEANUT CAKE WITH MOLASSES

This recipe from George Washington Carver, of Alabama's Tuskegee Institute, makes use of two Southern staples: molasses and peanuts.

YIELD: 12 TO 16 SERVINGS

2 cups ground peanuts
2 teaspoons cinnamon
½ teaspoon ground cloves
¼ nutmeg, grated
1 heaping teaspoon baking soda
4 rounded cups flour
2 cups molasses
1 cup firmly packed dark brown sugar
1 cup lard
2 cups hot water
1 egg, lightly beaten
Confectioners' sugar

Preheat the oven to 350°. Mix the peanuts, cinnamon, cloves, nutmeg, and baking soda with the flour. Mix the molasses, brown sugar, lard, and water; stir into the flour mixture. Add the beaten egg. Pour into a shallow dripping pan or broiler pan and sprinkle with confectioners' sugar just before putting in the oven. Bake for 30 minutes, or until done.

The Historical Cookbook
of the American Negro
National Council of Negro Women
Washington, D.C.

100-YEAR-OLD BLUEBERRY CAKE

From Charlottesville, home of Thomas Jefferson, arguably the nation's first gourmand, comes this cake with a long, proud lineage.

YIELD: 10 TO 12 SERVINGS

⅓ cup unsalted butter
⅚ cup sugar
1 egg
1⅔ cups flour
⅓ teaspoon salt
1 rounded teaspoon baking powder
⅓ cup milk
1 cup blueberries, picked over

Preheat the oven to 375°. Grease a 9x9-inch square pan.

Cream the butter and sugar in a large bowl. Add the egg and mix until light. Sift together the flour, salt, and baking powder. Add to the butter mixture alternately with the milk. Fold in the berries. Pour into the prepared pan. Bake about 40 to 45 minutes.

The Best of the Bushel
Junior League of Charlottesville
Charlottesville, Virginia

FRESH ORANGE CAKE

Oranges, once a Christmastime indulgence in the Upper South, are now more mundane fare.

YIELD: 6 SERVINGS

1 stick (¼ pound) unsalted butter or margarine
¾ cup sugar
Juice and finely grated zest of 1 orange
1½ cups self-rising flour
Pinch of salt
2 large eggs, lightly beaten
2 tablespoons milk
Whipped cream, for garnish
Fresh orange sections, for garnish

Preheat the oven to 350°. Grease a 7-inch cake pan well.

Cream the butter and sugar in a large bowl. Add the orange juice and zest; beat until light and fluffy. Sift the flour together with the salt; set aside. Combine the eggs and milk. Add to the orange mixture alternately with the flour, beating well after each addition. Bake for 30 minutes or until lightly browned. Remove from pan when cool. Spread with whipped cream and decorate with orange sections.

The Stoney Creek Recipe Collection
Independent Presbyterian Church
McPhersonville, South Carolina

LADY BALTIMORE CAKE

In 1906, Owen Wister wrote Lady Baltimore, *now considered a Southern classic. Of the many legends surrounding this cake, one has it that Wister received it as a gift from a young woman and later chronicled the cake in his novel.*

YIELD: 12 TO 16 SERVINGS

2½ cups cake flour
2½ teaspoons baking powder
½ teaspoon salt
1 stick (¼ pound) unsalted butter (or use half butter and half shortening), at room temperature
1½ cups sugar
1 cup milk
1½ teaspoons vanilla
4 egg whites, stiffly beaten
Icing (recipe follows)
Fruit-Nut Filling (recipe follows)

Preheat the oven to 350°. Grease and flour two 8-inch cake pans.

Sift together the flour, baking powder, and salt in a bowl. Cream the butter and sugar in a large bowl. Add the dry ingredients to the butter mixture alternately with the milk, mixing well after each addition. Stir in the vanilla. Fold in the beaten egg whites. Pour into the prepared pans. Bake for 30 to 35 minutes. Let cool.

Prepare the icing, then prepare the filling. Spread each layer with filling. Then spread one layer with a thin layer of icing and put the layers together. Cover the entire cake with the remaining icing.

Icing

1½ cups sugar
⅔ cup water
1 tablespoon light corn syrup
2 egg whites, stiffly beaten
1 teaspoon vanilla

Combine the sugar, water, and corn syrup in a saucepan. Boil until an 8-inch thread spins from spoon (242°). Beating constantly, pour the hot syrup slowly into the beaten egg whites. Add the vanilla. Continue beating until mixture is fluffy and will hold its shape.

Fruit-Nut Filling

⅓ cup raisins
⅓ cup figs, cut into small strips
½ cup chopped walnuts

Combine the ingredients with one-third of the icing.

What's Cooking for the Holidays
Irene Hayes
Hueysville, Kentucky

Lane Cake

Named for Erma Rylander Lane, of Clayton, Alabama, who published the original recipe in her cookbook, Some Good Things to Eat, *this layer cake is a pure Southern favorite.*

Yield: 12 to 16 servings

2 sticks (½ pound) unsalted butter, at room temperature
2 cups sugar
3¼ cups sifted flour
2 teaspoons baking powder
1 cup milk
8 egg whites, well beaten
1 teaspoon vanilla
Filling (recipe follows)
Icing (see recipe, this page)

Preheat the oven to 375°. Grease and flour well four 8-inch or 9-inch cake pans.

In a large bowl, cream the butter and sugar together until very light. Sift the flour and baking powder 3 times and add alternately with the milk to the creamed mixture, mixing well after each addition. Fold in well-beaten egg whites and vanilla. Pour into the prepared pans and bake for 20 to 25 minutes. Spread the filling between the cake layers. Frost the entire cake with icing.

Filling

1 stick (¼ pound) unsalted butter
1 cup sugar
8 egg yolks, lightly beaten
½ cup brandy
1 teaspoon vanilla
1 cup pecans, chopped
1 cup golden raisins

Cream the butter and sugar together. Add the yolks, brandy, and vanilla. Cook in a double boiler, stirring constantly, until thick. Stir in the pecans and raisins. Let cool and spread between the cake layers.

Tea-Time at the Masters
Junior League of Augusta
Augusta, Georgia

MISSISSIPPI MUD CAKE

According to Nathalie Dupree, author of, among other works, New Southern Cooking, *this cake should be cracked and dry-looking, like Mississippi mud in the hot, dry summer.*

YIELD: 10 TO 12 SERVINGS

2 sticks (½ pound) unsalted margarine
½ cup cocoa powder
2 cups sugar
4 eggs
1 teaspoon vanilla
Pinch of salt
1½ cups flour
Miniature marshmallows
Frosting (recipe follows)

Preheat the oven to 350°. Grease a 9x13-inch pan.

Melt the margarine with the cocoa and sugar in a saucepan. Mix well. Remove from the heat. Add the eggs, vanilla, and salt. Beat together. Add the flour; mix well. Pour into the prepared pan. Bake for 25 to 35 minutes. Sprinkle

miniature marshmallows on hot cake. Frost immediately.

FROSTING

1 pound confectioners' sugar
½ cup milk
⅓ cup cocoa powder
½ stick unsalted margarine

Mix all the ingredients together about 10 minutes before cake is done. Pour over hot cake.

The Pastors Wives Cookbook
Memphis, Tennessee

1-2-3-4 CAKE

So named due to the amount of ingredients . . .
1 cup butter, 2 cups sugar . . .

YIELD: 12 TO 15 SERVINGS

1 cup (2 sticks, or ½ pound) unsalted butter
2 cups sugar
4 eggs, separated
3 cups flour
2 teaspoons baking powder
1 cup milk
1 teaspoon vanilla
Frosting

Preheat the oven to 375°. Cream the butter and sugar in a large bowl. Beat in the egg yolks. Sift together the flour and baking powder. Add the flour mixture and the milk alternately to the creamed mixture, mixing well after each addi-

tion. Add the vanilla. Beat the egg whites until stiff and fold them into the batter. Spoon into a greased and floured 9x13-inch baking pan. Bake for 20 to 25 minutes, or until the cake is golden and springs back when touched. Frost as desired.

The Charlotte Cookbook
Junior League of Charlotte
Charlotte, North Carolina

KING'S CAKE

According to John Mariani, author of the Dictionary of American Food and Drink, *"Before the Civil War, American King Cakes often contained gold, diamonds or valuables instead of beans. After the war, with the end of the gala Creole balls in Louisiana, peas, beans, pecans, and coins were used, and in 1871 the tradition of choosing the queen of the Mardi Gras was determined by who drew the prize in the cake." Today, from Mobile, Alabama (where they throw Moon Pies rather than beads from their Fat Tuesday floats), to New Orleans, King Cakes promise good luck in the coming year to the person fortunate enough to bite down on the prize and not lose a tooth in the process.*

YIELD: 10 TO 12 SERVINGS

1 package active dry yeast
¼ cup warm water
6 tablespoons milk, scalded and allowed to cool
4 cups flour
2 sticks (½ pound) unsalted butter, plus additional, melted, for brushing the top of the dough
¾ cup sugar, plus additional for decorating cake

¼ teaspoon salt

4 eggs

Corn syrup, for decorating cake

Food coloring, for decorating cake

In a bowl, dissolve the yeast in the warm water. Add the milk and enough of the flour, about ½ cup, to make a soft dough. In another bowl, combine the butter, sugar, salt, and eggs with an electric mixer. Remove from the mixer and add the soft ball of yeast dough. Mix thoroughly. Gradually add 2½ cups of the remaining flour to make a medium dough that is neither too soft nor too stiff. Place in a greased bowl and brush the top of the dough with melted butter. Cover with a damp cloth and set aside to rise until doubled in bulk, about 3 hours.

Use the remaining 1 cup flour to knead the dough and to roll with hands into a rope shape. Place on a 14x17-inch greased cookie sheet and form the "rope" of dough into an oval shape. The center should be about 7x12 inches. Connect the ends of the dough by dampening with water. Cover with a damp cloth and let rise until doubled in bulk, about 1 hour. (A bean or a tiny figure of Jesus may be placed in the cake if desired.)

Bake at 350° for 35 to 45 minutes, or until slightly browned. Decorate by brushing the top with corn syrup and alternating 3-inch bands of purple-, green-, and gold-colored granulated sugar. (To color the sugar, add a few drops of food coloring to the sugar and shake in a tightly covered jar until the desired color is achieved.)

Recipes and Reminiscences of New Orleans
Parents Club of Ursuline Academy
New Orleans, Louisiana

SPONGE CAKE

YIELD: 10 TO 12 SERVINGS

5 egg yolks

4½ teaspoons fresh lemon juice

1½ teaspoons grated lemon zest

2 tablespoons water

5 egg whites

¼ teaspoon salt

¼ teaspoon cream of tartar

1 cup sugar

1 cup flour

Preheat the oven to 350°. Have ready two ungreased 9-inch cake pans.

Beat the egg yolks until thick; add the lemon juice, the zest, and the 2 tablespoons water. In a large bowl, beat the egg whites with the salt and cream of tartar until stiff and dry. Gradually add the sugar to the yolk mixture and with a wire whisk blend the yolks into the whites. Sift the flour over the egg mixture and blend in very gently. Bake in the prepared pans for 25 minutes. Let cool in pans and use a spatula to remove.

Southern Legacies
Nancy Patty Walker
Starkville, Mississippi

Angel Food Cake

So light, so ethereal, so sublimely celestial that it was thought to be the food of angels, this cake is as white as devil's food cake is dark.

Yield: 12 servings

1 cup sifted cake flour
1½ cups sifted sugar
1¼ cups egg whites (9 to 11 eggs)
¼ teaspoon salt
1¼ teaspoons cream of tartar

Preheat the oven to 350°. Add ½ cup of the sifted sugar to the sifted cake flour and sift four more times.

In a large bowl, beat the egg whites and salt with a wire whisk until foamy. Sprinkle in the cream of tartar and beat until the egg whites stand in peaks but are not dry. They should be soft and glossy. Sprinkle the rest of the sifted sugar (1 cup) over the egg whites, 4 tablespoons at a time. Beat 10 strokes after each addition. Sprinkle ¼ of the flour mixture over the egg mixture and beat 15 times, turning the bowl slightly. Keep adding the flour mixture as above until it is all gone.

Pour the batter into an ungreased angel food pan.

Bake for 30 to 35 minutes. Invert the pan and balance on the neck of a bottle for 1 hour before removing the cake from the pan.

Family Secrets
Lee Academy
Clarksdale, Mississippi

Devil's Food Cake

Yield: 10 to 12 servings

1½ sticks unsalted butter
1½ cups sugar
3 egg yolks, lightly beaten
2 ounces unsweetened chocolate
⅓ cup water
1¾ cups flour
2 teaspoons baking powder
Pinch of salt
¾ cup milk
½ teaspoon almond flavoring
1 teaspoon vanilla
3 egg whites, well beaten
Angel Icing (recipe follows)

Preheat the oven to 375°. Butter well two 9-inch cake pans.

In a large bowl, cream the butter and sugar; add the beaten egg yolks. Melt the chocolate with the water and let cool slightly. Add to the butter mixture. Sift together the flour, baking powder, and salt. Add to the butter mixture alternately with the milk, mixing well after each addition, beginning and ending with the dry ingredients. Add the almond flavoring and vanilla and fold in the well-beaten egg whites. Pour into the prepared pans and bake for about 25 minutes. Test with a cake tester and do not overcook. When cool, frost with the icing.

Angel Icing

1½ cups sugar
⅔ cup water

²/₃ teaspoon cream of tartar

4 egg whites, stiffly beaten

1 teaspoon vanilla

½ teaspoon almond flavoring

Put the sugar, water, and cream of tartar in a saucepan. Heat, stirring, until the sugar dissolves and the mixture comes to a boil. Put a lid on the pan and cook 2 minutes more so that the sugar crystals on the side of the pan dissolve. Remove the lid and cook until the syrup reaches 242° on a candy thermometer (medium-ball stage). Pour the syrup slowly into the stiffly beaten egg whites, add the vanilla and almond flavoring, and continue to beat until thick and stiff.

Southern Legacies
Nancy Patty Walker
Starkville, Mississippi

CARAMEL CAKE

YIELD: 12 SERVINGS

1 stick (¼ pound) unsalted butter

1½ cups sugar

2 large eggs

1 teaspoon vanilla

2 cups sifted cake flour or all-purpose
   flour

¼ teaspoon salt

1 cup buttermilk

1 teaspoon baking soda

1 tablespoon vinegar

Icing for Caramel Cake (recipe follows)

Preheat the oven to 350°. Grease and flour two 8-inch cake pans.

In a large bowl, cream the butter and sugar. Beat in the eggs, one at a time, beating well after each addition. Continue beating until fluffy. Add the vanilla and blend well. Sift the flour and salt together and add gradually to the butter mixture, alternating with the buttermilk. Dissolve the baking soda in the vinegar and add to the mixture.

Pour the batter into the prepared pans. Bake for 25 minutes. Remove from the oven when the cake springs back when lightly touched in the center. Let cool on wire racks before removing from pans. Frost with the icing.

ICING FOR CARAMEL CAKE

1 stick (¼ pound) unsalted butter

1 pound light brown sugar

⅛ teaspoon salt

²/₃ cup evaporated milk

1 teaspoon baking powder

1 teaspoon vanilla

Melt the butter in a heavy saucepan or small cast-iron skillet. Add the brown sugar and salt and blend well. Add the evaporated milk and cook, stirring frequently, to the soft-ball stage. Remove from the heat and let stand 5 minutes. Add the baking powder and stir. Add the vanilla. Beat until the mixture reaches spreading consistency.

Good Cookin' from the Heart of Virginia
Junior League of Lynchburg
Lynchburg, Virginia

RED VELVET CAKE

Glowing red and white like a beacon on the sideboard, this cake is fueled by a healthy dose of food coloring. We wouldn't have it any other way.

YIELD: 12 TO 15 SERVINGS

½ cup vegetable shortening
1½ cups sugar
2 eggs
1 teaspoon vanilla
1 teaspoon butter flavoring
3 level tablespoons cocoa powder
1 bottle (1½ ounces) red food coloring
1 teaspoon salt
1 tablespoon vinegar
1 teaspoon soda
1 cup buttermilk
2½ cups cake flour, sifted
Frosting (recipe follows)

Preheat the oven to 350°. Grease and flour 3 8-inch round cake pans.

In a large bowl, cream together the shortening, sugar, eggs, vanilla, and butter flavoring. Combine the cocoa and food coloring in a small bowl; mix into a paste and add to the egg mixture. Mix the salt, vinegar, and soda together and add to the buttermilk. Beat the flour alternately with the buttermilk into the egg mixture. Blend well after each addition. Pour into the prepared cake pans. Bake for 20 to 25 minutes. Let cool and frost with the frosting.

FROSTING

3 tablespoons flour
½ teaspoon salt
1 cup milk
1 cup vegetable shortening
1 cup sugar
2 teaspoons vanilla
¼ teaspoon butter flavoring

Cook the flour, salt, and milk in a saucepan until thick. Let cool. Cream the shortening and sugar in a bowl. Add the vanilla and butter flavoring. Stir the flour mixture into the shortening mixture. Beat well. Spread between the layers and on the top and sides of the cake.

More Calf Fries and Caviar
Janel Franklin and Sue Vaughn
Tahoka, Texas

COCONUT CREAM CAKE

Perhaps more aptly called coconut dream cake, for this was the stuff of childhood fantasy in a time when coconuts were a rare indulgence

YIELD: 10 TO 12 SERVINGS

1 stick (¼ pound) unsalted margarine
½ cup vegetable shortening
2 cups sugar
5 eggs, separated
1 teaspoon baking soda
1 cup buttermilk
2 cups flour
1 (4-ounce) can shredded coconut
1 cup chopped pecans
Cream Cheese Icing (recipe follows)

Preheat the oven to 350°. In a large bowl, cream the margarine, vegetable shortening, sugar, and egg yolks together. In a small bowl, add the baking soda to the buttermilk. Add the flour and the buttermilk mixture alternately to the margarine mixture, mixing thoroughly after each addition. Add the coconut and nuts. Beat the egg whites until stiff and fold into the batter. Pour into 3 greased and floured round cake pans. Bake for 25 minutes, or until done by the straw test. Frost with the icing.

CREAM CHEESE ICING

1 (8-ounce) package cream cheese
1 stick (¼ pound) unsalted margarine
1 pound confectioners' sugar, sifted

Blend the cream cheese and margarine until light. Gradually add the confectioners' sugar, beating well after each addition, until fluffy and light.

Waddad's Kitchen
Waddad Habeeb Buttross
Natchez, Mississippi

COCA-COLA® CAKE

A remnant of the World War II era, when sugar was rationed and the dark sticky syrup used for fountain Cokes was pushed into service as a dessert sweetener.

YIELD: 8 SERVINGS

1 cup sugar
1 cup flour
½ teaspoon baking powder
1 stick (¼ pound) unsalted butter
2 tablespoons cocoa powder
½ cup Coca-Cola
¼ cup buttermilk
1 egg, beaten
1 teaspoon vanilla
Frosting (recipe follows)
½ cup broken pecans

Preheat the oven to 350°. Grease and flour an 8x8-inch cake pan.

Mix the sugar, flour, and baking powder in a bowl. Bring the butter, cocoa, and Coca-Cola to a boil in a medium saucepan, stirring to blend well. Pour over the dry ingredients gradually, mixing well. Combine the buttermilk, egg, and vanilla in a bowl; mix well. Add to the batter; mix well. Spoon into the prepared pan. Bake for 25 to 30 minutes, or until a cake tester inserted in the center comes out clean. Turn the cake out onto a platter. Pour the hot frosting over the warm cake; top with the pecans. Let stand until cool.

FROSTING

½ stick unsalted butter
1½ tablespoons cocoa powder
¾ cup Coca-Cola
2¼ cups confectioners' sugar
1 teaspoon vanilla

Bring the butter, cocoa, and Coca-Cola to a boil in a medium saucepan, stirring to blend well; remove from the heat. Stir in the confectioners' sugar and vanilla. Pour over the warm cake.

True Grits
Junior League of Atlanta
Atlanta, Georgia

DR PEPPER® CHOCOLATE CAKE

Created in 1885 by pharmacist Charles Alderton of Waco, Texas, and named for Dr. Charles Pepper of Rural Retreat, Virginia, Dr Pepper is a western cousin to Dixie's favorite soft drink, Coca-Cola.

YIELD: 2 TUBE PANS OR 72 CUPCAKES

4 cups flour
½ cup cocoa powder
3 teaspoons cinnamon
1 teaspoon salt
2 teaspoons baking soda
4 cups sugar
1 pound unsalted butter
2 cups Dr Pepper

4 eggs

1 cup buttermilk

4 teaspoons vanilla

Dr Pepper icing (recipe follows)

Preheat the oven to 350°. Grease and flour two tube pans, or line 72 cupcake cups with paper cupcake liners.

In a large bowl, sift together the flour, cocoa, cinnamon, salt, baking soda, and sugar.

Heat the butter and Dr Pepper in a large saucepan until the butter melts. Add the eggs, buttermilk, and vanilla; mix well. Add the liquid to the dry ingredients and beat until smooth. The batter will be very thin. Pour into the prepared pans and bake for 60 minutes, or into the lined cupcake cups and bake for 15 minutes. Frost the warm cake(s) with Dr Pepper Icing.

DR PEPPER ICING

1 stick (¼ pound) unsalted butter

½ cup Dr Pepper

6 tablespoons cocoa powder

1 cup chopped pecans

2 teaspoons vanilla

2 pounds confectioners' sugar

Heat the butter and Dr Pepper together; do not boil. Add the remaining ingredients and mix well.

A Taste of South Carolina
Orangeburg, South Carolina

BOURBON-CHOCOLATE TIPSY CAKE

Bourbon sweetens and deepens the taste of this Bundt cake while chocolate sounds the bass note.

YIELD: ONE 9-INCH BUNDT CAKE (12 SERVINGS)

2 sticks (½ pound) unsalted butter, at room temperature, plus extra for greasing pan

Cocoa powder, for dusting pan

2 cups sifted flour

1 teaspoon baking soda

¼ teaspoon salt

¼ cup dry instant coffee or espresso

Boiling water

Cold water

½ cup bourbon, plus 2 tablespoons additional for sprinkling finished cake

1½ teaspoons vanilla

2 cups sugar

3 large eggs

3 ounces unsweetened chocolate, melted

2 ounces German's sweet chocolate, melted

Confectioners' sugar

Sweetened whipped cream, for garnish

Fresh strawberries, for garnish (optional)

Preheat the oven to 325°. Butter a 9-inch Bundt pan and dust with cocoa powder.

Sift together the flour, baking soda, and salt.

In a 2-cup glass measure, dissolve the coffee in a small amount of boiling water. Add cold water to the 1½-cup line and stir in the ½ cup bourbon.

Cream the butter in a large bowl. Add the vanilla and sugar and beat to mix well. Add the eggs, one at a time, beating until smooth after each addition. Add the two melted chocolates and beat until smooth.

Add the sifted dry ingredients to the butter mixture in three additions, alternating with the bourbon mixture in two additions.

Pour the batter into the prepared pan. Bake for 1¼ hours, or until a pick inserted in the middle of the cake comes out clean and dry. Let the cake cool in the pan 15 minutes, then remove to a wire rack and sprinkle with the remaining 2 tablespoons bourbon. To serve, dust with confectioners' sugar and garnish with whipped cream, and with strawberries if desired.

Come On In!
Junior League of Jackson
Jackson, Mississippi

PINEAPPLE UPSIDE-DOWN CAKE

Y I E L D : 6 T O 8 S E R V I N G S

2 sticks (½ pound) unsalted butter, at room
  temperature
½ cup firmly packed light brown sugar
7 to 8 slices canned pineapple
1 cup granulated sugar
1 teaspoon vanilla extract
2 eggs
2 cups flour
1 teaspoon baking powder
⅔ cup milk

Preheat the oven to 350°. Melt 1 stick of butter in a 10-inch cast-iron skillet. Add the brown sugar

and cook on low heat, stirring constantly, until the sugar dissolves. Remove from the heat. Arrange the pineapple slices in one layer in the sugar mixture.

Cream the remaining stick of butter with the granulated sugar and vanilla in a large bowl. Add the eggs, one at a time, beating well after each addition. Sift the flour and baking powder together. Add the flour mixture and the milk mixture to the butter mixture alternately, starting and ending with the flour mixture. Pour the batter over the pineapple slices in the skillet.

Bake for 40 to 45 minutes or until the cake is golden and a toothpick inserted in the center comes out clean. Run a knife around the edge of the pan. Hold a large serving plate upside down over the skillet. Turn the skillet and plate upside down. After the cake drops out, wait for a minute to let the brown sugar sauce drip down the sides before removing the skillet.

Cookin' Up a Storm
Jane Lee Rankin
Louisville, Kentucky

POUND CAKE

Y I E L D : 1 2 T O 1 6 S E R V I N G S

2 cups flour, sifted
1¾ cups sugar
½ cup vegetable shortening.
1 stick (¼ pound) unsalted butter
1 teaspoon baking powder
5 eggs
5 tablespoons milk
Pinch of salt

RONNI LUNDY

THE FAMILY REUNION

Although I was born in Corbin, Kentucky, my family was a part of the Hillbilly Diaspora. We moved north to Louisville when I was just one year old, but through my childhood and right up until my teens, I was still very involved with southeastern Kentucky culture.

Each summer my parents went home for two weeks. That was my father's vacation, and we seemed to always time it so that we could be back home for the family reunions of both his family and my mother's. Both were held at Levi Jackson State Park, just north of Corbin. It would have been unthinkable to miss either one.

I recall my father at the center of those reunions. And I was a little planet around his sun. People gravitated to him, attracted by his storytelling and his warmth of heart. He was a wonderfully quick-witted man who never saw an event or heard a fragment of a story that he couldn't turn into a full-blown anecdote that was both funny and instructional. Sometimes I think I was raised by Aesop.

At home, my mother was the center of the cooking universe, but at the reunions, she took a back seat. That was all right, because there were extraordinary cooks on both sides of the family. No matter who cooked what, and what tasted best, everybody tried to be very polite. At my dad's reunion it was Aunt Ariel's jam cake that tested everyone. It was the best, bar none. Usually, the first couple of people down the line would say they were coming back for dessert. But everybody knew that if you went back late, you didn't stand a chance of getting a slice of her jam cake. So somebody—it was usually a man—would get desperate and slice into the cake. From that point on, nobody went for anything else until it was all gone. We are an incredibly polite people. And no one wanted to hurt anyone's feelings, especially about food. As in most primitive food cultures, to give food was to give of your lifeblood. In Hillbilly culture you would not say to somebody, "I don't like this." To refuse food would have been a horrible thing. Nobody would say, "I want Ariel's jam cake." But since it was the one cut into, everybody would say, "Oh, this is already cut into. I'll just take a piece of this." So the first people down the line got Ariel's jam cake—and then you went on to the rest.

A native of Corbin, Kentucky, Ronni Lundy is the author of numerous works on food, including Shuck Beans, Stack Cakes, and Honest Fried Chicken *and* Butterbeans to Blackberries: Recipes from the Southern Garden.

1 teaspoon vanilla

1 teaspoon lemon flavoring

Have all the ingredients at room temperature. Preheat the oven to 300°. Grease and flour a tube or Bundt pan.

Put all the ingredients at a large mixing bowl. Beat at medium speed for 15 minutes. Pour the batter into the prepared pan and bake for about 1 hour, or until slightly browned and beginning to pull away from the sides of the pan.

Candlelight and Wisteria
Lee-Scott Academy
Auburn, Alabama

BUTTERMILK POUND CAKE

YIELD: 12 TO 16 SERVINGS

2 sticks (½ pound) unsalted butter, at room temperature

2 cups sugar

4 eggs

3 cups flour

½ teaspoon baking soda

¼ teaspoon salt

1 cup buttermilk

1 teaspoon lemon extract

1 teaspoon vanilla

Preheat the oven to 325°. Grease and flour a 10-inch tube pan.

Cream the butter in a large bowl; gradually add the sugar, beating until well blended. Add the eggs, one at a time, beating well after each addition.

Combine the flour, baking soda, and salt. Add to the creamed mixture alternately with the buttermilk. Stir in the lemon extract and vanilla. Pour the batter into the prepared pan. Bake for 1 hour.

Holiday Foods
Lafayette County Extension Homemakers
Oxford, Mississippi

LEMON POUND CAKE

YIELD: 12 TO 16 SERVINGS

1 stick (¼ pound) unsalted margarine, at room temperature

1 stick (¼ pound) unsalted butter, at room temperature

½ cup vegetable shortening

3 scant cups sugar

5 large eggs

3 cups flour

1 cup warm milk

½ teaspoon baking powder

¼ teaspoon salt

1 teaspoon vanilla

½ teaspoon orange extract

½ teaspoon lemon extract

Glaze (recipe follows)

Grease and flour a tube pan.

Cream the margarine, butter, shortening, and sugar in a large bowl. Beat in the eggs one at a time. Add the flour alternately with the milk, adding baking powder and salt to the last flour addition. Add the vanilla, orange extract, and lemon extract. Pour into the prepared pan. Put the cake in the oven, turn the oven to 350°, and let the cake bake for 1 hour and 15 minutes (do not preheat the oven).

Pour the glaze over the cake while the cake is still warm. Let the cake stand at least 5 minutes before removing from the pan. Put the cake in a tight cake holder; cover immediately. After 10 minutes, remove the lid and wipe out the moisture. Re-cover the holder tightly until ready to eat.

GLAZE

2 tablespoons milk
2 tablespoons unsalted butter
2 cups sifted confectioners' sugar
2 tablespoons fresh lemon juice
1 teaspoon grated lemon zest

Heat the milk and butter in a small saucepan until the butter melts. Put the sugar in a bowl, pour the milk mixture over the sugar, and stir until smooth. Add the lemon juice and zest and blend well.

Windows
Brenau College Alumnae Association
Gainesville, Georgia

PRIZE FRUITCAKE

YIELD: 2 LOAVES

1 pound candied cherries
1 pound candied pineapple
½ cup bourbon or sherry
2 sticks (½ pound) unsalted butter

1 cup sugar
6 eggs
1 teaspoon nutmeg
4 cups flour
1 teaspoon baking powder
½ teaspoon salt
2½ cups shelled pecans

Let the candied fruit soak overnight in the bourbon.

Preheat the oven to 250°. Line 2 loaf pans with greased brown paper.

Cream the butter and sugar in a large bowl. Add 4 of the eggs, one at a time, beating thoroughly. Add the nutmeg and ½ cup of the flour. Combine the remaining flour with the baking powder and salt. Then alternating, add the other 2 eggs and the flour mixture. Fold the nuts and soaked fruit into the batter. Mix thoroughly.

Pour into the prepared pans and bake for 2 hours. To prevent dryness, place a small pan of water in the oven during baking. If the cake still seems dry after it is done, pour a little bourbon on top. Store in a cool place in a sealed cake tin, and this cake will keep for a long time.

Christmas Favorites
Mary Ann Crouch and Jan Stedman
Charlotte, North Carolina

MARIE RUDISILL

FOR THE LOVE OF FRUITCAKE

Today, people just don't know what real fruitcake is. The abominations they try and pass off as fruitcake today are, quite frankly, horrible. When I was growing up, we loved them. They were the queen of cakes!

Not long ago, I came across a cache of fruitcake recipes that belonged to one of my relatives, Sook Faulkner. I found eighteen—eighteen different fruitcake recipes—each different, each lovely. There was peacock fruitcake, which when you cut into it revealed a plume of color like a peacock's tail. And Civil War fruitcake. And 1866 fruitcake, the kind she would pack up and send to the president. And bride's fruitcake, white like a bride's wedding dress. They all taste best after they have aged for at least two or three months, and they do nothing but improve with time if regularly sprinkled with sherry, bourbon, or maybe brandy. (I like Courvoisier.)

As a child we knew exactly where to find the fruitcakes—hidden on the top shelf of the walk-in kitchen closet, stored in these old tins that were used year after year. We would reach up there and gouge out a chunk with our finger, knowing full well that when they were opened—usually around Christmastime—we would be found out.

But my, we loved them. We used to have a gully back behind our house where, in the late fall and winter, we would swing from the old trees on vines, swinging from one side of the gully to the other. You know a child has never really lived until they have swung on a vine across a gully and then sat down beside a little campfire to drink hot cocoa and eat a slice of fruitcake. They just haven't lived!

Marie Rudisill, a native of Alabama now living in Florida, is the author of Sook's Cookbook, *a work that began as a joint project with her nephew, author Truman Capote, who spent his childhood summers in Monroeville, Alabama.*

Fruitcake

1 pound of flour
1 dozen eggs
1 pound of sugar
1 pound of butter
1 cup of port wine
2 teaspoons of baking powder
1 tablespoon ginger
2 tablespoons of vanilla extract
1 tablespoon cloves
1 tablespoon cinnamon
2 pounds of raisins
2 pounds of almonds
1 pound of citron, or watermelon rind
   preserves
1 pound of currants
1 pound of coconut

The raisins must be chopped and the currants carefully washed. Roll both thoroughly in flour. Blanch the almonds and chop the citron, or watermelon rind; slice very thinly and cut in small pieces. Grate the coconut carefully. All spices are pulverized. Cream the butter and sugar together carefully. Add well-beaten yolks of the eggs. Sift flour and baking powder together and add slowly. Add wine alternately with the flour. Beat in spices and flavoring, fold in well-beaten egg whites, then add prepared fruits. Bake three hours in a moderate to low oven.

Collected by Kate C. Hubbard in Possum & Pomegranate *for the Federal Writers Project "America Eats"*

WHITE FRUITCAKE

A native of Jackson, Mississippi, Miss Eudora Welty is among the most revered writers of the twentieth century—and a fine baker to boot.

YIELD: 3 MEDIUM-SIZE TUBE CAKES OR 1 LARGE AND 1 SMALL

1 pound crystallized pineapple, clear
1 pound pecan meats, halves preferably
1 pound crystallized cherries, half green,
   half red
Some citron or lemon peel (optional)
Flour for fruit and nuts
3 sticks (¾ pound) unsalted butter, at room
   temperature
2 cups sugar
4 cups sifted flour
2 teaspoons baking powder
Pinch of salt
6 eggs, separated
1 cup bourbon
1 teaspoon vanilla
Nutmeg (optional)
Additional whole pecans for garnish

Prepare the tube pans by greasing them well and lining them with greased waxed paper.

Prepare the fruit and nuts: Cut the pineapple into thin slivers and the cherries in half. Break the pecan meats, reserving a handful or so shapely halves to decorate the top of the cakes. Put the pineapple, cherries, citron, and nuts in separate bowls and dust them lightly in siftings of flour to keep them from clustering together in the batter.

Preheat the oven to 250°. Cream the butter

very lightly in a large mixing bowl; then beat in the sugar until all is smooth and creamy. Mix the flour with the baking powder and salt and sift into the butter mixture a little at a time, alternating with the unbeaten egg yolks added one at a time. When all this is creamy, add the floured fruits and nuts gradually, scattering them lightly into the batter, stirring all the while, and add the bourbon and vanilla in alternation, little by little. Add nutmeg if desired. Last, whip the egg whites into peaks and fold in. Pour the batter into the cake pans (remembering that they will rise). Decorate the tops with pecans.

Bake for 3 hours or until the cakes spring back to the touch and a straw inserted in the center comes out clean and dry. Cover lightly with foil if the tops brown too quickly. When done, the cakes should be a warm golden color. When cool enough to handle, run a spatula around the sides, cover the pan with a big plate, turn the pan and plate over, and slip the cake out. When the cakes are completely cool, they can be wrapped in cloth or foil and stored in a tightly fitting tin box.

From time to time before Christmas, you can improve these with a little more bourbon dribbled over the top of cake to be absorbed and so ripen the cake before cutting. This cake will keep a good while, in or out of the refrigerator.

Eudora Welty
White Fruit Cake
Albondocani Press

TRADITIONAL SCRIPTURE CAKE

Y I E L D : 1 6 S E R V I N G S

1 ½ cups plus 2 tablespoons flour (1 Kings 4:22)
2 teaspoons baking powder (1 Corinthians 5:6)
1 teaspoon ground cinnamon (1 Kings 10:25)
½ teaspoon ground nutmeg (1 Kings 10:25)
½ teaspoon salt (Leviticus 2:13)
¼ teaspoon ground ginger (1 Kings 10:25)
2 cups sugar (Jeremiah 6:10)
2 sticks (½ pound) unsalted margarine or butter, at room temperature (Judges 5:25)
2 tablespoons honey (Proverbs 24:13)
6 eggs, separated (Isaiah 10:14)
½ cup milk (Song of Solomon 4:11)
2 cups chopped almonds (Numbers 17:8)
2 cups chopped dates or figs (Nahum 3:12)
2 cups raisins (1 Samuel 30:12)

Preheat the oven to 300°. Grease and flour a 10-inch tube pan.

Mix the 1 ½ cups flour and the baking powder, cinnamon, nutmeg, salt, and ginger in a medium bowl. Beat the sugar, margarine, and honey in a large bowl with an electric mixer on medium speed until light and fluffy. Add the egg yolks, one at a time, beating well after each addition. Add the flour mixture alternately with the milk, beating after each addition until smooth.

Beat the egg whites in another large bowl with the electric mixer using clean beaters on high speed until stiff peaks form. Gently stir into the batter. Toss the almonds, dates, and raisins with the 2 tablespoons flour in a small bowl. Stir into the batter. Pour into the prepared pan.

Bake 2 hours and 45 minutes or until a

toothpick inserted into the center comes out clean. Let cool 10 minutes; loosen from the sides of the pan with a spatula or knife and gently remove the cake. Let cool completely on a wire rack.

Celebrating Our Mothers' Kitchens
National Council of Negro Women
Washington, D.C.

CRUNCH CAKE

YIELD: 12 TO 16 SERVINGS

2 cups sugar
1 cup vegetable shortening
6 eggs
2 cups cake flour
½ teaspoon vanilla
½ tablespoon lemon flavoring.

Preheat the oven to 300°. Grease and flour a tube pan. Cream the sugar and shortening in a bowl. Add 3 of the eggs, one at a time, beating well after each addition. Add 1 cup of the flour, the 3 remaining eggs, and then the remaining cup of flour. Add the vanilla and lemon flavoring. Pour into the prepared pan. Bake for 1 hour.

Favorite Recipes of the Deep South
Montgomery, Alabama

LUSCIOUS KEY LIME PIE

Found growing in Florida, the Key lime is a small round fruit that is usually more yellow than it is green.

YIELD: 8 SERVINGS

1 tablespoon plain gelatin
1 cup sugar
¼ teaspoon salt
4 eggs, separated
½ cup fresh lime juice
¼ cup water
1 teaspoon grated lime zest
A few drops green food coloring
1 cup heavy cream, whipped
1 (9-inch) pie shell, baked, or cracker crumb
   shell

Mix the gelatin, ½ cup of the sugar, and the salt in a saucepan. Beat the egg yolks well; add the lime juice and water. Stir into the gelatin mixture. Cook over low heat, stirring constantly, just until the mixture comes to a boil. Remove from the heat; stir in the grated zest and coloring. Chill, stirring occasionally, until the mixture mounds slightly when dropped from a spoon.

Beat the egg whites until soft peaks form. Gradually add the remaining ½ cup sugar, beating until stiff. Fold into the chilled gelatin mixture. Fold in the whipped cream, reserving some for a topping, if desired. Pour into the prepared crust. Chill until firm.

The Gasparilla Cookbook
Junior League of Tampa
Tampa, Florida

CANTALOUPE PIE

Known to some Southerners as the muskmelon, the cantaloupe is often eaten at breakfast. Here the dusky orange fruit plays up its sweet side in this simple pie.

Y I E L D : 8 SERVINGS

1 large cantaloupe
1 cup sugar
2 tablespoons cornstarch
3 eggs, separated
¼ teaspoon salt
1 (9-inch) pie shell, baked
¼ cup sugar
¼ teaspoon vanilla

Cut the cantaloupe in half, remove the seeds, cut up the pulp, put it into a double boiler with the sugar, and cook over hot water until the sugar is dissolved. Mix the cornstarch with a little cold water, add the mixture to the cantaloupe, and continue cooking until the mixture thickens. Beat the egg yolks and salt, add to the cantaloupe mixture, and cook a little longer. Let cool.

Preheat the oven to 325°. Pour the cantaloupe mixture into the baked pastry. Spread with meringue beaten from the egg whites and ¼ cup sugar, flavored with vanilla. Brown the pie in the oven. Let cool before serving.

The Historical Cookbook of the American Negro
National Council of Negro Women
Washington, D.C.

SOUTHERN PECAN PIE

No one knows for sure who made the first pecan pie, though you can be almost assured it was a Southerner, what with the wealth of pecan trees that span the southern belt of our region.

Y I E L D : 6 TO 8 SERVINGS

2 tablespoons unsalted butter
2 tablespoons flour
½ cup sugar
Pinch of salt
2 eggs, lightly beaten
1 cup light corn syrup
1 teaspoon vanilla
1 cup chopped pecans
1 (9-inch) pie shell, unbaked

Preheat the oven to 350°. Cream together the butter, flour, sugar, and salt in a large bowl. Gradually add the eggs and beat until smooth. Add the corn syrup gradually and beat until smooth. Stir in the vanilla and pecans. Pour into the unbaked pie shell and bake for 35 to 40 minutes.

Huntsville Entertains
Historic Huntsville Foundation
Huntsville, Alabama

CHOCOLATE PECAN PIE

YIELD: 8 SERVINGS

1 stick (¼ pound) unsalted butter or margarine,
    melted
1 cup sugar
2 eggs
½ cup flour
1 teaspoon vanilla
1 cup chopped pecans
1 (6-ounce) package chocolate chips
1 (9-inch) pie shell, unbaked
Whipped cream or ice cream

Preheat the oven to 350°. Combine the butter and sugar in a large bowl. Cream well. Add the eggs, one at a time, mixing well after each addition. Stir in the flour, vanilla, and pecans. Sprinkle the chocolate chips over the bottom of the pie shell. Cover with the filling. Bake for 40 to 45 minutes. Serve warm with whipped cream or ice cream.

Windows
Brenau College Alumnae Association
Gainesville, Georgia

BLACK BOTTOM PIE

This pie, known throughout the South, gets its name from the chocolate crust that forms the bottom. Though this recipe is from North Carolina, Majorie Kinnan Rawlings, a Floridian, was perhaps the primary proponent of this treat. In her book Cross Creek Cookery, *she writes that it is "so delicate, so luscious, that I hope to be propped up on my dying bed and fed a portion. Then I think that I should refuse outright to die, for life would be too good to relinquish."*

YIELD: 8 SERVINGS

1 cup sugar
1 tablespoon cornstarch
2 cups milk, scalded
4 egg yolks, lightly beaten
6 ounces chocolate bits
1 teaspoon vanilla
1 cup heavy cream, whipped
1 (9-inch) pie shell, baked
1 envelope unflavored gelatin
¼ cup cold water
4 egg whites
Shaved chocolate, for garnish

Combine ½ cup of the sugar and the cornstarch. In the top of a double boiler, slowly add the scalded milk to the lightly beaten egg yolks. Stir in the sugar mixture. Cook over hot water until the custard coats a spoon. To 1 cup of the custard, add the chocolate bits and stir until melted. Add the vanilla; stir and pour into the pie shell. Chill.

Soften the gelatin in the cold water; add to the remaining hot custard. Stir until dissolved, then chill until slightly thickened. Beat the egg whites, gradually adding the remaining ½ cup of sugar, until stiff peaks hold. Fold the gelatin-custard mixture into the egg whites and pour over the chilled chocolate layer in the pie shell. Chill until set. Garnish with shaved chocolate.

Charlotte Cookbook
Junior League of Charlotte
Charlotte, North Carolina

CHESS PIE

There are as many variations on the story of how this pie got its name as there are recipes. Foremost among the theories is that of John Egerton, author of Southern Food, *who postulates that the dessert owes its name to the pie chests in which they were stored, with chess pie taking on the title thanks to a lazy Southern tongue.*

YIELD: 6 TO 8 SERVINGS

1 stick (¼ pound) unsalted butter
2 cups sugar
6 eggs
¾ cup milk
1 teaspoon vanilla
Pinch of salt
1 (9-inch) pie shell, unbaked

Set an oven rack in the low position. Preheat the oven to 350°. Cream the butter and sugar in a bowl until light and fluffy. Add the eggs, one at a time, beating well after each addition. Add the milk, vanilla, and salt. Pour into the pie shell. Bake for 15 minutes on the low rack of the oven; lower the heat to 325° and continue baking for 50 to 60 minutes.

High Cotton Cookin'
Marvell Academy Mothers' Association
Marvell, Arkansas

PEANUT BUTTER CHIFFON PIE

From Sybil Carter, wife of President Jimmy Carter's brother Billy, comes the uptown treatment of the Carter family's downhome crop, the peanut.

YIELD: 8 SERVINGS

1 envelope gelatin
1 cup cold water
2 egg yolks, well beaten
½ cup sugar
½ teaspoon salt
½ cup creamy peanut butter
2 egg whites
½ teaspoon vanilla
1 (9-inch) pie shell, baked

Soften the gelatin in ¼ cup of the cold water. Combine the egg yolks, ¼ cup of the sugar, ½ cup of the remaining water, and the salt in the top of a double boiler; blend well. Add the gelatin mixture. Place over boiling water, and cook, beating constantly, until thick and fluffy; let cool.

Place the peanut butter in a bowl; add the remaining ¼ cup cold water, beating until smooth. Add the egg mixture and vanilla; mix well. Chill until slightly thickened.

Beat the egg whites until foamy; add the remaining sugar. Beat until stiff peaks form. Fold into the chilled peanut butter mixture. Pour into the pie shell. Chill until firm.

Plains Potpourri
Plains Junior Woman's Club
Plains, Georgia

LEMON MERINGUE PIE

YIELD: 8 SERVINGS

1 cup plus 6 tablespoons sugar
½ cup all-purpose flour
½ cup water
½ cup fresh orange juice
½ cup fresh lemon juice
3 eggs, separated
½ stick unsalted butter
1 (9-inch) pie shell, baked

Preheat the oven to 400°. Sift 1 cup of the sugar and the flour into a medium-sized pot. Add the ½ cup water, a little at a time, stirring until well combined. Add the orange juice and lemon juice and stir. Beat the egg yolks and add to the mixture. Add the butter. Cook over low to medium heat, stirring constantly and making sure to get around the edges, while the butter melts. Soon after the butter has melted, the pudding will begin to thicken. Pour it into the crust.

Beat the egg whites at medium speed until they are very foamy. Beat at high speed, pausing to add the 6 tablespoons remaining sugar 1 tablespoon at a time, until the mixture forms stiff peaks. Spoon the meringue on top of the lemon filling. Spread the meringue to the outer edges and form decorative peaks.

Bake on the top rack of the oven for about 4 minutes, until the meringue starts to turn golden brown. Watch carefully and rotate the pie halfway through browning.

Cookin' Up a Storm
Jane Lee Rankin
Louisville, Kentucky

QUICK CHOCOLATE BROWNIE PIE

YIELD: 8 SERVINGS

1 stick (¼ pound) unsalted margarine
1 square unsweetened baking chocolate
1 cup sugar
2 eggs
½ cup flour

Preheat the oven to 325°. Melt the margarine and chocolate in the top pan of a double boiler. Let cool slightly and beat in the remaining ingredients.

Bake in a greased pie pan for 35 to 40 minutes. Top with ice cream to serve.

The Pastors Wives Cookbook
Memphis, Tennessee

HOKA HOT FUDGE PIE

From Ron Shapiro, Oxford, Mississippi, gonzo movie buff and promoter of all things funky, comes this deep, dark rich slice of decadence.

YIELD: 6 TO 8 SERVINGS

1 stick (¼ pound) unsalted butter
1 cup self-rising flour
6 tablespoons cocoa powder
1 cup sugar
1 teaspoon vanilla
1 egg
1 (9-inch) pie crust, unbaked (recipe follows)
Vanilla ice cream, for serving

Preheat the oven to 350°. Melt the butter; let cool. Mix the flour, cocoa, and sugar together in a bowl. Add the vanilla to the cooled butter. Mix the butter mixture into the dry ingredients, then add the egg. Pour the fudge mixture into the crust. Bake for 35 to 40 minutes. Serve with vanilla ice cream.

CRUST

1 stick (¼ pound) unsalted butter
1½ cups self-rising flour
3 tablespoons water

Melt butter in a pie pan; let cool. Mix the flour and water with the butter. Mold the dough around the pan.

Cookin' in the Little Easy
Oxford-Lafayette Humane Society
Oxford, Mississippi

BUTTERMILK COCONUT PIE

YIELD: 8 TO 10 SERVINGS

1½ cups sugar
2 tablespoons flour
1 stick (¼ pound) unsalted butter, melted
3 eggs, well beaten
½ cup buttermilk
1 teaspoon vanilla
1 heaping cup grated fresh coconut, or 1 (3¼-ounce) can grated coconut
1 (9-inch) pie shell, unbaked

Preheat the oven to 350°. In a large bowl, mix together the sugar, flour, butter, eggs, buttermilk, vanilla, and coconut. Pour into the pie shell. Place the pie on a cookie sheet and bake for 1 hour, or until firm. If the crust starts to brown too rapidly, tent it with foil.

Some Like It Hot
Junior League of McAllen
McAllen, Texas

SWEET POTATO PIE

Shakespeare wrote of sweet potatoes in the Merry Wives of Windsor, *and by the close of the sixteenth century, sweet potato pies were an English dessert treat. But down South, they have always been among the most plebeian of desserts.*

YIELD: 2 PIES

3 to 4 large sweet potatoes
1 stick (¼ pound) unsalted butter or margarine, at room temperature
2 cups sugar
4 eggs
½ teaspoon salt
½ teaspoon nutmeg
½ teaspoon cinnamon
1 teaspoon vanilla
1 (12-ounce) can evaporated milk
2 (9-inch) pie shells, unbaked
Whipped cream, for topping

Preheat the oven to 425°. Boil the sweet potatoes until soft. Let cool slightly and remove the skins. Beat the potatoes with a mixer until smooth. Stir in the butter and sugar. Beat in the eggs, one at a time, mixing well after each addition. Mix in the salt, nutmeg, cinnamon, vanilla, and evaporated milk.

Pour into the unbaked pie crusts and bake for 20 minutes. Lower the heat to 325° and bake for 30 to 45 minutes more, or until a knife inserted near the center comes out clean. Let cool. Serve with whipped cream topping.

Sensational Seasons
Junior League of Fort Smith
Fort Smith, Arkansas

BUTTERMILK PUMPKIN PIE

Southerners dote on buttermilk as much for its tangy good taste as for its lengthy storage time compared with white, or sweet, milk. To combine a bit of buttermilk with our native pumpkin is to make a heavenly match.

YIELD: 12 SERVINGS

2 tablespoons unsalted butter, at room temperature
1½ cups buttermilk
1 cup fresh pumpkin or canned pumpkin purée
3 large egg yolks, well beaten
2 tablespoons flour
1 teaspoon cinnamon
½ teaspoon nutmeg
½ teaspoon cloves
¼ teaspoon soda
1 cup sugar
2 (8-inch) pie shells or 1 (9-inch) deep-dish shell, unbaked

Preheat the oven to 400°. Blend the butter, buttermilk, and pumpkin together in a large bowl. Add the egg yolks. Combine the flour, cinnamon, nutmeg, cloves, soda, and sugar in a small bowl. Add to the pumpkin mixture, mixing until thoroughly blended.

Pour into two unbaked 8-inch pie shells or one unbaked 9-inch deep-dish pie shell. Bake for 10 minutes. Reduce the heat to 350°. Bake for 45 minutes longer, or until a knife inserted near the center comes out clean.

What's Cooking for the Holidays
Irene Hayes
Hueysville, Kentucky

APPLE PIE

YIELD: 8 SERVINGS

1¼ cups sugar
½ cup flour
2 teaspoons cinnamon
½ teaspoon nutmeg
¼ teaspoon cloves
Pinch of salt
5 cups sliced peeled apples
¼ cup milk, plus additional for brushing the
*   crust*
2 tablespoons fresh lemon juice
2 teaspoons butter flavoring
1 (10-inch) pie shell, unbaked, plus enough
*   pastry for a 10-inch top layer*

Preheat the oven to 425°. In a large bowl, mix 1 cup of the sugar and the flour, cinnamon, nut-

meg, cloves, and salt. Stir in the apple slices. Combine the milk, lemon juice, and butter flavoring in a small bowl. Add to the apple mixture. Pour into the pie shell; top with a layer of pastry. Brush generously with additional milk and sprinkle with the remaining ¼ cup sugar. Cut decorative slits in the crust for air vents. Bake for 20 minutes; reduce the oven temperature to 350° and bake 30 minutes longer, or until done.

The Pastors Wives Cookbook
Memphis, Tennessee

PEACH PIE

Melissa Faye Green, in her account of coastal Georgia life, Praying for Sheetrock, *wrote that a "Georgia peach, a real Georgia peach, a backyard great-grandmother's orchard peach, is as thickly furred as a sweater, and so fluent and sweet that once you bite through the flannel, it brings tears to your eyes." This recipe comes from Tennessee, where the fruit is just as fluent.*

YIELD: 1 (9-INCH) PIE

1 (9-inch) pie shell, unbaked
1 cup sugar
1 tablespoon flour
1 tablespoon unsalted butter, melted
1 egg, well beaten
6 peaches, peeled and sliced

Bake the pie crust at 450° for 8 minutes. Lower the oven temperature to 275°. Combine the sugar, flour, and butter in a mixing bowl. Add the egg and mix well. Place the peaches in the pie crust. Pour the sugar mixture over the peaches. Bake at 275° for about 1 ½ to 2 hours. A crustiness forms over the top when done.

From the Kitchen Door
Nashville, Tennessee

VINEGAR PIE

A healthy slug of vinegar gives this pie a sweet-sour tang.

YIELD: 8 SERVINGS

½ stick unsalted butter, at room temperature
2 cups sugar
½ teaspoon cinnamon
½ teaspoon nutmeg
½ teaspoon allspice
¼ teaspoon cloves
4 egg yolks
3 tablespoons apple cider vinegar
1 cup chopped seedless raisins
4 egg whites
Pinch of salt
1 (9-inch) pie shell, unbaked

Preheat the oven to 425°. Cream the butter and sugar in a large bowl. Add the cinnamon, nutmeg, allspice, and cloves, blending well. Beat in the yolks until smooth and creamy. Add the vinegar; beat until smooth. Stir in the raisins. Beat the egg whites with the salt until stiff. Slide the egg white mixture into the yolk mixture. Cut and fold until lightly but thoroughly mixed. Place the filling in

the pie shell. Bake for 15 minutes; reduce the heat to 300° and bake for 30 minutes, or until the top is brown and the center of the filling is jellylike.

A Good Heart and a Light Hand
Ruth Gaskins
Alexandria, Virginia

JEFF DAVIS PIE

Named for the president of the Confederate States of America, this rich dessert is a favorite down Dixie way.

YIELD: 6 TO 8 SERVINGS

1 cup sugar, plus additional sugar to add to the
   egg whites (optional)
3 tablespoons flour
3 eggs
1 cup heavy cream
1 cup milk
1 teaspoon cinnamon
1 teaspoon cloves
1 teaspoon vanilla
2 tablespoons unsalted butter
1 (9-inch) pie shell, baked

Preheat the oven to 350°. In a large bowl, combine the 1 cup sugar and the flour, the 3 egg yolks and 1 of the whites, and the cream, milk, cinnamon, cloves, vanilla, and butter. (Reserve the remaining 2 egg whites for the meringue.) Pour the mixture into the pie crust.

   Beat the 2 egg whites until stiff peaks form. Add sugar, if desired. Spread over the pie. Bake for about 30 minutes, or until meringue is light brown.

Recipes from Old Virginia
Virginia Association for Family
   and Community Education
Hume, Virginia

TRANSPARENT PIE

So named for its almost transparent body, this pie is an up-South favorite.

YIELD: 6 TO 8 SERVINGS

1 heaping tablespoon unsalted butter
1 cup sugar
1 egg
1 teaspoon vanilla
1 (9-inch) pie shell, unbaked
Whipped cream, for serving

Preheat the oven to 400°. Cream the butter and sugar in a bowl. Add the egg and vanilla, beating until well mixed. Pour into the crust and bake about 30 minutes. Serve with whipped cream.

Recipes from Old Virginia
Virginia Association for Family
  and Community Education
Hume, Virginia

FRIED PIES

A baptism in hot oil leaves these blankets of dough crusty and oozing with fruit flavor.

YIELD: 5 DOZEN LARGE
OR 8 TO 9 DOZEN SMALL PIES

4 cups flour
1 teaspoon salt
1 teaspoon sugar
2 teaspoons baking powder
1 (13-ounce) can evaporated milk
1 egg, well beaten
⅔ cup vegetable shortening, melted (do not use oil), plus additional for frying
Peach, strawberry, apple, or other preserves or cooked fruits
Glaze (optional; recipe follows)

In a large bowl, combine the flour, salt, sugar, baking powder, evaporated milk, egg, and ⅔ cup shortening. Chill for about 2 hours.

Remove about one-third of the dough from the refrigerator at a time. Keep the rest of the dough chilled. Pinch off enough dough to roll into a circle about the size of a saucer when rolled thin. Place your favorite fruit filling or preserves in the center of the circle. Prick one side with a fork and fold over. Seal the edges well.

Fry in hot but not smoking shortening. Cook until golden brown, turning only once, to prevent sogginess. Drain well. (Can also be baked, to save on the calories.) Add glaze, if desired.

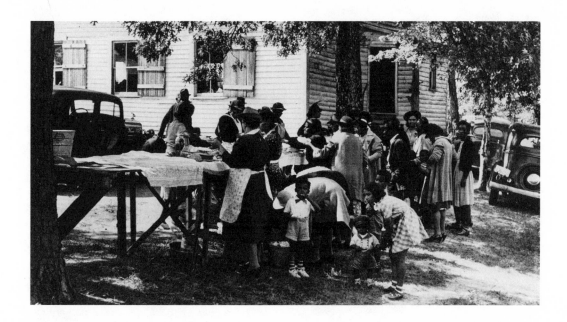

½ cup confectioners' sugar
1 tablespoon unsalted butter, melted
1 tablespoon milk

Combine all the ingredients in a small bowl. Spread on the hot pies.

Calf Fries to Caviar
Janel Franklin and Sue Vaughn
Tahoka, Texas

NEVER-FAIL PIE CRUST

Pie crusts are the backbone of the sweet Southern larder, and after a lifetime of practice, some still fail. With this recipe as your guide, you're halfway there.

YIELD: 1 (9-INCH) PIE CRUST

1½ cups flour
½ teaspoon salt
1 tablespoon unsalted butter
½ cup vegetable shortening
White of 1 small egg
¼ cup cold water
Cream or milk

Preheat the oven to 450°. In a large bowl, lightly mix the flour, salt, butter, and shortening. In a small bowl, beat the egg white and water. Add gradually to the flour mixture and mix well. Roll out the crust and fit in a pie plate; brush the crust with a little cream or milk. Bake for 15 minutes.

Woman's Exchange Cookbook II
Woman's Exchange
Memphis, Tennessee

HOT-WATER PIE CRUST

YIELD: ENOUGH FOR 2 (9-INCH) PIE CRUSTS

½ cup vegetable shortening
¼ cup boiling water
1¾ cups flour
½ teaspoon baking powder
½ teaspoon salt

Place the shortening in a large bowl. Add boiling water and beat until creamy and cold. Sift the flour, baking powder, and salt together; add to the shortening mixture. Stir until the dough forms a smooth ball. Wrap and chill until firm. Roll out between sheets of wax paper.

Houston Junior League Cookbook
Junior League of Houston
Houston, Texas

FUDGE MACAROONS

YIELD: 4 TO 5 DOZEN

4 ounces unsweetened baking chocolate
½ cup vegetable oil
2 cups sugar
4 eggs
2 teaspoons vanilla
2 cups flour
2 teaspoons baking powder
Confectioners' sugar

Melt the chocolate in the top of a double boiler and stir in the oil. (Or combine the chocolate and oil in a large bowl and melt together in the microwave.) Stir in the sugar. Beat in the eggs one at a time. Add the vanilla, flour, and baking powder. Chill the mixture.

Preheat the oven to 375°. Form the mixture into small balls and roll in confectioners' sugar. Place on a greased cookie sheet and bake 12 to 15 minutes.

Dining by Fireflies
Junior League of Charlotte
Charlotte, North Carolina

FORGOTTEN TEA CAKES

Zora Neale Hurston, the birth mother of African American women's fiction, named the male protagonist of her novel Their Eyes Were Watching God *Tea Cake. A man branded by the town of Eatonton, Florida, as not having "doodly squat," he is, however, appreciated by the heroine, Janie, for his sweetness.*

YIELD: 12 TEA CAKES

½ cup vegetable shortening
½ cup plus 1 teaspoon sugar
1 egg
1 teaspoon vanilla
2 cups flour
2 teaspoons baking powder
¼ teaspoon baking soda
¼ teaspoon salt
¼ cup buttermilk
¼ teaspoon nutmeg

Preheat the oven to 375°. Grease a cookie sheet.
Combine the shortening and ½ cup of the

sugar in a large bowl. Beat at medium speed in an electric mixer until light and fluffy. Beat in the egg and vanilla. In another bowl, combine the flour, baking powder, baking soda, and salt. Add to the creamed mixture alternately with the buttermilk at low speed. Mix well after each addition.

Roll the dough out to a ½-inch thickness on a lightly floured surface. Cut with a floured 2½-inch round cutter. Place on a cookie sheet. Combine the 1 teaspoon sugar and the nutmeg. Sprinkle over the tops of the tea cakes.

Bake at 375° for 10 to 12 minutes. Remove to a cooling rack. Serve warm or at room temperature.

Black Family Reunion Cookbook
National Council of Negro Women
Washington, D.C.

GINGERSNAPS

YIELD: 4 DOZEN

¾ cup vegetable shortening
1 cup sugar
¼ cup light molasses
1 egg
2 cups flour
¼ teaspoon salt
2 teaspoons baking soda
1 teaspoon cinnamon
1 teaspoon cloves
1 teaspoon ginger
Sugar, for dipping

Preheat the oven to 375°. Cream the shortening and sugar in a large bowl. Add the molasses and egg; beat well. Sift together the flour, salt, baking soda, cinnamon, cloves, and ginger. Add the sifted dry ingredients to the shortening mixture.

Roll into small balls, dip in sugar, and place 2 inches apart on a greased cookie sheet. Bake for 15 minutes.

Smoky Mountain Magic
Junior League of Johnson City
Johnson City, Tennessee

FORGOTTEN KISSES

Chasteness and taste meet in this recipe from a clutch of churchwomen in North Carolina.

YIELD: 2 DOZEN

2 egg whites
⅔ cup sugar
Pinch of salt
6 ounces chocolate chips
¾ cup chopped nuts (optional)

Preheat the oven to 400°. Beat the egg whites with the sugar (adding the sugar a spoonful at a time until thoroughly incorporated) and salt until stiff peaks form and hold. Fold in the chocolate and the nuts if desired. Drop the batter by teaspoonfuls on a greased cookie sheet. Place in the oven and turn the oven off. Leave 6 hours or overnight. Do not open the oven.

In Order to Serve
Christ Episcopal Church Women
Charlotte, North Carolina

AUNT NETTIE'S ROCKS

Mrs. P. K. Lutken of Jackson, Mississippi, writes, "This recipe is over 100 years old. When I was a bride, Aunt Nettie taught me to make these cookies so I could have them at Christmas as she had for many years and her Mother before her. She made them by ear—not measuring a thing—so, as she made them one time, I carefully measured each ingredient she put in and wrote it down."

Y I E L D :   3   O R   4   D O Z E N

3 sticks (¾ pound) unsalted butter
1½ cups sugar
3 eggs
3¼ cups flour
1 teaspoon each cloves, allspice, ginger, and cinnamon
1 teaspoon salt
1½ teaspoons baking soda
3 tablespoons warm water
2 cups raisins
2 cups currants
4 cups chopped pecans and brazil nuts
2 cups dates, chopped fine
2 cups cut up watermelon rind preserves
Grated zest of 1 orange

Preheat the oven to 325°. Cream the butter and sugar in a large bowl. Add the eggs, flour, cloves, allspice, ginger, cinnamon, and salt. Dissolve the baking soda in the warm water; add to the mixture. Add the raisins, currants, nuts, dates, watermelon preserves, and orange zest. Place by teaspoonfuls on cookie sheets. Bake until done.

Inverness Cookbook
All Saints Episcopal Church
Inverness, Mississippi

MORAVIAN SUGAR COOKIES

This recipe is thought to have been brought over by the first Moravian family to settle in Salem, North Carolina.

YIELD: ABOUT 15 TO 20 DOZEN

3 pounds light brown sugar
3 teaspoons white sugar
1½ pounds unsalted butter
15 eggs, separated
Flavoring (such as vanilla) to suit taste
Flour to make a good-handling dough
  (maybe 8 to 10 cups)

Preheat the oven to 375°. Cream the brown sugar, the white sugar, and the butter in a large bowl. Add the egg yolks; mix well. Add the flavoring, mix well. Beat the egg whites until frothy. Fold into the butter mixture alternately with the flour (add flour gradually until you have a good handling dough). Roll out thin; cut into desired shapes, and bake on a greased cookie sheet for 8 to 10 minutes, or until lightly browned.

Favorite Recipes Old and New
The North Carolina Federation
  of Home Demonstration Clubs
Raleigh, North Carolina

PECAN TASSIES

YIELD: 2 DOZEN TARTS

3 ounces cream cheese, at room temperature
9 tablespoons unsalted butter, at room temperature
1 cup sifted flour
Cooking spray
1 egg
¾ cup firmly packed dark brown sugar
Pinch of salt
1 teaspoon vanilla
⅔ cup coarsely chopped pecans

Blend the cream cheese and 8 tablespoons of the butter together. Stir in the flour. Chill the mixture for 1 hour.

Preheat the oven to 325°. Spray 2 dozen miniature muffin tins with cooking spray so the tarts can be easily removed. Press the chilled dough into the tins.

Beat together the egg, the brown sugar, the remaining tablespoon of butter, the salt, and the vanilla. Put the pecans in the bottom of the pastry cups. Pour the egg mixture over them. Bake for 25 minutes.

Concerts from the Kitchen
Arkansas Symphony Orchestra Society Guild
Little Rock, Arkansas

Wedding Cookies

Pure and pretty like the flowing white drape of a wedding dress on a spring day in Dixie.

YIELD: 2 ½ DOZEN

1 stick (¼ pound) unsalted butter
2 tablespoons sugar
1 teaspoon vanilla
1 cup flour
½ cup finely chopped pecans
½ cup confectioners' sugar

Preheat the oven to 350°. Cream the butter, sugar, and vanilla in a large bowl. Add the flour and the pecans. Roll into tiny balls and place 1 inch apart on a greased cookie sheet. Bake for 15 to 18 minutes. Remove from the sheet and roll immediately in confectioners' sugar. Let cool on a wire rack; then roll again in confectioners' sugar.

In Order to Serve
Christ Episcopal Church
Charlotte, North Carolina

Lemon Bars

A great dessert when cut into large squares, topped with vanilla ice cream or whipped cream, and garnished with a lemon slice and a mint sprig.

YIELD: 24 SQUARES

2 sticks (½ pound) unsalted butter, at room temperature

1 scant cup confectioners' sugar, plus additional for sprinkling
2¼ cups flour
4 eggs, well beaten
2 cups granulated sugar
1 teaspoon baking powder
8 tablespoons fresh lemon juice

Preheat the oven to 350°. Cream the butter, the scant cup confectioners' sugar, and 2 cups of the flour in a large bowl. Spoon into a 13x9-inch baking pan. Bake for 20 minutes. Remove from the oven and reduce the oven temperature to 325°.

Meanwhile, combine the eggs, the 2 cups granulated sugar, the baking powder, the remaining ¼ cup flour, and the lemon juice in a bowl; mix well. Pour over the baked shell. Bake for 30 to 35 minutes. Sprinkle with confectioners' sugar. Allow to cool before cutting and removing from pan.

Christmas Favorites
Mary Ann Crouch and Jan Stedman
Charlotte, North Carolina

Divinity

White and pure—and decadently sweet—this holiday candy belies its name.

YIELD: ABOUT 30 PIECES

2 cups sugar
½ cup water
¼ cup light corn syrup
2 egg whites

½ teaspoon pure vanilla

1½ cups chopped pecans

Combine the sugar, water, and corn syrup in a heavy two-quart saucepan and bring the mixture to a boil over a high heat, stirring the sugar until it is dissolved. Then cook briskly, uncovered, for ten to fifteen minutes, until the syrup reaches a temperature of 255 degrees on a candy thermometer or until a drop spooned into ice water immediately forms a brittle ball.

In a deep bowl, beat the egg whites with a wire whisk until they are stiff enough to stand in unwavering peaks on the whisk when it is lifted from the bowl.

As soon as the syrup reaches the proper temperature, remove the pan from the heat. Whipping the egg whites constantly with the whisk, pour in the syrup in a very slow, thin stream. (Do not scrape the saucepan; the syrup that clings to it is likely to have gone to sugar.)

Add the vanilla and continue to beat for about ten minutes longer, or until the candy begins to lose its gloss and is thick enough to hold its shape almost solidly in a spoon. Stir in the pecans at once.

Without waiting a second, drop the divinity by the tablespoon onto waxed paper, letting each spoonful mound slightly in the center (make a peak). Place a whole half pecan on top of each piece. Allow the candy to sit undisturbed until it is firm. (When divinity was served at weddings, it was customary to place a whole cherry on top.)

Sook's Cookbook
Marie Rudisill
Monroeville, Alabama

CREOLE PRALINES

Once sold on the streets of Louisiana towns by Creoles of color, these buttery, sweet indulgences are now enjoyed throughout the Deep South.

YIELD: 3 DOZEN

3 cups sugar

1½ cups whole milk

¼ cup light corn syrup

3 cups chopped pecans

2 tablespoons unsalted butter or margarine

1 tablespoon vanilla

Mix the sugar, milk, syrup, and pecans together in a deep, lightweight pot. Bring to a boil, stirring constantly. Cook to the soft-ball stage (234° to 240°). Remove from the heat and add the butter. Set aside to cool. Add the vanilla and whip with a spoon until creamy. Spoon out quickly onto waxed paper. Let set until firm.

Louisiana Legacy
Thibodaux Service League
Thibodaux, Louisiana

PLAINS PEANUT BRITTLE

From Lillian Carter, mother of President Jimmy Carter, known to most everyone as Miz Lillian, comes this quintessential take on a shatteringly brittle favorite.

YIELD: ABOUT 2 POUNDS

3 cups sugar

1½ cups water

1 cup light corn syrup

3 cups raw peanuts

2 teaspoons baking soda

½ stick unsalted butter

1 teaspoon vanilla

Bring the sugar, water, and corn syrup to a boil in a heavy saucepan and boil until a thread can be spun; add the peanuts. Stir continuously until the syrup turns golden brown. Remove from the heat; add the baking soda, butter, and vanilla and stir until butter melts. Pour quickly onto two cookie sheets with sides. Pull until the brittle begins to harden around the edges.

Plains Potpourri
Plains Junior Woman's Club
Plains, Georgia

CREAM PULL

Kissing cousin to the saltwater taffies up New Jersey way, this is a treat for strong Southern arms.

YIELD: 4 DOZEN

4 cups sugar

1⅓ cups boiling water

1 cup heavy cream

2 tablespoons unsalted butter, plus additional for buttering the marble slab

Add the sugar to the boiling water. Cook to the soft-ball stage (234° to 240°). Gradually add the cream. Cook to the hard-ball stage (250° to 265°), but just before reaching that stage, add the butter. Butter a marble slab and pour the mixture onto the buttered slab. As quickly as you are able to handle the mixture, pull until it sets. Twist into ropes and cut individual pieces with scissors.

The Stuffed Griffin
Utility Club
Griffin, Georgia

POPCORN BALLS

YIELD: ABOUT 2 DOZEN

3 cups sugar

1 cup water

6 tablespoons unsalted butter

4 quarts popped corn

Cook the sugar and water in a saucepan, without stirring, until light brown or to the hard-ball stage (250° to 265°). Remove from the heat, add the butter, and pour the mixture over the popcorn. Form quickly into balls.

De Bonnes Choses à Manger
St. Matthews Guild
Houma, Louisiana

PEACH LEATHER

1 peck peaches, peeled and mashed through colander

12 ounces sugar for each gallon of peach pulp

Additional sugar

To each gallon of peach pulp, add 12 ounces of sugar in a very large saucepan. Bring to a boil. Remove from the heat and spread on tin pie plates. Place in the sun to dry, about 3 or 4 days; bring in at night. Peach leather is done when dry enough to peel it from the plate. Sprinkle with sugar, cut into strips, and roll into wafer-like pieces of preferred length. Will keep in tins.

The Savannah Cook Book
Harriet Ross Colquitt
Savannah, Georgia

BOURBON BALLS

Bourbon, the South's native drink, fuels these potent little confections, which are holiday favorites.

YIELD: 12 TO 18 SERVINGS

1 cup finely crushed vanilla wafers
1 cup chopped pecans
2 tablespoons cocoa powder
¼ cup bourbon
1½ tablespoons light corn syrup
1 cup confectioners' sugar

Combine the wafers, pecans, and cocoa in a bowl. Combine the bourbon and syrup in a bowl and add to the dry ingredients, mixing thoroughly. Form into balls. Roll the balls in confectioners' sugar. Keep cool until ready to serve.

What's Cooking for the Holidays
Irene Hayes
Hueysville, Kentucky

CHOCOLATE ICE CREAM

YIELD: 12 SERVINGS

2 ounces unsweetened baking chocolate
2 cups milk
1 cup sugar
⅛ teaspoon salt
1½ teaspoons vanilla
1 cup heavy cream, whipped
1 cup half-and-half
7 cups milk

Melt the chocolate in the milk in the top of a double boiler over hot water. Stir in the sugar and salt. Remove from the heat and whip with a whisk until cool and fluffy. Add the vanilla. Fold in the whipped cream and half-and-half. Place in a 1-gallon freezer container, and store in the refrigerator overnight. When ready to freeze, add about 7 cups milk to fill the container three-fourths full. Freeze according to manufacturer's instructions; remove the dasher, cover, and repack in ice and salt for a couple of hours to ripen.

Cotton Country Collection
Junior League of Monroe
Monroe, Louisiana

VANILLA ICE CREAM

YIELD: ABOUT 12 SERVINGS

5 eggs, separated
2½ cups sugar
¾ cup water, boiling
1 quart heavy cream

2 quarts milk
1 tablespoon vanilla

Beat the egg yolks until light. Add the sugar and beat well. Add the boiling water very slowly and stir well. (If this is lumpy, strain it, but it will be smooth if the boiling water is poured slowly enough.) Add the cream, milk, and vanilla and pour into the ice cream freezer. Beat the egg whites until stiff; stir into the mixture in the ice cream freezer and freeze according to manufacturer's instructions.

Variation: If a fruit ice cream is desired, blend the fruit in a blender and decrease the amount of milk.

The Pastors Wives Cookbook
Memphis, Tennessee

CHOCOLATE MINT ICE CREAM

An uptown take on a hand-cranked treat—ice cream with a kick from crème de menthe.

YIELD: 12 SERVINGS

5 eggs
3 cups heavy cream
4 cups milk
1 cup sugar
½ cup light corn syrup
2 teaspoons vanilla
½ teaspoon salt
⅔ cup green crème de menthe
4 to 5 squares semisweet chocolate, shaved

Beat the eggs with a mixer until light, about 4 minutes. Add the cream, milk, sugar, syrup, vanilla, and salt; mix until the sugar dissolves. Add the crème de menthe and fold in the chocolate. Freeze in an ice cream freezer with 1 part rock salt to 4 parts ice. (This ice cream will not harden.)

Pearls of the Concho
Junior League of San Angelo
San Angelo, Texas

PEACH ICE CREAM

YIELD: 6 TO 8 SERVINGS

2 cups peeled and chopped peaches
1½ cups plus 3 tablespoons sugar
2 cups milk
1 small (5-ounce) can evaporated milk
1 cup half-and-half
1 cup heavy cream
1 heaping tablespoon sifted flour

Sprinkle the peaches with the 1½ cups sugar and let stand a few hours at room temperature. Heat the milk, the evaporated milk, the half-and-half, and the cream in the top of a double boiler. Mix the flour and the 3 tablespoons sugar together and add to the milk mixture. Add the peaches and stir with a wooden spoon until heavily coated. Freeze in ice cream freezer according to manufacturer's instructions.

Little Bit Different!
St. John's Episcopal Church
Moultrie, Georgia

LEMON BUTTERMILK ICE CREAM

The tangy taste of buttermilk tempers the sweetness and the bite of lemon in this Southern take on an American standard.

YIELD: 8 SERVINGS

1 quart buttermilk
2 cups heavy cream
1½ cups sugar
7 tablespoons fresh lemon juice
Grated zest of 1 lemon
Salt to taste

Combine all the ingredients in a large bowl; mix well. Pour into the ice cream freezer container and freeze according to the manufacturer's instructions.

True Grits
Junior League of Atlanta
Atlanta, Georgia

WATERMELON SORBET

Long a Southern summer treat, watermelons are called August hams by many. This recipe takes the African fruit a notch higher—and the topping of sesame seeds nods once again to the African continent from which they came.

YIELD: 10 SERVINGS

1 watermelon (small)
1 quart simple syrup (equal parts sugar and water heated until the sugar dissolves)
2 lemons

Remove the rind and seeds from the watermelon. Purée the pulp in a blender and strain it. Add the juice of the 2 lemons and enough simple syrup to sweeten (the amount depends on the sugar content of the fruit). Freeze in an ice cream freezer according to the manufacturer's instructions.

SERVING WATERMELON SORBET

5 limes
2 tablespoons sugar
1 tablespoon black sesame seeds
10 mint leaves

Slice the limes in half lengthwise and remove the inner pulp. Sprinkle the cavity with sugar. Fill with watermelon sorbet. Sprinkle the top with black sesame seeds. Garnish with mint leaves.

A Taste of Memphis
Share Our Strength
Memphis, Tennessee

ORANGE ICE

A Southern take on Italy's granita, this will cool the palate and soothe the sweating brow on a hot summer day.

YIELD: 1 TO 1½ QUARTS

2 cups water
1 cup sugar
Juice of 12 oranges
Juice of 2 lemons

Boil the water and sugar 5 minutes. Let cool; add to strained fruit juices. Freeze in an ice cream freezer according to manufacturer's instructions.

Woman's Exchange Club Cookbook I
Woman's Exchange
Memphis, Tennessee

BANANA PUDDING

Bill Neal, author of Biscuits, Spoonbread, and Sweet Potato Pie, *says banana pudding is "a corruption of a classic English trifle." Call it a corruption. Insist that the wafers be of the packaged variety. Do what you will. This dessert is a favorite of young and old.*

YIELD: 6 SERVINGS

⅓ cup flour
⅔ cup plus 3 tablespoons sugar
2 cups milk
3 egg yolks, beaten

¼ teaspoon salt
2 tablespoons unsalted butter
1¼ teaspoons vanilla
1 package vanilla wafers
5 to 6 bananas, sliced
3 egg whites

Preheat the oven to 350°. Combine the flour and the ⅔ cup sugar in a saucepan. Gradually stir in the milk, then the egg yolks and salt. Cook over medium heat until thickened, stirring constantly. Remove from the heat and add the butter and 1 teaspoon of the vanilla. Let cool slightly. Layer the vanilla wafers, bananas, and pudding mixture one-half at a time in a deep baking dish. Beat the egg whites with the remaining 3 tablespoons sugar and the remaining ¼ teaspoon vanilla in a mixer bowl until stiff peaks form. Spread over the pudding, sealing to the edge. Bake for 15 minutes, or just until the meringue is light brown. Serve warm.

Apron Strings
Junior League of Little Rock
Little Rock, Arkansas

TRIFLE

Among the most elegant of Southern desserts, the trifle is of English origin.

YIELD: 12 TO 16 SERVINGS

2 cups heavy cream
1 cup milk
6 eggs
½ cup sugar

¼ teaspoon salt

1 teaspoon vanilla

½ teaspoon almond extract

1 pound cake

¾ cup raspberry preserves, plus additional for
   decorating trifle

½ cup cream sherry

Whipped cream

Toasted almonds

Scald the cream and milk in a heavy saucepan. Beat the eggs in the top of a double boiler with a wire whisk. Add the sugar and salt. Gradually stir in the scalded cream. Cook over hot water over medium heat, and stir until the mixture coats a metal spoon. (Don't cook too quickly, because this causes the custard to curdle.) Remove the mixture from the heat and let cool. Add the vanilla and almond extract. Cut the cake into ¼-inch slices. Spread with the preserves. Place one layer of slices in a 2-quart serving dish and sprinkle with sherry. Add a little custard. Repeat the layers until all the ingredients are used. Chill overnight. Before serving, decorate with preserves, whipped cream, and almonds.

Charlotte Cooks Again
Junior League of Charlotte
Charlotte, North Carolina

1920 RICE PUDDING

Syrup rather than the traditional sugar was a wartime necessity in 1920. Today, it simply makes for good eating.

YIELD: 4 TO 6 SERVINGS

5 tablespoons raw long-grain rice

4 cups milk

½ cup cane syrup

½ teaspoon salt

½ teaspoon ground cinnamon

½ cup raisins

Preheat the oven to 250°. Wash the rice. Mix the rice with the milk, syrup, salt, cinnamon, and raisins. Grease a baking dish; pour the mixture into the dish. Bake for 3 hours, stirring often to prevent sticking during the first hour. Serve hot or cold.

Forgotten Recipes
Jane Rodack
Memphis, Tennessee

PERSIMMON PUDDING

YIELD: 4 TO 6 SERVINGS

2 quarts chopped persimmons

2 cups sour milk

2 eggs, lightly beaten

1 cup milk

2 cups firmly packed dark brown sugar

1 teaspoon cinnamon

1 teaspoon ground allspice

½ teaspoon nutmeg

2 cups flour

1 teaspoon baking soda

2 sticks (½ pound) unsalted butter, melted

Whipped cream, for serving

Preheat the oven to 350°. Butter a baking pan well.

Mash the persimmons through a colander. Add the sour milk. Add the eggs, milk, brown sugar, cinnamon, allspice, nutmeg, flour, baking soda, and butter. Blend well. Bake in the prepared pan for 45 minutes, or until firm. Serve with whipped cream.

1982 Official World's Fair Cookbook
Phila Hach
Knoxville, Tennessee

BAKED CUSTARD

Y I E L D : **6** S E R V I N G S

2 eggs
⅓ cup sugar
¼ teaspoon salt
2 cups milk, scalded
1 teaspoon almond or vanilla flavoring

Preheat the oven to 350°. Beat the eggs, sugar, and salt slightly to mix. Pour the hot milk into the egg mixture. Strain into 6 custard cups or a 1½-quart casserole. Set in a pan of hot water (1 inch up on cups or casserole). Bake for 20 to 35 minutes, or until a silver knife thrust into the center of the custard comes out clean. Let cool and serve.

Family Collection
Mona Roussel Abadie
Edgard, Louisiana

BREAD PUDDING

A Louisiana favorite and a resourceful use of yesterday's bread.

Y I E L D : **8** T O **10** S E R V I N G S

3 extra-large eggs
1 quart milk
1 quart coarsely crumbled stale bread
    (French bread or good-quality American
    white bread)
¾ cup sugar
¼ teaspoon cinnamon, plus extra for
    topping
1 teaspoon vanilla
1 tablespoon unsalted butter, at room
    temperature

Preheat the oven to 350°. Butter the bottom and sides of a baking dish.

Break the eggs into a 3-quart mixing bowl. Beat the eggs slightly. Add the milk and blend well. Add the crumbled bread to the egg mixture; stir. Set aside to soak, stirring occasionally, until the bread is soft.

Combine the sugar and ¼ teaspoon cinnamon. Add to the softened bread mixture. Stir until the sugar is dissolved. Blend in the vanilla. Pour the pudding mixture into the prepared baking dish. Sprinkle evenly with cinnamon. Bake for 1 hour or until golden brown.

Remove the pan from the oven and place on a wire rack. Run a knife around the sides of the pan; this loosens the pudding and allows it to settle evenly. Let cool on a wire rack. Serve warm or cold.

Variation: If desired, ⅓ cup raisins or 2 cups coarsely chopped Golden Delicious apples can be added to the pudding before baking. Delicious when topped with Whiskey Sauce (see below).

Marie's Melting Pot
Marie Lupo Tusa
New Orleans, Louisiana

WHISKEY SAUCE

YIELD: ABOUT 2 CUPS

1 cup water
1 cup firmly packed dark brown sugar, or
   1 cup granulated sugar
3 tablespoons cornstarch
¼ teaspoon nutmeg
1 tablespoon fresh lemon juice
¼ teaspoon grated lemon zest
2 tablespoons unsalted butter
½ to ¾ cup whiskey

Heat the water in a small saucepan until tiny bubbles appear. Blend together the brown sugar, cornstarch, and nutmeg in a bowl. Stir into the water. Cook over medium heat, stirring constantly, until the mixture begins to thicken. Add the lemon juice, zest, and butter. Cook, stirring constantly, until the sauce thickens and returns to a boil. Add the whiskey and cook 1 minute, stirring constantly. Serve over Bread Pudding (page 312), Pound Cake (page 281), or Angel Food Cake (page 275).

Variation: Omit the whiskey and substitute cognac, brandy, or rum.

Marie's Melting Pot
Marie Lupo Tusa
New Orleans, Louisiana

CHOCOLATE BREAD PUDDING

What was once a resourceful use of yesterday's bread by New Orleans cooks goes uptown and unctuous with the addition of chocolate.

YIELD: 6 SERVINGS

2 cups plain bread crumbs
4 cups scalded milk
2 heaping tablespoons cocoa powder
¾ cup sugar
¼ teaspoon salt
1 teaspoon vanilla
2 eggs
Sauce (recipe follows)

Preheat the oven to 350°. Add the bread crumbs to the milk in a large bowl. Combine the cocoa, sugar, salt, and vanilla in a small bowl. Stir in the eggs; mix well. Add the cocoa mixture gradually to the bread mixture. Pour into a greased baking pan. Bake 45 minutes to 1 hour. Serve with the sauce.

SAUCE

2 cups firmly packed dark brown sugar
3 heaping tablespoons unsalted butter
1 egg

Mix the ingredients well in a saucepan; heat, stirring constantly, until thickened.

Smoky Mountain Magic
Junior League of Johnson City
Johnson City, Tennessee

MEXICAN BREAD PUDDING

Y I E L D : 1 2 S E R V I N G S

1 loaf French bread or good-quality white sandwich bread
2 sticks (½ pound) unsalted butter, melted (optional)
3 cups firmly packed dark brown sugar
1½ tablespoons whole cloves
5 (3-inch) cinnamon sticks
1½ tablespoons anise seeds
1 cup unsalted shelled peanuts
20 colaciones (candied peanuts), about 2 (⅞-ounce) packages (optional)
1 cup raisins
2 cups shredded white cheddar or Monterey Jack cheese

Prepare the bread: Preheat the oven to 400°. Grease two cookie sheets. Arrange the bread on the cookie sheets and bake until golden. Turn and continue baking until both sides are toasted. Using a pastry brush, coat or drizzle the bread with melted butter, if desired.

Make the syrup: In a small pot, combine the brown sugar, cloves, cinnamon sticks, and anise seeds with 8 cups water. Bring to a boil and cook, uncovered, stirring occasionally, until the sugar dissolves. Reduce the heat and simmer vigorously, uncovered, until the liquid reduces to a syrup, about 25 minutes.

Prepare the casserole: Preheat the oven to 350°. Butter a 13x9x2-inch baking dish. Place a layer of bread on the bottom. Slowly pour 1 cup of syrup evenly over the bread layer and allow the bread to soak up the syrup. Sprinkle with a third of the peanuts, a third of the raisins, and a third of the cheese. Repeat the layers twice, ending with cheese. Pour the remaining syrup over the casserole.

Cover and bake for 30 to 45 minutes, or until the cheese has melted. During the last 10 minutes, uncover the casserole and top it with additional *colaciones,* if desired.

Celebración
National Council of La Raza
Washington, D.C.

PASSOVER APPLE KUGEL

Y I E L D : 1 0 S E R V I N G S

6 eggs, separated
1⅓ cups sugar
Pinch of salt
4 cups grated peeled apples
⅔ cup matzo meal
4 teaspoons grated lemon zest
2 tablespoons slivovitz (plum brandy), or wine
½ cup ground pecans

Preheat the oven to 350°. Beat the egg whites in a large bowl until stiff; set aside. Beat the egg yolks, sugar, and salt in a bowl until thick and lemon-colored. Stir in the apples, matzo meal, lemon zest, and slivovitz. Fold in the stiffly beaten egg whites and pour into a greased 10-inch springform pan. Sprinkle the nuts on top. Bake for 35 minutes, or until brown and firm. Let cool before removing the sides of the pan.

From Generation to Generation
Sisterhood of Temple Emanu-El
Dallas, Texas

CHARLOTTE RUSSE

Long a favorite of the Ladies Who Lunch, Charlotte Russe was created by the French chef Antonin Carême while he was working for Czar Alexander I.

YIELD: 8 SERVINGS

2 eggs
2 cups milk
1 cup sugar
1 teaspoon vanilla

1 envelope unflavored gelatin
¼ cup cold water
1 cup heavy cream, whipped
8 to 10 ladyfingers
Sherry (optional)
Additional whipped cream (optional)

Beat the eggs well in a bowl; stir in the milk and sugar. Cook in the top of a double boiler until the mixture coats a spoon; add the vanilla. Let cool.

Sprinkle the gelatin over the cold water in a small saucepan. Stir constantly over low heat until the gelatin dissolves. Add to the egg mixture. When the mixture is completely cooled, fold in the whipped cream.

Line a 2-quart casserole with split ladyfingers. Sherry can be sprinkled over the ladyfingers, if desired, before the custard is poured. Pour the custard slowly over the ladyfingers. The ladyfingers will tend to float to the top. (For looks only, you may want them all up or all down.) Refrigerate several hours. The Charlotte Russe can be served with whipped cream on top, if desired.

The Stuffed Griffin
Utility Club
Griffin, Georgia

PEACH-BLUEBERRY COBBLER

Its name perhaps derived from the phrase "to cobble something together," this Southern amalgam of fruit and crust is sure to please.

Y I E L D : 8 S E R V I N G S

⅓ cup plus 1 teaspoon sugar
1 tablespoon cornstarch
¼ cup fresh orange juice
1½ cups fresh or frozen peach slices
1 cup fresh or frozen blueberries
½ cup all-purpose flour
½ cup whole-wheat flour
1½ teaspoons baking powder
⅓ cup skim milk
3 tablespoons vegetable oil

In a small saucepan, stir together the ⅓ cup sugar and the cornstarch; add the orange juice. Cook, stirring, until bubbly. Add the peaches and blueberries; cook until the filling is hot. Keep warm.

Preheat the oven to 425°. Stir together the all-purpose flour, the whole-wheat flour, and the baking powder in a large bowl. Add the skim milk and oil; stir until the mixture forms a ball. On a floured surface, pat the dough into an 8-inch circle. Cut into 8 wedges. Spoon hot berry mixture into a 9-inch pie plate; immediately top with the pastry wedges. Sprinkle the top with the 1 teaspoon remaining sugar. Bake for 25 to 30 minutes or until the pastry wedges are brown. Serve warm.

Southern But Lite
Jen Avis and Kathy Ward
West Monroe, Louisiana

TENNESSEE BLACKBERRY COBBLER

YIELD: 8 SERVINGS

4 cups fresh blackberries or 24 ounces frozen,
    thawed and drained
1½ cups plus 1 tablespoon sugar
2 cups plus 3 tablespoons flour
1 tablespoon fresh lemon juice
3 tablespoons unsalted butter
¼ teaspoon salt
1 tablespoon baking powder
1 cup heavy cream, whipped

Preheat the oven to 400°. In a large bowl, toss the berries with the 1½ cups sugar and the 3 tablespoons flour. Spoon into an ungreased 9-inch baking dish. Sprinkle the berries with lemon juice and dot with butter, set aside.

Combine the 2 cups flour and the salt and baking powder in a large bowl. Gently fold the whipped cream into the flour mixture. Place the dough on a floured board and knead for 1 minute. Roll the dough to a ½-inch thickness. Cut into lattice strips or place the entire sheet of dough on the cobbler. Sprinkle with the 1 tablespoon sugar. Bake for 10 to 12 minutes, then reduce the heat to 325° and bake another 20 minutes, or until golden brown.

Miss Daisy Celebrates Tennessee
Daisy King
Nashville, Tennessee

AMBROSIA

Known as the food of the gods to those with a background in Latin, or to those who have put a spoonful of this nectar to their lips.

YIELD: 1 GALLON

3 to 4 dozen oranges
1 to 1½ pounds grated coconut, fresh or frozen
2 cups sugar

Using a sharp knife, peel the oranges, removing the rind and all the outside white membrane from the sections. Separate the sections and remove the seeds. Place the orange sections and any juice in a large bowl. Add the coconut and sugar; mix well. Cover tightly and refrigerate until time to serve.

Note: This is best prepared 24 hours in advance, and it keeps for weeks.

*How to Cook a Pig
and Other Back-to-the-Farm Recipes*
Betty Talmadge
Lovejoy, Georgia

Blackberry Dumplings

This dish is not made with piecrust but with ordinary biscuit dough made just a trifle shorter than usual. Roll the dough out a little thinner than for biscuit, on a well-floured cloth. Cover the top of the dough with a thick layer of fresh ripe blackberries. Roll the dough and berries up and tie the whole in the cloth on which it was rolled. Put the whole thing in a pot of briskly boiling water. Bring it back to boiling point as quickly as possible and then cook steadily till done. While the dumplings boil make a sweet sauce as follows: Take one and a half cups of top milk, one cupful of sugar, ¼ cup of butter, cook together thoroughly and flavor by putting in sprigs and leaves of mint which have been bruised. Remove the mint leaves before serving the sauce, which should be served hot on slices of the boiled dumplings.

Collected by Kate C. Hubbard in Possum & Pomegranate *for the Federal Writers Project "America Eats"*

BAKLAVA

A Greek treat goes Southern with the addition of pecans.

Y I E L D : 2 4 S E R V I N G S

1 pound walnuts or pecans, finely
   chopped
⅓ cup sugar
1 teaspoon cinnamon
½ teaspoon cloves
½ teaspoon nutmeg
1 pound phyllo
1 pound unsalted butter, clarified, melted, and
   warm
Whole cloves (optional)
Syrup, warm (recipe follows)

Preheat the oven to 325°. Combine the nuts, sugar, cinnamon, cloves, and nutmeg. Trim the phyllo to pan size. Place 6 phyllo sheets in a buttered 13x9-inch baking pan, brushing each sheet generously with butter. Sprinkle a thin layer of nut mixture evenly over the phyllo. Cover with 4 buttered phyllo sheets. Continue alternating phyllo, butter, and nut mixture until all the nuts are used. Top with 8 buttered phyllo sheets. Cut into diamonds or squares. If desired, stud each piece with a whole clove.

Bake for 30 minutes; then lower the oven temperature to 300° and bake 30 minutes longer, or until golden brown. Pour the warm syrup over the hot baklava. Let stand for several hours or overnight. Store in airtight containers in a cool place; it will keep for several weeks. The baklava freezes well. Thaw to room temperature and serve.

SYRUP

3 cups sugar
2 cups water
1 stick cinnamon
Juice of ½ lemon
2 to 3 tablespoons honey
   (optional)

Combine the sugar, water, cinnamon stick, and lemon juice and gently boil for 20 minutes, or until a candy thermometer reaches 230°. Remove from the heat; if desired, stir in the honey.

The Grecian Plate
Hellenic Ladies Society
St. Barbara Greek Orthodox Church
Durham, North Carolina

LADYFINGERS

1½ sticks unsalted butter
¼ cup confectioners' sugar, plus extra for rolling
2 cups plain flour
1 tablespoon ice water
1½ teaspoons vanilla
1 cup finely chopped nuts

Preheat the oven to 325°. In a large bowl, cream the butter and sugar. Add the flour, water and vanilla, then the nuts. Pinch off in small bits. Roll between your palms into strips and curve slightly. (Chilled dough is easier to roll.) Place on a greased cookie sheet and bake until light brown. Remove from the pan and roll in confectioners' sugar.

Recipes for Creative Living
John C. Campbell Folk School
Brasstown, North Carolina

MENUS

....

MYRLIE EVERS WILLIAMS

THE TRACTOR MEETING

There was, each August, something called a tractor meeting, and after we were married, Medgar took me to one. It was held on a Sunday at the picnic grounds of a church far out in the country, and from just after dawn, families would begin to arrive from all over that part of the state. It seemed to me that all of the families were huge and that somehow all were related, for nearly everyone you met was introduced as a cousin. Each family brought with it what seemed a ridiculous amount of food, and what developed was a sort of all-day picnic, with preaching and singing groups from different churches competing with one another.

A family would set itself up at a picnic table and spread out its food; three or four different kinds of cake, meats, vegetables, everything imaginable. During the day, whole families or groups of two or three would drift from table to table, from family to family, carrying baskets of food, sampling the delicacies of others and leaving something in return to be sampled.

The primary reason for the success of the affair was that it served as a sort of reunion. This was where you found relatives and friends seen only once a year. It was where you learned who had married whom, who had died, who had graduated, and who had had another child. It was where the men discussed their crops and their jobs and the price of cotton and the impossibility of making a living cropping shares. It was where the women compared recipes and children and the white families they worked for and, I suppose, their husbands. It was where the ministers looked over one another's congregations and choirs and preaching techniques, and where the teachers talked about their schools and their students. Above all, it was where the genealogists in each family spent a happy day untangling the exact relationships of sixth cousins four times removed.

In a way these tractor meetings were both a time of renewal of bonds and a release from the drudgery of a year of hard work. They were the only real means of communication among the Negro families in that part of Mississippi. They represented the only large social gathering of the year, and there was a special sadness in going home when they were over.

Myrlie Evers Williams was the wife of NAACP field secretary Medgar Evers at the time of his assassination. She is now the Chairperson of the NAACP. This excerpt, set in Decatur, Mississippi, is taken from her book For Us, the Living, *originally published in 1967.*

Lowcountry Boil

Where seafood is as plentiful as an everyday garden vegetable, neighbors share their bounty. The host sets large pots filled with water to boil over a backyard pit lined with hot coals. The catch of the day is dropped in. Dishes are set on newspaper-covered picnic tables. The shrimp blushes to a beautiful pink. And soon comes the call to eat, "Help yourself!"

Frogmore Stew
Hush Puppies
Coleslaw
Butter-Roasted Corn
Vinegar Pie
Buttermilk Coconut Pie

Hunt Breakfast

As the early morning mist covers the ground, the dogs gather, their masters mounted on horse-back. The hunt is blessed. Off they go, anticipating a return to a large hunt table laden with a feast.

Betsy's Sherried Doves
Country Ham with Red-Eye Gravy
Breakfast Sausage Casserole
Garlic Cheese Grits
Sweet Potato Biscuits
Curried Fruit

Holiday Open House

Come December, in every Southern community— large and small, urban and rural—hosts throw open their doors, welcoming friends and family, co-workers and neighbors, for an evening of merrymaking. Often held on Christmas Eve, these parties offer everyone a chance to drop by and partake of a bit of holiday cheer.

Pickled Shrimp or *Spiced Pecans*
Baked Ham
Pecan Tassies or *Lemon Pound Cake*
Winter Wassail
Holiday Eggnog

Garden Wedding Reception

By late spring, Southern gardens are ablaze with color as azaleas and dogwoods burst forth from their winter slumber. On the appointed day, white chairs are set in front of a makeshift altar decorated with bouquets of flowers picked from the garden.

Cheese Straws
Cucumber Sandwiches
Hot Crab Meat Puffs
Chicken Salad
Angel Food Cake or *Wedding Cookies*
Aunt Nettie's Rocks
Champagne Punch

Dinner on the Grounds

The Sacred Harp Singers, known for the shape-note singing (gospel harmony), perform in the blazing sun just outside the church doors while members gather nearby under the shade trees to feast. Young and old alike walk around folding tables filled with home-cooked food known through the hill country to be as good as the singers.

Buttermilk Fried Chicken or *Jimmy's Meat Loaf*
Potato Salad or *Green Beans* or *Pear Salad Delight*
Chow-Chow
Corn Light Bread
Red Velvet Cake or *Banana Pudding* or *Fried Pies*
Sweet Mint Iced Tea or *Lemonade*

Funeral Wake

When a loved one passes away, people come from far and wide to pay their respects. And they do not come emptyhanded. With them they bring proof of their love, their loss. They bring food. It is the Southern way of caring.

Chicken and Dumplings
Vegetable Soup
Fried Green Tomatoes
Southern Pecan Pie
Old-Fashioned Pound Cake
Pecan Butter Chiffon Pie
Hoka Hot Fudge Pie
Lemonade

Box Social

To raise funds, the ladies of the congregation often prepare a box or a basketful of the South's savoriest and sweetest treats, to be auctioned off to the highest bidder. Here's a real winner, sure to command top dollar.

Fried Chicken
Tomato Salad or *Cornbread Salad*
Buttermilk Biscuits
Mustard Pickles or *Okra Pickles*
Divinity or *Crunch Cake*
Sun Tea

Cake Walk / Ice Cream Social

The ladies' guild offers a perfect weekend fundraiser for every generation. Ice cream is sold by the scoop or bowl. The center of attraction, however, is the Cake Walk. Members spend days baking "their family secrets." Tickets are sold. Participants of all ages walk "the line," which is a curving sidewalk of numbered steps, to background music. When the beat stops, the winning number is called. The cake of choice is the prize.

Chocolate Ice Cream
Lemon Buttermilk Ice Cream
Orange Ice
Watermelon Sorbet
Peach Ice Cream
Lane Cake
1-2-3-4 Cake
Coconut Cream Cake
Traditional Scripture Cake
Peanut Cake with Molasses

Summer Porch Party

In the swelter of summer we gather on wisteria-sheltered porches for the Southern equivalent of afternoon tea. We may say that we have just dropped by to visit, but most Southerners will not decline a taste or a tipple when offered.

Tomato Sandwiches
Radish Sandwiches
Vidalia Onion Dip with crackers
Stuffed Celery
Baked Custard
Forgotten Tea Cakes
Planter's Punch

WILL D. CAMPBELL

COUNTRY HOSPITALITY

In the summer of 1941, I took a trip to visit with a congregation about thirty or forty miles outside Alexandria, Louisiana. I had to hitchhike to get there, riding through what seemed a veritable wilderness to get to this little community. I can't even recall the name of the place.

I arrived late on Saturday evening, and so I spent the night with one of the local families. I woke up the next morning before sunrise but even at that early hour I could hear them all outside. It was still a couple hours before breakfast, but the whole place was alive. They were milking cows and killing chickens, because the little preacher had come to visit.

The smell of coffee got me to stirring. (They had parched the beans that morning and then ground them in a hand grinder mounted on the wall.) And when we finally sat down to eat, the table groaned under the weight of the feast: they had fried squirrel and chicken with white milk gravy. And of course we had milk to drink—whole milk still warm from the cow. And coconut pie. We had coconut pie for breakfast. We had butter beans and rice and mashed potatoes, too. I remember the mashed potatoes so well. There was a mound of them in a fairly big bowl, and I noticed that as each person passed the bowl around the table, they would take the spoon, make an indentation, and then dip down deep into the bowl for their potatoes. I got to wondering what was so special down deep in the bowl. When the mashed potatoes were passed to me, I realized what had been going on: the top was all flyspecked. They were dipping underneath the flyspecks!

Flyspecks or not, we feasted. The preacher had come. And it didn't matter if I had come for breakfast or dinner or supper. If the preacher was there, you fed him! So we feasted on fried squirrel and fried chicken and flyspecked mashed potatoes.

A longtime defender of civil rights and civil liberties, Reverend Will D. Campbell, a native of Amite County, Mississippi, is the author of Brother to a Dragonfly *and* And Also With You: Duncan Gray and the American Dilemma, *among other works.*

Texas Barbecue

Sitting under the trees at a redwood picnic table, listening to easy laughter and conversation of friends and neighbors, and taking in the aromas of a Texas night—a setting for the perfect barbecue is in place.

Texas Caviar
Guacamole with blue corn chips
Grilled Brisket
Southwestern White Chili
Hot Potato Salad with Bacon
Jalapeño Cornbread
Fried Pies

New Orleans Jazz Brunch

Nothing compares to a Sunday afternoon in the Big Easy, listening to jazz on Bourbon Street or joining your friends for a potluck brunch— New Orleans style, of course.

Crawfish Bisque
Seafood Medley
Wilted Lettuce
Grillades and Grits
Jambalaya
Dirty Rice
Baked Custard
Creole Pralines
Buttermilk Pound Cake
Sazerac
Café Brûlot

Family Reunion

The Southern mealtime is the taproot of the African American family. Relatives drive for days, arriving with photos, scrapbooks, and memories to share. The organizers often have custom T-shirts, complete with a family logo, ready for all ages. Prizes are given for who came the longest distance, the "best preserved," most children, and so on.

Benne Seed Wafers
Fried Catfish
Spicy Fried Chicken
Creamy Macaroni and Cheese
Green Beans
Crunchy Cabbage Apple Slaw
Peach-Blueberry Cobbler
Scripture Cake

Passover

During Passover, by tradition, a seat is saved at the table for a stranger. Now if that's not Southern hospitality, what is?

Fluffy Matzo Balls
Passover Brisket
   Stuffed with Spinach and Carrots
Passover Apple Kugel

New Year's Day Brunch

New Year's Day may be the one day when almost all Southerners endeavor to eat the same meal. Tradition dictates that, if you are to have a prosperous New Year, you must eat black-eyed peas and greens for the noontime meal, with the black-eyed peas representing the coins that will jangle in your pocket, and the greens representing the folding cash soon to be stashed in your wallet or purse.

Hoppin' John
Limpin' Susan

Hominy Cassserole
Baked Ham or *Beaten Biscuits*
Hot-Water Cornbread
Milk Punch or *Magnolias*

La Quincenera

The fifteenth birthday of a daughter is a sacred day for the Latino family, as grandparents, aunts, uncles, cousins, friends, and neighbors come with gifts to celebrate her passage into womanhood. Grounded in a religious ceremony, the Quincenera begins with a Catholic mass, witnessed by godparents and fifteen attending couples. The lunch or dinner reception includes music, dancing, and a feast.

Southwestern White Chili
Pinto Beans "From the Pot"
Aberdeen Spanish Rice
Mexican Bread Pudding

Chittlin Strut

Chittlin struts were once a common occurrence in the homes of black Southerners, usually taking place in the fall, soon after the first pigs were slaughtered and the first batches of chittlins cleaned. Time was, these feasts were house parties, staged to raise money, with the hosts selling a plate of chittlins and all the fixings to neighbors and friends, the proceeds going toward next month's rent, or this month's doctor bills. Some advertised their chittlin struts by wandering about the community, singing:

Good fried chittlins, crisp and brown,
Ripe hard cider to wash 'em down.

Coleslaw, cold pickle, sweet potato pie,
And hot corn pone to slap your eye.

Fried Chitterlings
Chittlins (boiled)
Cabbage with Pork
Hot-Water Cornbread
Mustard Pickles
Pecan Tassies
Sweet Potato Pie
Coleslaw

Tailgating in the Grove

Tailgating, the sharing of food and drink before a college football game, was once a simple affair, when friends and family gathered around the tailgate of a truck or car for a pre-game meal. But today, the feasts can be elaborate, the gatherings protracted. Perhaps the finest feast, the ne plus ultra of tailgating, takes place on Saturdays in Oxford, Mississippi, where alumni and students gather in the tree-shrouded Grove at the heart of the Ole Miss campus. Candelabra are not unheard of. Beautiful sprays of fresh flowers blanket the tables covered in red and blue cloths. And everyone shows up dressed to impress— and eat.

Hot Sausage Balls
Dill-Stuffed Deviled Eggs
Artichoke Dip with Chips
Fried Chicken
Cornbread Salad
Pimiento Cheese Sandwiches
Devil's Food Cake
Southern Pecan Pie
Chess Pie

GLOSSARY

Corn is not a grain. Macaroni and cheese is not a starch. Barbecue is a noun, not a verb. And this glossary is subjective, in that these definitions emanate from the collective Southern mind rather than the annals of Brillat-Savarin, Dumas, or Larousse.

absinthe An anise or licorice-flavored liquor once made with wormwood, a hallucinogen now believed to have induced insanity in its partakers. It was once very popular in New Orleans, where its modern-day substitutes—Pernod, Ojen, and anisette, among others—are still consumed.

alligator pear Southern slang for the avocado, attributable to the fruit's reptilian skin.

ambrosia Loosely translated as "food of the gods," ambrosia is a kitchen-sink conglomeration of fruits, the most popular being oranges and coconuts. Ambrosia is served as a side dish and, most often, as a winter holiday dessert.

andouille Though this sausage, popular in Cajun Louisiana, takes its name from the chittlin-stuffed *andouillette* sausage of France, this version contains no chittlins. Instead, look for a chunky mixture of pork meat and fat, heavily spiced and smoked. Andouille is often used in gumbo and jambalaya.

barbecue Meat (most often pork) that has been slow-smoked over a hardwood-fueled fire. Though there are myriad stories as to the origin of the term, the most credible is that Spanish explorers, upon encountering Amerindians of the Caribbean roasting meat on a frame made from green timber, gave the name *barbacoa* to the cooking frame, and thus, inevitably, to the food.

barbecue sauce There is no "one" barbecue sauce. Ranging from vinegar-spiked with a few hot peppers to ketchup, molasses, and mustard amalgams, in the South, barbecue sauce varies from region to region, state to state, even county to county. Pitmasters are known to guard the ingredients in their secret sauce with a zeal that borders on the fanatical. "Somewhat like religious tenets," wrote Katherine Zobel in an article for the magazine *Southern Exposure,* "barbecue sauces are touted as being essential while, at the same time, being declared unknowable."

Benedictine spread First made by Louisville, Kentucky, caterer Jennie Benedict, this spread of cucumbers, onion, mayonnaise, cream cheese, and salt is most often served on crackers or as a sandwich filling. It is little seen outside Kentucky.

benne A seed nowadays often called sesame, *benne* (from the Wolof tribe of Africa's word) is a common Lowcountry ingredient, most popularly used in cocktail wafers.

biscuit There are as many varieties of biscuits as there are cooks in the South. Basic categories are based on leavening agents—or lack thereof.

  angel biscuits utilize both yeast and baking powder for a high-rising biscuit.

  beaten biscuits are from a time when leavening agents were little known and the dough was beaten with a mallet or the side of an ax until the dough blistered with air pockets, and when baked, rose

  buttermilk biscuits benefit from the interaction of acids in the buttermilk with the leaveners baking soda and baking powder.

black-eyed pea Also known as the cowpea, this legume is native to North Africa and was introduced to the South during the period of slave trade, most probably by Spanish traders intent on feeding captive slaves in an economical and comparatively palatable fashion.

boudin A sausage made of rice, hot peppers, various spices, and pork offal, stuffed in casings, and most often found in Cajun Louisiana. Take a drive along the back roads of the Cajun parishes and you will see signs proclaiming their availability: Hot Boudin and Cold Beer! There are two varieties: boudin *blanc* and boudin *rouge.* The latter gets its name and its color from the addition of pig's blood.

bourbon A whiskey made from at least 51 percent corn that has been distilled to a maximum of 160 proof and then aged for at least two years at no more than 125 proof in charred new oak barrels earns the right to be called bourbon. Do at least the aging in Kentucky and you've got Kentucky bourbon.

Brunswick stew This was originally a huntsman's stew made with squirrel. Modern versions now substitute chicken, beef, or pork for the squirrel and add a multitude of vegetables including, but not limited to, potatoes, tomatoes, corn, and lima beans. Brunswick, Georgia; Brunswick County, Virginia; and Brunswick County, North Carolina, claim to be the origin point, though the myriad creation stories seem to all reek of the apocryphal.

burgoo The Kentucky cousin of Brunswick stew, traditionally heavy on mutton rather than squirrel.

butter bean Southern name for the lima bean, a cream- to light-green-colored bean known to have been cultivated in the Caribbean before Columbus's arrival.

buttermilk A by-product of buttermaking, this is the liquid that remains after the milk fats solidify and form butter. In the days before refrigerators were widespread, buttermilk was preferred, for it kept longer than fresh milk, often called sweet milk.

Cajun cooking Hearty foods from the Acadian parishes of southwestern Louisiana, most often one-pot dishes that are a melding of French, Native American, and, to a lesser extent, African-American ingredients and techniques. Though a Cajun craze swept the United States in the 1980s, dishes like blackened redfish are not the products of Cajun home kitchens but the inventions of enterprising chefs like Paul Prudhomme.

catfish Once dismissed as a "trash fish" because of its tendency toward bottom dwelling and bottom feeding, the whiskered catfish is now most often raised in ponds and fed a diet of grain. Richard Schweid's book *Catfish and the Delta* is a masterful examination of the cultural, political, and gastronomical importance of this Southern mainstay.

chess pie According to Elizabeth Sparks, author of *North Carolina and Old Salem Cookery,* chess pie takes its name from the town of Chester, England. John Egerton, in *Southern Food,* offers up a number of possible sources for the name, including one wherein it is a mutation of chest pie—a treat stored in a pie chest or pie safe. No matter, this Southern concoction of sugar, eggs, and butter is a perennial favorite.

chicory A salad green whose roots are dried and ground into a powder. Chicory was once used as an extender when coffee was scarce, but the bitter bite of chicory is now valued as a flavor enhancer.

chittlins Properly called chitterlings, though few who consume them would argue the point, chittlins are the small intestines of the hog. A vestige of the day when poor Southerners ate "every part of the hog but the squeal," chittlins require thorough cleaning and are served either boiled and napped with vinegar or fried.

cornbread In good times and bad, cornbread has sustained the South. Though there are any number of variants, from slender corn sticks, to muffins, to pie-shaped cakes and partly fried patties, most Southerners prefer white corn to yellow, eschew the addition of sugar, and endorse the addition of lard or butter. But there are deviations. . . .

cracklin' When lard is rendered from the fatty carcass of a pig, the little bits of meat that do not turn to liquid float to the bottom, where cracklin' lovers scoop them up and eat them either out of hand or in a batch of cracklin'-laced cornbread.

crawfish Like catfish, crawfish are now being farmed in Louisiana fields once dedicated to rice. Usually between 2 and 6 inches long, these freshwater shellfish resemble tiny lobsters. Fresh crawfish are available from late winter through early summer.

cream of mushroom soup The duct tape of culinary creation, used by many Southern cooks to bind casserole ingredients. Though mushroom is the most-often-used variety, there are numerous others; none will show up in this cookbook.

deviled eggs Though elsewhere the term *deviled* might well pertain to the addition of some sort of hot pepper, in the South it almost always means a healthy dollop of mustard has been added, as in deviled eggs. To make deviled eggs, hard-cooked eggs are halved; the yolks are removed and then mashed with mustard, perhaps a bit of mayonnaise, and maybe a bit of chopped pickles; and the yolks are stuffed back into the white halves and dusted with a shake of paprika.

dinner and **supper** Traditionally, dinner was the sit-down, midday meal of Southerners, with supper being a lighter meal that followed in the evening. Lunch, says author, activist, and preacher Will Campbell, was what you took to work.

dirty rice A composed rice dish made "dirty" by the addition of chopped chicken livers, gizzards, or other browned meat, dirty rice is popular in the Acadian parishes of Louisiana.

dressing Though the rest of the country calls this side dish of stale cornbread, stock, and vegetables stuffing, down South it is more often referred to as dressing. And it is often baked in a separate casserole dish rather than being stuffed into the cavity of a bird. Down Louisiana way, French bread might be added to oysters and seasoned pork, or rice might replace the bread altogether.

fatback Literally, fat from the pig's back, fatback is most often preserved by salting and is also referred to as "white meat." Fatback is often employed as a "seasoning meat" when cooking vegetables.

filé Ground leaves from the sassafras tree, filé is used as a thickening agent in dishes like gumbo, imparting an herbaceous muskiness in the process.

Frogmore stew A Lowcountry seafood boil usually consisting of shrimp, hot link sausage, corn, and seasoning, such as Old Bay. In other parts of the South similar dishes are known, though of late this unusual moniker has eclipsed their usage.

geophagy According to the *Encyclopedia of Southern Culture,* references to the consumption of soils date as far back as 40 B.C. Known colloquially as "dirt eating," the practice refers to the eating of specific clays, not the random consumption of everyday dirt. Some Southerners believe that the ingestion of clays, specifically kaolin-rich clays, calms upset stomachs and provides pregnant women with needed nutrients.

greens Collard, mustard, and turnip greens are the most popular Southern greens but by no means the only ones consumed. Lamb's quarters. crow's toes, creeces, dock, and rape are eaten as well. Not to mention poke sallet, dandelion, kale, and chickweed. No matter the green, the most common preparation technique is to braise the vegetables in a stock suffused with some sort of pork—whether it be pig tails, hock, or fatback—and serve the greens swimming in their own potlikker and sprinkled with a dash of pepper sauce.

grits Grocery store grits, the kind most modern-day Southerners were weaned on, are made by soaking hard kernels of corn in a lye-based solution to remove the outer hull. The resulting soft nubbin is called hominy. Dry and grind the hominy and you have grits. Stone-ground grits are another animal (well, okay, a grain) altogether, made by grinding the dried whole kernels of corn. The coarse product is sold as grits, the finer grind as corn flour. And yes, Southern stone-ground grits and Italian polenta are much the same thing, though we Southerners prefer white corn and the Italians prefer the yellow variety.

gumbo Reference point for the most overused food metaphor applied to the South ("Louisiana is a gumbo of cultures"), as well as quite possibly the archetypal Louisiana dish, gumbo is a stew of various ingredients, maybe rabbit and andouille sausage or shrimp and crab, thickened with either okra or ground sassafras, the latter often referred to as filé gumbo. Those who argue that gumbo isn't gumbo without okra are quick to point out that the dish gets its name from the Bantu peoples of Africa, whose name for okra is *quingombo.*

ham Salt-cured, smoked, hung to sweat in the summer heat, and aged for around a year or so, country-cured hams are hard to find these days, but they've been pleasing Southern palates for hundreds of years. According to John Egerton, author of *Southern Food,* around Smithfield, Virginia, folks claim that as early as 1650, hogs brought from England were fed peanuts from Africa and cured by means of Native American techniques. Among other top-producing ham locales are the Ozark Mountains of Arkansas and the piedmont of Kentucky.

head cheese A pâté of sorts made from pork offal, especially the meat and gelatinous matter from a pig's head.

hoecake Alternately a cornmeal cake originally cooked on a hoe or a large and irregularly shaped wheaten biscuit, hoecake is Southern bread at its simplest.

hominy See GRITS.

hoppin' John A rice dish most popular in the Lowcountry of South Carolina, composed of black-eyed peas and rice. Karen Hess in her seminal work *The Carolina Rice Kitchen* suggests that the name is a corruption of a French/Caribbean term, *pois à pigeon,* meaning pigeon peas.

hot brown A sandwich of chicken and bacon, topped with a tomato slice and drenched in a cheese and cream sauce, created in the late 1920s or early 1930s by chef Fred Schmidt of the Brown Hotel in Louisville, Kentucky.

hush puppy A deep-fried fritter composed of cornmeal, eggs, and any number of other ingredients, including, but not limited to, bell peppers, hot peppers, and onions. Though the tale reeks of the apocryphal, the name may have come from the practice of tossing fried bits of meal to silence dogs gathered around a campfire. When you consider that hush puppies resemble other dishes, like "dog bread," a simple fried bread made from boiling water and cornmeal once used to feed dogs, the tale seems more plausible.

jambalaya Another composed rice dish, etymologically linked to *jamón,* the Spanish word for ham. As served in Louisiana, jambalaya is a sort of "dry stew" often studded with many of the same ingredients as in gumbo, minus the okra or filé.

lard The rendered fat from a slaughtered pig, lard is considered by many Southern cooks to be a superior frying medium and the perfect oil for pie crusts and biscuits. Until recently, lard was, according to one scribe, the very grease of Southern life.

light bread Southern slang for wheat-based loaf bread, also known as wasp-nest bread.

macaroni and cheese This may well be a starch, but you will never convince a Southerner of that. To Southerners, it is a vegetable, and though it may well have been featured in antebellum receipt books, it did not gain widespread acceptance until the arrival of Kraft macaroni and cheese dinners in the 1930s.

maque choux A Cajun concoction of corn, onions, peppers, and milk similar to the pan-Southern side dish called succotash, which typically includes lima beans as well.

Mason jar A glass canning container used by Southerners for "putting up" pickles, conserves, and vegetables, the Mason jar was patented November 30, 1858, by New Yorker John Mason. Mason's version of the canning jar quickly became the standard, for his threaded neck and zinc lid made for a better seal than previous versions that relied on cork. Twenty years later, when Mason's patent ran out, the

Ball Brothers improved on the initial design, and it is their jar that has since been most often used by Southern canners.

mint julep As much a Southern symbol as a potable, mint juleps are a mixture of bourbon, sugar, mint, and ice. Though the identity of the first man to ever put "greens in his whiskey" is lost to the ages, it is generally accepted that the states of Virginia and Kentucky are the capitals of mint julep consumption. There is much discussion as to whether the mint should be crushed, merely bruised, or left alone. Judge Joule Smith, who lived in Lexington, Kentucky, during the late 1800s, believed that "like a woman's heart, it gives its sweetest aroma when bruised."

moonshine So named for the practice of operating stills at night with only the moon for light, home-stilled moonshine is most often a corn-based liquor that in addition to slaking the thirst of many a mountaineer, can be said to have had a part in the birth of stock car racing when bootleggers began to test the speed of their souped-up sedans on an oval track in addition to the back roads of the South.

mullet Like catfish, a Southern favorite long considered inferior, this oily fish is well suited to smoking and is most popular in the Gulf Coast region.

muscadine A grape variety indigenous to the South, of which the most common species is the scuppernong. Equally popular for making wines and jellies, muscadine grapes have a musky-sweet taste.

muskmelon Southern term for cantaloupe, so named for its dank yet sweet taste.

okra Kissing botanical cousin to cotton, okra is a talisman of African American cooking. According to culinary historian Jessica Harris, "wherever okra points its green tip, Africans have been." Europeans once called these furred, mucilaginous pods ladyfingers.

peach First cultivated in China, peaches came to the South by way of Spanish explorers. Commercial profitability was not reached until the 1870s, when Samuel Rumph of Marshaville, Georgia, cultivated the Elberta peach. Described by Melissa Faye Green, author of *Praying for Sheetrock,* as being "thickly furred as a sweater, and so fluent and sweet that once you bite through the flannel, it brings tears to your eyes," peaches are, arguably, the quintessential Southern fruit.

peanut Also known as the groundnut or ground pea, this Southern favorite is actually a legume rather than a nut. Peanuts were South American in origin, but they first came to Dixie by way of Africa, and though long a popular staple, were not as widely eaten until George Washington Carver found myriad uses for them during experiments in the early years of the twentieth century.

pepper sauce A condiment made from cayenne, sport, rooster spur, or other common peppers and vinegar, most often served at the table and sprinkled on collard, mustard, turnip, or other greens. Also called hot pepper sauce.

pimiento cheese Most commonly a sandwich spread made from grated cheddar cheese, mayonnaise, and mild red peppers, this is a dish that gained popularity with the advent of the country store and the easy availability of hoop cheese.

poke sallet A roadside weed that, when picked young, has a flavor similar to spinach. The berries and roots, however, are poisonous. Even those who have never tasted poke know the Tony Joe Royal song "Poke Sallet Annie."

pone A much manipulated word, originally *apone,* and of Amerindian origin, today *pone* can refer to both the simplest and the most seductively complex of cornbreads. In antebellum days pone signified a bread made of cornmeal, water, a pinch of salt, and a bit of grease that was baked on a hearth or wrapped in vegetable leaves and submerged in ashes.

porgy A variety of bream, favored by African American fisherman and made famous by DuBose Heyward's novel and, later, George and Ira Gershwin's opera, both of which were titled *Porgy and Bess* and featured a character named Porgy as the male lead.

possum Correctly opossum, but few save the effete pronounce it that way, the possum is a marsupial hunted after dark. Upon threat of being captured, the possum will freeze, as if "playing dead," hence the old Southern term "playing possum."

potlikker The liquid essence left in a stew pot after cooking vegetables with pork, potlikker most commonly refers to the broth from cooking greens but can also be applied to other vegetables like black-eyed peas.

praline A confection popular in the Deep South, especially around New Orleans, pralines (pronounced "prawlines" by those in the know) are most often a wafer of caramel and pecans, though almonds or hazelnuts were once common.

ramp A wild onion common to the Appalachian South, the ramp has a flavor similar to, albeit stronger than, that of the scallion.

red beans and rice Traditionally prepared on "wash day" in New Orleans because a potful could burble away on the back of the stove while other work was done, red beans and rice is, quite simply, red kidney beans cooked with pickled or smoked pork and a few vegetables before being ladled over a base of white rice.

red rice A dish of rice, tomatoes, other vegetables, and a bit of bacon, most often served along the Georgia and Carolina coasts.

rice Rice was once one of the South's staple crops, and rice cultivation owes its initial success to the acumen of African American slaves who worked the fields of coastal Georgia and South Carolina. For an authoritative examination of rice culture in the South, see Karen Hess's *Carolina Rice Kitchen.*

roux Many a Cajun recipe begins with these instructions: "First you make a roux." This is a base or binder used most often in stewlike dishes, made by slowly browning flour in oil, butter, or some sort of rendered animal fat.

rutabaga Many Southerners refer to these orange-yellow tubers as yellow turnips.

Scripture cake A cake made with ingredients cited in particular Bible verses, often employed by a mother in hopes of teaching a daughter the way around both the church and the kitchen.

she-crab soup A seafood-and-cream-centered soup inextricably linked to its birthplace, Charleston, South Carolina, she-crab soup relies upon roe from the female, or she, crab for both flavor and color.

shortenin' bread Not just what "Mammy's little baby loved," but also a "quick" bread made with butter or lard and often a foil for strawberries and other fruits.

smothered chicken Sautéed chicken that has been covered, or smothered, in a gravy made from its own drippings. The étouffées of Cajun Louisiana are prepared in a similar fashion, among them crawfish étouffée.

sop A verb, used to describe the use of bread—most often cornbread but also, on occasion, biscuits—as a sponge to absorb the liquid in a soupy vegetable dish or a meaty gravy.

spoon bread The most often repeated story about this dish's etymology is that spoon bread is so named because a spoon is required to serve this egg-rich, cream-heavy side dish.

squash From the Amerindian word *asquatasquash,* this family of indigenous vegetables includes zucchini, pumpkin, pattypan, and acorn squash, among others.

streak o' lean So named because the fatty portion of salt pork is often streaked with a bit of lean meat, streak o' lean is often used for a "seasoning meat."

supper See *dinner and supper.*

sweet potatoes No, they're not the same as yams. Yams are big hairy tubers native to Africa. Sweet potatoes, on the other hand, are indigenous plants, tubers that are about the same size as white potatoes (what many Southerners call Irish potatoes), with flesh that ranges from pale yellow to bright orange. In addition to his work with peanuts, George Washington Carver found many unconventional uses for sweet potatoes, and today NASA is testing sweet potatoes for possible use on longer-term space travel.

Tabasco Not a universal class of hot sauces but a singular concoction of Tabasco peppers and vinegar made by the McIlhenny family of New Iberia, Louisiana. Tabasco is the most popular of the commercial hot sauces, but home cooks make innumerable variations.

tasso A highly spiced, smoked ham common to Cajun Louisiana and often used as a flavoring meat.

tomato Musician Roy Clark summed it up when he sang that the "only two things in life that money can't buy are true love and homegrown tomatoes." Ever the pride of the Southern garden, tomatoes are one of the true delights of summer. Aficionados have been known to carry a salt shaker out to the garden, pluck a tomato from the vine, and eat it then and there, with the juices running down their forearms.

Vidalia onions First grown in Toombs County, Georgia, in the 1950s, these super-sweet onions are grown in a twenty-county region surrounding the south Georgia town of Vidalia.

watermelon A native of Africa, this fruit gets its name from its high water content. Because of their availability in a time of scarcity, some Southerners call watermelons "Depression hams," while others, in tribute to the rosy color and time of harvest, know watermelons as "August hams."

EPILOGUE

....

The three of them spoke to me, in their own way, using the language of food. Each of their messages was very different, but as I look back on my days as a little girl, the threads come together to create the fabric of my life. I recognize now, perhaps as all women do, the importance of what the three of them taught me: *In the setting where food is grown, prepared, and served, there is the sacred.* I learned, too, that in the mystery of the meal table there is a priceless truth: *I had a safe place where my family's values, beliefs, and traditions were passed on.*

My maternal grandmama, Ellen Knighton Rainer, was the picture of a proud countrywoman: piercing brown eyes, white hair pinned up, simple floral-print dresses, and sensible laced-up shoes. She and my grandfather bought a boardinghouse during the Depression, so many relatives had a place to live from time to time. She learned to live off the land there in lower Alabama. I really don't remember her talking much. She would just take my hand, and we would ease into the backyard to gather speckled eggs that she placed in her clean apron cupped under her arm. She always let me carry one in each hand so I could feel the warmth of their freshness. Sometimes we would pick figs from the garden trees just beyond the rusting fence. She taught me to make tomato sandwiches on white Sunbeam bread. We scraped yellow corn using the back of a knife, then would fry a panful in the skillet. We snapped fresh beans while sitting on the back porch or fed grain to the hens and their rooster, who had pretty free range of the yard. I remember particularly the Sunday I counted one less hen, yet I knew not to ask questions of this importance, as it was a day of rest. I intuitively understood that Grandmama had forced her "life-and-death" connection to the fried-chicken platter. Even as a young child, I realized that the abundance from the backyard and our family times around the large table had a deeper meaning than I could fathom.

My paternal grandmother, Majorie Yerger Robinson, was more of a city woman, even though it was in a small Mississippi Delta town where she ruled the manor on Catalpa Street. Although stylishly turned out in high heels with silk hose, she always wore black or gray, as she was in eternal mourning because of the untimely death of her only daughter. She believed God had brought me here to take little Margie's place, so she had to make up for so much untaught motherly wisdom. She devoted herself to sharing her lessons of gentility with me during the frequent Saturday nights and Sundays that I spent with her.

Grandmother and I shared many hours together carefully placing settings for twelve at the dining room table. I learned about the position of silverware and a centerpiece, and napkin folding. No details were left unattended, right down to the crystal iced tea coasters and tiny cut-glass salt and pepper shakers. We two were simply doing women's work, as we talked our way around the table and prepared for the Sunday meal, when my family and my cousins' family gathered for dinner after church.

By choice—her own or that which her society dictated—my grandmother did not undertake the actual food preparation; rather, her role, she explained, was the art of ritual, table manners, and conversation. (The kitchen belonged to that third member of the triumvirate so influential in my understanding of the foodways of the South, Artie Parker. But she has yet to make her appearance.)

So in her self-appointed role as doyenne, on each Sunday, shortly after high noon, Grandmother rang the tiny silver bell to summon us to the table. In my assigned seat—always to her right—I sat with a crisp cloth napkin across my lap, hands folded and back straight to await the serving of the meal. Grandfather, at the opposite end of the table, was regal in his heavily starched shirt and maroon tie. Following the blessing, he carved the well-done roast, then meticulously placed each serving of meat on a china plate from the stack in front of him. The ritual of passing began counterclockwise around the table. As the adults started to chat among themselves about the morning's sermon or the weather, the rhythm of forks being lifted and glasses raised shifted upward as we dug into the aspic salad on a Bibb lettuce bed, the first of many courses.

In keeping with the hallowed dictate that children should be seen and not heard, we were silent for the most part. Still, my brothers and cousins and I were caught up in the melody of the escalating conversation—politics, family matters, jokes, and particularly the sparring between my aunt and Daddy. Occasionally we'd share knowing, secretive glances across the table, creating a special kind of conspiracy of our own.

Then suddenly the kitchen door swung open. And Artie, majestic in her blue-and-white uniform, entered bearing the first of her many perfected dishes: silver bowls filled with sweet potato topped with browned marshmallows, an asparagus casserole, rice and gravy or mushy eggplant with cracker crumbs. Artie's beaten biscuits—the most humble yet most essential part of the meal—were always greeted with appreciative nods and smiles. Yet in a twinkling, the finale would arrive with a swift clearing of the dishes, and a stack of dessert plates were placed before Grandmother, who would then stand to serve angelic ambrosia from a frosted bowl. (Although the dessert offering varied from week to week, sometimes pecan pie with sherried whipped cream or chocolate or store-bought ice cream, it is the ambrosia that I choose to remember.)

In my memory of this weekly ritual in which my grandparents and Artie Parker each played their finely choreographed parts, nothing ever changed—the table, the conversation, the food. For this eager child, those wonderful Sunday afternoons told me that all was right with the world.

Artie arrived at my grandmother's house each day around seven in the morning from her room above the funeral home on Issaquena Street to work until after seven at night. The window box fan in the hot kitchen turned ceaselessly and the little radio, caked with dried dough, was always on. Of all the children, I was the one who probably spent the most time with Artie. During our time together, she would be working steadily, singing along with the gospel tunes on the radio and telling me that I was her "chosen one." And I certainly believed that I was. She wanted me to learn her magic. The blending of yolk and oil in mayonnaise would only work if the clouds in the sky were fluffy white. The scallop thumbprints on the pie crust had to be mashed to the rhythm of the music. And the biscuit dough could only be flattened properly when her arthritic hands cupped over mine as we worked the rolling pin across the marble-topped table. In between mixing and stirring and chopping and cleaning, we talked about food and life and God: where it all came from and where we all were going.

When I think of Grandmama, Grandmother, and Artie, I understand most profoundly how each of us is a collection of our life experiences. As a child in the Deep South, I was blessed to have my mind, body, and spirit fed at the tables of these three women. As a woman of the South, I have also come to understand, through the lessons of these three women, that I am one of the keepers of the flame. And I believe that from the beginning of our lives, Southern women, or for that matter all women, pass this flame on at the meal table. Thanks to these women, making cookbooks and making a meal are ways I have to come to know myself.

The recipes in this book, culled from community cookbooks dating back to the Civil War, and the words of those whose recollections appear within these pages, not only embody the essence of Southern foodways but also reveal the dramatic changes that have come about in our society in the past century. These changes, married to the rhythm of time, come no matter what. So it is increasingly important that I pass to my daughters, Amy and Ellie, the values that have shaped my life. This book, then, is part of my legacy to them so that they too can go forward into the twenty-first century with a firm grounding in the best of the traditions that make the South unique.

A good cookbook is a storybook compiled to document a time and place, revealing how we live in such intimate relationships. No matter what the food or the meal or the circumstance, when two or more are gathered at the meal table, we are connected—to the past, to one another, and to the future. This is why we eat in the South.

Ellen Robinson Rolfes
Oxford, Mississippi

P.S. No self-respecting Southern woman could talk about the foodways of the South without at least a passing reference to her mother. My mother did not adopt the country ways of her mother or inherit the mantle of social director that was her mother-in-law's. Even by then, times had changed. But I do recollect the lemon pies that she baked every Saturday. I see so clearly the tangy confection piled high with golden meringue. It is part of a still life as it cools on a sheet of newspaper near the window next to three pairs of small white high-tops that she had polished ready for Sunday school. This memory says to me that there are good cookbooks still to be written.

THE CENTER FOR THE STUDY
OF SOUTHERN CULTURE

The Center for the Study of Southern Culture was established at the University of Mississippi in 1977. Since then, the Center has become a focal point for innovative education and research by promoting scholarship on every aspect of Southern culture and encouraging public understanding of the South through publications, media productions, lectures, performances, and exhibitions.

The Center offers both B.A. and M.A. degrees in Southern Studies. The pioneering curriculum, comprising more than forty courses taught by faculty from ten departments in the College of Liberal Arts, combines innovative, interdisciplinary instruction with traditional approaches to the study of the South. A grant from the National Endowment for the Humanities in 1979 helped launch the curriculum, and a Ford Foundation grant funded a three-year (1986–1989) project to strengthen Southern Studies at the University and other institutions in the region by bringing distinguished visiting faculty and faculty fellows to the campus.

Research is integral to the Center's academic program, as faculty and students collect information, analyze it, and write about the South. Their efforts in documenting the region's culture are creating a notable body of scholarship that will be the Center's great legacy to future efforts to study the South. An integral part of the Center's documentary and educational activities, the Southern Media Archive, has accumulated an outstanding collection of photographs, videos, and distinctive home movies that document the South's visual traditions of the twentieth century and reach out to a wide audience.

Other Center activities bridge the gap between the University and the broader public. Among the nationally recognized programs sponsored or cosponsored by the Center are the Faulkner and Yoknapatawpha Conference, the Porter L. Fortune Chancellor's Symposium in Southern History, the Oxford Conference for the Book, and two national civil rights symposia that brought scores of distinguished journalists and jurists to the University to participate in nationally televised panel discussions. In May 1998 the Center hosted its first Southern Foodways Symposium. This unique meeting focused on the theme "The Evolution of Southern Cuisine" and interspersed formal sessions with cooking demonstrations and community meals.

The Center is well known for its varied programs and for its publications. The *Encyclopedia of Southern Culture,* edited by Charles R. Wilson and William Ferris, was published in 1989. This award-winning 1,634-page reference work has been widely hailed as a major contribution to the multidisciplinary study of the South and was a phenomenal publishing success. The National Endowment for the Humanities and the Ford Foundation generously supported the project. *The South: A Treasury of Art and Literature,* compiled and edited by Lisa Howorth, appeared in 1993. Other Center publications include Dorothy Abbott's anthology, *Mississippi Writers: Reflections of Childhood and Youth,* volume five of which has been adopted as a state textbook; the 636-page *The Blues: A Biliographical Guide;* several other books, including *Lower Pearl River's Piney Woods: Its Land and People;* the bimonthly magazine *Living Blues;* and the semiannual journal *Mississippi Folklife.* Friends of the Center follow its activities through its quarterly newsletter, *The Southern Register.*

To provide needed resources the Center has assisted the University's John Davis Williams Library and the University Museums in developing collections on the South. The Center raised matching funds for a National Endowment for the Humanities challenge grant to establish the Blues Archive and to endow a fund to purchase library materials in Southern Studies.

A second NEH challenge grant was awarded to the Center for the renovation of Barnard Observatory. This grant helped raise matching funds to preserve the long-neglected building, restore its original architectural features, and transform the antebellum observatory into an exemplary place for studying the South.

ACKNOWLEDGMENT OF SOURCES

The authors gratefully acknowledge the cooperation of and permissions from the following sources whose recipes are reprinted in this work:

Abadie Family Collection. Edgard, Louisiana.
Acadian Bi-Centennial Cookbook. Acadian Handicraft Museum, Jennings, Louisiana.
Almost Heaven. Junior League of Huntington, West Virginia.
Ambrosia. Junior Auxiliary of Vicksburg, Mississippi.
Among the Lilies. First Baptist Church, Atlanta, Georgia.
And Roses for the Table. Junior League of Tyler, Texas.
Apron Strings. Junior League of Little Rock, Arkansas.
The Artful Table. Dallas Museum of Art League, Dallas, Texas.
Augusta Cooks for Company. Augusta Council of the Georgia Association for Children and Adults with
        Learning Disabilities, Augusta, Georgia.
Bayou Cuisine. St. Stephen's Episcopal Church, Indianola, Mississippi.
The Best of the Bushel. Junior League of Charlottesville, Virginia.
Bless Us Cooks. Grace–St. Luke's Episcopal Church Women, Memphis, Tennessee.
Cajun Cooking. Angers Publishing, Lafayette, Louisiana.
Calf Fries to Caviar and *More Calf Fries to Caviar.* Janel Franklin and Sue Vaughn, Tahoka, Texas.

Calvary Church Circle Cookbook. Calvary Episcopal Church, Memphis. Tennesseee.

Candlelight and Wisteria. Lee-Scott Academy, Auburn, Alabama.

Cane River Cuisine. Service League of Natchitoches, Louisiana.

Celebración and *Mother Africa's Table.* Main Street Books/Doubleday, New York.

Charleston Receipts and *Charleston Receipts Repeats.* Junior League of Charleston, South Carolina.

Charlotte Cookbook and *Charlotte Cooks Again.* Junior League of Charlotte, North Carolina.

Christmas Favorites. Mary Ann Crouch and Jan Stedman, Charlotte, North Carolina.

Classic Catfish. Evelyn and Tony Roughton, Indianola, Mississippi.

Come On In! and *Southern Sideboards.* Junior League of Jackson, Mississippi.

Concerts from the Kitchen. Arkansas Symphony Orchestra Society Guild, Little Rock, Arkansas.

Cook with a Natchez Native. Bethany Ewald Bultman, Myrtle Bank Publishers, Natchez, Mississippi.

A Cook's Tour of the Azalea Coast. New Hanover–Pender County Medical Society Alliance, Wilmington, North Carolina.

A Cook's Tour of Shreveport. Junior League of Shreveport, Louisiana.

A Cookbook of Pinehurst Courses. Moore Regional Hospital Auxiliary, Pinehurst, North Carolina.

Cookin' in the Little Easy. Oxford-Lafayette Humane Society, Oxford, Mississippi.

Cookin' Up a Storm. Jane Lee Rankin, Grace Publishing, Louisville, Kentucky.

The Cooking Book and *Cordonbluegrass.* Junior League of Louisville, Kentucky.

Cooking for Food. M. D. Anderson, University of Texas, Houston, Texas.

The Cotton Country Collection and *Celebrations on the Bayou.* Junior League of Monroe, Louisiana.

Cross Creek Cookery. Marjorie Kinnan Rawlings, Charles Scribner's Sons, New York.

De Bonnes Choses à Manger. St. Matthew's Guild, Houma, Louisiana.

Delta Dining, Too. Delta Academy, Marks, Mississippi.

Dining by Fireflies. Junior League of Charlotte, North Carolina.

Dinner on the Diner. Junior League of Chattanooga, Tennessee,

Dodwell's Cookbook. Mary Dodwell, New Orleans, Louisiana.

Drop Dumplin's and Pan-Fried Memories Along the Mississippi. Angie Thompson Holtzhouser, Lilbourn, Missouri.

Family Secrets, Best of the Delta. Lee Academy, Clarksdale, Mississippi.

Fare by the Sea. Junior League of Sarasota, Florida.

Favorite Recipes of the Deep South. Montgomery, Alabama.

Favorite Recipes Old and New. North Carolina Federation of Home Demonstration Clubs, Raleigh, North Carolina.

Festival Cookbook. Humphreys Academy Patrons, Beltoni, Mississippi.

Food for Body and Soul. Highway 5 Church of God, Nauvoo, Alabama.

Foods à la Louisiane. Louisiana Farm Bureau Women's Committee, Baton Rouge, Louisiana.

From Generation to Generation. Temple Emanu-El Sisterhood, Dallas, Texas.

From North Carolina Kitchens: Favorite Recipes Old and New. North Carolina State College, Raleigh, North Carolina.

From Rose Budd's Kitchen. Rose Budd Stevens, University Press of Mississippi, Jackson, Mississippi.

The Gasparilla Cookbook and *Tampa Treasures.* Junior League of Tampa, Florida.

Global Feasting, Tennessee Style and *1982 Official World's Fair Cookbook.* Phila Hach, Knoxville, Tennessee.

Good Cookin' from the Heart of Virginia. Junior League of Lynchburg, Virginia.

A Good Heart and a Light Hand. Ruth Gaskins, Fund for Alexandria, Virginia, Simon & Schuster, New York.

Gracious Goodness. Memphis Symphony League, Memphis, Tennessee.

The Great American Writers' Cookbook. Yoknapatawpha Press, Oxford, Mississippi.

Great Performances. Symphony League of Tupelo, Mississippi.

The Grecian Plate. Hellenic Ladies Society, St. Barbara Greek Orthodox Church, Durham, North Carolina.

Heart and Soul, The Memphis Cookbook, and *Party Potpourri.* Junior League of Memphis, Tennessee.

High Cotton Cookin'. Marvell Academy Mothers' Association, Marvell, Arkansas.

The Historical Cookbook of the American Negro. National Council of Negro Women, Washington, D.C.

Holiday Foods. Lafayette Extension Homemakers Cookbook, Oxford, Mississippi.

Hospitality. Harvey Woman's Club, Palestine, Texas.

Houston Junior League Cookbook. Junior League of Houston, Texas.

How to Cook a Pig and Other Back-to-the-Farm Recipes. Betty Talmadge, Lovejoy, Georgia.

How to Grow the Peanut . . . (Bulletin 31) and *How the Farmer Can Save His Sweet Potatoes* (Bulletin 38). George Washington Carver, Tuskegee Institute, Tuskegee, Alabama.

Howorth Family Collection. Oxford, Mississippi.

Huntsville Entertains. Historic Huntsville Foundation, Huntsville, Alabama.

Impressions. Auxiliary to the Memphis Dental Society, Memphis, Tennessee.

In Order to Serve. Christ Episcopal Church Women, Charlotte, North Carolina.

Inverness Cookbook. All Saints Episcopal Guild, Inverness, Mississippi.

Irwin S. Cobb's Own Recipe Book. Irwin S. Cobb, Louisville, Kentucky.

La Cocina Cubana Sencilla. Paul Adams, M.D., Louisville, Kentucky.

La Piñata and *Some Like It Hot.* Junior League of McAllen, Texas.

Little Bit Different. St. John's Episcopal Church, Moultrie, Georgia.

Louisiana Legacy. Thibodaux Service League, Thibodaux, Louisiana.

Louisiana Wildlife Magazine. Baton Rouge, Louisiana.

The Magnolia Collection. Gene Westbrook, Millbrook, Alabama.

Mam Papaul's Country Creole Basket. Nancy Tregre Wilson, Baton Rouge, Louisiana.

Marie's Melting Pot. Marie Lupo Tusa, T&M Publications, New Orleans, Louisiana.

Mirations and Miracles of Mandy. Natalie Scott, New Orleans, Louisiana.

Miss Daisy Celebrates Tennessee and *From the Kitchen Door.* Hillsboro Press/Providence House, Franklin, Tennessee.

Miss Lillian and Friends. Beth Tartan and Rudy Hayes, New American Library/Signet, New York.

Mountain Measures and *Mountain Measures: A Second Serving.* Junior League of Charleston, West Virginia.

Mrs. Wages® New Home Canning Guide. Precision Foods, Inc., Tupelo, Mississippi.

My Mother Cooked My Way Through Harvard with These Creole Recipes. Oscar Rogers, Natchez, Mississippi.

Necessities & Temptations. Junior League of Austin, Texas.

The New Orleans Cookbook. Rima Collin and Richard Collin, New Orleans, Louisiana, Alfred A. Knopf, New York.

North Carolina and Old Salem Cookery. Elizabeth Hedgecock Sparks, Kernersville, North Carolina.

Out of Kentucky Kitchens. Marion Flexner, Nashville, Tennessee.

Outdoor Tables and Tales, Celebrating Our Mothers' Kitchens, Forgotten Recipes, The Pastors Wives Cookbook, Wild About Turkey, Homemade Christmas, Campsite to Kitchen, Black Family Dinner Quilt, and *Black Family Reunion Cookbook.* Tradery House Books, Memphis, Tennessee.

Peachtree Bouquet and *Puttin' On the Peachtree.* Junior League of DeKalb County, Decatur, Georgia.

Pearls of the Concho. Junior League of San Angelo, Texas.

The Picayune's Creole Cookbook. The Times Picayune Publishing Corporation, New Orleans, Louisiana.

Plains Potpourri. Plains Junior Women's Club, Plains, Georgia.

(The James K.) Polk Cookbook. James K. Polk Memorial Association, Columbia, Tennessee.

Possum & Pomegranate. Kate C. Hubbard, Mississippi historical recipes.

Possum on the Half-Shell. Possum Kingdom Chamber of Commerce, Possum Kingdom Lake, Texas.

Recipe Jubilee and *One of a Kind.* Junior League of Mobile, Alabama.

Recipes and Reminiscences of New Orleans, vols. 1 and 2. Parents Club of Ursuline Academy, Metairie, Louisiana.

Recipes for Creative Living. John C. Campbell Folk School, Brasstown, North Carolina.

Recipes from Old Virginia. Virginia Association for Family and Community Education, Hume, Virginia.

River Road Recipes, Recipes II, Recipes III. Junior League of Baton Rouge, Louisiana.

The Savannah Cookbook. Harriet Ross Colquitt, Savannah, Georgia, Colonial Publishers, Charleston, South Carolina.

Savannah Style Cookbook. Junior League of Savannah, Georgia.

Sensational Seasons. Junior League of Fort Smith, Arkansas.

The Share-Cropper. Central Delta Academy Parent-Teacher Organization, Inverness, Mississippi.

The Smithfield Cookbook. The Smithfield Junior Woman's Club, Smithfield, Virginia.

Sook's Cookbook. Marie Rudisill, Longstreet Press, Atlanta, Georgia.

Soul Food. Albert Ikner, San Jose, California.

Page 20: *Soft drinks slake the summer thirst at a picnic.* Irwinville, Georgia, 1939. Courtesy Library of Congress. Marion Post Wolcott, photographer.

Page 24: *Grinding cane for syrup on a fall afternoon.* Orange County, South Carolina, 1939. Courtesy Southern Historical Collection, University of North Carolina Library at Chapel Hill. Marion Post Wolcott, photographer.

Page 31: *A slice of watermelon is a heavy but welcome burden on a sunny summer afternoon.* Manning, South Carolina, 1939. Courtesy Library of Congress. Marion Post Wolcott, photographer.

Page 40: *Soft white wheat flour is best for Southern baked goods.* Almance County, North Carolina, 1939. Courtesy Southern Historical Collection, University of North Carolina Library at Chapel Hill. Dorothea Lange, photographer.

Page 48: *Churning ice cream on a sultry summer day in North Carolina, 1939.* Courtesy Southern Historical Collection, University of North Carolina Library at Chapel Hill. Marion Post Wolcott, photographer.

Page 56: *A picnic on cemetery-cleaning day.* North Carolina, 1965. Courtesy North Carolina Collection, University of North Carolina Library at Chapel Hill.

Page 59: *Everybody gets a piece of watermelon at this picnic.* Crisp County, Georgia, 1939. Courtesy Vanishing Georgia Collection, Georgia Department of Archives and History.

Page 60: *Snapping beans and peeling carrots is a family affair.* 1940s. Courtesy Caufield & Shook Collection, University of Louisville Photographic Archives.

Page 67: *Making moonshine by the light of day.* Rabun County, Georgia, early 1900s. Courtesy Vanishing Georgia collection, Georgia Department of Archives and History.

Page 73: *A family reunion beneath the boughs brings everyone out in Sunday best.* Daisy, Georgia, 1915. Courtesy Vanishing Georgia Collection, Georgia Department of Archives and History.

Page 78: *Canning green beans is a group effort at the Jefferson County Community Cannery.* Courtesy Library of Congress. Howard Hollem, photographer.

Page 88: *An oyster roast draws a crowd to Pine Harbor, Georgia, 1936. Courtesy Vanishing Georgia Collection, Georgia Department of Archives and History.*

Page 94: *Chinese grocery stores, like this one in Vicksburg, Mississippi, were fixtures in many Southern communities, 1960s.* Courtesy Ferris Collection, Special Collections, University of Mississippi.

Page 101: *Peeling potatoes on the porch to escape the heat of the infernal kitchen.* Mississippi Delta, 1960s. Courtesy Ferris Collection, Special Collections, University of Mississippi.

Page 106: *Picking over berries on a summer day.* Mississippi Delta, 1960s. Courtesy Ferris Collection, Special Collections, University of Mississippi.

Page 116: *Sharing the bounty of the lunch bucket in the schoolyard.* Breathitt County, Kentucky, 1940. Courtesy Library of Congress. Marion Post Wolcott, photographer.

Page 121: *Grinding fresh French-roasted coffee.* Bayou Pierre Part, Louisiana, 1946. Courtesy Standard Oil Company Collection, University of Louisville Photographic Archives. Arnold Eagle, photographer.

LIST OF PHOTOGRAPHS

Page ii: *A proud Carolina couple with preserves and ham to stay them through the winter.* Zebulon, North Carolina. Courtesy Library of Congress. Arthur Rothstein, photographer.

Page iii: *Stocked up for winter with the bounty of summer.* Yanceyville, North Carolina, 1940. Courtesy Library of Congress. Marion Post Wolcott, photographer.

Page x: *Preparing the Mason jars for putting up vegetables.* Date and place unknown. Courtesy Caufield & Shook Collection, University of Louisville Photographic Archives.

Page xii: *A Fourth of July fish fry on the Cane River near Natchitoches, Louisiana, 1940.* Courtesy Library of Congress. Marion Post Wolcott, photographer.

Page xviii: *Keeping a watchful eye on a skillet full of chicken.* Escambia Farms, Florida, 1942. Courtesy Library of Congress. John Collier, photographer.

Page 8: *The race goes to the swiftest eater at the annual Crowley Rice Festival.* Crowley, Louisiana, 1940. Courtesy Library of Congress. Marion Post Wolcott, photographer.

Page 15: *A student at Bethune-Cookman College carries a heaping tray of cornbread to a waiting lunchtime crowd.* Daytona Beach, Florida, 1943. Courtesy Library of Congress. Gordon Parks, photographer.

Page 18: *Hulling rice the old-fashioned way, with a mortar and pestle.* Near Crowley, Louisiana, 1939. Courtesy Library of Congress. Russell Lee, photographer.

Page 254: *Religious belief informs all facets of Southern life, even that of truck patch farms.* Mississippi Delta, 1960s. Courtesy Ferris Collection, Special Collections, University of Mississippi.

Page 260: *Sharing news of the day while the food settles at a church supper.* Caswell County, North Carolina, 1939. Courtesy Southern Historical Collection, University of North Carolina Library at Chapel Hill. Marion Post Wolcott, photographer.

Page 263: Mississippi Delta, 1960s. Courtesy Ferris Collection, Special Collections, University of Mississippi.

Page 264: *Sunday morning in the kitchen, learning to make cookies under mother's watchful eye.* Escambia Farms, Florida, 1942. Courtesy Library of Congress. John Collier, photographer.

Page 269: *Churning butter on the porch.* Randolph County, North Carolina, 1939. Courtesy Southern Historical Collection, University of North Carolina Library at Chapel Hill. Dorothea Lange, photographer.

Page 272: *Many mouths to feed—and a few cats as well.* North Carolina, 1939. Courtesy North Carolina Collection, University of North Carolina Library at Chapel Hill.

Page 277: *A fisherman's lunch by the seashore.* North Carolina, 1939. Courtesy North Carolina Collection, University of North Carolina Library at Chapel Hill.

Page 289: *A produce wagon brings the farm to town.* Tennessee, 1930s. Courtesy Tennessee State Archives, Nashville.

Page 293: *Gathering the leftovers after a dinner on the grounds.* North Carolina, 1939. Courtesy North Carolina Collection, University of North Carolina Library at Chapel Hill.

Page 299: *Noontime intermission brings the crowd to dinner on the grounds during a ministers' and deacons' meeting.* Near Yanceyville, North Carolina, 1940. Courtesy Library of Congress. Marion Post Wolcott, photographer.

Page 302: *A game of checkers played with bottle caps and a slice of melon makes for an afternoon of summer fun.* Courtesy Library of Congress. Cox, photographer.

Page 315: *Beekeepers tending to their charges.* Tennessee, 1930s. Courtesy Tennessee State Archives, Nashville.

Page 319: *First birthday with family and friends.* Clarksdale, Mississippi, August 1947. Courtesy Ellen E. Rolfes.

INDEX